Art, Nature, and Religion in the Central Andes

Joe R. and Teresa Lozano Long Series
in Latin American and Latino Art and Culture

Art, Nature, and Religion in the Central Andes

Themes and Variations from Prehistory to Present

Mary Strong

UNIVERSITY OF TEXAS AUSTIN

Printed in the United States of America
First edition, 2012

Requests for permission to reproduce material from this work should be sent to:
Permissions
University of Texas Press
P.O. Box 7819
Austin, TX 78713-7819
utpress.utexas.edu/about/book-permissions

♾ The paper used in this book meets the minimum requirements of
ANSI/NISO Z39.48–1992 (R1997) (Permanence of Paper).

LIBRARY OF CONGRESS CATALOGING-IN-PUBLICATION DATA

Strong, Mary, 1947–
Art, nature, and religion in the central Andes : themes and variations from prehistory to present / Mary Strong. — 1st ed.
p. cm. — (Joe R. and Teresa Lozano Long series in Latin American and Latin art and culture)
Includes bibliographical references and index.
ISBN 978-0-292-75425-6
1. Indian art—Andes Region 2. Indians of South America—Andes Region—Religion. 3. Indians of South America—Andes Region—History. 4. Indians of South America—Andes Region—Social life and customs. I. Title.
F2230.1.A7.S79 2012
980'.01—dc23

2011042861

First paperback printing, 2013

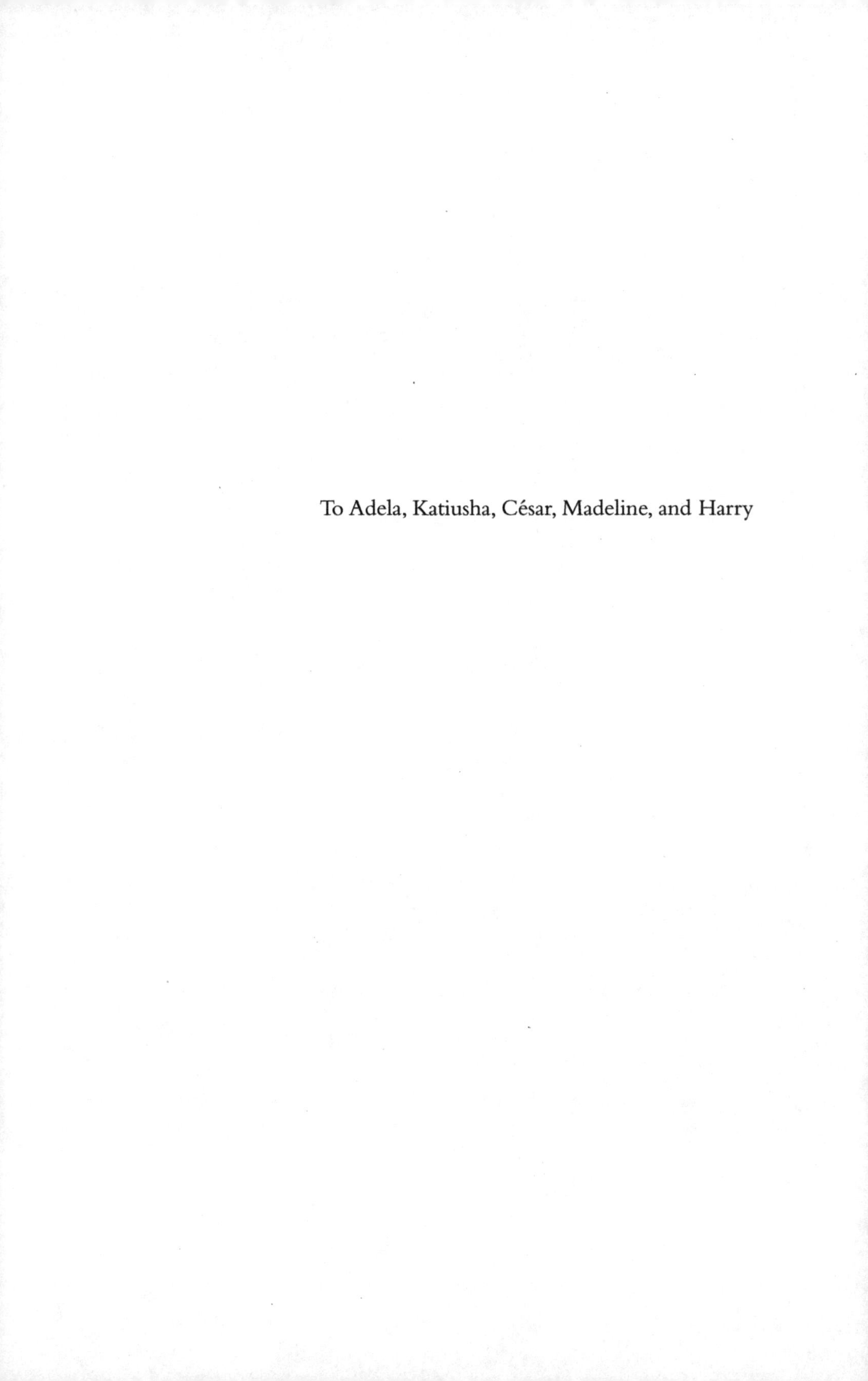

To Adela, Katiusha, César, Madeline, and Harry

Contents

Acknowledgments

The author wishes to thank the following artists, scholars, supporters of the arts, and people in other fields for their immeasurable contributions to this book.

Adela Katiusha Barrio Tarnawiecki de Batticani, Adela Tarnawiecki (Saco) de Barrio, César Barrio Mendoza, Marta Betty Herrera Altamirano, Lucy Núñez Rebaza, Antonio Vásquez, Patricia Moyano, Máximo Damián, Jaime Guardia, Luis Oscco, Carlos Flores, Basilio Pichihua, Ysabel Asto, Elsa Damián, Joachín López Antay, Alberto Ayala, Edwin Pizarro, Ignacio López Antay, Eulalia Bustamante, Magdalena Aymi, Roberto Contreras Montero, Delia García Ynga, Donato Enríquez, Rolando Enríquez, Vidal Gutierrez Cordero and son Juan, Arístedes Quispe López, Felicitas Quispe López and daughter, Primitivo Evanan Poma, Santiago Huarcayo and wife Mari, Grimaldo Escalante, Victor Paredes, Adolfo Quispe, Roberto Huarcayo, Teodoro, Samuel, Maxidomio Palomino Torres and wife, Teófilo Araujo, Antonio Prada Cuadros, Teófilo Araujo Choque, Juan Araujo Choque, Rebeca Gómez, Julio Galvez, Edgar Gálvez, Raúl García Zárate, Manuelcha Prado, Najwa Adra, Steven Syrop, Kathleen Price, Edward Ochsenschlager, Stuart Schaar, Paul Doughty, Peter Biella, Rafael Domingo, and Madeline and Harry Strong, Ann, Joan, Ned, and Don Strong and their families.

The writer would not have been able to take on the task of producing this book were it not for Theresa J. May, editor-in-chief of the

University of Texas Press. Her constant positive support and practical help as well as that of her very capable staff made this project come to pass in concrete form. Special thanks to Victoria Davis, Tana Silva, Kaila Wyllys, and Kay Banning.

Note: Pseudonyms rather than artists' proper names are used in this book for their own protection. All translations were made by author.

Art, Nature, and Religion in the Central Andes

Introduction

This volume is a broad look at the cultures of the Andes and their arts. Readers will find an introduction to the subject here that will encourage further exploration of these fascinating and beautiful traditions. Following is a general ethnohistory of symbolic meaning in a selection of Peruvian religious art motifs relating to the natural world. The geographic and cultural focus is the central Andean region of Peru, especially in Huamanga (also known as Ayacucho) and its environs. This book is different from others in several ways. First, it concentrates on "folk art" images, but it also traces how contemporary "folk" traditions relate back to the arts of the Andean past (note 1). Second, rather than trying to seek out a tiny and supposedly isolated community where "pure" Indigenous forms have been somehow preserved despite tumultuous incursions of sociocultural change, this study looks at a major art production center and acknowledges outside influences coming from cultural interchanges in the Indigenous period, European colonialism, economic and political change later in history, and most recently the life-altering introduction of new telecommunications technologies. Third, in partial response to a "further research needed" request made a half-century ago by the renowned anthropologist José María Arguedas, these chapters show how aspects of the arts of today as well as the belief systems they express have been heavily influenced by Spanish cultural traditions as well as Indigenous ones. Fourth, rather than concentrating only on famous senior artists and their work, this book considers younger art makers and contemporary influences on their thought, art, and means of making a living.

1. The term "folk" can be problematic for some artists because to them the word implies that their work is not as good or sophisticated as mainstream or "art world" pieces. For this reason, I do not use the term "folk" commonly in this book. In Peru and the Spanish-speaking world generally, the word *popular* (*arte popular*) is used to refer to folk art. This does not translate with the same meaning into English, so in the book I also avoid that term.

Geography

The corpus of images in the study derives from a selection of Indigenous, or "Andean" in this book (note 2), art forms traditional to the region in and around the city and department (similar to a province) of Ayacucho, originally called Huamanga, in Peru's central Andes mountains. The city of Huamanga is known as an art center and has been famous for its creative work especially since European colonial times. The people living in the environs around the city trace their art inheritance into the deep Indigenous past. This area constitutes the main geographic focus in the study. Artists in the book have their roots in Huamanga, but their lived experience can include a much broader swath of the nation and regions overseas. These artists know about or have traveled to other art centers in Peru, including Huancavelica, Apurimac, Junín, Cuzco, Lima, and Lurín. A few have gone abroad, some to New York City and other world capitals. Many younger artists maintain sporadic contact with international areas through Internet cafes with wireless capability and cell phones. With these wonderful tools for communication, the previous requirements for literacy and wire-based electricity are no longer necessary for some degree of inclusion in global conversation because users can employ visual and voice media over satellite networks (Jayasinjhi Jhala, personal communication, 2007). The Internet is replete with Web sites where formerly remote communities now post their cultural heritage in complex detail. Andeans incorporate artistic influences from these media and national and international locations into their work. Artists' own relatives and friends now living and working in other parts of Peru and in Brazil, Spain, the

United States, Japan, and other foreign lands serve as additional conduits for new, creative inspiration.

2. The term "Andean" is used in this book to mean the culture and arts of the Indigenous and Mestizo (mixed European and Indigenous descent) peoples of the Andes mountains as well as the adjoining jungle and coastal regions of Peru. The word "Andean" is used in this way by Peruvians.

The themes and variations prevalent in Andean visual art and described in this book derive from the very extensive work carried out by archeologists, ethnographers, and artist-ethnographers cited here. Suggestions as to how and why it is that these themes and variations are expressed through time and space is the work of this study and based on bibliographic and field research by the author.

This book examines images in a few of the domestic and village-based art forms characteristic of Huamanga and the department of Ayacucho: the scissors dance (*danza de tijeras*), home altars (*retablos*), carved gourds (*mates*), board painting (*tablas de Sarhua*), tin arts (*hojalatería*), and alabaster carving (*piedra de Huamanga*). There is also a limited view of particular representations in the well-studied Andean high arts of textiles and ceramics. Within these traditions, this book looks specifically at images showing certain aspects of the natural environment. The motifs under study include selections from the animals, plants, earth forms, astral bodies, meteorological conditions, and, to a lesser extent, human beings that prevail in the central Andean environment.

The time frame for field and documentary research upon which this book is based extends from the late 1960s to the first decade of the twenty-first century.

The book deals with "themes," or relatively unchanging spiritual forms and meanings, as well as "variations," or forms and meanings that change over time. This volume goes beyond the usual anthropological literature staple of "continuity and change" studies, however, in several ways. Andeans have a particular idea of the workings of time and space and how they interrelate. Time and space have a political dimension both for Andeans and outsiders. Andean artists utilize special tactics to speak religiously and politically to insiders and outsiders simultaneously in ways that please both audiences. Three of these ploys are inversion, disjunction, and dual subjectivity. Artists make use of such techniques by taking advantage of the ambiguous character of visual media. They use visual art to countermediate outsider views about Andean culture and assert their own ethnic pride and ideology.

Borrowing and Incorporation

Andean imagery often incorporates elements from various deities, religious traditions, regions, and time periods into one piece of work. This was done in the past and continues in the present. Since prehistoric times, Andean motifs and art categories have exhibited multiple symbolic referents, types of construction materials, designs, historical periods, and geographic regions. Andean images often contain various symbols within one form. These motif hybrids can take the shape of chimeras, which may be serpents, pumas, rainbows, bolts of lightning, eagles, and jaguars all at once. A ceramic object can take on images and decoration more characteristic of textiles, for example, or a wooden art form can incorporate stone elements in terms of materials. The freewheeling Andean tendency to borrow and incorporate disparate elements has only increased today due to the ubiquity of modern telecommunications.

This cultural penchant for borrowing and incorporating has contemporary implications for research and researchers. Time periods matter little when artists can access images from archeological sites, books, and the Internet. In this way, the past, present, and future share space in their work. Nor does geographic delimitation constitute a boundary around ethnographic study for similar reasons. In fact, regionalism was probably never very strong in Andean art traditions because of the ritual and trade networks evidently fostered by the chronological chain of empires even preceding those of the Incas and Europeans. What binds this work together, then, are the artists the author knows who self-identify as being from Huamanga (Huamanguinos) and their work, which shows influences from across broad areas of history, geography, and ideological traditions.

Andean Time and Space

> The eternal equilibrium of things is great, and the eternal overthrow of things is also great.
>
> —Walt Whitman, "Leaves of Grass"

The Andean art tradition of borrowing and incorporation relates to a particular concept of time and space that artists express visually. How pictures, images, and concrete forms appear to encase Andean thought better than written words is still somewhat of a mystery. An artist once said to the author as he tried to explain the meaning of his work, "I cannot say it to you, but you and I both know what it is." Andean thinking has been analyzed by experts as being three-dimensional or metaphorically spatial. Andean thought also incorporates the fourth dimension, time, particularly through a notion of repeating cycles that is embedded both in language and cosmology. In the Andean conception of reality, time and space appear to intersect. There are certain aspects of time/space that are cyclic and others that allow for aberrations and changes as each cycle repeats back upon itself. Celestino (1997, 1998) and others discuss the most dramatic instance of aberration in cycles known as a *pachacuti* (loosely translated as "world turned upside down"), or cosmic inversion that is expected to occur from time to time in Andean cosmology. The languages Quechua and Aymara, the two major Andean Indigenous tongues, have notions of blended time/space built into them, according to linguists (Faller and Cuellar 2009, Nuñez and Sweetser 2006). Nuñez and Sweetser, following Gifford (1986), find that the Aymara and Quechua languages construct time in a very particular way. Their research shows that native speakers of the two languages seem to be looking "forward" toward "past" events, while the "future" lies behind them. Faller and Cuellar studied the same linguistic phenomena but perhaps interpret the data in a way that is more comprehensive because in addition to being cognitive linguists they are native speakers of Quechua. They posit that Andean languages conceive of time as a circular process. In this way the relative positions of "future" and "past" blend into one another. These authors contend that time consists of movement but that it is also a kind of container that can take on new elements each time it repeats its circular journey. An apt metaphor for this idea might be a child on a carousel who takes an additional gold ring each time she passes the same point in her rotation. Thus, say the researchers, Andean time encases the old while incorporating the new. Here readers can see how space and time seem to blend in this culture. Faller and Cuellar go further in that they contend that this spatial/metaphoric time sense relates very much to the ever-repeating diurnal and annual sun cycles so important in Andean religion and the complex agricultural systems that traditionally have formed the basis of their existence.

Andean concepts of time and space call up images of Einstein's obscure lectures about such conundrums as what happens at the speed of light. Pictures for Andeans are the best and perhaps only way to deal with these kinds of thought systems since they defy the usual possibilities allowed by spoken and written language. In the political realm, pictures also serve their makers well, especially when dealing with problematic outsiders who are not picture-oriented in a primary way.

The Influence of the Colonial and Postcolonial Experience: The Political Dimension in Concepts of Time and Space

> A fish said to another fish,
> "Above this sea of ours there is another sea with creatures swimming in it—they live there even as we live here."
> The other fish replied,
> "Pure fancy! Pure fancy! When you know that everything that leaves our sea by even an inch and stays out of it, dies. What proof have you of other lives in other seas?"
>
> —Khalil Gibran, "Other Seas," *Collected Works*

Why, one might ask, should Andeans choose to invoke a kind of circular timelessness in their verbal and visual expressive forms? Mircea Eliade describes the process very well in his 1949 book *Le Mythe de l'eternel retour* (*The Myth of the Eternal Return*, 1954). According to Eliade, myths and rituals are vehicles of an "eternal return" to a mythical age. Religious narrations, images, objects, and practices are a means for attaining a sacred dimension that gives life value and meaning. Victor Turner, in his classic study *The Ritual Process* (1969), finds that ritual and its accoutrements allow people to attain a state he calls "communitas." Communitas is an unstructured community in which all people are equal. This ideal level of being is most important to maintain among all people, but especially those who have been demeaned, colonized, or discriminated against. Eliade contends that people try to keep themselves in the eternal, timeless realm of the sacred (corresponding to Turner's communitas) in order to avoid being trapped in the linear, progressive dimension called "history." Historical time moves ever forward like a speeding arrow flying through space. Some questionable Western theories of social "progress" depend on the historical linear time metaphor. Social evolutionists of this type posit that culture and society change through time, always "improving." There is also embedded in social evolutionist thought an often unspoken assumption that the cultures of the powerful (to which these theorists, of course, belong) represent a later and therefore better stage of social evolution than those of the less powerful.

Social evolutionists often equate the future with what is "better" or "best" in human civilization and the past with what is underdeveloped, primitive, and not so good. Politically, these ideas have served militarists, colonialists, and empire builders well because they can justify imposing their regimes on other peoples in terms of providing "progress" and "betterment" for those they conquer. Nineteenth-century European colonialists justified their "white man's burden" of "bettering ignorant masses" over which they wished to impose power. Twentieth- and twenty-first-century imperialists have followed suit. Peoples who have been conquered and colonized thus become part of a misty, timeless, and aimless "past" wherein reside populations considered by the powerful to be part of the primitive "Other," that is, probably not as fully human and complex as they (the powerful) are. Edward Said presents this idea in depth in his book *Orientalism* (1979), and so does Johannes Fabian in his book *Time and Other* (1983).

How Religion and Politics Come Together in Andean Imagery

Many Andean scholars agree that pictures and three-dimensional forms are vital to that culture, in which thought systems are so different from those of many outsiders (whether or not they are exploitive) including researchers. Since Andean thought is nonlinear in nature, the all-at-once quality of pictorial representation may express the artists' mental patterns better than spoken and written language, a linear communication mode. Imagery in this culture has another aspect as well that is both religious and political. Andean pictures and forms not only "stand for" something in the symbolic role pictures usually have in other cultures. It seems that pictures for Andeans also actually "stand in" for what they represent (Jackson 2008, Salomon 2004b). This, say scholars in the field, requires a special kind of semasiography, or method for creating form for and deciphering meaning inherent in images. The term "semasiography" is a derivation applied to images of the word "semasiology," or the philosophical and scientific study of meaning in linguistics.

Margaret Jackson studied the art of the Moche, one of several major pre-Inca cultures. She defines semasiographic images as graphic scripts or representations that do not directly reflect speech. She states that there is no reason to automatically classify pictures at the primitive extreme of human communication systems and alphabetic writing at the opposite or most advanced end. Semasiographic systems can represent ideas directly, but their ordering is different from what generally are considered language forms as such (2008:82) The Moche are famous for their realistic representations of beings and objects in nature. Jackson asserts that such close rendering of palpable forms created meaning for this culture.

Frank Salomon studied contemporary *quipu*, or knotted-rope systems that served the Incas as well as some modern Andeans as a way of keeping important records. Knotted ropes are an extremely abstract and, some believe, mathematical mode of visual representation. However, even here, Salomon concludes that these complex arrangements of ropes and knots are not just symbols that simply *stand for* something else but actually *stand in* for actual features of reality. Salomon goes on to say that the quipus and what they represent are the same essence. They are stand-ins for each other without the mediation of words (Salomon 2004b:176, 280).

It appears, then, that images for Andeans, whether naturalistic or abstract, are much more real than the words in this book are to readers. Because most images are sacred in some sense, they animate the minds of their viewers in the know with a sense of the holy.

Pictorial systems such as the Andean one present themselves in a simultaneous or all-at-once manner. Pictures and forms make artful use of positive and negative space; they indicate two and three dimensions through perspective and other representational conventions that push images forward and backward in space. Pictures placed on a frieze, scroll, or any area of space include the fourth dimension of time since they are meant to be "read" by viewers in a certain order or even no particular order. The process of "reading" produces a narrative sequence or story that can have one plot or many alternate plots depending on where and in what order the viewer looks. In this last case of no particular order, pictures allow themselves to be open to multiple interpretations.

This study shows how images can have spiritual power in themselves (Strong 2003a); in other words, spiritual power both inhabits and projects from images. This book uncovers a few tips of the icebergs that perhaps will eventually reveal themselves about how this form of communication functioned and still functions so well for the people who invented it.

Pictures work for Andeans regardless of their mimetic correspondence, since some look very much like their models in nature while others are highly designed abstractions.

Tactics Employed by Andean Artists

> Guile is the sword and shield of the oppressed.
>
> —Thornton Wilder, *The Eighth Day*

Artists use special tactics or ploys to communicate their praise and honor of Andean traditions to Andean audiences, at the same time hiding these messages from discriminatory outsider audiences. This research shows some of the subtle tactics artists employed to survive the onslaught of European colonization and still use today to overcome marginalization, the recent effects of a twenty-year civil war (Ulfe 2005), and the vicissitudes of the global economic system (Henrici 2003).

María Eugenia Ulfe wrote a dissertation about retablos, or home altars, made in Huamanga by one of the extended families well known for this work. Some retablo and other local art forms depict the terrible violence and tragedy that centered in Huamanga during the two last decades of the twentieth century due to a situation of civil war (described in chapter 4). Many people still suffer from the effects of this period during which family members were killed, people left in financial ruin, and the rule of law ignored. As a result, even now Huamanga's residents suffer from violence, poverty, high unemployment, lack of trust in local institutions, fragmentation of civil society, loss of religious traditions, alcoholism, street gangs, and abandonment of customs and festivals (Ulfe 2005:260). Ulfe follows Rowe and Schelling (1993:179) in saying that making art about these horrible events helps people distance themselves from them enough to begin thinking about ways to promote societal change for the better.

Visual images and forms seem to accomplish this task of healing and transformation effectively. Pictures also work well as survival tools because Andeans' adversaries and outsiders to their belief system have trouble understanding them. Non-Andeans are often limited by language systems that correspond to speech and writing. Outsiders also may live within time concepts with rigid present, past, and future time demarcations. This means that the full religious and political import of images escapes outsiders to the degree that they can become a useful secret code for insiders. Artists employ visual depictions that are ambiguous enough to allow for multiple viewer interpretations (Strong 1998, 2009). Not only do they represent their concept of "inversion," or pachacuti described above, but also "disjunction" (Stastny 1981) and "dual subjectivity" (DuBois 1994).

A simple communication model will help to explain what is meant by inversion, disjunction, and dual subjectivity. A communication system basically involves a sender, a message, and a receiver. The artist is the sender, the artwork is the message, and the viewer is the receiver. Experts in the field say that any communication system and thus any message includes a certain amount of "noise," or interference with the clear reception of the message. In telecommunications, for example, solar storms create noise or static, which interrupts the free flow of messages sent by means of transmitters that are then bounced off satellites to finally reach various kinds of receivers. The art messaging system in this book involves a kind of noise created intentionally by artists and perceived according to a traditionally agreed-upon code cipher by special groups of receivers. This operates somewhat like the codes used in wartime like the "Enigma" manual scrambler used by the Germans in World War II, which notably had certain unchanging aspects as well as others that changed over time. Computer encryption programs also have these characteristics enhanced a thousandfold.

The artist employs calculated noise, or visually ambiguous code, to assert her pride in and support of her culture in an environment of social and ethnic discrimination. Indigenous Andeans, though the numerical majority in many highland regions, are nonetheless a sociopolitical minority in Peru and part of the "third and fourth world" of marginalized peoples from a global perspective. These "minority" artists must, however, appeal to and market their work to their own kind as well as to those who look down upon them in the national and international social structures. In order to do this, they must communicate effectively with two and sometimes more audiences with widely differing expectations. The artist presents a benign surface in her work meant for elite buyers, one that belies the critical messages lurking in its symbolic depths. These deeper ideas have to do with cultural pride and social protest, and they focus on a special in-group of viewers.

Artists' well-planned and calculated noise or intentional ambiguity allows them to communicate with multiple audiences simultaneously. The artists clearly show preference for one of their message systems: the one that exalts the lifeways and values of their own cultural tradition. In this manner, artists avoid a common and devastating pitfall characteristic of groups of people living in discriminatory societies. W.E.B. DuBois (1994) discusses this danger when he describes the idea of dual subjectivity. The minority person living in a state of dual subjectivity perfects the skill of existing in two almost opposite value systems at the same time: his own culture and that of the social majority that oppresses his own culture. DuBois warns that this delicate balancing act can lead an individual to internalize the discriminatory ideology of the powerful in society and to develop a corresponding self-hate for his own background. As this insidious process advances, the individual takes on the values of the majority and leaves his own minority ideology, which he now considers worthless, behind.

Despite many historical layers of colonial and economic rule in their ethnohistory, Andean artists consistently avoid DuBois' pitfall. They live and produce art in multiple dimensions in ways that escape detection and thus avoid the destruction of their culture at the hands of outsiders. They employ tactics such as disjunction, described by Andean folk art historian Stastny as the process of depicting historical or nonmainstream imagery under the guise of acceptable or contemporary customs and mores. An example of disjunction drawn from European art history might be a typical eighteenth-century painter's tendency to clothe figures in a painting about a Greek myth in eighteenth-century fashionable attire rather than the togas and sandals the classical Greeks actually wore. Andean artists often play with disjunction and reverse disjunction.

Another common ploy is the use of inversion in addition to the pachacuti or cosmic inversion discussed above. Inversion is a concept discussed at length in several ways by Celestino (1997, 1998). Inversion in art makes negatively valued aspects of society into positive ones. The weak in official society become powerful in art. An example of this is the Andean preference to depict fighting bulls with condors riding their shoulders, making the Andean sacred bird superior to the Spanish colonial mystical animal. The exalted become downtrodden and the downtrodden exalted. Another example is the high respect given the poor and the heavy criticism of the rich in Andean art. One of the biggest cataclysmic inversions of the universe was the European colonial period and its aftermath. Since Andeans' idea of time involves periodic inversions, their art shows a future time when they will reinvert their world and once more be in charge of their own destinies.

This ethnohistory draws from the both the research literature on these subjects as well as what artists themselves say and do. Artists speak about their work as they make it in their workshops. They comment on the effects of recent changes in art and society. They offer observations and practical suggestions regarding art making as well as economic and spiritual survival in the twenty-first century (chapter 4; Henrici 2003).

Final Thoughts

Andean traditional use of a sacred visual language not directly translatable to words and the postcolonial employment of images as survival tools in the face of difficult outside influences are connected concepts. Religion, art, and politics all relate to the concept of ethnic identity and pride. In postcolonial times the politics of discrimination keep the powerful elements in the nation and the world in an elite position by justifying their innate superiority. Andean religious art as a mode of communication counteracts this status quo because it makes Andeans spiritually powerful. This spiritual power is deeply connected with the natural world, which for Andeans contains the essence of life's meaning. Andean art as an assertion of spirituality, pride, and culture is ambiguous enough to be fully appreciated by insiders while being a message hardly seen or understood by outsiders.

This study presents ways in which the Andean empire builders, especially the Incas, marshaled the force of a pan-Andean corpus of visual symbols to consolidate their empires under uniform sets of religious beliefs. During the colonial and postcolonial periods, Andeans have used a similarly widespread image and design system to both resist and adjust to external forces. The post–Inca empire Andeans, bereft of their central state apparatus and social elite, were compelled to relegate their language of imagery to the small arts of the farm and home. After that period, they imaged coded messages among themselves to maintain their identity and even their very existence. Now, in the twenty-first century, these images take not only an Andean but a worldwide stage through telecommunications technology and transnational migration. In each of these three historical periods, the book describes and explains how pictures promote Andean basic values (themes) while they adjust to evolving circumstances (variations).

In sum, this book asks two questions about Andean religious images. First, how do they depict continuing cultural values (themes) on the one hand and adjustment to change (variations) on the other? Second, how does Andean art exhibit the strategies and ploys artists use to hide their true intentions from outsiders while conveying a strong message to cultural insiders? Another way of phrasing the second question would be: How do Andean artists construct their work so that it countermediates negative outsider concepts of their value and worth, and how do they assert their pride in a way that is hidden from these same outsiders? The answers the book offers are partial, but they will perhaps provide a beginning for further thought and study.

Part I

Themes

Themes are ideas embodied in art that took shape, probably, at an early time in regional Andean cultural development. The local natural environment combined with religious conceptions of space and time inspired these themes in art. The themes were taken up and elaborated upon by civilizations that built cities and colonized other regions. These basic Andean art concepts have continued through time into the present period. Chapter 1 in this section examines some of these religious motifs within the pre-Inca and Inca cultures. Chapter 2 explores Andean modes of thought in terms of space, time, and nature and shows how these ideas took form in a few of the many nature symbols common in Andean art.

CHAPTER 1

Pre-Columbian Andeans

Pre-Columbian Andeans include all Indigenous peoples who lived in the region before the coming of the Europeans in the fifteenth and sixteenth centuries. This chapter concentrates on some of the later cultures, notably those of peoples who built cities and established empires or had panregional influence over neighboring cultural groups in terms of art. The first part presents the general environmental context, next the peoples before the advent of the Inca civilization, and then the Incas themselves.

The Natural Environment

Religious ideas expressed in art flow from a special relationship Andeans feel with their natural surroundings. For this reason, a general look at the lay of the land, the climate, and living creatures that inhabit the Andean region provides some groundwork for understanding why Andean arts take their particular shapes, forms, colors, and materials. One of the best sources for understanding the richness of this environment is the Peruvian geographer Javier Pulgar Vidal (1968, 1987), upon whose lectures and writings this discussion has been based.

Peru is a country of very diverse climatic zones, each with distinct earth features, weather, plants, and animals. These rich and varied surroundings allowed for the existence of a long line of empires and urban settlements. Some of the area's civilizations remained limited to one region, while others, such as the Chavín, Huari, and Inca, extended their influence over several regions and topographies.

Peru has three major and quite distinct climatic and geographic zones: the coast, the mountains, and the jungle. Human groups living in each zone have adapted in characteristic ways to their environment and at the same time have often taken advantage of the benefits offered by the other zones through trade, travel, religious pilgrimage, military conquest, and colonization. Peru lies in tropical latitudes but has part of the second-highest mountain range on the globe and one of the world's driest deserts cooled by an inversion effect of the cold ocean current close offshore. The Amazon basin to the north and east surrounds the country's shoulders in its warm and humid mantle (figure 1.1).

Coast

The desert coast (*costa*) is on the leeward face of the Andes range. Prevailing east-to-west trade winds drop their moisture in the form of rain on

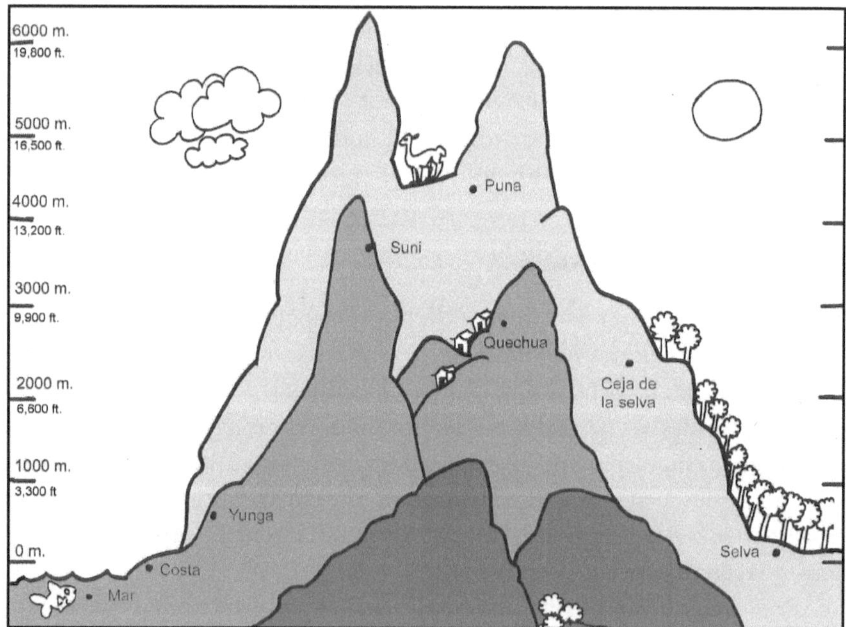

1.1 Andean geography. Altitudes and principal climatic zones (left to right: coast, mountain, jungle) are shown in a vertical slice of topography, with local terms for some environmental niches. Drawing by the author.

the windward side of the Andean *cordilleras*, ranges or literally "backbones." The mountains are so tall that the water never makes it over them to the Pacific-facing coast. Just off the coast to the leeward side, the cold Humboldt ocean current brings an "inversion effect" that creates a relatively cool and foggy maritime climate on land and a wealth of seaborne food sources. The cold upwellings off Peru's coast provide one of the richest sources in the world of fish, marine mammals, and birds. It is this cold current that allowed ancient Indigenous cultures to build and support the concentrated populations living in their seaside cities. The Spanish built the city of Lima, one of the two co-capitals of their colonies in the Americas, on this coast. Most large cities and most of Peru's population occupy the coast today.

Agriculture along the banks of the short rivers flowing west down from the mountains produces good yields of foods and cotton fiber for cloth in limited econiches. A number of early civilizations developed on this thin strip of otherwise dry land walled on one side by the Andes and lapped on the other by a life-giving sea full of resources. Among these Indigenous coastal cultures were Paracas, Nazca, Moche, Chimú, and Pachacamac. The oceanside climate of the coast precludes extremes of temperature, though in winter many areas are blanketed in thick coats of fog. In fact, one product of the coast is vegetation that grows well in desert fog zones, such as epiphytes (plants deriving nutrients and hydration from the air and from host plants, such as orchids) and crops that thrive in small riverine floodplains. The *yunga*—lands at slightly higher altitudes than sea level and facing the water, or leeward side of the Andes—offered coastal peoples more microclimates for special uses such as gourd farming. Coastal cultures, accordingly, had pantheons of divinities that included sea creatures whose images they painted into ceramics, wrought in metal, and wove into cloth. Seashells, sharks, dolphins, marine birds, fish, and other coastal denizens, plus ideas attached to them, spread to other regions as coastal peoples traded their home-produced arts for goods native to and made in other areas.

Mountains

The mountains encompass three major ranges that course through a broad diagonal swath of Peru. The mountains include a multitude of microclimatic zones. Some of these depend on altitude, which can range from the always frigid and snowy peaks at 22,000-plus feet above sea level to deep tropical valleys at or below sea level and named after the rare insect-borne diseases lurking within them. Other zones depend on latitude, or relative distance from the equator, location on either the leeward or windward slope, or a combination of all these factors. The Pacific-facing yunga and the *ceja de la selva* (eyebrow of the jungle) fronting the Amazon basin provide mountain peoples with tropic and subtropic zones and cultigens to add to the richness of animals and plants farmed at temperate to cool zones in higher elevations. A farmer can often tend crops and animals by walking up or down a few thousand feet in altitude to work in his various *chacras*, small farm plots, at different levels. Mountain peoples, according to Pulgar Vidal, prefer to live between about 8,000 and 13,000 feet of altitude, where they enjoy a temperate climate, often experiencing almost all seasons of the temperate year every twenty-four hours. This region, thought to be ideal for human habitation, is called the *quechua* zone, and the same term often applies to the peoples of this region as well as to their spoken language. Here, people grow staple food crops and pasture animals at slightly higher altitudes. Pulgar describes the higher altitudes of the *puna* (14,000 to 16,000 feet or more in altitude) as a pleasant land of lakes and pastures and the *jalca* (at 13,000 to 18,000 feet) as having bird-filled and subtle air, with parades of llamas, alpacas, vicuñas, and guanacos—varieties of Andean camellids—grazing there (Pulgar Vidal 1968:16, 102; 1987).

Major cultures that developed in the mountains were the Chavín, Pucará, Huari, Tiahuanacu, and Inca. The mountains provided major empire-building traditions with a midpoint location from which to benefit from the exchange of foods, materials, arts, manufactured and natural goods, religious and profane ideas, and migratory populations flowing between the mountains and other regions. At a more local level, the myriad environments of the mountains allowed villages, settlements, and extended families to seek marriage partners, goods, and ideas in a kind of "vertical exchange" (Murra 1972) that was beneficial as much between small communities as between those of larger scale. This book concentrates primarily on the peoples of the mountains and views the other regions from the perspective of those living in the mountains.

Jungle

The jungle includes the subtropical yunga and eyebrow as well as the river-laced tropical lowlands. The eyebrow of the jungle is a transition between the mountains and jungle zones. The eyebrow lies on the western, windward side of the Andes and overlooks the Amazon basin, the "eye." This region is humid and green, and it lies in a subtropical to tropical zone a few hundred to a couple of thousand feet above sea level. It receives some of the rains that never reach the dry seacoast to the lee of the Andes chains, and it is a place where important condiments including spicy peppers, fruits, much-desired items like coca and other medicinal plants, sugarcane, and such warmer-climate staples as corn are grown and gathered.

The rain-soaked viridian sward of the jungle occupies one-third of Peru's total area, and yet it is the least explored by nonnative peoples. Indigenous and later European explorers ventured little into its intimidating green vastness. Though some experts suggest there may have been cities and full-blown agriculture in the lowland tropics, there is little beyond intriguing explorers' and travelers' accounts providing corroboration for such ideas (Roosevelt 1999). Most jungle people seem to have practiced hunting, gathering, and small-scale horticulture for much of their history. They live in small groups and speak localized tongues. Some of the mountain empire-building cultures did have a degree of relationship with the jungle area. The art of the powerful Chavín and Huari, for example, suggests that they had settlements or even origins in the jungle. However, the extremely wet climate does not favor artifact or organic preservation, so archeologists await the discovery of more evidence to reveal the prehistory of the jungle region. For this reason, the present chapter focuses on a few of the pre-Inca traditions of the coast and mountains and only areas where dry conditions have favored artifact preservation.

Environmental Influence on Cultures

The Andean region has been an area of constant cultural change and interchange. Different civilizations in eternal search for water and places to gather and grow food in a difficult environment have been in continual contact with others on the same quest. Besides the need for food and water, another determinant of human existence in the region is the unpredictability of the weather and the specific nature of the land and ocean. The Andes environment on land is a zone of frequent earthquakes and volcanic activity since it lies along a major geologic fault line where tectonic plates meet that both created the mountains and yearly add to their height. El Niño is a periodic climatic event originating in the Pacific

Ocean. The effects of El Niño can cause climates to be reversed, that is, rain at times and places that otherwise would be dry, dryness instead of rain, cold in place of heat, and the reverse. El Niño thus causes periodic floods, droughts, famine, and disease among Andeans. The need for political stability and religious fervor as hedges against calamity thus became very important to peoples in this naturally volatile region. Being able to anticipate the future became vital as well and promoted the importance of prophecy and prediction in Andean religions. This led to the development of pilgrimage centers where oracles assured migrants about their immediate future. In this way, religion was as important as trade, military activity, and agricultural colonization as a contributor to cultural mixtures. Religion promoted the honing of artists' skills in the creation of religious pieces with multiethnic influences since very early periods in Andean history.

In homage to the unifying peoples—Chavín, Huari, and Inca—this overview begins with a general description of a few of the major mountain traditions first and then some of the coastal populations.

Before the Incas

The art ethnohistory of the Peruvian Andes is long and diverse. There is a corpus of images and ideas that dates back to the earliest complex

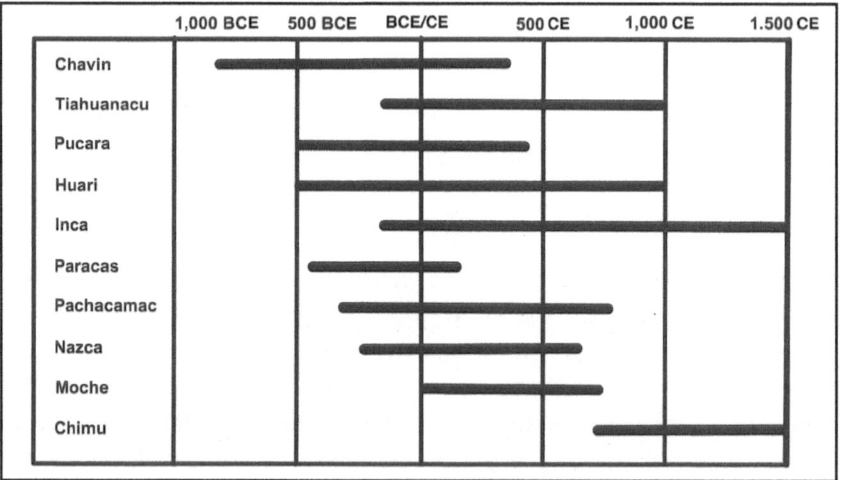

1.2 Andean cultural time lines. Approximate beginning and ending dates are shown for regional domination by cultures named on the left. During temporal overlaps civilizations probably influenced each other. Drawing by Rafael Domingo.

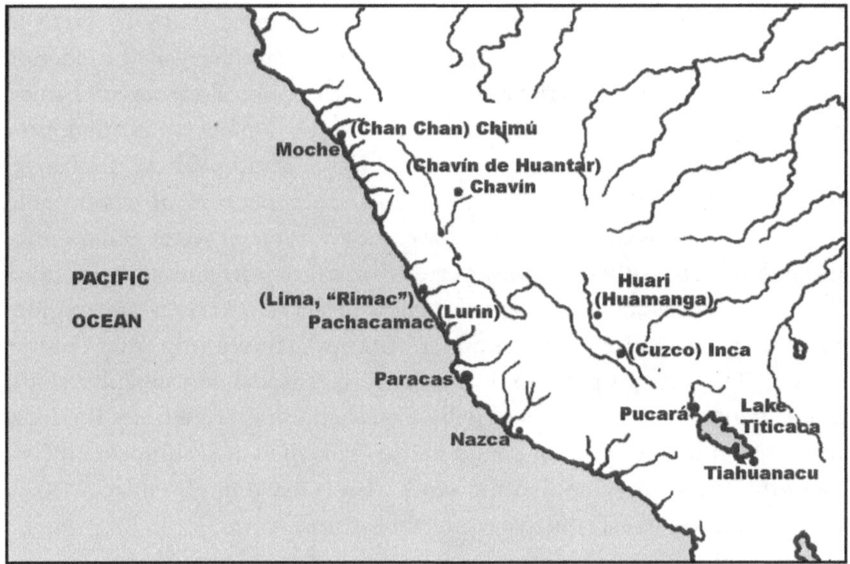

1.3 Culture map of civilizations' geographic centers. Cultures contiguous in space and time presumably interacted, though Andeans' travels, religious pilgrimages, and colonization campaigns could trump contiguity in fostering cultural exchange. Drawing by Rafael Domingo.

civilizations in this environment and continues to this day. This chapter examines the work of a few of the major Indigenous cultures whose legacy still appears in contemporary Andean art. The Europeans encountered the geographically vast and populous Inca empire, and it is with the Incas that many contemporary artists tend to identify. More than ten million Native American Quechua and Aymara speakers, descendants of the Incas, constitute the largest Native American ethnic and language grouping in the Americas. Millions more bicultural and bilingual Mestizos also keep Andean traditions alive in the twenty-first century. This population occupies and spills over the borders of seven modern nation-states once contained within the Inca regime.

However, the Incas are only the last inheritors in a long historical line of civilizations, including empire-building cultures that occupied the mountains, jungle, and coast of Peru 15,000 to 12,000 years before the present era. Some scholars dispute these dates, saying that human entry in the Andes occurred 5,000 to 8,000 years earlier (note 1). Early civilizations raised and worked cotton by 3,000 years ago and produced baskets and gourd implements as well as preceramic items by 3000 to 2000 BCE. Pre-Inca cultures contributed to one another's art production technologies as well as to the religious and philosophical ideologies behind shared imagery by means of cultural exchanges fomented by migration, trade, encounters at religious sites, and colonization. These exchanges took place both through time and across space because of travel, trade, militaristic expansion, the need to have good sources of water and produce more food, and other reasons. Periods of overlap in these civilizations' histories and favorable topography allowed certain periods and regions to become particularly rich in the creation of arts resulting from cultural contact. The Inca empire would later absorb regional and subcultural arts as it expanded just as previous civilizations had done. Sometimes the Incas imported entire colonies of conquered artisans such as Chimú ceramicists, and other times they copied the work of revered though endangered or extinct cultures like Tiahuanacu and Pachacamac.

1. The dates used here for pre-Inca civilizations are taken from Moseley 1992. There is hardly ever absolute accord among experts about prehistorical dating, and new research constantly calls time lines into question. However, these dates do represent a general consensus.

There are also differences of opinion about when and how human beings came to the Americas and specifically to the Andes in the first place. Archeologists and biological anthropologists native to the Andean region say humans inhabited the Andes by 20,000 BCE, or 10,000 years after the first human entry to the American continent via Beringia. Other scholars contend that the Andes were settled much later in time and that human beings may have come to the Americas from different origin points, in several waves of migration, and by means of a series of land and sea routes.

"Before common era" (BCE) refers to times before the birth of Christ (BC). "Common era" (CE) refers to times after the death of Christ (AD). The use of BCE and CE is an example of dating-designation systems created to apply globally. In this way, references to a particular religion can be avoided. For similar reasons, archeologists sometimes use the designation "before present" (BP); the number of years BP is determined by counting backward from the present.

Mountain Cultures

Chavín

Richard Burger's book *Chavín and the Origins of Andean Civilization* (1992) is an especially useful general study of this ancient and in many ways Ur-culture of the highland Andes. The Chavín constitute the oldest major urban civilization in the mountain zone. They resided in the north central Andes from about 800 BCE to 400 CE (note 1). The best-known Chavín city is Chavín de Huantar, the capital. Artistic motifs and technologies invented by the Chavín spread far and wide through the mountains and coast during their time because they colonized other regions to meet their own need to find additional food and water sources. However, it was the religion known by archeologists as "the Chavín cult," with its characteristic imagery, that unified these disparate regions. Chavín religious ideas expressed in art styles echoed through history such that it is difficult to find an Andean art tradition in any medium that is untouched by Chavín influence even today. Andean religions feature astral bodies and local animals and plants and with spiritual power. For example, coastal cultures depict orcas, crabs, seabirds, and fish—all sea or littoral organisms. Mountain people created images of llamas, pumas, condors, foxes, deer, and hummingbirds, all denizens of the high sierras. Chavín art shows the caiman (crocodile), harpy eagle, monkey, jaguar, and a serpent that is probably a python. These jungle creatures lived far from Chavín de Huantar, and it is the prevalence of such images that fuels archeological speculation about the possible jungle origins of the Chavín. Artists of today depict pumas with jaguar or perhaps jungle serpent spots, paying in this and in many other ways unknowing respect to their Chavín ancestors' use of motifs based on creatures of the Amazonian basin.

The Chavín innovated many visual symbolic traditions inherited by Andean cultures that followed them in history. Many of the major innovations, even abstract ideas, passed through Andean history by the Chavín made their material presence felt in art. The Chavín may have been the originators of the primacy of the visual in Andean communication systems. Archeological excavations of Chavín de Huantar reveal a particular kind of burial known as a "shaft tomb." The shaft tomb's construction makes the theological idea of *ushnu*, or the connections of human beings, the underworld, and ancestors, into a three-dimensional stage set. (Zuidema 1977–1978:165 and chapter 2 of this volume present the structure of the Andean cosmos.) The kind of monumental construction characterizing

Chavín sites attests to the social and spiritual value placed on public-labor projects. These values would be passed down in Andean history, celebrated in art, and recorded on visual devices for storage. The organization of imagery into units of two contiguous equal but opposite concepts attests to a belief in symbolic duality, which in art and thought is a strong inheritance clearly present in contemporary arts. For the Chavín, textiles were the highest art, just as they were under the Incas and probably among Andeans today as well, with ceramics coming in a close second. Very finely cut stone indicated high-status architecture for the Chavín as well as many of the civilizations that came after them. Precious metals were valuable only in terms of the divine principles they represented, and the elites in society were associated with gold and silver objects only after these were wrought into art of religious significance. European colonialists would much later fail to appreciate that Andeans did not value the precious metals melted down into bars as did Europeans.

In other areas of endeavor, the Chavín pioneered classic Andean economic and political systems. They created technology-intensive, high-altitude, irrigation-based agriculture utilizing multiple ecozones and supplemented by camellid herding, the images and forms of which would pass through history in the arts. They concentrated on large-scale infrastructural maintenance rather than mechanical improvement. Andeans today celebrate in multimedia art forms the cleaning of irrigation canals, the construction of rope-bridge spans over chasms, and the building of homes.

Chavín religion was the factor that unified peoples living in disparate regions that they colonized and influenced with their religious beliefs. Burger finds that this took place as an indirect consequence of the Chavín prime motivation, the need for food and water. The Andean tradition of expansion to encapsulate enough of the region's varied ecozones to ensure a complete and reliable diet was pioneered by the Chavín and celebrated in their art, which depicted, among many other subjects, produce, even the lowly potato, an Andean staff of life. The Chavín were conveniently located in the highlands in a place easily accessible to both the jungle and the coast. This greatly facilitated the spreading of their agricultural, religious, and artistic influence into these adjoining areas.

Archeologists trace Chavín empire-building history by following the trail of the spread of the religious art iconography and design style they used in all their materials and media, from stone to pottery to textiles. One example of this is the Lanzón (early form) and the Raimondi Stone (later form) of what is known as the "staff god" image that continued through history, geography, and multiple Andean cultures after its innovation by the Chavín. The Chavín developed an impressive type of polychrome pottery that led to its highest florescence centuries later, when it was inherited by the Nazca and Huari. Chavín designs appeared in the textiles and ceramics of these and other peoples.

The Chavín pictorial and sculptural style had a kind of simplified, slightly geometrized realism similar to Art Deco. The Chavín combined elements of naturalistic forms, for example of sacred animals, creating chimera whose purpose was to refer to multiple supernatural powers or aspects simultaneously. The Chavín design decision to employ "kennings," or limitless variations on a small number of themes, also constitutes a system of multireferencing. A third way to do the same thing would be to use a common general shape for single or multiple messaging. For example, a zigzag, or *qenqo* in Quechua, could signify lightning, a snake, simply a zigzag, or all those at once. The city of Chavín de Huantar contains carvings showing the physical symptoms involved in imbibing *epene*, a hallucinogen typical of jungle peoples' religious practice. Some stone figures show the large amount of mucous discharge caused by the drug during the nasal imbibing process. Final-stage carvings show human beings completely transformed into sacred animals once the drug takes full effect (Burger 1992:158, figures 147–155). These carved series express another form of multireferencing as well as the close spiritual interchangeability of humans and sacred animal beings. The Chavín presented their images using "contour rivalry," showing the profile and frontal view at the same time, as Picasso would do many centuries later. They divided their forms and shapes, such as a round clay pot, into equally sized vertical and/or horizontal bands within which they placed designs. The Chavín employed bilateral symmetry, echoing their belief in symbolic dualism. Design grids and symmetries like these still appear in contemporary Andean art.

Tiahuanacu

The Tiahuanacu culture held sway on the Bolivian side of Lake Titicaca between 100 BCE and 1000 CE. The Huarpa culture developed into Tiahuanacu, and the Moche and Nazca existed alongside it in time. The capital city of the same name was one of the highest in the ancient world, at 12,630 feet. The earlier Chavín culture very much influenced Tiahuanacu. The Huari also would influence Tiahuanacu, followed by a period of mutual cultural exchange between these two groups. The Huari and later Inca cultures incorporated Tiahuanacu images into their own visual repertoire, skewing proportions and details probably to suit their own purposes (Morris and Von Hagen 1993:102, 111; Moseley 1992:218–219).

Tiahuanacu religious beliefs and the arts in which they took form spread widely. There was an emphasis on sky and gateway divinities, and Tiahuanacu architecture in their walled city featured gateways in the form of intricately carved, enormous stone arches as well as theatrical spaces for the enactment of large-scale rituals. Tiahuanacu excavations reveal many items related to the use of alcohol and other drugs, probably having to do with religious activity. Huge statues taken from the city of Tiahuanacu now stand in La Paz, Bolivia, and the skid marks from moving the enormous stones the Tiahuanacu architectural engineers used for their titanic buildings and statues are still visible from the air.

Like the Chavín, the Tiahuanacu struggled to feed themselves in the cold, dry environment that characterizes much of the highlands. They constructed swales or troughs running parallel to the shore of the sea-like inland Lake Titicaca to provide fresh water for themselves and irrigation for their crops. Also like the Chavín, they colonized warmer regions so they could grow needed foods and find materials not available in the higher altitudes. These colonizations spread Tiahuanacu religious beliefs and imagery over a broad geographic area. The Inca took on the Tiahuanacu myth of origin, though they would eventually subjugate it to their own Cuzco-centered history of beginnings. Design elements used by Tiahuanacu include very detailed kennings, split representations, and mirror images. These and other visual traditions influenced the Huari and some of today's artists in the Huamanga region and had a direct relation to the prized Inca *cumbi* weaving style. Andean artists of today integrate creative versions of Tiahuanacu imagery into their own work. The force of Tiahuanacu visual thought still exerts great influence on the contemporary Aymara cultures of Bolivia.

Pucará

The Pucará culture, located on what is now the Peruvian side of Lake Titicaca, existed between 500 BCE and 475 CE. Pucará was influenced by Tiahuanacu and in turn influenced the Huari. Pucará has long been known as a ceramics center. Archeologists have found Pucará clayware at both the site itself and near Huari. Today Pucará is still a well-known ceramics center and the major place for the manufacture of bulls of Pucará, described in chapter 8.

Huari

Huari is the second of the three great Andean unifying cultures, like the Chavín before them and the Inca to follow. All three of these civilizations had true state economic and political formations. The Huari are especially important in this book because they are the local artistic forebears of the Huamanga-area people of today. The Huari lived between 500 BCE and 1000 CE in the city of Huari, between the contemporary city of Huamanga and the town of Quinua. The city was large even in its early stages, occupying about 250 acres. The preceding Huarpa culture grew into both the Tiahuanacu and Huari traditions, and these inheritors of Huarpa beliefs and behaviors exchanged cultural elements with one another. Huari artifacts resemble those of the coastal Moche, who lived during the same historical period, though the Moches' vibrant color designs also echo their Paracas and Nazca contemporaries. Like Tiahuanacu, the city of Huari was surrounded by walls.

Huari visual imagery drew heavily from Tiahuanacu. The Huari made "gateway god" or "staff god" images, humanoid figures carrying a staff in each hand. Unlike the Tiahuanacu originals, the Huari added legs and feet. Huari versions of Tiahuanacu architectonic stone divinities in general were often skewed and truncated, perhaps to fit better into an overall design scheme meant for textiles and pottery rather than stone. The Huari used warp patterning in their textiles, and they spread this technique through interregional colonization. Warp patterning was eventually to become a hallmark of Indigenous weaving techniques throughout the highlands. Warp-patterned textiles tend to favor abstract and angular geometric shapes and soft transitions between colors. Yet the innovative Huari also perfected a brilliantly colored tapestry weave technique, perhaps in part borrowed from their ancestors and coastal colonies where it was used during pre-Columbian times. Tapestry weaves include curved designs and feature strong immediate transitions from one color to another. Huari tapestries feature bold designs, both curved and angular, in heavily saturated color, similar to the types of motifs also found in Huari ceramics (note 2). Europeans were eventually to promote tapestry weavings in the textile factories (*obrajes*) in which they employed Andean craftspeople.

Thus Huamanga today may be noted for tapestry techniques because of the local Indigenous forebears as much as for its Spanish colonial history. The Huari made large, multicolored pots as part of their ceramic repertoire. Some of the most ornate of these were "sacrificed" by breaking them as part of religious rituals. They used *quipu*-like cord bundles to communicate and keep records, but instead of the meaningful knots used by the Incas, the Huari relied primarily on color to carry signification.

2. The Huari weavers used both warp patterning, which spread far in the region, and tapestry weave. The Huari are particularly known for the brightly colored, clearly delineated designs of their woven tapestries and ceramics. Huamanga weavers of today, regional descendants of the Huari, pride themselves especially on their tapestries.

The Huari capital, like Chavín de Huantar, was conveniently located between breaks in the mountains that facilitated access to the coast and the jungle. This made the highland imperative of finding more sources of water and food through colonization of other ecozones relatively easy. The Huari continued the development of Chavín-like multizone agricultural techniques that the Incas would later use on a large scale. They constructed satellite towns and further developed the Chavín systems of multiple exchanges among ecozones, about which Murra would write centuries later (1972) with regard to modern Andeans. The Huari colonized and influenced many far-flung regions and facilitated the exchange of art styles and the religious beliefs they expressed, along with food, water, and practical technology. Archeologists have found their artifacts in several coastal areas: Cajamarquilla, a cemetery east of Lima; Pachacamac, a sacred coastal city near contemporary Lurín; Nazca sites on the South Coast; and late-phase Moche sites on the North Coast. Huari wanderings established a way of life requiring periodic travel and migration that passed through the centuries to the present time.

Interim Period

Between the periods of the Tiahuanacu and Huari and the Incas who followed them in central highland history was an interim during which small-scale warring groups lived in the mountainous areas. These groups defended what scholars call small "resource archipelagos" (Moseley 1992:14, 15); they were eventually quelled but not beaten down by the Incas. Two of these groups were the Chanca and the Huanca.

The Huanca occupied the area where Lake Junín feeds into the Mantaro and the highlands to the east in the Rio Tarma headwaters. The contemporary town of Huancayo is named after them, and there is still a distinguishable art style known as *huanca* in this area and in the Huamanga region.

The Chanca, according to Inca conquest tradition, began to attack Cuzco, the Inca capital, from the northwest under the reign of the Inca leader Viracocha (a word used in three ways—to indicate this historic individual, a name for a high Inca deity, and a term used as a general honorific). Viracocha failed to defend the capital, and it was his younger son, eventually called Pachacutec Yupanqui (note 3), who repulsed the Chancas.

Another name for one of these interim cultures used in the Huamanga region today is Huanta, which refers to a contemporary native of the city of Huamanga (Ayacucho). The city of Huanta is a principal population center in the valleys and high mountains near the Mantaro River. People of contemporary Huamanga call themselves Huanta. This is a cultural designation rooted in the past and a reference to the area generally known as the Huanta River Valley, where Huamanga is located.

3. Pachacutec, or Pachacuti Yupanqui, was known and revered for his extraordinary military prowess. His first name derives from the term for "inversion of the universe." Thus he is the one who turns the world upside down through his extensive conquests.

Specifically in the Huamanga or Ayacucho area, the Incas conquered the local Huanca, Chanca, and Huanta peoples. The Chanca and Huanca, with a reputation for being indomitable, still retain a distinctly noncolonial style in their arts, which favor Indigenous design and iconography. The Huanta, on the other hand, prefer Spanish motifs and methods since they inherited a legacy of intense historical acculturation. A major reason for this is the development of art and trade schools to train Indigenous artists in European traditions during colonial times. Contemporary artists from all three of these subgroups still actively seek out the imagery and technology of their local pre-Inca Huari ancestors.

Coastal Cultures

The Incas inherited cultural traditions and technologies not only from neighboring mountain civilizations but also from the coast. This multi-regional contribution was due in great part to the previous Chavín and Huari expansions that extended to coastal areas.

Some of the major civilizations of the coast came in contact with the highland state societies. As a result, coastal cultures and arts crossed currents with highland traditions in a process of mutual exchange and interchange. Major coastal traditions, in order of appearance, are Paracas, Pachacamac, and Nazca on the central and southern coasts and Moche and Chimú on the North Coast.

Archeologists have a much more profound idea about coastal cultures than about the other two regions. The extreme dryness of the desert climate preserves artifacts, even the most fragile textiles and robes made of bird feathers, in almost perfect condition. Natural mummification preserves human and animal remains. Cities made almost entirely of adobe still stand today after thousands of years.

Paracas

The Paracas tradition developed on the South Coast between 475–300 BCE and 100–200 CE. Paracas is perhaps best known today for intricate textile work, particularly difficult production techniques such as looping to produce tiny three-dimensional figures that often fringe especially fine pieces. The slit tapestry technique is typical, and Paracas weavings integrate feathers and other ornamental materials into fiber pieces. Paracas textiles are among the finest in the world. Weavers combined their techniques, integrating ornate embroidered designs into their woven patterns. Though the Paracas people did not raise their own camellids, they wove in wool as well as cotton. They traded for wool with highland cultures that provided the fiber already dyed in a wide range of colors (Moseley 1992:47).

Artists also produced impressively formed and colored ceramics that reached a zenith in their Nazca and Moche daughter cultures. Paracas may be the, or one of the, origin points for ceramic stirrup jars and perhaps whistling jars.

Pachacamac

Pachacamac is a stone and adobe city on a beach near the present-day town of Lurín, near Lima. The Chavín influenced this culture, which flourished between 400 BCE and 800 CE. The city was primarily a religious center to which pilgrims came from long distances to consult an important oracle. As a result, food, art, and ideas came to Pachacamac and were exchanged among people of different local ethnic groups. Branch oracle deities eventually took up residence in other ecozones, spreading the ideological influence of Pachacamac culture. The influence of Pachacamac grew to the degree that the Incas preserved the religious character of the center without undue interference during their conquest of the coast. The Incas' laissez faire attitude toward the site was due to their extreme respect for it as a sacred location, even though the city was probably long since abandoned by the time their conquering armies arrived.

Nazca

Nazca, on the South Coast, flourished from 250 BCE to 650 CE. It inherited the artistic tradition of Paracas and is especially well known for its brightly colored ceramics and huge earth formations commonly called the Nazca Lines. Nazca artists placed the same images in the lines that they did in their pottery and textiles, and many of these came from the marine and coastal environment.

Nazca artists placed most emphasis on polychrome design and pattern in their pottery painting and textiles. Rather than emphasizing form in their pottery, the Nazca made simple shapes and concentrated on using pots as a plain canvas for their complex and multichrome painted designs. Their debt to Paracas can be seen in the early Nazca pots that have painted figures similar to Paracas textiles from what archeologists call the Necropolis phase of Paracas cultural history. Painted figures from later periods became more abstract.

The Nazca Lines consist of very large drawings of animals, plants, humans, and some abstract designs. Many of these are hundreds of feet square and constructed by removing the dark top layer of desert soil to expose a light-colored undersurface. Scholars including Zuidema (1964, 1990), Aveni (2000), and Reiche (1993) assert that the lines have religious significance similar to and perhaps preceding or part of the *ceques* (note 4), a system of radiating sacred lines characteristic of Cuzco and very likely other locations as well. The Nazca Lines probably connect sacred points, or *huacas*, which are at the same time *ushnus*, or gateways between different Andean cosmic levels (explained in chapter 2). Even now people keep the lines clean, and some walk along them, in a sense reading the sacred landscape the lines delineate. In addition, there is some relation between these designs and water, the source of life.

4. *Ceques* are sacred lines of force that radiate from special points of spiritual power called *huacas*. The Andean natural environment is full of ceques that radiate from center points like the spokes of multiple wheels. Some ceques mark pilgrimage routes. Ceques are a kind of map of the spiritual landscape overlying the natural lay of the land. The German scholar Maria Reiche (1993) speculated that the Nazca Lines were probably related to ceques; see also Bauer (1998).

Nazca imagery included marine and coastal creatures such as orcas, hummingbirds, sharks and other fish, crabs, and creatures they admired, including the tiny but fierce spider. Nazca arts and artists had a strong influence on art styles in many other regions of Peru. They received influence, in turn, from the Huari culture when the Nazca came in contact with the central highlands through Huari expansion.

Moche, North Coast

The Moche existed between 1 CE and 750 CE, approximately. Ancestral to the Moche and contributing to their arts were the Vicus and Recuay cultures. The descendant Chimú culture would eventually grow directly from Moche roots. Though they were perhaps best known for their ceramics, the Moche were expert artists in all media. They constructed cities and pyramids. They were also fine metalworkers who employed techniques such as *repoussé* to produce their pieces. One of the archeological sites most known for metalwork is the recent excavation of the Moche royal burials at Sipán. The Sipán burial contains many fine examples of Moche metalwork and use of precious stones. Moche two-dimensional art includes depictions of warrior-cult religious traditions in images of sacrifice rituals, probably of prisoners. Moche textiles were finely wrought, and weavers produced elaborate clothing using sophisticated techniques.

In ceramics the Moche were masters of the modeled form. Moche ceramic ware was often either natural clay color or minimally slipped or partially decorated on its sculpted surface. For the Moche, shape was all, in contradistinction to the Nazca, for whom surface decoration was the primary emphasis, such that pots (aside from their practical uses) seem to have served in large part as supports for Nazca paintings. Moche pot shapes were utilitarian in that they were used as containers, and at the same time they had decorative qualities. Pot forms depicted every aspect of Moche life, such as livestock herding, building styles, rituals, crop planting, plants, animals, and people of all ages and ranks engaged in both public and intimate activities. Moche style was primarily realistic, so much so that experts contend some "portrait pots" were depictions of actual individuals. The Moche may have invented "whistling pots," although the Paracas culture is another candidate for the invention. Whistling pots have two spouts, sometimes connected by a bridgelike handle to each other. When liquid pours out of one of the spouts, the pot makes a whistling sound. The Moche were among the first to use molds to mass-produce ceramic ware.

By about 600 CE, the Moche moved inland from their coastal location. Archeologists find that the timing of this move corresponded with a severe drought in the Andes. The Moche wanted to be nearer irrigation-canal intakes to ensure their survival during this very dry period.

Chimú

The Chimú lived approximately in the same area as the Moche and inherited many art traditions from them. Some archeologists call them the Moche/Chimú for this reason. The Sicán people were the immediate predecessors of the Moche/Chimú, and they are famous for types of figures commercially known today as *tumis*. These are figures with humanoid faces and full body forms that have comma-shaped eyes, large headdresses, and truncated limbs. The body of such a figure forms the handle of a semilunar-shaped "sacrificial" cleaver atop the head. Tumis have become as much common and stereotypic icons of the tourist industry as tikis in

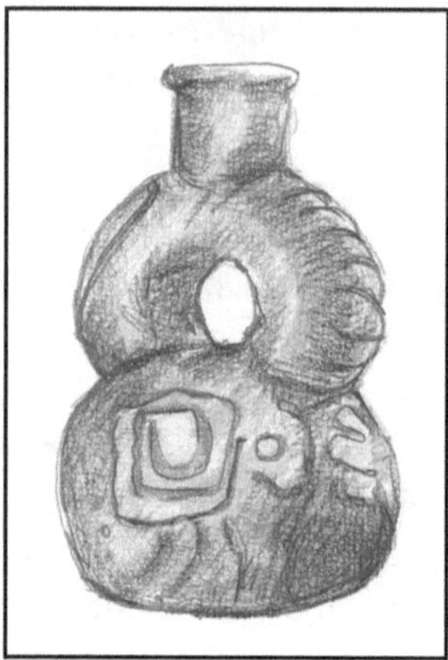

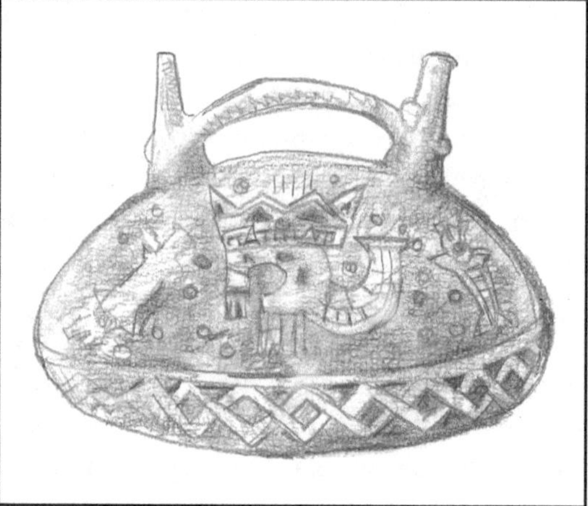

Figures 1.4, 1.5 Stirrup jar and whistling jar. Drawings by the author after Moseley 1993, photo #46, attributed to Rafael Larco Hoyer.

Hawaii, totally divorced from their true history and meaning. The tumi is actually a ceremonial knife depicting a seated Sicán lord, thus the truncated limbs. Tumis can have a variety of shapes and proportions (Morris and Von Hagen 1993: figure 206), and some individuals in Sicán burials have tumis in their hands.

The Sicán also innovated certain traditions having to do with sacred objects that would continue to echo through Andean history. They probably noticed that the spiny oyster known as spondylus populated their beaches in far greater numbers during rainy El Niño years. This was because warm waters with spondylus in them flowed south as a part of El Niño events. However, the Sicán saw the spondylus as bringers of water, a resource so hard to come by that it became sacred. By association so did the spondylus shell, which was imported afterward from the beaches of Ecuador and employed in religious rituals along with the shell of the strombus, a type of conch that is sometimes blown like a trumpet by modern Andeans. Sicán and Moche/Chimú religious use of strombus and spondylus shells continues today in the sacred ceremonies of modern Andean religious practitioners.

The huge, primarily adobe city of Chan Chan, the Chimú capital, was more than two miles square; its walls were densely decorated with designs also used in Chimú pottery and textiles. Chimú textiles were of highly varied types and had feathers, beads, and metal ornaments attached to the fiber weavings.

Chimú pots resemble those of the Moche in their emphasis on form over surface decoration and in their depiction of every imaginable aspect of human life. Fine craft production in many media appears to be one of the major activities in Chimú culture. The Inca conquerors appreciated this and imported large numbers of Chimú artists to their capital of Cuzco. There, Chimú artists formed new styles that mixed Inca and Chimú elements. The typical Inca pot, large-beakered and low-bellied with handles on its "hips," began to take on Chimú decorative elements as imported artists integrated forms and motifs from both cultures in their production of ceramic ware.

Incas

Like the Chavín and Huari before them, the Incas were a highland "unifying" culture. Experts can only infer information about the Chavín and Huari from artifacts and organic remains. For this reason they can at best make educated speculations about the prime motivating factor in these cultures' expansion and multiregional influence. Did these three traditions spread throughout the Andean coast, mountains, and jungle primarily to search for food and water, to promote religious traditions, or to reap the benefits of colonialism and conquest? We do not know for certain in the case of the Chavín and Huari. The Inca case is easier to decipher. For the Incas, historians have both artifacts and the advantage of access to written accounts based on firsthand narratives that Europeans and people of mixed descent or having command of both European and Indigenous languages recorded during early Spanish colonial times. These histories, diary entries, and hero tales as well as other documents reveal the military and expansionist emphasis in Inca civilization and the subsequent cultural and artistic blending that resulted from Inca acculturative influence over conquered peoples. Like all acculturative processes, however, influence moved in more than one direction. The "conquered" could have a mighty influence over the conquerors. This was particularly true when the spiritually awed Inca armies approached the ruins of mythic Tiahuanacu or the great oracle of Pachacamac. So it was, as well, when Inca military might came in contact with the fine workmanship of Chimú artists and craftspeople. The Incas added these jewels of civilization to their own crown of ethnic identity.

The Incas of pre-Columbian times gave primacy to visual ways of communicating, as previous Andean civilizations had done. Inca graphic and plastic works expressed their manner of thinking, which was also visual, rooted in referents to the natural world, and organized in terms of spatial metaphors. The Incas externalized their way of thinking through the use of images. The Incas' descendants of today inherit this strong visual legacy. Information in this section derives from "chronicles"—histories, diaries, and letters written in Quechua and Spanish during the early period of Spanish conquest—as well as from archeological research and verbal traditions among the Incas' descendants. One of the most comprehensive of the chronicles is the illustrated, bilingual, bicultural account by Felipe Juan Guamán Poma de Ayala in 1603. Also very important are the writings of the Spanish soldier Pedro Cieza de León in the mid-sixteenth century and missionary Bernabé Cobo one hundred years later. "El Inca" Garcilaso de la Vega wrote an important history that was first published in the early seventeenth century, and others including colonial governors and functionaries recorded their observations as well (note 5).

5. Guamán Poma's chronicle is particularly valuable because it was written by a person of Spanish as well as Indigenous descent who was both bilingual and bicultural. There is some bias toward official Spanish policy and ideology because Guamán worked as an employee in the colonial government during the period when the crown's policy was to forcibly remove and erase Indigenous traditions. The chronicle includes the author's mixed thoughts and feelings about this campaign and his place in it. The manuscript is bilingual in Spanish and Quechua and is heavily illustrated. Guamán's work offers rare written as well as visual accounts of the early colonial period.

The stage was set for the rise of the final Native American empire in the Andes, that of the Incas. The first dates for the Incas as a recognizable cultural tradition, before they became a conquest state, are in some dispute. The Peruvian authority Luis E. Valcarcel (1967) places the birth of the Incas as a cultural group at about 100 BCE, while North American and European scholars seem to pay most attention to the defeat of the Chancas by Pachacuti Inca Yupanqui in 1438. The Incas themselves were reputed to say that they existed as a state society nine generations before 1400 CE European time. The Incas expanded their territories in a very short period. This came about because of military prowess as well as an effective means of colonial government.

The Empire and the Colonial System

The Inca realm eventually grew to a size encompassing seven modern Latin American nations during the reigns of three emperors, perhaps with greatest expansion under the Inca Pachacutec. Pachacutec's son Topa Inca brought the empire to almost its full extension in terms of size. Within two to three generations, then, the Inca empire swept from Ecuador to Chile. It stretched from coast to mountains to ceja (eyebrow of the jungle) in breadth, as well as over the southern high plains of Peru. The empire was called Tahuantinsuyu, which means "all directions."

Efficient methods of conquest and control contributed greatly to the rapid expansion of the empire. The Inca military machine was phenomenal. The imperial armies used effective tactics such as siege and carried

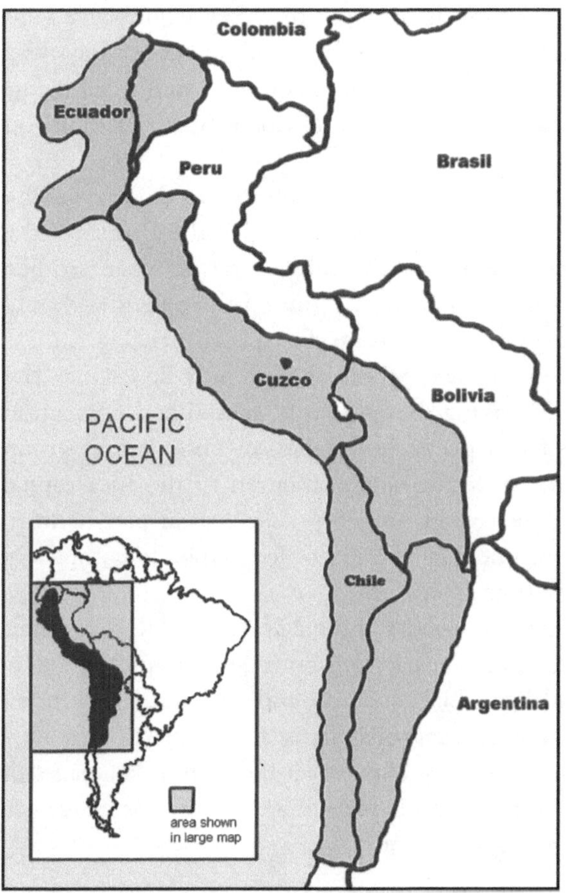

1.6 Map of Inca empire. Shading on map and inset indicates extent of the empire superimposed over modern political boundaries. Drawing by the author.

weapons made of the hardest metal yet used in the Americas: a kind of bronze called copper-tin. Eventually just hearing that Inca soldiers were advancing on a town would induce flight or surrender among peoples the Inca armies intended to conquer. On the positive side, being taken into the fold of the Inca empire had advantages unavailable outside it. The new rulers provided a constant supply of food assured by prominent storehouses as well as homes, employment, medical attention, education, child care, and security in old age. These benefits were rare in the hardscrabble lives that most non-Incas led at the time in addition to the earthquakes, volcanic explosions, El Niño events, and other unpredictable cataclysms endemic to the Andean environment that made life precarious.

The Incas took care to install reassuring visual symbols in prominent places throughout their colonies. They built large food-storage towers on high ledges above colonized farming villages. The constant sight of these structures comforted people with the thought that they would have food in hard times. The conquering empire served, in this and other ways, as a cushion against calamities. Once the rhythm of conquest was in full swing, even the mighty Chan Chan, capital of the rival Moche/Chimú empire on the North Coast of Peru, fell.

Another important factor that favored stability in the expanding empire was the Inca method of colonial control. Like the British of the modern era and the ancient Romans, the Inca exercised what is called "indirect rule." When the Incas conquered a group of people they would train local rulers in Inca ways. In exchange for special privileges, these leaders would in turn rule their own people, though now under Inca law. This had the advantage of making it appear to a vanquished population that no real change had taken place. Sometimes an obstreperous group would require the removal of local leaders' children to the Inca capital for total indoctrination. This would not only keep fearful parents from attacking but would ensure a new generation of local nobility completely acculturated into Inca traditions.

The new empire builders consolidated their power by imposing their tongue, Quechua, as the lingua franca, by promoting religious conversion, and by teaching new and beneficial technical and agricultural methods. Quechua is almost uniformly spoken today in areas once part of the empire, and it is now the most widely spoken of all Indigenous languages of the Americas. Such standardization and long duration of a language are testimony to the efficacy of Inca control.

The Incas had another method of control, that of employing the *mitmaqs* or *mitimaes*. The mitmaqs were ecological communities consisting of groups of agriculturalists, educators, and technicians sent far from their homes to the new colonies. These emissaries would introduce and grow varieties of edible and useful crops and bring domesticated animals, craft and construction techniques, language, and cultural traditions into recently conquered territories, vastly increasing predictable supplies of water, food, cloth fiber, and other community needs. Mitmaqs' work in the instruction of the state language, Quechua, the state religion, and Inca technologies made them primary instruments in the spread of religious art styles into the frontiers of the Inca realm as it grew. The Inca were later to view the Spaniards as mitmaqs of their royal capital in Spain (Adorno 2000).

The Social System

On an empirewide scale, Inca society was strictly hierarchical, with much privilege at the top of its many social levels. In contrast, egalitarianism characterized village life. Laws governing land, labor, and taxes along with a good system of communication and a predictable and forgiving yearly calendar of activities kept the imperial system functioning smoothly. The social system was orderly as well. It was created to ensure agricultural and craft production and distribution and to guarantee the construction and maintenance of public works and services. The social structure mirrored the religious system in that it had many levels and granted great authority and privilege to those at the top.

The Inca emperor never wore the same clothes twice. The royal family's rich woven raiment was testament to the high value placed on textiles as a fundamental basis of wealth. As mentioned earlier among the Incas' ancestor cultures, precious metals and jewels were considered of lesser value and prized only when wrought into religious artworks. The chronicler Cieza de León speaks of the emperor as having a large garden in Cuzco of metal "corn plants" (1945), a staple considered sacred, exquisitely wrought of silver for the stalks and gold for the ears of grain. Among these shining stands of corn wandered living llamas, all snowy white in color. All this and more was for the emperor's personal contemplation. At the beginning of the planting season, as testament to the religious importance of nature and agriculture, the emperor would lift a spade of metallic "earth" in a sacred gesture that would start official agricultural activity throughout the realm. Besides intricate textiles of the most highly prized designs and techniques, the royal leader wore gold and silver decorations and extremely large earrings. So large were they that when the Inca emperor or high nobles and provincial governors would remove their earrings, the stretched earlobes were said to dangle over their chests. Today, in Peru, people of high status are still called *orejones*, or "big ears." Below the level of the Inca emperor were many stairsteps of power. Regional governors, generals, and priests ruled over their provincial counterparts, who in turn ruled over groups of villages.

The vast majority of the people, on the other hand, lived in small agricultural and craft communities. These villages came to be called *ayllus*, though this term is a kinship designation related to the idea of clan or lineage. Thus a village can and often did have several exogamous, competing, but also interdependent ayllus. Ordinary people performed agricultural work, art and craft production, construction and maintenance of buildings and highways, and military and other social services. Most of these tasks were divided into local, provincial, and state levels. Some of the services performed for the state as a whole facilitated the incorporation of new populations into the empire. Inca supervisors made sure that

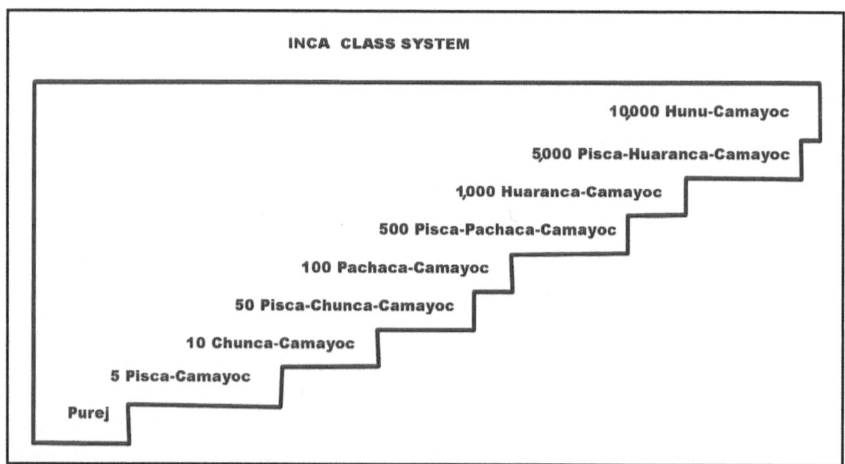

1.7 Inca class system. Numbers in ranks designate how many families respective officers supervised. The lowest rank, *purej*, was head of a single family. Above the Hunu-Camayoc, head of 10,000 families, were even higher dignitaries, powerful religious and military officials, with the Inca royal family at the top. Divisions in multiples of 5 are typical of Inca numerical systems. Drawing by the author after Luis E. Valcarcel 1967:116.

people accomplished their work by recording each person's productive activities (or lack of them) on the knotted-rope systems called *quipus*, mentioned earlier. (Salomon 2004b shows contemporary use of this system.) Such careful record keeping constituted a strong sanction to promote hard work as a basic value.

The large-scale versus small-scale societal structures in opposition maintained a kind of equilibrium. Other factors also kept the vast machine of the empire running efficiently. These included a land distribution system, tax and labor regulations, networks of roads, celebrations, communal values, and different sorts of sanctions that promoted desired behaviors.

Commoners, then, had to work the lands of the Inca emperor and local community lands before being allowed to work their private plots. These plots were called *tupus*. Each man, however humble, inherited a full tupu (about two-thirds of an acre) and each woman a half-tupu. The inheritance system was such that men and women inherited from the ayllu as individuals. When a married person died, his or her lands would revert to the ayllu. The word *tupu* means in a general sense "measure." It is used today to refer to the spoonlike pins Andean women use to secure their best-woven shawls, worn on ceremonial occasions. These pins can be used as grain measures. The mass of the population had to pay taxes to at least three levels of the state organization. That could take the form of proportions of crops or craftwork or labor service. An example of labor service was the necessity to maintain the extensive and well-constructed system of roads and bridges that netted the coast and mountains. Many of these bridges were hanging spans made of plant fiber that swung in the wind between mountains. The most famous of this kind is probably the bridge two hundred feet long crossing the Apurimac River that became Thornton Wilder's *Bridge of San Luis Rey* (1927). Some of these rope bridges—more recently built and maintained—still exist.

The life of an ordinary Inca villager, then, was one of almost constant toil and a rigidly predictable yearly calendar. In return for this labor, each person was guaranteed food, a home, a job, the care of a solicitous community, and a restful retirement in old age. The pressure of unremitting labor was somewhat relieved by yearly celebrations that fell at the solar solstices and equinoxes. Hard-working souls could then let loose with feasting, drinking, dancing, elaborate ritual, or perhaps an extramarital affair now and again. These celebrations served as a pressure valve, encouraging the people to focus on the benefits of membership in the Inca state. Today, Andean feasts and rituals are characterized by heavy consumption of food, *chicha* or *aja* (corn beer of varying alcoholic content), and *trago* (strong alcoholic drink), otherwise unpermitted sexual behavior, and social and religious dancing (Meyerson 1990).

Some authorities describe Inca society as communistic or communal. It certainly was anything but ideal communism when the lives of nobles and commoners are compared. However, given reports that there was no hunger, no homelessness, and no unemployment for any Inca, the system as a whole reflected communal values to a greater degree than, say, the situations in many modern industrial countries of the "developed" world in the twenty-first century. Where communism in close to the ideal sense perhaps existed was among members of a given agricultural village, or ayllu. Village members practiced the concept of *ayni*, or reciprocal labor. This is a form of work pooling that resembles the modern concept of cooperativism. Groups of farmers would form joint crews to break ground, plant, cultivate, and harvest each other's crops on a rotating basis. Organizations of craftspeople would collaborate on ceramic or weaving production. Another form of group labor consisted of crews of men (*mita*) or crews of men and women (*minka*) required to perform public-works duties such as road construction and building repair. Chroniclers have written that mita crews might be taken away from home for long periods. Minka projects (evidently then as now) involved lighter work near home and enjoyments such as feasting.

Excessive disparities in wealth within a village were prevented by morally sanctioned aid to poor villagers and a local patronage system for celebrations. Village celebrations had to be financed by villagers or groups of villagers thought to be most prosperous in a given season or year. Sponsors thus had to pay for food, drink, and other expenses. The system of charity and sponsorship, then, served to even out differences resulting from individual effort, luck, and other factors. The overarching ethic of economic equality created and maintained something close to a Marxian community at the village level. Interestingly, the Spanish system of *fiestas patronales* (patron-saint feast days), which came later in Andean history, had a similar economic philosophy at the village level (note 6).

6. The chronicles surviving from early colonial times attest to this arrangement as being Inca in origin. Salomon's study of modern-day use of quipus (2004b) suggests that records of individuals' labor in these knotted-rope accounting systems determined traditional Indigenous

sanctions intended to vigorously maintain communal customs. However, the rotating sponsorship of village celebrations is also a tradition in Spain. It is certain that the Spanish colonial government shifted sponsorship from individuals with the support of their kin group (ayllu) to sponsorship by craft guilds or religious brotherhoods (*cofradías*). It was in the interest of the colonial government to diminish the ayllu system of reciprocal exchange in favor of social units under its political control.

Religious sanctions encouraged sharing and redistribution of wealth. One example is a version of a fable with a narration about the accreted Inca god Pachacamac; this personage glosses somewhat Cuni Raya Vira Cocha in the Huarochiri Manuscript, translated by Salomon and Urioste (1991), named after the coastal culture the Incas so admired. He is described as often taking human form, disguising himself as a beggar, and asking for alms. If Pachacamac did not receive the charity he requested, he might turn the ungenerous soul involved to stone. Generous people, in contrast, received great rewards from the shining son of Viracocha, considered by some experts as the Incas' highest divinity. Because any poor beggar might be Pachacamac in disguise, people felt constrained to care for such people out of a combined fear of divine punishment and hope of divine and human social approval. There is a resemblance between this story and some narratives within the European classical tradition, indicating possibly a mixed cultural origin. Contemporary Andeans, perhaps out of knowledge from oral tradition or due to feelings of nostalgia for a lost ideal, recount a way travelers through the mountains would greet one another: "Do not lie, do not steal, do not cheat, work hard, good morning" or other time of day. This greeting conveys prevailing Andean values in a nutshell: honesty toward others, the necessity to pull one's weight to accomplish group tasks, and the importance of diligent and constant labor. Today, the hands of Andean art makers are seldom at rest, and support of one's family and community comes before self-promotion.

In Inca empire times and today, festival sponsors have tended to serve their own ayllu, which sometimes constitutes the population of an entire town or a great part of one along with one or two other ayllus. In a sense, the village communalism is really just taking care of one's own, though ayllus are much larger than most of the lineages or clans that anthropologists study. Ayllus compete with one another at celebrations, trade goods, and exchange marriage partners within and between villages. A person cannot marry within her ayllu because that would be incest, though the family ties include members like distant cousins who would be allowable marriage partners in the United States. Ayllu trading partners allow several of these large families to benefit from, say, ayllu 1's alpaca wool and textiles, ayllu 2's potatoes and ceramics, and ayllu 3's onions, corn, and woodcrafts. These types of goods would otherwise be out of reach due to each clan's location in a different ecozone or economic specialty (a custom explored in depth in Murra 1972).

The Family and the Life Cycle

The family constitutes a basic and most important unit in any society. Beliefs and practices within the family reveal much about the Incas' sociocultural values. As individuals passed from one stage of life to another, they shared common rights and responsibilities. The way Inca individuals lived within their families reflected the values of the society as a whole. From birth to death, a person lived a life of service compensated by a natural and social environment that provided for every need while also imposing certain strict limitations, especially for those in the lower social echelons.

When children were born, special care was given to the umbilicus in order to prevent harm to the child. A hair-cutting ceremony marked official membership in society at the age of three or four. Biologists who have studied remains of pre-Columbian Inca populations note that in general the group had a very long life expectancy and good health. However, there was a marked tendency for infant death before the age of three or four. This may be due to the physical stress of living at high altitudes or to other factors. The Incas obviously made the same observation and perhaps for this reason put off weaning and officially naming their children until they had lived through this critical period.

Guamán's chronicle describes how children's work progressed from sweeping the hearth or feeding small animals at the age of six to going out with llama or alpaca herds at nine or ten to protect them while they grazed. There was evidently a system requiring schooling for children as well that emphasized learning Inca religious and social traditions and agricultural and craft skills. Senior village members watched over infants while the children's young parents performed services required of them by the empire. As they grew older, youngsters learned to perform increasingly responsible tasks for their families and communities.

Puberty was marked by special clothing and appearance such as new ear ornaments for boys and different hairstyles for girls. Youth would go through special rites of passage during which they were removed from their everyday communities and then returned wearing such symbols of their more mature status. These ceremonies took place at the ages of twelve to fourteen; upon returning from them boys and girls were no longer children but now in the category of young adult. It was at this time of life that youthful Incas engaged in a custom called "trial marriage." Inca society was not concerned with condemning premarital sex or even out-of-wedlock babies among their own people. The Incas felt that sexual experimentation among the young was normal. This usually took the form of one or two serial monogamous relationships before official marriage. Babies resulting from this behavior were cared for by mature members of the ayllu so that issues like contemporary paternity litigation had no importance. This constellation of behaviors would shock the Spanish during European colonial times, as their values along these lines were distinct in the extreme. Modern descendants of the Incas continue to practice trial marriage to the consternation of law enforcement and social service professionals who work within a very different national system of family law largely inherited from European traditions.

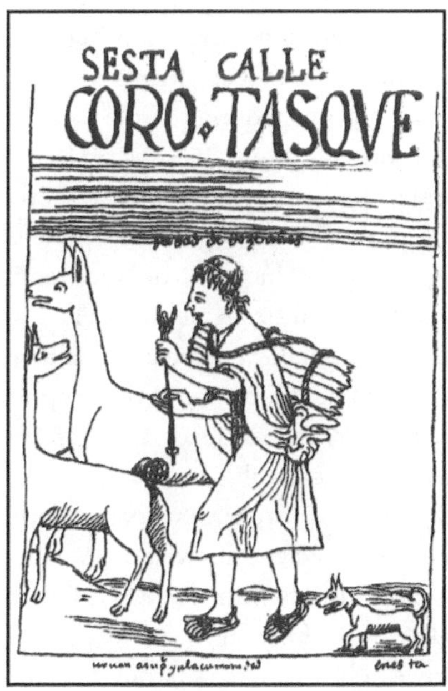

1.8 Childhood among the Incas. In this seventeenth-century drawing Guamán Poma illustrates an activity of adolescent girls in a series depicting Inca children's activities from birth to maturity. Guamán Poma de Ayala 1988:200, figure 225.

Childhood was a time of gradually increasing work and other responsibilities along with relative social freedom for youth. Figure 1.8 shows a teenage girl herding llamas. She contributes serious labor to her family and community, and she is of an age to participate in a "trial" marriage. However, when it came to formal adult marriage, Inca sanctions promoting exclusivity and faithful partnerships for life were severe and exacting. Despite the apparent strictures marriage represented, most Inca youths chose life partners by their early twenties. The married state rewarded couples with individually assigned tupus of land (the young men and women inherited land independently of their marriage partners, though they worked the joint lands together), gave them official adult status in the community, and made them eligible to sponsor village celebrations. A string of successful sponsorships could eventually lead to leadership positions and elder status for the wedded pair. These benefits were great encouragements for marriage.

The Inca state did well strategically to protect the marriage bond because it formed the foundation of governmental control and strengthened the basic unit of production in this society based on agriculture, craft manufacture, and military conquest. Accordingly, punishment for adultery was very severe: death by stoning for the offending parties. Both the man and the woman were thought equally guilty. Also during this stage when young people approached adulthood, men would perform military service for the constantly expanding empire. While the soldiers were away, young women learned specialized forms of fine weaving and pottery. When the soldiers came home, young people formed pairs in earnest and began to have families. Judging by customs still observable, young people would announce their intentions to marry, and parents would then usually approve. The period of young adulthood as a married pair constituted the most productive years in terms of labor, craft production, taxpaying, and building toward the political role of elder.

Youngsters who were considered especially talented received advanced training, and some were sent to Cuzco, the capital and center of the empire, to complete their education as military or governmental leaders. Religious specialists learned their vocations at sacred centers. Religious leaders were both male and female. However, the Spanish explorers were particularly taken with the *ñustas*. Ñustas were, according to Spanish writers, beautiful and intelligent young women who served the divinities and who were said to have remained virgins. Some folk tales and mythical stories feature ñustas whom Inca emperors chose as wives. The emperor's family was the only one practicing polygamy. Emperors and empresses were often married to blood siblings, the rationale being that since they were divine they could only marry each other. However, chronicles tell of both male and female royal spouses having a good number of unofficial marriage partners as well as an extremely large number of children.

By the time Incas reached their forties and fifties, according to many experts, they were considered senior citizens. By that time, they had earned the right to rest. Seniors lived in special neighborhoods in villages and towns, sometimes performing light work or child care while young parents toiled in the fields and craft centers. Seniors were much respected, especially those whose exemplary behavior and generous sponsorship of local celebrations earned them elder status.

When death came, family members carried the deceased around to places they enjoyed in life. The family took care to bury the dead person in a special holy grave knowing that they could continue to communicate with their family member's spirit.

Families prospered and grew in a healthy environment that provided them with a varied and nutritious diet. The extensive empire provided a wide range of climatic zones in which numerous foodstuffs grew well. This plus efficient systems of trade provided extraordinarily rich nutritional sources to people living within the empire's boundaries. Those who survived the crucial early years of infancy suffered little from disease. The dry coast and high mountains were especially healthful environments. Of course, the peoples of the Americas had an advantage in that they did not experience the degree of disease exchange and spread characteristic of the contiguous continents of Asia, Africa, and Europe. According to Guamán Poma, many Incas lived into their eighties, making them exceptionally long-lived as a population, especially at that time in human history.

Their arts celebrated the Incas' manner of thinking, values, and religious ideas. Arts of the empire featured images of the natural and spiritual world and forms and scenes from a daily life replete with meaningful and productive tasks.

Communication Systems

The Incas had mastery over advanced scientific and technological knowledge. They excelled in mathematics and engineering, and their high development of astronomy and geometry related very much to their religion. However, they had no writing system of the kind Europeans could recognize on initial contact. Inca numerical accounts and messages recorded on quipus could be carried rapidly by messengers called *chasquis* who ran in relays along the well-built Inca highways. These runners could rest in shelters called *tambos* that were placed at strategic distances. Relay runners then intercepted quipu messages and sped on toward their final destinations. According to Lanning (1967:166), the lack of writing—with its forms in quintuplicate (today we would say the need for extensive backup files) and other ungainly time- and space-consuming aspects of bureaucracies with written records—may have contributed to the efficiency of the Inca state. The Incas recorded many kinds of information in quipu and graphic form, including poetry, accounting, history, astronomical cycles, and agricultural data. Narrations based on these records were translated into Spanish and Quechua (using the European alphabetic system) in the chronicles and other colonial documents compiled by Spaniards and bicultural Andeans in the 1500s and 1600s. The famous Spanish chronicler Cieza de León notes:

> In the capital of each province there were accountants whom they called "quipucamayocs," and by (means of) these knotted ropes (quipus) they kept the account of the tribute paid by the natives of that district in silver, gold, clothing, flocks, down to wood and other insignificant things, and by (reading) these quipus, at the end of the year, or ten or twenty years, they gave a report to one whose duty it was to check the accounts so exact that not even a pair of sandals was missing . . . and I was at once amazed there by . . . the wars, cruelties, pillages, and tyranny of the Spaniards [which] had been such that if these Indians had not been accustomed to order and providence, they would have all perished . . . and after the Spaniards had passed through, the chieftains came together with the keepers of the quipus, and if one expended more (labor or crop/craft production) than the other, those who had given less made up the difference, so that all were on an equal footing. (In Gaur 1992:77)

There are other ways in which Andeans, culminating in the Incas, used visual systems to communicate. The pre-Inca Moche evidently used beans painted or marked with combination of dots and lines rather than knotted ropes. They put these beans in small bags carried by runners, who in Moche art often have animal, bird, or insect heads. These marked beans may have had numerical or verbal meaning or a combination of the two.

The custom, then, of visual record keeping was probably widespread and existed before the Incas' time. Figure 1.9 presents *tocapu* symbols, which appeared in several Inca art genera and may have functioned as units of communication.

In weaving, tocapus are often executed using the most highly esteemed *cumbi* method. Various scholars assert that tocapus constitute a visual system of communication. Among them, Thomas Barthel scrutinized tocapus on *keros* cups; he studied four hundred script signs and deciphered fifty, according to a paper he presented in Lima in 1970. Barthel employed notes and chronicles made by Spanish missionaries. With regard to these designs Gaur writes,

> It is improbable that each design corresponded to a character. However, tocapus (fairly standardized visual symbols usually encased within a rectangular format) may have contained phonetic elements found in many forms of memory aids, such as Ashanti proverbs, Yoruba love letters . . . and the embryonic script signs found in some Olmec clothing. (1992:79)

The chronicler Cieza wrote that the term *tocapu* or *tucupu* means "king's robes." This indicates perhaps at least a rank designation apparent

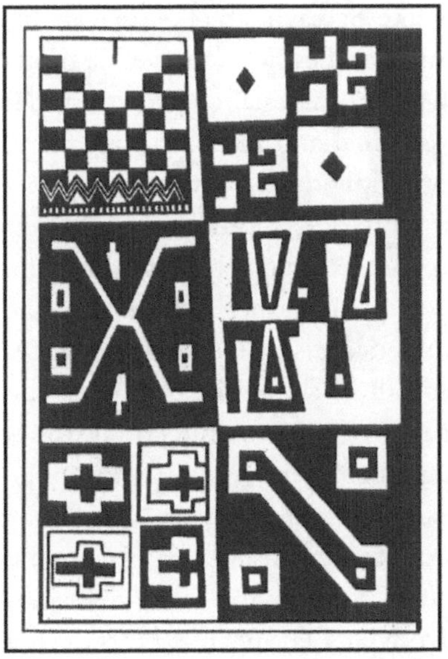

1.9 Tocapus. These emblems adorned wooden keros cups, ceramics, wall paintings, and textiles, particularly clothing and accoutrements of high-ranking Incas. Drawing by Rafael Domingo, after Phipps, Hecht, and Esteras Martín 2004: catalogue figure 18.

in Inca weaving. The idea that weaving designs, murals, and other arts containing tocapu designs might constitute a graphic code is widespread among archeologists and contemporary ethnographers. Bonavia states that mural decoration is "the expression of a symbolic language, only minor aspects of which we have been able to understand" (1985:6). Bastien says, in reference to textiles, that Andeans "dress like the mountain that gives them their clothes and the designs for their clothes" (1978: xxv). While most murals have disappeared, weavings continue to be made and worn by contemporary Andeans. Certain symbols in textiles appear to have definite meanings, as will be discussed in chapter 10, though no outsider has yet fully translated the system.

Science and Technology

Incas' technical know-how, in contrast to the inscrutability of their writing system, inspires respect among scientists of today. Some examples of their skillful work include stone masonry, water engineering, metallurgy, transportation networks, and medical practices. Even in practical and technical work the Incas left a characteristic esthetic stamp that was very much related to their natural surroundings.

Inca houses were either of stone with hexagonal windows and doors and roofs of wood or of plant material. Inca stone masonry, particularly in important religious and political sites like Sacsayhuaman, Coricancha, and Macchu Picchu, stands out as a technical and esthetic marvel. Specialists in the Inca cultural tradition, particularly in material culture, find that stonework may well be the Incas' most original and important art form. The stones, some tremendous in size, were individually cut with external and internal grooves so as to interlock with one another in the finest examples of this art. The most important Inca buildings have faced-stone blocks, often irregular in size and shape yet put together without mortar. Wedged between very large worked boulders are small, triangular pieces meant to help the walls sway rather than fall in the event of one of the frequent regional earthquakes. The outer face of many architectural stones is rounded, with an almost melted appearance. There is often a knoblike protuberance interrupting the otherwise smooth outer surface. These protuberances may have functioned as aids in stone transport or placement. The technique is still not fully understood. It is one of the many mysteries in Inca tradition that outsiders cannot solve. Many Peruvian experts as well as individuals like Rigoberta Menchu, an Indigenous Maya winner of the Nobel Prize, posit that Native Americans continue to keep secrets like this to themselves.

The Inca built irrigation systems especially for maintaining coastal agriculture but for some mountain areas as well. Many irrigation tunnels cut through the interiors of mountains. Entire mountain ranges were carved into terraces for farming. Many of these were faced with stone and are still in use. Terraces at Macchu Picchu contain elaborate below-surface structures and layered materials constructed to prevent mudslides that might have destroyed the citadel during the rainy seasons (PBS, *Nova* 2010). Towns had systems of running water with separate sources of spring water especially for drinking as well as systems for drainage and waste disposal. The level of daily hygiene was similar to that of modern urban life. Inca irrigation systems are represented by intricate stone models, some the size of a large beach ball. A person can demonstrate how the irrigation systems of a particular region function by pouring water through these working models. Modern agronomists have successfully put this ancient water engineering to work again for the benefit of farmers and householders. A number of major festivities among Andeans today revolve around cleaning and maintaining these complex water-delivery systems.

Bronze and the bronzelike metal called copper-tin were the hardest metals the Incas used. Military weapons and agricultural implements were made of this bronze. Soldiers wore quilted armor and carried slings, clubs, bolas, spear throwers, and bows and arrows. Work in other metals such as gold, silver, copper, and combinations of these was primarily decorative. The Incas knew how to electroplate without having the benefit of electricity. Some experts say the Incas used lightning or chemical methods. Gold and silver were basic components of economic wealth for Europeans. By contrast, the Incas, as previously noted, valued these metals only when they were transformed into religious, utilitarian, and/or decorative pieces. It was fine textiles that constituted the Inca "gold" standard rather than gold itself.

Since there were no heavy draft animals, plowing, carrying, and traveling were done largely by people on foot. Llamas can carry small backpacks of about one hundred pounds but are too delicate for other work. Burger (1992), however, has found that large groups of llamas carrying small packs can actually transport quite a bit of freight in valuable trade goods. Some Inca artworks show small people, perhaps children, mounted on llamas.

There are also some accounts of military campaigns involving sentinels astride llamas, notably in chroniclers' narrations about the war between the Caranquí and the Otavaleños. But llamas were not generally used as riding animals. Oddly, the Inca did not use the wheel; in this they were similar to the Aztecs (Mexica) and Mayas, with the peculiar exception in all three cultures of wheels in children's toys.

Inca roads were very well constructed in a manner similar to the techniques of ancient Romans. A major connecting road spanned the length of the empire, a distance of more than three thousand miles, and hundreds of others criss-crossed the realm. On these roads, armies, quipu-carrying chasqui runners, traders, herders, religious pilgrims, and many other groups, probably including llama caravans, traveled quickly and efficiently.

According to some archeologists who have studied pre-Columbian marine trade, the Incas carried on seagoing commerce with other Pacific coastal civilizations as far north as Central America. Inca boats were of two kinds. Woven reed boats of various sizes were used for both freshwater and ocean travel. Large balsa rafts with sails and oars were used for marine voyages up and down the coast. The author Thor Heyerdahl built a raft similar to those used for ocean travel by Polynesians as well as Andeans. With this he sailed across the Pacific in the mid-twentieth century, showing that there may have been travel and migration between the islands and the continent (Heyerdahl 1950). Boats and rafts made of reeds are still in use on the coast, some rivers, and Lake Titicaca.

Inca medics practiced "trephaning," or making holes in the skulls of fracture victims to release pressure from the brain. A large number of people suffered such fractures from club blows in war. Inca battle strategy favored close one-to-one combat with clubs, so many soldiers sustained such injuries. Inca surgeons probably used sedatives derived from coca, scrupulous hygiene, and a sort of blood transfusion method similar to that employed in the Western world in the nineteenth century. They made neat holes around the fractured bone fragments, removed them, and protected the brain with gold plates over which the bone healed nicely at the edges. Judging from the evidence, some experts say that fifteenth-century Inca medics had a very high success rate at this surgery in contrast to nineteenth-century European physicians, who lost 90 percent of their patients as a result of the procedure (Gross 1999, New York Academy of Medicine 1865) Inca surgeons were greatly helped by dealing with a population with an almost uniform blood type. Europeans had every genetic type imaginable among their patients, whose ancestry included the results of thousands of years of cross-migrations across Asia, Africa, and Europe.

Inca medical experts also performed dentistry. They filled infected teeth with gold and silver and used their advanced metallurgical skills to build dental bridges, caps, crowns, false teeth, and tooth implants. Some military generals had sets of false teeth made from alabaster, quartz, and other stones in various colors including green and purple.

Art and Esthetics

Art, as Valcarcel says (1967:181), is the expression or language of the Inca religion. The Incas were able to support grand-scale art production, including the importation of artists from conquered populations, because they had mastered the necessarily previous art of feeding and sheltering their growing population. Music, weaving, metalwork, pottery, mural painting, and stone carving are notable Inca arts, many styles and techniques of which were inherited fully or partially from ancestor traditions. The arts were a primary communicative mode for this people without writing. Following is a short summary of some of the Inca achievements in this area.

Music and Performance

The musical format used in Tahuantinsuyu (Land of the Four Directions, the name given by the Incas to their empire) and still among musicians emphasizing the Indigenous roots of their music is the five-note system in minor scale employed also by East Asians. The Incas played a large variety of pipes and flutes, pan pipes (*zampoñas*), and single-tube instruments (*quenas*). These ranged from palm size to the height of a man. There were a number of drum types and ocarinas. Conch shells, *pututus*, served to call groups together, as their sound carries well in the mountains. Songs were based on *urpi* poems (very short pieces somewhat like Japanese haiku), ballads, stories of romance and tragedy, and hero tales. People still sing these and constantly invent new versions. Contemporary Andeans engage in elaborately costumed dance-dramas as part of their traditional celebrations. These productions are full of humor as well as criticism of historical and recent events (Mendoza 2000). Other musical productions still performed can be both religious and competitive in nature; one of these, the scissors dance of Huamanga, is the subject of chapter 5.

Material Culture

Inca weaving was used for clothing and domestic adornment as well as for ritual purposes. Many of the same motifs used by the Incas' predecessors appear in their textiles. The best pieces have fine thread, dense weave, and small, well-wrought designs in brilliant colors. The Incas preferred abstraction to realism, and this is apparent in their textiles as in other art media. Inca clothing, consisting of long togas and shawls for women and short togas for men as well as waist sashes and head coverings, often had border designs (note 7). The royal family's clothing and that of high officials featured tocapu designs that were probably rank designations as well as symbols relating to nature, agriculture, and the supernatural. A chronology of the Inca royal family in Guamán's heavily illustrated chronicle shows emperors and empresses wearing finely made sashes (*chumpi*, crafted with cumbi technique), headbands, tunics, shawls, and dresses replete with these designs. Huamanga weavings of today are described in chapter 10; some of them display Inca imagery.

> 7. Andean "traditional" clothing styles consist of wide skirts, shawls, and braided hair for women, and ponchos, knee pants, knitted hats with ear flaps, and bowl haircuts for men. These derive from styles among Europe's peasants during the colonial period in Peru. Fedoras and bowler hats for both genders became stylish during the postcolonial period marked by railroad and mine development by Germans and British who wore such headgear. Particular shapes and forms of these hats complete with different types of sashes mark regional identity, especially for women. Today many Andeans, particularly the young, dress as do youth the world over.

Inca-era pottery, like wooden keros cups, weaving, and murals, had sculptural and/or painted versions of meaningful designs. Like the Moche/Chimú, Inca potters showed many aspects of human life and forms from nature in their work. Like the Nazca, the Incas made use of two-dimensional applied designs. There are certain pot and ceramic shapes and motifs that experts recognize as Inca, but much was acquired from conquered peoples and from ancestral cultures. Contemporary pottery in Huamanga will be described in chapter 8.

Inca metalworkers made jewelry and decorative items as well as weapons and tools from a variety of metals and metallic mixtures. They used stones such as the green Andean turquoise to decorate headdresses, nose pieces, earrings, necklaces, and other body adornments made of gold, silver, copper, and combinations of these and other metals. A characteristic Inca technique was that of pounding out thin sheets of metal over a mold to achieve the desired shape. Metal artists also worked in filigree to achieve an open-weave effect from the interlacing of fine filaments. The hard metal called copper-tin allowed the Inca to make tools and weapons as hard as iron. Much of the Inca repertoire in precious metals has been lost due to the Europeans' policy of melting down metal pieces into bars. Contemporary work in Huamanga in only one metal, tin, will be described in chapter 11.

Murals, or very large wall paintings, often consisted of correspondingly large, blown-up versions of tocapu designs (Bonavia 1985). Painters arranged these designs in overall or alternating patterns often following a checkerboard or parallel striped design grid. The paints were made from natural pigments, and a kind of fresco technique was used by muralists. The importance of murals for the Incas and their danger to colonial governments is described in chapter 3. Discussion of contemporary and perhaps inherited traditions in painting appears in chapter 9.

Some art experts consider Inca stonework to be the culture's finest achievement esthetically and technically. Inca stonework possesses an esthetic quality similar to that of certain traditions in Japanese art. Preference for natural forms in both systems shows a very light touch from the hands of human beings. A description of contemporary work in one type of stone, alabaster, appears in chapter 11.

Concepts of Beauty

In their original styles and their many borrowings, the Incas' esthetic sense shows notable characteristics. They favored the linear, angular, and geometric over the curvilinear, rounded, and pictorial. These preferences may derive in part from the high regard they placed on weaving and the technical demands of their particular tools and techniques, such as warp patterning, in relation to the textile medium.

In the arts of stonework and some instances of landscape architecture, the Incas left a picture of their thoughts about the relation between art and nature. Their idea of beauty in these grand-scale arts entails making small and subtle changes in natural forms in such a way that stone buildings almost appear to be made by nature itself. Inca homes, like many Andean domiciles today, offered simple, rustic shelter. Buildings and cities fit into their natural backdrops as if they had always been in those particular places. At Macchu Picchu, sacred areas were carved to mirror the shapes of the mountain range behind them. In the Sacred Valley (Valle Sagrado) near Cuzco, enormous land sculptures were gently shaped to resemble such forms as a reclining llama and a soaring condor.

This is, after all, a culture for which the sacred is in nature itself. The role of the artist is simply to reveal this relationship, though never in a way so obvious that the original feeling of awe and mystery in untouched nature disappears.

CHAPTER 2

Andean Thinking

This chapter presents some aspects of the way Andeans think by using their own art or approximations of the images in their minds with regard to nature and religion. For this reason, attention to the illustrations is just as important as the verbal text in this chapter.

The Inca religious belief system and how it finds expression visually is still alive in the minds of Huamanguino artists today. Inca ideas, in turn, came from an amalgam of traditions previous to their reign and from the peoples they conquered. The first part of this chapter describes and explains as much as possible pan-Andean ideas about origins, space, and time as these concepts relate to the structure and function of the cosmos, divinities, life after death, and the sacred in nature. The second part gives some background on a selection of nature symbols on which this book concentrates.

Origins

Inca religious beliefs include a number of origin myths gathered as the empire expanded. Other concepts important to the Inca system of sacred thought have roots in the natural spaces and time cycles of the Andean region. The Incas' penchant for abstraction reduced many concepts to mathematical and geometric mental models they employed, like many other of the world's peoples, to contemplate the cosmos. Though supernatural, this cosmos anchored itself in the empirically observable world of nature.

Science and religion were one and the same for the Incas. This mode of religious thought applied to the empire as a whole, but each local community had its own personal version based on its unique experience of nature in the immediate environmental context. Thus a particular village had its own sacred mountains, hills, waterfalls, springs, lakes, and rivers and made observations relevant to the agricultural cycle within the local geography. Villagers would observe the movements of astral bodies with respect to landmarks within their own particular valley and imbue these with sacred and practical significance.

Myths of origin and sacred beings multiplied as the empire grew and accreted the beliefs of conquered peoples. However, it was vital to the justification of their hegemony that Incas' beliefs be focused on their own capital of Cuzco (Brundage 1975). There are a number of traditional origin myths, each tied to a distinct geography. Two of the most important of these are the Lake Titicaca myth and the Hermanos Ayar myth. The civilization of Tiahuanacu, on the southern shore of Lake Titicaca, predated the Incas by four hundred years. When the Inca empire was in place, the ruins of Tiahuanacu spoke of a past glory that impressed the rulers of the new regime. The Incas therefore incorporated some aspects of the Tiahuanacu origin myth and religious ideas into their own but gave precedence to their preferred story of origin, which was strongly linked to the geography of Cuzco and its surroundings. According to the Lake Titicaca myth, it was at Tiahuanacu that the great god Viracocha first displayed the created heavens and earth. There is a very sacred island in the southern part of the lake called Rock of the Cat. It was here that, according to pre-Inca mythic tradition, the first light shone out of eternal darkness (note 1).

1. A related story about light and darkness, perhaps from the Inca tradition, recounts how Viracocha's son and child of light Tawapaca, later called Supay, inverted his father's *huaca* (sacred power). Supay would later become responsible for disharmony in the world and come to live in and operate from the dark World of Inside. The Rock of the Cat featured in the Tiahuanacu myth of origin as the place where light first came out of the darkness may gloss with the Pumapunku (Quechua for "door of the puma"), a structure in the ruins of Tiahuanacu that may represent a doorway, or ushnu, between two or more of the three Andean vertical cosmic levels.

When Topa Inca conquered this region, he took pains to worship at the famous shrine of Tiahuanacu. However, it was in Topa Inca's interest to increase the power centered in his own contemporary capital at Cuzco no matter what historical interest the Titicaca sites might have. Thus, he needed to reinterpret history such that the cosmic events connected with the sacred place he was visiting be closely attached to the first Inca ruler, Manco Capac, and his unquestioned dominion over the universe. Topa therefore created a new myth that justified the Incas' right to rule. The Inca heroic founder, Manco Capac, had three brothers, and each of the four male siblings, called the Hermanos Ayar, had a wife. (The founding pairs were brothers and sisters in some versions of this myth, a tradition that gives credence to brother/sister marriage in the Inca royal family.) Each of these couples rose out of clefts in the rocks at Paucarictambo and represented one of four founding tribes or lineages. The sun god, Inti, had made Manco Capac his son. Manco would found Cuzco as the capital of a future empire when the gold digging stick of his wife, Mama Ocllo, sank itself into the ground at the Cuzco site. It was from this point that Inca power would eventually spread to include hegemony over what the Incas considered to be the four corners of the world (Brundage 1975).

For the Inca and probably for many of the peoples they conquered, victory was less a military than a religious phenomenon. Victory was the conquest of the Inca divinities over the Chimú gods, for example. (This concept, shared by Incas and later Spaniards in Peru, would smooth the way for European conquest.) The Incas would remove images and figures of local gods and transport them to the Inca capital. In this way the Incas forced conquered peoples to face Cuzco rather than their own temples to pray. This strengthened Cuzco's position as a sacred center. The religious aspect of Inca indirect rule made it inordinately strong. According to some scholars, however, the Incas either were predisposed or found it useful in addition to moving images to assimilate some of the new divinities of conquered peoples into their own, now official religion. Brundage contends (1975) that the god Viracocha may have been invented by the Incas or made more important than in the pre-Inca past for military reasons.

The Incas added a number of new divinities to their pantheon as the empire grew. The addition of Pachacamac, mentioned before, serves as an example. Long after Pachacamac, an ancient coastal city, was an abandoned ghost town, it was held in high regard by Incas and their descendants (Lanning 1967). The pre-Inca god Pachacamac, whose name means "the earth's double" in Quechua, at some point became featured in myths describing him as taking the form of a human being physically like a European, with light-colored skin and a beard, while Andean males, like Asians, tend to have little facial hair. The Inca Pachacamac, son of Viracocha, soon came to resemble Christ in the syncretic religious process following encounters with the Europeans. He was said to have walked on water and tested the generosity of human beings while in the guise of a poor beggar. Thus, the Incas' religious tradition grew in complexity as they incorporated aspects of new belief systems they encountered among conquered groups and at ancient revered historical sites.

Space, Time, and Nature

Natural formations and the spatial arrangement of their world were very important to the Incas. Andeans had long viewed the physical space around them and its natural features in religious terms. The earth and sky constituted a large living organism nourished by waterways. In exchange for the privilege of residing in this cosmos, human beings had to share labor and resources with the divine beings and with each other to maintain everything in good working order. Sharing ensured survival and well-being for all dwellers in the cosmos. This view of reality is described beautifully by Paul Trawick in an article titled "The Moral Economy of Water" (2001) about Andean irrigation systems. Here he speaks of the profoundly other-oriented and generous Andean way of thinking and behaving.

> I cannot say where the model comes from, whether from the ground and water up or "the Spirits"—the human mind and Spirit—down. Contrary to what one might think, if forced to choose, I would opt for the latter . . . It partially reflects necessity, the impact of material constraints, but it is also, in the final analysis, an expression of certain eternal elements of human desire and intent. In the Andes, this way of life and world view emerged long ago in the sharing of water, and irrigation has helped to preserve it and hold it fast ever since. (374)

As we shall see in the following sections, water is the lifeblood of Mother Earth for Andeans; it is perhaps the most precious treasure they have. Water courses through time and space, keeping all the creatures of the earth and the universe alive and strong. Though external guises change, the power within the natural world remains.

The traditional Andean view of the universe in pre-Inca and Inca times utilized spatial and temporal metaphors employed in visual and verbal communication forms. Symbolic oppositions like male/female, sun/moon, gold/silver, and *hanan/hurin* (note 2) implied both temporal fluctuation and spatial balance. Part of the role of human beings was to help maintain this balance through proper behavior such as labor exchange and other forms of reciprocity, worship rituals, and sacrifices in the form of difficult trials as well as animal and sometimes human offerings (note 3).

2. *Hanan* (upper) and *hurin* (lower) constitute a spatial metaphor that can relate to altitude, social class, the structure of the cosmos, or reciprocal relations between ayllus (lineages) in towns at different elevations. Relations between ayllu towns are ideally represented in the Inca graphic tradition as tripartite stairsteps, which gloss with the symbol for mountain.

3. Whether Incas practiced human sacrifice and if they did to what extent are in dispute. Some of the pre-Inca Andean cultures very probably did sacrifice human beings. The Sicán people, predecessors of the Moche and Chimú, show human sacrifice in their arts.

There have been recent discoveries of Inca-period mummy burials, and media coverage connected with these has intimated that the mummies were sacrificial victims. Evidence shows that elaborately dressed children and adults died at high altitude, but just what took place remains unclear. Guamán Poma describes human sacrifice, though he had been heavily influenced by European clerics and colonial governors. These colonialists have been known to exaggerate the importance and scale of customs they found shocking to justify their conversion and governing activities.

Among modern Andeans in some regions there certainly are seasonal pilgrimages featuring dangerous physical trials. In several of these, unprotected climbers purposely put themselves in danger should the mountain divinities wish to take their lives in tribute. In other religious rituals such as the scissors dance, practitioners likewise can put themselves at considerable physical risk.

Inca believers imbued natural surroundings, animals, and plants with sacred meaning. Nature inspires fear and confidence simultaneously, since it both provides to and takes away from human beings for its own inscrutable reasons. It is then the job of people to seek harmony with nature, whether the outcome of their effort be for good or ill. Science and religion were glossed concepts for the Incas. These aspects of thought did not occupy different mental dimensions as they do for many modern Western people. Inca cosmology combined science and religion and gave high priority to astronomical observations. For that reason, directionality, geometry, and movements of the heavenly bodies were very meaningful. The Inca universe had three levels and four directions. Different mountain altitudes on the cosmic level where people live were considered separate and oppositional from a symbolic perspective. These altitudes corresponded to kin groups that exchanged marriageable individuals and to craft- or crop-producing groups that exchanged goods and produce (Bastien 1978). Andean peoples of today follow these symbolic patterns in their religious and philosophical thought.

The Inca religion gave high priority to the idea of foretelling the future. This was done in part through astronomical calculations. The sacred center of Macchu Picchu has a sun observatory, among other astronomical structures, the purpose of which is to measure and time the sun's path as it changes duration and position throughout the year. Other prophecies and curing ceremonies were carried out by observing certain bones and the entrails of sacrificial animals, consulting with the mummies of deceased individuals, observing animal behavior and weather conditions, and the like. Prophecy also gave Andeans reassurance in their seismically and climatically unpredictable world.

Abstractions about sacred space and time related directly to the concrete world of observable nature. Environmental features, plants, and animals exhibited repeating ecological cycles from one year to the next. The Inca concept of time and the practice of prophecy had to do with agriculture. To this end they studied the repeating patterns in nature in great detail. Minute studies of sunlight duration and directional patterns and the predictable cyclical patterns of plants and stars led to the efficient timing of agricultural activities. Life itself depended on these observations.

Certain shapes, or visual metaphors, that aid Andean religious thought also appear in art and ritual. Rhomboids are found in weaving, trapezoids in architecture, and the U and spiral or zigzag formations in sacred dance. Many of these geometric thought aids started in pre-Inca times. The U shape described by Burger (1992) as a Chavín visual metaphor for opposing forces probably passed through time to the Inca period. Meyerson

(1990) describes farmers sitting in the same U shape during agricultural ceremonies at the time of her research.

Visualization of the Cosmos and Its Temporal Cycles

The next three figures graphically show the major form of the Andean cosmos and some of the temporal processes taking place within it. The detailed text that follows each explains different aspects of the drawings.

Figure 2.1 shows the universe as if viewed in cutaway from the side, so that the three levels of existence can be scrutinized.

The cosmos has three vertical spatial dimensions divided by horizontal levels of reality. It is helpful to think of each of these levels as being floored by planes stretching infinitely in all directions. The World of Above, the top layer, contains celestial bodies and other divinities. The celestial bodies include the sun, moon, stars, and planets. Of particular importance is the Milky Way, which at certain times is observable as forming an X in the sky with its center over Cuzco. This mirrors the middle-level World of Here's division into four parts (Urton 1979, 1986). Major deities include

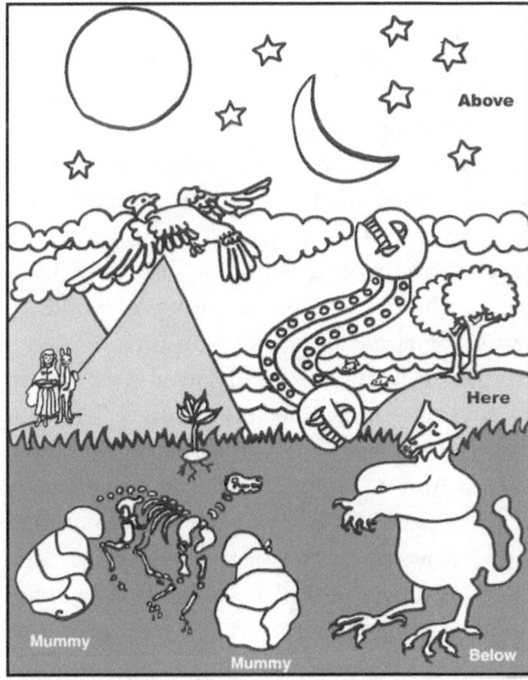

2.1 Worlds of Above (Hanan Pacha), Here (Kay Pacha), and Below or Inside (Uku Pacha). Drawing by the author.

Pachamama (Mother Earth), Pachacamac (son of Viracocha whose name means "the earth's double"), Mother Moon, and Viracocha, the unseen male god whose full name is Apu (supreme ruler) Kon (fire) Titi (all things) Vira (land) Cocha (water), according to Valcarcel (1967:157).

The central zone, the World of Here, is where people, animals, plants, geographic features, and meteorological processes exist (in short, the perceptible world). This plane is itself divided into four parts or directions based on the trajectory of Inti, the sun divinity, and a line drawn perpendicular to the sun's daily path (figure 2.2). Cuzco marked the center of the X or cross form delineated into these divisions.

The bottom realm, the World of Below, is sometimes translated as the World of Inside. This dimension encompasses two opposite symbolic concepts: it is the place of death on the one hand and new life on the other. Supay (note 1) resides in the Below world along with mischievous figures like Pishtaco, who escapes to the World of Here to feed on people's and animals' vital forces. The bodies of the dead were wrapped like plant bulbs and buried in this realm while their souls labored there (figure 2.3). These human seeds, along with those of animals and plants, have the potential to sprout new life in the World of Here. *Huacas*, or sacred tombs of ancestors with associated artifacts (*huacos*) and animal remains, also lie in this dimension.

In and between these vertical zones are points of transition from one level to another, and there are beings who specialize in moving between worlds. The deity Pachamama, residing in the Above world, is known to visit the World of Here in serpent form. Minor divinities like Condor and Rainbow travel between zones and facilitate cross-dimensional human communication. Condor has wings and so can potentially take the prayers of humans from Here to the Above world. Rainbow has two heads equipped with teeth for grasping the division planes between worlds in order to assist human prayer. Geographic points of transition between worlds make them particularly sacred to Andeans and sites for their most important rituals. Mountains physically unite the three worlds. The tops of mountains are optimum places for prayer and the gathering of sacred water in ice form, being close to Above. The insides of mountains contain extensions of the World of Below (figure 2.3). Caves in the ground unite the worlds of Here and Below, as do the ocean, springs, streams, rivers, waterfalls, lakes, and lagoons. Caves and places where water flows or is contained have the potential to be *ushnus*, portals between cosmic realms. Elements of weather like rain, snow, and lightning extend from the

Above world into the realm of people and so indicate the deities' changing reactions to human behavior.

Figure 2.2 shows Tahuantinsuyu, the central plane where human beings live, as if viewed from above.

Tahuantinsuyu's four directions or suyus—Antisuyu (east), Contisuyu (west), Chinchaysuyu (north), and Collasuyu (also spelled Qollasuyu, south)—were determined by the line of the sun's daily trajectory bisected by its perpendicular. Figure 2.2 represents some aspects of the World of Here plane of reality in the horizontal dimension. The city walls around the Inca capital of Cuzco were built in the shape of a puma. These walls represented in miniature the belief that the entire World of Here (Kay Pacha) existed on the back of an enormous puma earth deity. A small park with illustrative plaques in the city today shows the outlines of this wall. Figure 2.2 shows the puma transected by the lines dividing the city and the Inca empire into four parts, with the crossing point indicating the navel of the world or center of the universe in the heart of the feline-shaped urban capital. Scholars point out that the Incas discriminated between different parts of their realm and the people residing in them. Those who were members of the original Inca lineages and lived primordially in and near Cuzco held highest prestige. Some areas of the city, near the cat's head (where the Sacsayhuaman fortress is shown in figure 2.2) and the central body (where the Coricancha, or Temple of the Sun, sacred enclosure signals the center of the universe), contained the abodes of the upper classes, while the lower rungs of society lived near the back and tail. The peoples of the jungle, the *chunchos* of Antisuyu, were and still

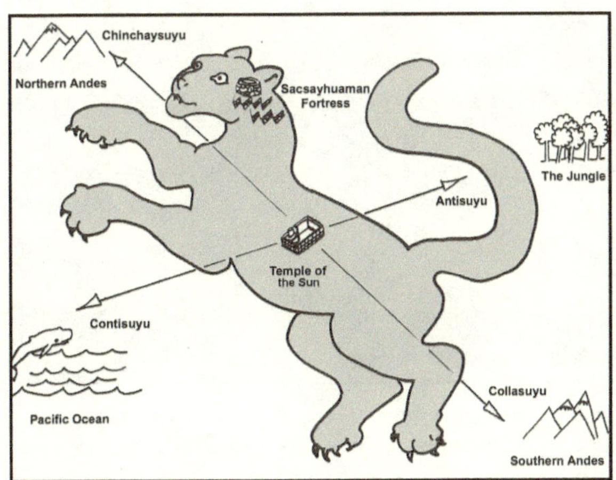

2.2 Tahuantinsuyu, Land of the Four Directions. Tahuantinsuyu was the name given to the Inca empire. Its four parts or *suyus* were Antisuyu (east), Contisuyu (west), Chinchaysuyu (north), and Collasuyu (or Qollasuyu, south). Drawing by the author.

are thought to be especially uncivilized, crude, and primitive but at the same time mysterious holders of ancient spiritual and medical wisdom (chapter 10).

Figure 2.3 shows what happens to a human being after death, according to Inca theology. As in figure 2.1, the viewer looks at the cosmos from the side so all three levels are visible. The numbers, explained below the figure, show temporal sequences of events.

Rather than being an illustration of spatial concepts like figures 2.1 and 2.2, figure 2.3 depicts one of the temporal/spatial cycles important in Andean thinking. In this progression as shown in figure 2.3, the deceased is being carried on a litter and held with tethers in squatting position for burial (1). Here the dead person's family carries him around to places he enjoyed in life. The deceased then is buried in a bulb-shaped mummy bundle with the kind of face mask sometimes found by archeologists (2). While inner wrappings for the body may be of rich textiles, the outer layers were often of rough cloth. The mummy bundle resembles a plant

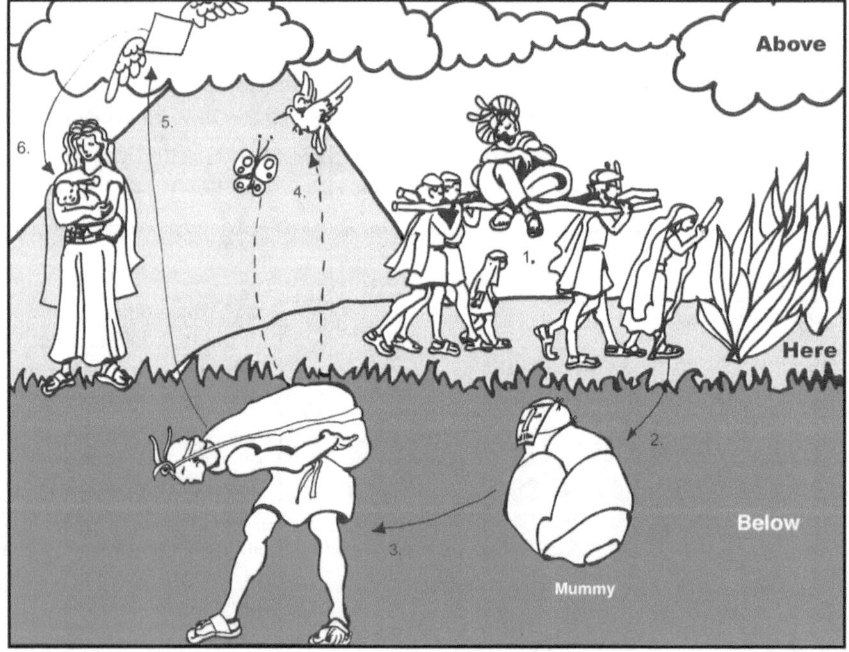

2.3 Progression of Souls. 1. Body carried on a litter. 2. Body buried. 3. Soul laboring Below. 4. Deceased visiting Here as hummingbird or butterfly. 5. Soul migrating to mountaintop. 6. Soul reborn as a human. Drawing by the author.

bulb in shape. The natural dryness of many coastal and mountain climates led to mummification without any special human intervention. Next, the soul is laboring in the World of Below (3). The soul operates, in a sense, apart from the body, and all souls of the deceased must perform arduous spiritual duties in the World of Below. This hard work in the afterlife finds artistic form in the shape of the snail burdened by its enormous shell. The soul shown in drawing 4 is returning temporarily to the World of Here in the form of a hummingbird or butterfly. If the family members of the deceased pray hard enough, they may be visited by their ancestor in the shape of these creatures. In drawing 5, the soul is migrating to the top of a mountain. Families in ancient times actually transported the mummies of their loved ones to caves in higher and higher mountain elevations. This advancement symbolizing the spiritual progress of the deceased in the World of Below's mountain extension up toward an eventual rebirth from the pinnacle. People would also temporarily remove the mummies of important Inca rulers and sages from their burial places for religious or political consultation. Finally, the soul of the ancestor is being reborn as a new infant (6), completing the life-death-life temporal cycle and its movement through sacred space.

Several illustrations and captions made by the chronicler Guamán Poma exemplify ways Andeans then and now have viewed some native animals and natural surroundings as they relate to repeating cycles in nature. Cycles inside each geographic zone and the subzones within it could be very different from one another because of the Andes' extraordinary diversity of climate. Ancient and modern Indigenes have solved this dilemma by developing their own particular local cosmological structures and cycles. These multiple sacred universes were adaptations to specific econiches while also echoing the rhythms of the larger-scale or empirewide religious tradition.

Writer-artist Guamán Poma's description of religious activities during different times of the year includes the drawing shown in figure 2.4 of a llama being prepared for sacrifice. It is raining, as it does in the Huamanga region from late February through April. Both the sun and moon deities hang in the sky. The accompanying verbal description of March illustrates the importance of water in this dry land, March being one of the wettest and greenest months in parts of the highlands:

> March is the month when the earth matures. In this month, they (the Incas) sacrificed black llamas to their idols and gods, whose names were

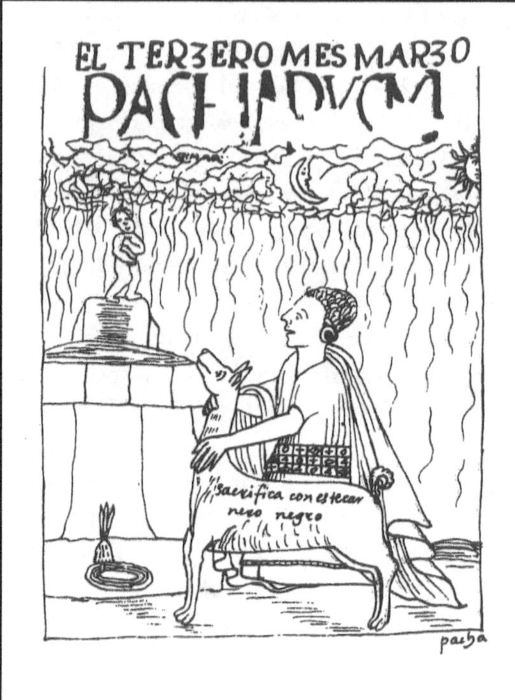

2.4 "The Month of March." Guamán Poma de Ayala 1988:214.

> Huacavilca and Orcocona. Religious leaders called walla wisas and conde wisas (high level sorcerers) along with bay coconas (witches who could speak with devils and according to custom would fast, not eat salt for many days, and refrained from sex, fruit, and sacred dance) engaged in ceremonies and idolatries. In this month, they would eat new potatoes, early corn, and ripe yuyos (water plants), which are healthy and good and do no harm. In this month, there was no hunger in the empire, and the animals had plenty of grass to eat. (Guamán Poma de Ayala 1988:215)

Guamán's use of the terms "sorcerers," "witches," and "idolatries" reflects the perspective of his European employers as well as a fear of the supernatural shared by Incas and Spaniards. He shows joy in the bounty of water and plant foods available at this time of the year. The Andean concept of nature encompasses both helpful and harmful aspects. Nature has raw power that can manifest in either benevolent or harmful form from the perspective of human beings. In a sense, nature demonstrates wisdom that human beings do not have the capacity to comprehend. As a result, people must respond by simply accepting the events and effects of nature, whatever they may be. The environment provides food, shelter, and other benefits, but it can also be a source of danger and illness.

Animals and other elements of nature have double personalities. On the one hand they have extreme and sometimes frightening spiritual potential. Certain creatures like the puma are said to prey exclusively on the souls or hearts of their victims. On another, more obvious level, animals are just ordinary creatures with earthly attributes. A panel by Guamán about the early growing season shows birds and animals eating a crop of young corn and a woman beating a drum to scare them away (1988:1032). This takes place at night, since Guamán has drawn a moon in the sky. The animals seem quite normal invading agricultural land as they do to get an easy meal.

Animals and plants endemic to the area formed part of the Inca religion, as did natural formations such as mountains and waterfalls. All aspects of nature appear in Andean ritual, especially those connected to annually repeating agricultural rhythms. The seasons in the Southern Hemisphere are the reverse of those in the north. Farming forms the bedrock of the Andean economy, so major ritual activity was reserved for times of low demand for agricultural labor such as winter. Correspondingly, farmers worked hard in their fields during the growing season, October through April, and engaged in major religious observance from May through September. The Inca calendar gave primacy to astronomical observations such as the equinoxes and solstices. For a sun-worshipping people, the winter solstice was a particularly fearful time. The winter solstice rituals, called Inti Raymi, were for that reason of great importance. During the Inti Raymi (meaning "sun-tying ceremony" in Quechua), worshippers tried to tie the sun to the earth so that it would not continue to fade away as it appeared to be doing in winter. The fluctuations of bright bodies like Venus, the ascendance of constellations such as Yacana (the Llama) and Chakana (the Southern Cross), and other stellar events were accompanied by important rites and associated practical activities. Inca ritual was grand in scope, carried out on a massive scale, and performed according to strict requirements.

Inca religious ritual in the empire period was marked by public displays featuring enormous numbers of people. Dance accompanied by music and song, often in chorus, was a major form of prayer. Hundreds, even thousands of ritual dancers wore elaborate clothing and props that figured strongly in their tightly choreographed displays. Offerings commonly included sacrificial animals such as llamas of the wool color prescribed for each ritual occasion. Evidently there were public confessions and acts of personal trial, usually physical feats, performed by specialists who had undergone years of spiritual preparation. These ceremonies were enacted for the redemption of society in general. Today, major regional festivals like those dedicated to local patron saints feature large-scale public displays. Well-drilled dance-drama teams compete with one another to best exhibit desired ritual skills and attitudes.

This very brief account gives a general sketch of the pre-Columbian way of thinking about the universe that is based on artifacts, records put together about Inca lifeways in early Spanish colonial times, and oral tradition collected by ethnographers. However, all of the narratives, written and visual, available today are partial and heavily influenced by colonial and postcolonial thought. The great Peruvian writer and anthropologist José María Arguedas (1985) lamented his inability to access truly untouched, that is, purely Indigenous Andean belief, and there are few, if any ethnographers of the past or present able to match the depths of his experience and understanding.

Nature Symbols in Art

This section presents descriptions of selected elements of nature important to Andeans past and present. The study in subsequent chapters will concentrate on the corpus presented here, which, though it represents only a small part of the whole, examines some of the more important images appearing in regional arts. Categories chosen include astral bodies, earth forms, and meteorological elements including weather- and climate-related phenomena as well as plants and animals.

Astral Bodies

Astral bodies include the sun, moon, planets, and stars that for Andeans reside in the World of Above. People observe most of them at night, but some of the most important ones characterize daylight hours as well.

The Sun (Inti, Sol)

For an agricultural people, knowledge about the daily and yearly cyclical positions of the sun, the angles of its rays, and the relative hours of daylight and darkness at different times of the year is vital for growing good crops (though differences in length of daylight are miniscule in the tropics). Andeans built elaborate sacred observatories like Macchu Picchu to track the sun's movements. In this way they could predict optimum times for planting, harvesting, wool shearing, and other agricultural activities. The sun in some weaving traditions is shown as a rhomboid with rays arranged according to its position in the sky. European colonial and postcolonial arts show the sun as a round circle with a face and a fiery aura, after the European style of the time. The sun relates to the idea of a yearly cycle of time, dryness and dry months of the year, daytime, and the masculine principle. Inti and the metal gold are coterminous, gold being the "sweat

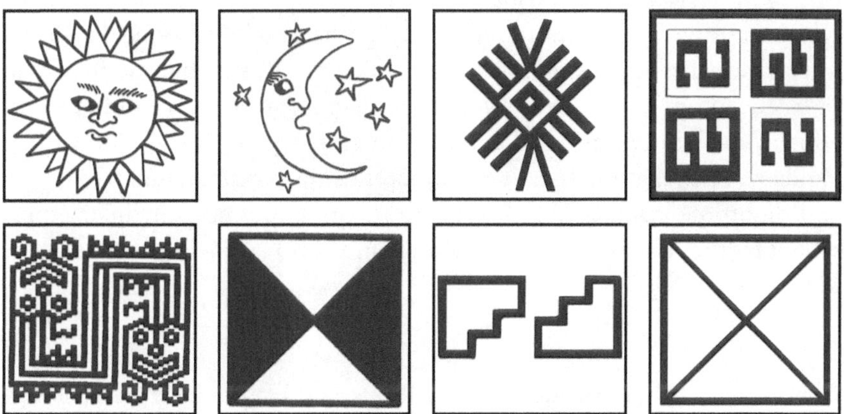

2.5 Sun (Inti, Sol). Drawing by Rafael Domingo after anonymous work.

2.6 Moon (Killa, Mama Pajsi, Luna). Drawing by Rafael Domingo after anonymous work.

2.7 Star (Ch'aska Quullur, Ch'ism Ch'aska, Lucero, Estrella). Drawing by Rafael Domingo after anonymous work.

2.8 Lightning (Illapa, Rayo) and Thunder (Trueno). Drawing by Rafael Domingo after anonymous work.

2.9 Rainbow (Amaru, Cuurmi, Arco Iris). Drawing by Rafael Domingo after Moseley 1993:109, figure 47.

2.10 Earth (Pachamama, La Tierra). Drawing by Rafael Domingo after anonymous work.

2.11 Mountain (Apu, Montaña). Drawing by Rafael Domingo after anonymous work.

2.12 Cultivated field, agricultural plot (Chacra, Chácara, Campo, Plantación). Drawing by Rafael Domingo after anonymous work.

of the sun" in some folk traditions. Inti is a major male divinity whose offspring founded Cuzco, the Inca capital, and it is the progenitor of the Inca imperial family.

The Moon (Killa, Mama Pajsi, Luna)

The moon is a major goddess, and the word *killa* also means "month." The moon's phases clearly relate to the length of a month, the menstrual cycles of women, the female principle, nighttime, and childbearing. The moon is important during the rainy months of the growing season and in art takes both abstract and realistic form in ways similar to the sun. European representations of the moon's phases influenced Andean artists who worked in a more realistic style during colonial times. The moon's metal is silver, which in some folk traditions represents the "tears of the moon." Art pieces often place the sun and moon and/or their metals side by side in a kind of balanced opposition. Jewelry and the decorative arts, for example, may contain the same number of elements in each type of metal. The scholar Zuidema finds that the Incas used an interlocking combination of daytime and nighttime calendars, each relating to the opposing principles represented by the sun and moon (in Morris and Von Hagen 1993:180–181).

Stars and Planets

Certain stars, groups of stars, constellations, and planets have spiritual significance for Andeans. Temporary disappearance of the open star cluster known as the Pleiades marked the period of thirty-seven days not accounted for by the two-calendar system.

The morning and evening star known as Lucero is actually the planet Venus, the brightest planet and the third-brightest object in the sky. Lucero's comings and goings as well as those of the sun and moon mark the beginnings of day and night, though at different times of the year. The word *lucero* in Spanish means "light giver" or "lighting the way," and the Spanish term is often used. The Quechua term *ch'aska* means "star" in the general sense. There are a number of designations for Venus, the morning and evening star. Among them are Ch'aska Quullur (daytime) and Ch'isin Ch'aska (nighttime). In Indigenous-period art and that of more remote communities today including textiles, this and other planets and stars can take a rhomboid shape with extended rays. In postcolonial art this type of heavenly body has five or six triangular points arranged in a circle familiar in European tradition. Venus is one of only three planets that rotates "backward," that is, from east to west. It appears to viewers on earth to move back and forth in the sky as it rotates around the sun. It disappears to earthly eyes for a little over a month between its role as announcer of morning and harbinger of evening. Because Venus is so visible and its movements so unusual, it became special to Andeans as it was to Mediterranean observers like the ancient Greeks, who thought it must be two different planets (National Audubon Society 1991:644).

Constellations

There are two types of Andean constellations: "dark cloud" and "starry." Dark-cloud constellations are areas in the night sky surrounded by stars. Andeans see in these spaces the outlines of animals and other shapes. The dark-cloud constellations include the Llama, Fox, Toad, and Snake. Starry constellations are ones in which the stars themselves indicate the shapes Andeans see. Some of the starry constellations include the Two Pumas, the Southern Cross, the stellar body called the Milky Way, and the Condor. Among the principal constellations for Andean observers were these: the Llama, Fox, Toad, Snake, Condor, Two Pumas, Milky Way, and Southern Cross. (Further details on the land creatures the first six represent are provided in the Animals section below.)

Yacana is the spiritual double (*camac*) of llamas. Llamas, in turn, are symbolic doubles or stand-ins for human beings. The Yacana constellation represents a female llama and her baby. These two figures constitute a dark-cloud or negative constellation in the Milky Way between the "coal sack" (located with Alpha and Beta Crux on one side and Alpha and Beta Centaurii on the other) and Epsilon Scorpii. One of several constellations of importance to Andeans, Yacana has a vital role. She must constantly drink seawater to keep the land safe from deluge by the ocean. *Yaku* means "water" in one of the Quechua dialects. The constellation appears to austral human eyes above the horizon at the time of llama fertility. In Andean art, llamas are associated with water, salt, femaleness, breeding, symbols including U shapes, rivers, springs, and small ducks and other birds. All these are mimetically related. Fertility ceremonies in springtime involved smearing llamas with red ochre in abstract shapes symbolizing these and other concepts (Berenguer and Martinez 1989:390–416).

The Fox (Atuq, Atoq) is in a dark-cloud area between Scorpio and Sagittarius.

The Toad (Sapo) is in the dark area between the Fly and Carina constellations.

The Snake (Machacuay Wayanara) extends through the dark areas from near the Southern Cross to Canis Major. The serpent constellation is visible during the rainy season. It may associate symbolically as the night version of the rainbow that comes out of the earth in the daytime after a storm. The Snake constellation is not visible during the dry season.

The Condor (Kuntu, Quntur) is the upper part of Scorpio.

The Two Pumas (Puma Yunta) constellation is known to Westerners as Gemini. Andean legend has it that one or the other of these pumas sometimes jumps at the sun or moon with the idea of eating it. This causes eclipses of the sun and moon.

Mayu means "river" in Quechua, "sky river" in this case. Mayu (the Milky Way) is a night-sky mirror of earthly waterways. It forms the shape of an X in the sky at certain times. The cross-point in the X indicates the sun's zenith point above Cuzco. The shape of the X also signals the idea of Tahuantinsuyu, Land of the Four Directions.

The Southern Cross (Chakana) also may carry this symbolic import. The cross or X form superimposes on the Christian cross as well, allowing for multiple and simultaneous interpretations of meaning. Chakana ascends from the horizon for nine months and determines the timing of important agricultural activities.

Sky Beings and Weather

During the day a number of features are seen in the sky—the sun, other stars, the moon, and planets—that have supernatural and sometimes divine qualities for Andeans. Most of these have to do with meteorological conditions, which are of vital importance to agriculturalists. Andeans believe weather conditions to be ordered upon them by the divine powers. Good weather indicates that the divinities are pleased and bad weather that people have behaved at less than the required level. Accordingly, farmers try to propitiate the divinities in order to receive weather that is most helpful for farming activities.

Lightning (Illapa, Rayo) and Thunder (Trueno)

Lightning (*rayo* in Spanish) is a mysterious and sometimes destructive force. Electrical storms at high altitude can destroy animals and people. They can fell trees and split boulders. Artists represent Rayo with zigzag lines. These same zigzags (*quenquo* or *qenqo*) can symbolize the idea of a supernatural being, which could be Amaru (figure 2.9) or even Pachamama (under Earth Forms, below) or all of these ideas at once. Illapa is the name of a sky being that sometimes combines the notions of lightning, lightning flash (*relámpago* in Spanish), and thunder. Thunder, Trueno, is the announcer of lightning but does not appear to take form in art, pending further research.

Rainbow (Amaru, Cuurmi, Arco Iris)

The minor divinity Amaru, or Rainbow, is an unusual spiritual entity in that he befriends human beings, as does Condor, in his role as connector and messenger god. Amaru can relay messages and concerns between the Here world and that of Above. His shining form consists of a ribbon of brightly colored stripes with a head at each end. One head grasps the Above world in its jaws and the other the Here world. Amaru in art is sometimes a striped, snakelike creature that coils in loops or zigzags. Other times the stripes have jaguar spots in them. The double heads may show serpentine forked tongues and/or may exhibit the interlocked eyeteeth, slit iris eyes, and ear shapes of large feline predators such as jaguars and pumas. Representations of Amaru, then, are multivalent symbolically and can range from abstract zigzag or undulating lines to much more naturalistic depictions.

As stated above, weather conditions and astral formations indicate how the divinities are feeling about human beings and their activities, especially whether the gods believe they have received sufficient ritual propitiation. Accordingly, divinities send good or bad weather conditions from their supernatural abode in the World of Above to the human home in World of Here as a reward or divine punishment. The idea of reciprocal exchange of labor and goods, the basis for the human moral code, extends to include the divinities and spiritual powers in general. Astral formations and cycles present fewer anomalies, but when they occur, as in the case of comets and eclipses, Andeans believe them to be highly significant.

Earth Forms

For Andeans, what may be called the "inanimate" aspects of nature are in fact very animated and sometimes appear to influence human lives even more than moving and growing creatures like animals and plants. Andeans imbue the physical aspects of the landscape with spiritual force.

Mother Earth (Pachamama, La Tierra)

Mother Earth is a goddess who is the life-sustaining earth itself. She sometimes takes the form of a large snake in Indigenous art and has the Virgin Mary as her syncretic alter ego during and after Spanish colonial times. Art shows parts of the goddess when it depicts agricultural fields of various types and states of use in tocapu emblems. Andean farmers depend on Pachamama for the continuing health and fertility of their families, domestic animals, fields, and crops. Caves and holes in the ground communicate with the Below world, so Andeans have traditionally buried religious art and "planted" clothed figures and bunches of flowers (*mallqui* representing ancestors) into Pachamama's surface for religious reasons. They offer prayers, sacrifices, and libations to the divinity often during major and minor rituals. She is a constant, all-pervading presence, the solid support upon which the World of Here rests.

Mountain (Apu, Montaña)

Mountains are formations in the World of Here that extend upward close to the World of Above. As such, they are the best places from which to pray and perform rituals, and the very best of these are the highest snow-covered peaks. The insides of mountains are extensions of the World of Below wherein reside the supernatural being Supay and at times the *huamani*, powerful spirit beings who often take the form of winged creatures. The souls of the dead must migrate through this Inside world extension to the tops of mountain peaks if they are to be reborn. Artists sometimes depict mountains with fiery extensions coming from their tops and sides. This may be a reference to the volcanic activity common to the region as well as to certain aspects of the nature of the World of Inside. Each community has its own sacred mountain, or apu, which it worships and within which its dead ancestors lie buried. Snow-topped mountains with associated high-altitude springs are the origin points for sacred and life-giving water.

Mountains may be triangular, as in European tradition, but they may also be stepped rectangles as shown in figure 2.11. The steps can stand for the three levels of the cosmos, ayllus living at three altitudes and interchanging goods and services, or both concepts at once.

Water (Unu, Yaku, Agua)

Water is the lifeblood of Mother Earth and a stand-in for the human circulatory system. Accordingly, ice from the tops of apus is sacred, and springs (*pacarinas*) are communication points with the World of Below and are thus sacred places where people conduct rituals. Streams, rivers, and to an extent irrigation canals correspond to human veins and arteries. Ponds, lakes, and the ocean are repositories of the vital sustenance provided by water. Waterfalls are much like caves, communication places between worlds, and Andeans use them as sites for special rituals.

Andean rituals involve water and the earth's hydraulic system and blood and the bodily circulatory system as conterminous symbolic concepts. Some fertility rituals involve throwing a llama heart (symbolically like a seed meant to ensure water supply and other benefits) into water, and public dance-dramas have actors wielding whips against others' unprotected legs, causing minor blood flow. In art, water/blood can take the form of parallel curving lines among Indigenes and realistic form in the colonial era.

Water in art may look like its natural referent, as in the European tradition of realism, or it may consist, according to some artists, of one or several parallel extensions of serpentine lines.

Agricultural Plot, Cultivated Field (Chacra, Chácara, Campo, Plantación)

There are hundreds of terms for different kinds of cultivated fields, the types of furrows made in them, seed beds, irrigation systems, and planting designs for crops grown. Andeans are an agricultural people, and this is a highly developed scientific technology in their tradition. A very simple indication for a plowed field is a square with an X in it. More complicated symbols can link cultivated lands with different extended families who work them.

Plants

The Andean environment provides fertile growing possibilities for many kinds of plants. Among food plants particularly important are the staples potatoes and corn as well as the high-protein grain quinua. Andeans love flowers. They raise them near their homes, wear them in their hats, and use them in religious ceremonies. Certain types of flowers have special significance. Many traditional love songs liken romantic partners to flowers. Trees and other plants are also important, though only a few are included here.

Flower (Tika, Flor)

Flowers as well as their stems and leaves can be represented in generalized geometric shapes or naturalistically. Spanish colonial–style flowers often serve as design templates and space fillers.

Potato (Papa, Patata)

Potatoes are the staple food of the cool mountain regions. They are highly nutritious and thus found at most meals. As the Andean staff of life they take major roles in religious activities similar to those of wheat and wheat products like bread in Europe and rice in Asia. The potato flower, the green plant, and the root itself take both realistic and abstract form in art. Andeans were the first people to domesticate the potato. Eventually they

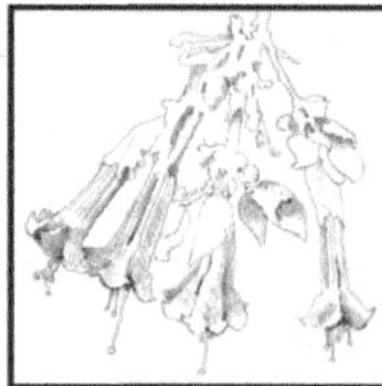

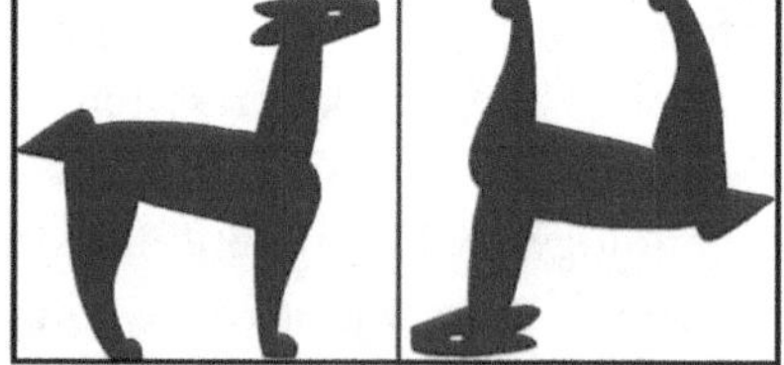

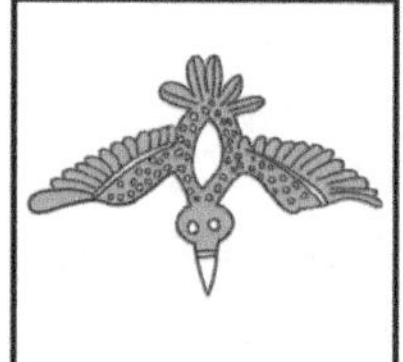

2.13 Potato flowers. Drawing by the author after anonymous work.

2.14 Cantuta flower. Drawing by the author.

2.15 Llama. Drawing by the author after anonymous work.

2.16 Hummingbird (*Qinchu, Qinti, Picaflor, Zumbador*). Drawing by the author after anonymous work.

developed myriad varieties, each growing particularly well in one of the many and varied econiches provided by the mountain habitat. Potatoes spread to Europe, where at first they were thought to have aphrodisiac qualities and therefore fit only for the elites. Eventually the tubers came to the tables of common folk on the continent. Eating a diet heavy in potatoes first supported and later destroyed the population of Ireland, whose growers were not prepared for a blight that obliterated the only variety of potato raised on the islands. From Europe the potato spread around the world as an important food.

Corn (Sara, Maíz)

Corn is a staple food particularly in warm temperate regions. Its plant, seed ears, flowers, and tassels appear in art. Corn accompanies meals, and it is featured in religious ceremonies. Corn was first domesticated in what is now Mexico and Guatemala by Mesoamerican cultures, probably ancestors of groups such as the Maya and Mexica. Andeans likely learned of corn cultivation though coastal ocean trade with these cultures, which developed myriad corn varieties from a primitive maize type. Andeans continued to develop varieties adapted to their climates, ranging from the enormous ears known as *choclo* to small and medium-size types with all sorts of seed shapes and colors. Corn cultivation and consumption spread from the Americas to Europe and from there around the world.

Quinua

Quinua is a high-protein grain that supplements Andeans' largely vegetarian diet. The characteristic large, red seed head of the quinua plant appears in art in pictorial and abstract representations as well as in border designs.

Ichu

Ichu is a grass eaten by many wild and domesticated animals. It grows in a characteristic bushy fan shape and appears in art in its green wet-season color and its golden dry-season appearance. Ichu grass can be used in house construction, and in burnt form it provides a good black color for use in making art. Andeans say that llamas and alpacas are not happy if they do not have ichu to eat.

Cantuta Flower

The bell shape of the lily-like cantuta suggests that it is related to a family of alkaloid-containing plants that serve to induce trance, sacred dreams, and sometimes hallucinations in religious specialists. The most famous of these are the jungle plants used as ingredients to produce the hallucinogen *ayahuasca*. The cantuta figures in Andean art in all periods, and in colonial and contemporary arts its depiction is an assertion of Indigenous pride. The long, bell-shaped flower has several color varieties including purple, pink, white striped, and yellow, but in art and life it is usually red. The cantuta tricolor variety has red petals, a yellow floral tube, and a green calyx. It is probably this variety that figures in the legend about a wedding between Rainbow and Cantuta that explains how the formerly white flower changed into a multihued bloom (Paredes Candia 1972). The cantuta is the national flower of both Peru and Bolivia.

Retama

This bright-yellow flower from a bush growing on riverbanks serves as a yellow dye, and its stems produce a pleasant green tint. The flower has medicinal qualities, serving to alleviate headache. The retama flower in Huamanga became a political symbol representing the common people during the violent period of unrest in the 1980s and 1990s. Singers and visual artists painted and spoke of the flower instead of the people it symbolized during that time and thus escaped reprisals from those fomenting violence.

Molle

The molle is a tree growing in the Huamanga and other areas. Its green leaves make various forms of commonly used yellow and green dyes. The female plant produces a characteristic pinkish-purple fruit that is used to make a drink, *chicha de molle*. The leaves, wood, and branches of the tree serve many rural uses; among these, the ground leaves are applied to help cure horses' and donkeys' saddle sores.

Maguey

This is a large succulent plant of the agave family with a woody trunk and tall, pointed leaves with spines on the edges. The trunk served historically as a construction material and to make art. The leaves contain fiber and could be used to produce cloth and a paperlike writing material. The spine at the leaf's end serves as a needle attached to one of the fibers as a thread. The leaves produce a sweet juice, and they can be employed to make substances that serve as soap and lotion.

Maguey plants often appear in art as background foliage and space fillers. Andean art makers use a combination of maguey wood and fiber plus other materials to make a kind of compressed "wood" for certain types of artifact construction (chapter 6). This was primordially one of the few woody plants that could grow in the high-altitude dry areas of the Andes. The eucalyptus tree now replaces the maguey as a wood source.

Cactus (Kaktu, Sankay, Cacto)

Several varieties of cactus grow in Huamanga. There are tall, branching types that produce flowers in November and December and a highly prized fruit during the rainy season in March and April. Art depicts people harvesting this fruit (*tuna*). A short and more flat-leafed variety growing on adobe and stone fences gets infected with cochineal insects that form white rust on parts of the leaf surface. Rubbing this rust between the fingers produces a bright-red dye. (Macera and Andázabal 1999 gives more detail on these cactus plants.)

Animals

Animals are fellow residents of the World of Here in which human beings find themselves. Divinities often take the form of animals, so unseen spiritual forces can easily be residing within what appears to be an ordinary creature. Animals are sentient beings that communicate with humans in various ways. For this reason, animals are perhaps the most important of the aspects of nature in this study.

Camellids

The family of New World camellids includes llamas, alpacas, guanacos, and vicuñas.

LLAMAS

Llamas serve the Andean people as pack animals. Their long wool is not as high in quality as that of its camellid cousins, but it can produce usable ropes and cords as well as rough cloth for daily wear. They also provide some milk and meat. A llama cannot carry more than 100 to 150 pounds. Though llamas appear in prehistoric art carrying small people, these are likely to be children. Children sometimes ride llamas today, though adults do not. This creature appears to be frail and delicate when compared to European draft horses or oxen, for example.

Burger (1992:210), however, points out that a llama caravan moving through the Andes might actually be a very efficient method of freight transport, given the difficult terrain. Llamas are native to the high puna elevation, but they adapt easily to other altitudes. Given enough food, a herd of pack llamas will follow a lead animal with the aid of very few people. One llama will carry 40 to 120 pounds for nine to twelve miles per day; fifty animals can then carry two tons per day under the supervision of only two or three herders. This means that in precolonial times a great deal of llama-back trade may have been going on in the region. Llamas are a highly regarded animal. They are somewhat independent, curious, graceful of movement, quick, and cantankerous when crossed. When angered, llamas spit a noxious liquid, as do all their camellid cousins. Llamas and people are spiritual stand-ins for one another in Andean religion. Llamas often talk in Andean myth (note 4), and llama fetuses represent human babies in ritual. The idea of llamas giving birth is parallel to humans giving birth (Mendoza 2000). Llamas accompany people to the World of Below, and the hearts of llamas, called "moist seeds," are sacrificed to streams and rivers for good crops (Bastien 1978). Llama fetuses were burned in sacrifice to the divinities, and evil spiritual forces like Pishtaco were known to kill people and llamas by taking their fat (note 5).

4. In a narrative known as the llama flood myth, collected by Bastien (1978:72–73), a talking llama warns his herder about an impending inundation. The herder at first refuses to listen and rudely throws a corncob at the llama. Later, when the water begins to rise, the herder goes to the top of a mountain with his family to wait out the flood. The llama herd, along with a menagerie of tame and wild animals, accompanies the human family to safety. This tale is probably another of innumerable examples of flood stories collected by folklorists

worldwide. However, an attached commentary written by its translator, a Spanish missionary, syncretizes the story with the biblical account of Noah. Mendoza (2000:193) describes a traditional dance-drama known as *inini* in which humans in the role of llamas give birth. In Andean lore, llamas generally vocalize "In! In!" when they wish to attract human attention or when they are in pain.

5. Being able to maintain adequate body fat is highly prized in a world that demands much hard physical labor in order to garner the basic necessities of existence. In addition, high altitudes exact a greater energy toll on the body than the same work at lower elevations. Thus, animals and humans in the high mountains burn more calories than if doing the same task at sea level. For these reasons, being too slender in the high Andes is dangerous to one's health. An Associated Press article published in the *New York Times* on November 20, 2009, "Peru's Police Say Gang Drained Victim's Fat," describes a criminal gang involved in illegal drugs that reportedly killed human victims, rendered their fat, and sold it to European cosmetics firms. However, the article points out that human fat is not a very important ingredient in cosmetics, according to dermatologists. This leads to the educated speculation that the gang's true purpose was to excite traditional fears in order to protect its drug business rather than contribute to developing a macabre cosmetics trade.

Llamas were sacrificed, according to Guamán's chronicle, at different times of the agricultural year to ensure that crops and animals could produce in abundance. The different stages of the growing cycle demanded ritual sacrifice of particular colors of llamas—pure black, red, or white, for example. Pied animals would not do. Sometimes jars (*canopas*) or small statues of llamas would be sacrificed in convenient replacement for the actual animals. Hollow llama-shaped jars also served as libation vessels during rituals and take that role at weddings today. Llamas' alter ego in the forms of bulls and horses can serve the same purpose in contemporary times (chapter 8).

ALPACAS

Alpacas appear in art as often as llamas, and their forms are distinguished by shorter, heavier bodies and coats of heavy wool that extend to the legs. During Indigenous times and to some extent today, alpacas have lived in a semi-wild state. They range over high-altitude pastures in the puna above the tree line eating grass and lichens, and some herders gather them into enclosures at night to guard against attacks by predators, at lambing time, and at shearing time for wool collection. They serve as wool-producing animals primarily and to some extent as sources of meat and milk. Alpaca wool has a rough outer layer and a fine, thick, lightweight inner layer. Weavers use this inner wool, especially of younger alpacas, to make garments and blankets of high quality. This clothing is lightweight, warm, and water-resistant, well suited to the climate.

Alpacas in art can be abstract or realistic, always distinguishable from llamas by their more truncated shape and heavy wool.

GUANACOS AND VICUÑAS

Guanacos and vicuñas are completely wild cousins of llamas and alpacas. Guanacos, with their distinctive red-brown and cream-colored fur, are very hardy, with a range extending south to Tierra del Fuego. They are medium-size and gracile animals. The Incas, according to chroniclers, rounded up guanacos and vicuñas at particular times of the year and sheared wool from their backs only. In this way the shearing did not compromise the animal's health because enough wool would grow back to assure protection during the harsh mountain winters.

Vicuñas resemble guanacos in color, but they are much smaller and very delicately built creatures. Their wool is so fine that artists can make cloth from it that resembles woven silk. Spanish chroniclers believed that some of the clothing worn by the Inca emperor must have been made from bat hair. It is likely that this cloth was, in fact, made from vicuña wool. Access to vicuña-wool cloth in Indigenous times was a privilege of the elites, and today it still commands a high price.

Guanacos and vicuñas in art appear clearly identified in painted form including as ceramic motifs. Otherwise, they are hard to distinguish from abstracted llama shapes.

Birds and Insects

Raptors such as vultures, eagles, hawks, and falcons are important in Andean religion. These birds are the primary avatars of the huamani (a term that also carries the meaning "hawk" in Quechua), or spiritual forces that emanate from the insides of sacred mountains—apus, upward extensions of the World of Below—and from other spiritual realms. Certain insects can also indicate the presence of huamani. For example, in Arguedas' work *La agonía de Rasu Ñiti* (1962), insects portend the scissors dancer's fate. This family of raptor birds, along with large felines and serpents, shares importance with other religions of New World Indigenous peoples.

HUMMINGBIRD (QUICHU, QUITI, PICAFLOR)

The tiny hummingbird, though not a raptor, is important to Andeans because the souls of departed relatives often take hummingbird form as well as the shape of certain butterflies. It is for this reason that the appearance of such creatures causes great delight among Andeans. One type of hummingbird, called Tchudi's Inca, was discovered by the scholar of that name near Huari in 1876. This species' iridescent colors include black, green, brown, purple, and white. The Central Andes host many species of hummingbirds, known as *zumbadores* or "buzzers" in Spanish because of the sound of their rapid wing beats and *picaflores* or "flower peckers" because of their habit of feeding on blossom nectar.

BUTTERFLY (CHAPUL, KAPILA, MARIPOSA)

Butterflies abound in the Andean region, which is home to one-third of the world's species. A number of these miniature beings abide at very high elevations. The Puna Clouded Yellow lives between 9,000 and 12,000 feet above sea level, and the dazzling, multihued Andean Painted Lady lives between 3,600 and 9,900 feet. Like hummingbirds, butterflies are ever-moving miniature sparks of color that animate their often brooding and intimidating mountain backdrops.

CONDOR (KUNTU, QUNTUR)

The Andean condor is the largest flying bird in the Americas. It soars among Andean peaks searching for carrion and small animals. With a wingspan of twelve feet, this vulture is capable of carrying off a baby llama. The condor's characteristic hooked beak, red comb, white-ringed neck in males, black and white body feathers, and large, clawed feet appear in both natural and abstract form in art. The condor is an intimidating predator that inspires respect in human beings, yet it also has helpful qualities. The

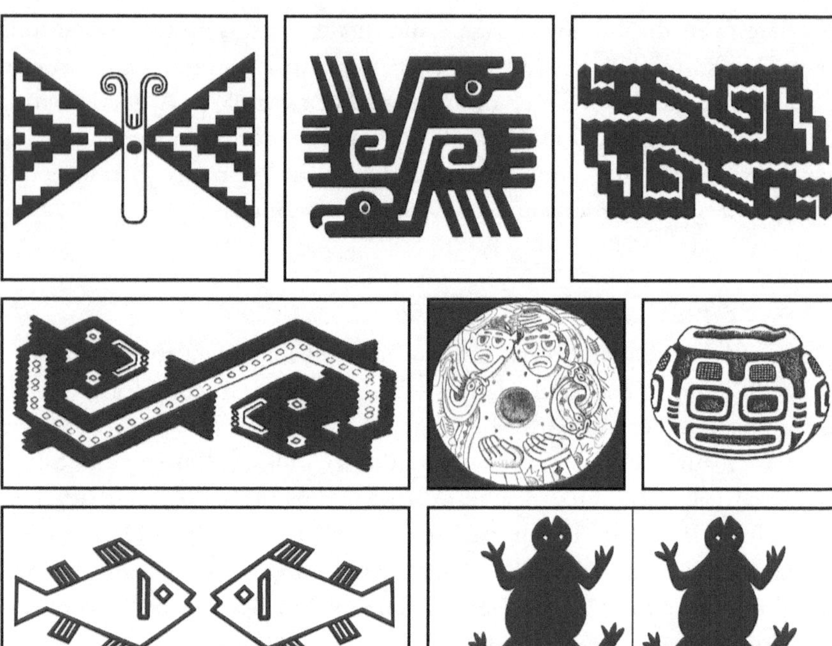

2.17 Butterfly (*Chapul, Capila, Mariposa*). Drawing by the author after anonymous works.

2.18 Condor (*Kuntu, Quntur*). Drawing by the author after Burger 1992:32, figure b.

2.19 Condor (*Kuntu, Quntur*). Drawing by the author after Burger 1992:32, figure c).

2.20 Snake (*Amaru, Culebra, Serpiente*). Drawing by the author after Moseley 1993:108, figure 46. Moseley considers the figure a fish or an eel. The image shares characteristics with two-headed serpents, zigzags, and rainbows.

2.21 Snakes and human faces on Nazca gourd. Drawing by the author after anonymous gourd carving, Stastny 1981:32, figure 133.

2.22 Puma on Chavín carved gourd. Drawing by Rafael Domingo after Miguel Covarrubias 1954:16, figure 2.

2.23 Fish (*Suche, Pez*). This type of fish resembles a flounder with many fins. It has a symbolic association with the Inca emperor. Taquile weavers and Huamanga artists use the motif in their work. Drawing by the author after anonymous work.

2.24 Frog (*Atarway, K'ayra, Hamp'atu, Rana*) or Toad (*Hamp'atu, Sapu, Sapo*). Drawing by the author after anonymous work.

condor and other huamani, since they have wings, can move among the worlds in the Andean cosmos. In this way, the condor can carry messages between the realm of the gods Above and the abode of human beings in the World of Here. Condors float and soar through the air above high pinnacles performing aerial ballets apparently with minimal effort. At close range they are startling in size and power.

EAGLE (ÁGUILA), HAWK (FALCÓN, HUAMAN), AND FALCON (HALCÓN, FALCÓN, GUAMÁN)

These classes of birds are also huamani with characteristics much like those of the condor. The Chavín, whose culture may have had jungle origins, carved images of the jungle-dwelling harpy eagle for their mountain city of Chavín de Huantar. This very large member of the eagle clan has a characteristic topknot of feathers on its head and flies in a specialized way so as to pull in and let out its wings rapidly to avoid colliding with jungle branches yet maintain speed and altitude as it hunts. The smaller hawks and falcons exhibit all the flying and hunting prowess of their big relatives with the addition of possible superiority in agility and diving ability in some cases.

In art, the head and hooked beak of typical raptors symbolize all of these types of birds and can refer to the huamani in general. Other distinguishing structures and colors in more realistic representations can signal reference to particular species.

Snake (Amaru, Culebra, Serpiente)

Snakes, avian raptors, and big cats represent the most important animals among the sacred beings of most of America's major Indigenous civilizations. Pachamama can take the shape of a large serpent, and jungle peoples of the Andes especially represent her this way in the form of one of the bigger members of the Amazonian boa family. The green anaconda is the largest member of this family and biggest snake in the world. It has irregular spots on its skin that appear as rounded and regularly placed in art. Other species more commonly called "boa" are also sizable animals. One of these has elongated stripelike spots on its skin that run crosswise over its body. In art, stripes can be crosswise or lengthwise in reference to these and other species and families of snakes.

Many of the serpents command respect if not fear in human beings because the largest ones are capable of hunting homo sapiens and other large prey. On the other hand, Pachamama, one of the most esteemed of divinities, chooses this form as her avatar. This negative and fearful while at the same time positive view of snakes as natural and spiritual beings is characteristic of a more general Andean religious belief. The serpent form, whether realistic or abstract, can have multiple symbolic referents to rainbows, zigzags, lightning bolts, water, and other natural elements as well as to snakes. The rainbow divinity Amaru's image can extend the number of references to include felines if the heads have interlocking eyeteeth and catlike ears, eyes, and nose forms.

Felines

Felines, along with raptor birds and serpents, commonly were worshipped among the first peoples of most of the American continent where local versions of these creatures abide. The Andes region is home to two major types of divine felines, pumas in the mountains and jaguars in the jungle.

PUMA

The puma, or Andean mountain lion, is a powerful earth divinity. This big cat can weigh in at several hundred pounds of bone and muscle, and it can make off with young livestock and small children, given the opportunity. Herders build special night shelters to protect their animals from pumas, especially at calving and lambing time. An Andean friend of the writer told her that pumas often take nothing but the hearts of their victims and that they wander about roaring and frightening man and beast. Puma is as much a potential soul snatcher as he may be a helper of human beings. Andeans interpret puma predation as a demand from the spiritual world that they must meet in return for general survival and well-being in their environment. Pumas appear throughout the history of Andean art in many media and in abstract and natural form. They sometimes exhibit body parts and markings of condors, anacondas, and llamas, following the common tradition of multiple symbolic referencing. Both jaguars and pumas have their large, overlapping eyeteeth exaggerated in art.

JAGUAR

The jaguar is a large, graceful, and awe-inspiring jungle cat with open spot markings on its body. Some jaguars, especially those living in a deep jungle environment, are black in color. Puma and jaguar forms often mix in art. The Chavín may originally have worshipped the jaguar and then the puma when they migrated from their possible place of origin in the Amazon basin to the mountain highlands. The people of Tiahuanacu believed the origin of the universe to be associated with a big and secretive Andean lion (puma) or jaguar that resided on the Rock of the Cat, an island in Lake Titicaca. Jaguars can live in a wide range of habitats, though most reside in humid jungle zones. Contemporary scientists assert that jaguar and puma habitats overlap, just as do their depictions in Andean art. *Otorongo* is a designation for an actual felid but also a name used for a gigantic mythical cat in Andean narrations.

Skunk (Añas, Zorilla, Zorrino)

The skunk and the fox are important alter egos for scissors dancers (chapter 5). The skunk, considered an especially admirable and agile creature, is said to stand on its hind legs like a person and wear dry turds on its head like hats. Groups of skunks gather at night to have dancing parties, according to Andeans (Macera and Andázabal 1999, Núñez Rebaza 1990). Biologists describe the creatures as jumping up and down and pawing the air with their forefeet as a way to catch insects for food. This hunting technique may account for the "dancing" behavior.

From a scientific perspective, the Andean skunk, known as Molina's hog-nosed skunk, has several kinds of black and white markings depending on the region. Carmelón Berrocal Evanán illustrates one that is black with two parallel white stripes running from forehead to tail tip (in Macera and Andázabal 1999:56). Andean skunks are carnivorous, eating worms such as the *lucia*, and nocturnal.

Fox (Atuq, Surru, Zorro)

The fox, like the skunk, is a trickster figure in Andean lore and another alter ego for scissors dancers (chapter 5). José María Arguedas, in his 1971 book *El zorro de arriba y el zorro de abajo* (The Fox from Above and the Fox from Below), makes his two protagonists, the scissors dancer and the factory owner, into foxes. The fox is a clever, quick, and graceful animal, capable of putting one over on human beings and divinities. Sometimes the fox can be tricked himself. There is a mythic tale, for example, about how the fox tried to keep basic Andean foodstuffs like corn for his own use. Fox was eventually tricked into carelessness so humans could have corn to eat, and in spite of himself, fox became the harbinger of food for humanity. (A poster illustrating this tale was distributed by *El Comercio* in 2003.) Foxes can cause major predation problems for Andean herders, who try to trap them to protect small domestic animals.

The Andean fox has red fur and a black-tipped tail. Fox's tail has a black tip because it got wet in the Andean version of the universal flood myth. In this narration, a talking llama convinces its herder to take his family and local animals to the top of a high mountain to escape a flood. Fox, contrary as usual, brings up the rear of the parade and gets his tail wet in the inundation.

Vizcacha

The vizcacha is a small rodent and member of the chinchilla family. The high-altitude variety is gray with white and black markings. It resembles a cross between a rabbit and a squirrel, with short forelimbs, long hind limbs, soft, long fur, and a long, bushy tail. It eats grasses and seeds and enjoys basking in the sun on rocky ledges, always ready to scurry to safety should a predator appear. According to folk tradition, this special animal is the "apu's mule" (Macera and Andázabal 1999).

Fish (Suche, Pez)

A number of fish species, such as the river trout and ocean-dwelling varieties, are important in the Andean diet and lore. The *suche* variety appears often in art. The term is used to refer specifically to a species living in Lake Titicaca and generally to small freshwater fish.

Frog (Atarway, K'ayra, Hamp'atu, Rana), Toad (Sapu, Hamp'atu, Sapo)

These two animals are sometimes not clearly distinguished; for example, the term *hamp'atu* can mean toad or frog. They both possess magical qualities having to do with spontaneous generation and reincarnation. The young of the frog, for example, appear to spring out of nowhere. These babies make themselves known on river and lake banks, that is, near gateways to the spiritual realm of the World of Below. The skin of some Amazonian amphibians produces the raw material for hallucinogens and

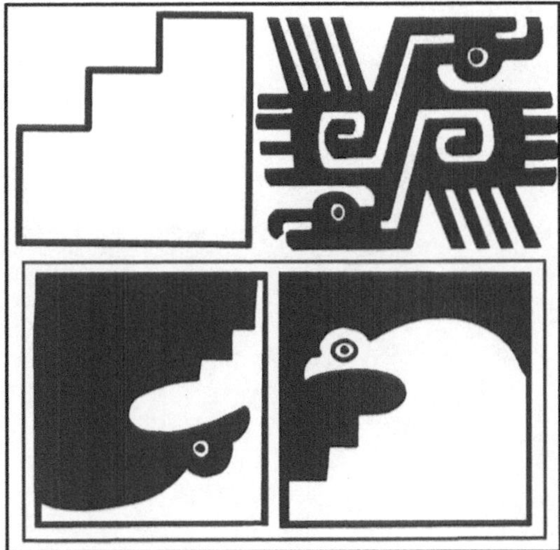

2.25 Mountain, condor, ayllu combination. The symbol in the lower right and left quadrants combines the forms of the mountain, the condor, and three ayllus in a reciprocal relationship. The apu, or sacred mountain (upper left), contains the condor (upper right). Drawings by the author after anonymous work.

medicinal substances used by religious specialists to prophesy and communicate with divinities.

Combinations

All nature motifs in art are combinations of natural forms and spiritual symbols, and many also make multiple references to both mundane and supernatural realms. The way some depictions of the rainbow divinity, Amaru, combine the idea of snake, cat, lightning, and rainbow is described above. Another example is the image standing for apu, condor, ayllus (figure 2.25).

There are numerous other natural symbolic referents in Andean art, and some of these will be explained briefly in the following chapters. This writing will concentrate, however, on the corpus of astral bodies, earth forms, climatic conditions, plants, and animals described here.

Part II

Variations

Variations on a theme in music or in visual art imply that continuity of thematic elements coexist with changes simultaneously through time and space. Listeners and viewers recognize references to the themes within the variations because the variations contain partial repetitions of the themes. This is a tried and true esthetically pleasing structure in artistic creation and perhaps in the development of cultures as well. The first very major variation in Andean traditions came about when Europeans founded colonies in the region from the fifteenth to nineteenth centuries. There were areas in which the two cultures blended easily because of their existing similar systems of belief and practice. At the same time there were points of deep opposition and conflict. These are the subjects described and explained in chapter 3, with emphasis on the tumultuous early part of this era. The first section presents cultural combinations, and the second section deals with Andeans' "adjustment" to changes imposed by the Europeans.

Chapter 4 presents the next great cataclysm in Andeans' universe, and that is the modern era from the twentieth century to the first decade of the twenty-first century. The first part of this chapter describes agrarian reform and resultant massive rural-to-urban migration; the second section includes a short history of the recent long period of civil war in Peru as well as an analysis of globalization and its effects on artists. The third part of chapter 4 provides details about twenty-first-century artists and their relation to contemporary events, international labor migration, and the telecommunications revolution. The fourth section presents artists' observations and suggestions about their work.

CHAPTER 3
The Spanish Colonial Period

The Incas interpreted the coming of the Spaniards as a pachacuti, or inversion of the universe. Pachacutis, as described previously, occur cyclically in the Andean concept of time. The Incas reacted to the Spanish colonization with the idea that if they became more strictly exacting about religious observance, the world would once more put itself right and Inca culture could again reign supreme. Consequently, the colonial period entailed not only massive acculturative processes but also revolts and millenarian movements. Out of this crucible came new and multilayered versions of Mestizo (culturally mixed) art forms that contain subtle and highly nuanced messaging. These ideas were embedded into the intensely chromatic geometries of Inca designs and the wild, curvilinear exuberance of the Spanish Baroque esthetic. The Spanish Baroque, assisted by similar predispositions in the Inca culture, became a major template for Andean art even in contemporary times (Baily 2010).

Peru participated in a global system for the first time as part of the world-skirting Spanish empire between the fifteenth and nineteenth centuries. There were enough similarities between Andean and Peninsular traditions of the time that the two cultures shared some commonalities. External visual forms common to the two civilizations, however, often retained distinct meanings and interpretations that coexisted simultaneously. Artists knew how to use ambiguity and camouflage to encourage multiple interpretations by various sets of viewers with distinct expectations. Some of these art types and styles persist into the present.

Early Stages of the Encounter

The first part of the following discussion looks briefly at what took place at the beginning of the period of culture contact. The second section of the chapter analyzes the longer-term effects after the initial meeting between two peoples who were similar in some ways and different in others.

Two Social Structures Coming Together

Spanish adventure seekers and soldiers of fortune craved the great sources of wealth rumored to abound in the Andean region. Many of these travelers had nothing to lose, having come from great poverty at the bottom rungs of a feudal society. The promise of gold and silver in the Americas drew them onward despite terrible risk and indescribable hardship. The military and technological aspects of the campaign for conquest had much less importance than the deadly introduction, at first inconspicuous, of Old World diseases among Indigenes with little biological resistance to the new illnesses. This tipped the balance heavily in favor of the Spanish. Once in control, the Spanish confronted cultural similarities and differences with the Indigenous people they encountered that respectively facilitated and undermined Spain's new government over the long run.

On Columbus Day people throughout the former Spanish global realm hark back to a time when "the sun never set" on Spanish holdings. When the Spanish empire was at its height, its colonies extended across the Americas to the Pacific and then to Asia and beyond. Spanish ships engaged in a robust trade among all of these regions. A notable example of the workings of this intercontinental network is the beautifully embroidered silk *mantón de Manila*, the long, colorful shawl worn by elegant women of Lima and Seville and draped over their shoulders and over balustrades at the bullring. The cloth was from China, embroidery was added in the Philippines, and Spanish galleons carried these and numberless other items across the seven seas among all the world's continents. Pierce and Otsuka's recent study (2006), for example, analyzes the influence of Asian art in Spanish colonial America due to this period of global trade made possible by the Iberian empire.

The Spanish conquering armies did not, however, enter empty lands. Stretching across seven modern Latin American nations was the formidable Inca empire. The Incas had imposed their language, religion, and even agricultural techniques on the largest of the Indigenous empires in the Americas. They sent colonizers, *mitimaes*, from the central state to newly conquered territories as long-term acculturation teams. They added to this technique a system of indirect rule that made their imposing presence seem not so foreign after a generation or two. In fact, the Inca governmental system was so effective that the Spanish left a good part of it in place. They substituted Spaniards for the Inca elites and relied on the generational forgetfulness of commoners remaining alive under Spanish rule to erase memories of Indigenous statecraft.

This hope for Indigenous memory loss on the part of the newcomers was only partially realized. The two traditions grew together in a syncretic exchange with the passage of time. Commonalities often outweighed a lack of fit between the two lifeways. Thinkers tried to rationalize the conflicts between the two cultures. This was at times done in quite creative ways. One example is the chronicler Guamán Poma's simple inclusion of two creation myths, Inca and Spanish (1988:42, 89), and making them fit together by piecing them chronologically as if they were a combined and mutant strand of DNA that indeed went on over time to replicate itself. Other conflicts required more dramatic tactics, like a number of

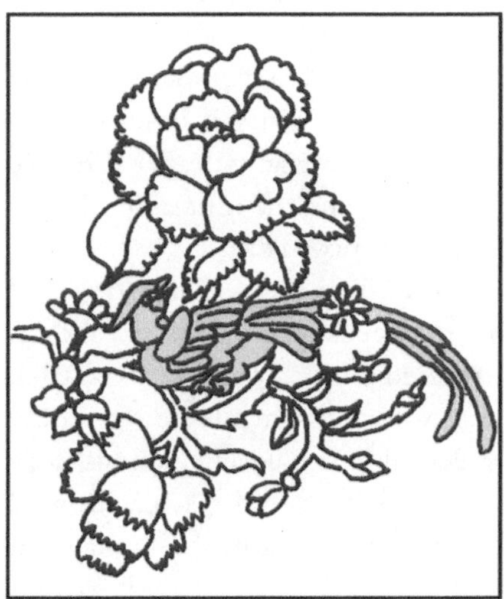

3.1 Embroidery detail, *mantón de Manila*. *Tapadas*, covered women, were stylish Creoles (often upper class and of ethnically mixed descent) of colonial Lima. They wore long shawls in the streets to maintain public modesty required by Spanish mores for honorable women but kept one flirtatious eye uncovered and might arrange clandestine meetings with men and sometimes scholarly or political gatherings otherwise forbidden to women of their time. Drawing by the author after a mantón in her personal collection.

Indigenous revolts that took form as both military action and millenarian movements.

It is likely that the prime motivation for Francisco Pizarro's entry into Peru was the report that the mythical El Dorado, or the golden ruler, resided there rather than in Mexico. The Incas and their predecessors had mined gold and silver as well as other metals for generations using techniques of excavating only surface areas. The Europeans were to introduce techniques for deep-shaft mining to the Andes. Large populations of Indigenes and Africans would eventually serve as mine workers along with Europeans. Of these miners, many would die of work-related lung disease, the stress of living at high altitude, and other maladies that were little understood at that time (Bowser 1974, Brockington 2000). The Spanish crown would realize wealth so fabulous it was almost beyond imagination. The discovery of Potosí, an entire mountain of silver in Bolivia, perhaps represented the culmination of exploration in terms of wealth. From this came an often-used phrase "It is worth a Potosí" (*Vale un Potosí*), meaning something of value impossible to measure.

However, the official justification for the colonial enterprise was much more idealistic. The discovery of the Americas represented an opportunity to incorporate vast numbers of people into the Spanish culture and the Christian religion. Like the Incas before them, the Spanish saw themselves as promoters of a new and better way of life for the peoples of the Andes.

Pizarro appeared in Peru in the early 1530s, a propitious time for him in Inca governmental history. It was the first instance of decentralization in Inca civic record. Rather than having only one capital, at Cuzco, the empire now had two capitals, at Cuzco and Quito. The old emperor Huayna Capac evidently loved one of his mistresses more than his official sister-wife. As a result, Atahuallpa, his son with the unofficial wife, ruled half of the empire from Quito, in present-day Ecuador, and the official son Huascar ruled the other half from Cuzco, in what is now Peru.

The Inca armies were so overconfident in their prowess and so sure of the divine nature of their emperors that the appearance of Pizarro and his retinue did not faze them at first. Pizarro used political techniques to trick both emperors in turn and to attack the two capitals while he was in the role of guest and observer of official welcoming rituals. The famous story of Atahuallpa filling an entire room as high as he could reach with gold artifacts to win release from being held hostage by Pizarro shows the great cultural difference in valuation of this shining metal. The Spanish soldiers immediately began to melt the beautifully wrought artifacts into gold and silver bars.

There is little doubt that the Spaniards' superior arms served them well against the Incas. They had iron and steel as opposed to the Inca bronze or copper-tin. They had arquebuses and cannons, while the Incas had clubs, spears, and other types of Roman-era weapons and war machines. Last but not least, the horse, mule, and ox helped the Spanish war effort immensely. These animals carried and pulled people, weapons, and basic supplies over great distances. The Incas relied on foot soldiers and llamas, whose delicate build does not permit heavy draft work.

Modern analysts of the colonial encounter in the Americas have found that the most important factor of all that favored the Spanish, however, was probably disease. The peoples of the Americas suffered from relatively few mortal illnesses due to their continental isolation as a biological group. Europeans, on the other hand, carried diseases from Africa, Asia, the Pacific, and Europe. These populations had criss-crossed one another's continents for generations exchanging goods, philosophies, religions, and illnesses. This intercontinental exchange of disease vectors created an Old World population with some immunity to the mortal ravages of a number of major human illnesses. By contrast, the peoples of the Americas were isolated by oceans from the rest of the world and exposed among themselves to relatively few diseases.

Within Pizarro's troops and among earlier sailors and explorers were individuals who carried smallpox, typhus, measles, and other diseases to which they were immune. These carriers had a dramatic effect on the populations of the New World. The Indigenous population in Peru, as elsewhere, began to sicken and die on initial contact with disease organisms brought by the newcomers. The population in Peru was reduced by 60 percent within one generation due to disease (Cook 1998, Diamond 1998, Dobyns and Dougherty 1976). This, of course, was not nearly as dramatic as the 97–98 percent reduction of Indigenes in the heavily ship-trafficked Caribbean of early colonial times. The rapid sickening of Indigenous populations led to the creation of the stereotype that they were physically "weak." This justified the large-scale importation of enslaved Africans carried on later by various European groups. The Indigenes did send a disease to Europe that was probably not very common there until American contact: syphilis. Syphilis caused problems for denizens of the Old World, but its effect was negligible when compared to the devastation caused by the diseases introduced into the Americas (note 1).

1. Medical historians have found a form of syphilis extant in the Old World by conquest times. However, the New World form of the disease caused health problems for the Old World when it was transported there by European explorers from the Americas.

Besides unintentionally bringing sickness to these new lands, the Spanish conquerors purposely took advantage of the divided state of the Inca empire under Atahuallpa at Quito and Huascar at Cuzco. They also enlisted the help of thousands of conquered peoples disgruntled with the Incas and their regime. These potentially revolutionary factions bolstered Spanish troop numbers enormously and were crucial to Spanish military success.

The Incas and Spanish shared some similarities in cosmological concepts, which facilitated the religious conversion process and took pictorial form in art. These similarities are discussed in some detail later in this chapter. Andeans dealt with the problem of monotheism (espoused by Europeans) versus polytheism (the Inca belief), for example, by converting the numerous Christian saints and angels into alter egos for Andean deities and spiritual beings.

In the area of statecraft, the Spanish utilized extant Inca structures for government that promoted their own regime. The taxation systems of the Incas, especially the custom of conscripting labor and construction crews, the payment of large quantities of craft items and crops as tax, and similar customs useful to the Spanish continued under the European reign.

In family life and kin-based social networks, a number of cultural conflicts arose. First, it was vital for Spanish local governments to break the power of the Inca ayllus or lineages. Attempts were made to refocus the Indigenous lineages toward the idea of a religious brotherhood, or *cofradía*, whose rights and obligations limited them to religious ritual. The Spanish also tried to substitute labor and craft guilds for the ayllu as a focus for member loyalty. These attempts had varying levels of success during the early colonial period.

Second, the custom of trial marriage among Inca young people flew in the face of Spanish notions of honor within the family. The colonial

Spanish shared an ancient Mediterranean idea that probably preceded the founding of Judaism, Christianity, and Islam. The notion was that an honorable family reputation within a community had much to do with what was considered proper sexual behavior. This meant ideally no sexual encounters before marriage for both genders but especially for women. Early Spanish explorers thus viewed trial marriage as reprehensible if not sinful behavior and Inca young women as shameless harlots. Incas viewed Spaniards as being unnatural in their officially sanctioned sexual reticence before formal marriage. Andeans and Spaniards continued to experience conflicts in this area over history. Today, the official laws of Peru conform to Spanish ideas of honor within marriage, while Indigenes still practice trial marriage in a way similar to pre-Columbian times. There are many other examples of cultural harmonies and conflicts. Those discussed here give an idea of the complexity of the interaction between the two cultural systems.

Despite the Spaniards' efforts to obliterate Inca tradition and impose their own culture, what took place over time was a gradual exchange and blending of beliefs and practices. The coming of the Europeans had long-term effects in the material as well as the ideological realm. The newcomers influenced population indices, systems of social ranking, and the natural environment. Little by little the two cultures began to take on each other's language, building styles, dress, rituals, foods, and other traditions. Just as the Incas ceded to their conquered populations as much as or more than they imposed themselves, so did the Spaniards during their colonization of the Andeans.

Early Spanish colonial governments tried as best they could to physically eliminate the Inca elite and promote ethnic intermarriage. As a result, many Andeans of today are descendants of the commoners within the old Indigenous empire. This may be a reason there is only dim memory among them of Inca elite cultural traditions.

The disease factor drastically reduced Indigenous populations of all social levels. Some of the monastic missionaries' attempts to save the Incas by concentrating them in close-knit communities (*reducciones*) only increased the spread of disease. Continuing and vertiginous population decline was of major concern to the Spanish colonial government after officials finally became conscious of it. Little was known, however, about the specific mechanisms for the spread of disease at that time, so the decline continued for a long period.

The building of empires, such as the European conquest of the Americas, often has tragic consequences for conquered populations in the short run. However, in the long run, empires tend to enrich conquerors and conquered alike through ideological and material exchanges of many kinds. These exchanges take the form of sharing domestic animals, crops, medicines, inventions, languages, philosophies, religions, and trade goods, to name a few examples.

The introduction of European animals into the environment of the Americas had both helpful and harmful effects. Cattle, pigs, sheep, goats, and chickens greatly increased the kinds of animal protein foods available to American populations. Oxen, horses, mules, and donkeys provided travel possibilities and help with heavy labor. These animals along with wagons, carts, plows, and other useful European machinery improved the quality of life. There was also a downside, however. Early Spanish settlers slaughtered llamas and alpacas for meat, making them unavailable as wool producers. As a result, European sheep outnumbered local camellids in some areas for a long time, though sheep wool does not provide the same lightweight warmth of camellid wool. Pigs, with their root-digging habits, denuded large swaths of countryside. Cattle turned mixed ecozones into vast semi-desert pampas.

The Americas contributed many nutrient-rich plant foods to the Old World. Important among these is the potato, which became a staple in some European countries, and corn, which is now eaten throughout the world. Europeans at first ignored Andean crops such as quinua, a grain recognized and used globally in very recent times because of its high protein content.

The European entry into the Americas meant a gigantic influx of exotic objects and images. The Europeans brought sailing ships, ploughs, carts, clocks, printed books, steel-making technology, oil-painting skill, and many other previously unknown wonders to the Americas. The Andeans used the wheel only in children's toys. European wheeled vehicles drawn by heavy draft animals greatly increased Andeans' capacity to work and travel. The Spanish established instruction centers where they taught Andeans to weave, paint, carve, and build in the European style. The introduction of European tools, techniques, and products, including looms and painting supports, brushes, and pigments, forced Indigenous artists to take new bodily positions in their work. The European horizontal loom meant a new way of working and different production methods as well as new motifs and designs for Andean weavers. The Spanish established significant fine arts and crafts schools in Cuzco and Ayacucho (Huamanga) in which they taught Andeans oil painting on canvas, one of several newly introduced European arts. At first, colonial laws promoted the replacement of Inca visual expressions by Spanish counterparts. When this proved unworkable, the two sets of arts repertoires began to blend and develop over time into an amalgam through the process of visual syncretism.

Religious Conversion, Ideology of the Spanish Colonial Government, and the Baroque Style

The Spanish empire in the Americas had as its ultimate justification the conversion of Indigenes and the later forcibly imported Africans to Christianity. However, often other motives were attached to this enterprise. The chronicler Francisco López de Gómara in 1552–1553 said it very well, stating that the most important reason for engaging in the discovery and exploration of the Americas was to spread the faith of Christ, even though power and money happened to go along with this objective. López concluded with the wry comment that the pursuits of religious conversion on the one hand and power and wealth on the other have a hard time coexisting. Herein is the crux, the underlying dilemma behind the building of this and many other empires. It is a high ideal that often serves as the official banner driving people forward to great and heroic deeds of conquest. After this first wave, however, baser instincts take over in some individuals, while others retain the original philosophies. It is well to keep in mind that this issue must remain within the framework of thought of those times, during which neither anthropology nor cultural relativity was a common concept. The right to convert others to one's own religion was not questioned any more than such a phrase as "Speak to me in Christian" (the Spanish language) remained unexamined as examples of ethnocentric thought.

The Spanish military, along with explorers and missionaries, entered Peru in the early sixteenth century. They brought with them mental paradigms created by their experiences in the recent history of Spain. At the same time, Spain participated in new thought created by the Renaissance. In fact, Spain and Italy were the first in Europe to experience the Renaissance due to monastic translations of Arabic, Greek, and Latin texts. Soon to appear on the horizon were the Golden Age, the Baroque period, and the Enlightenment. Of these intellectual currents, the legacy of the Spanish *reconquista* (Spanish rulers Ferdinand and Isabel's Reconquest, in the name of the Christian religion, of the Iberian Peninsula that had been colonized by Islamic peoples), Renaissance philosophy, and the Baroque are of great importance as a basis for understanding art forms created during this period.

In the late fifteenth century Ferdinand of Aragon and Isabel of Castile spearheaded the final movement culminating the process started centuries earlier known as the Reconquest; they began incipient state formation on the Iberian Peninsula out of what had been independently governed provinces and kingdoms, including regions known as *reinos de taifas* under Islamic rule. These monarchs decisively broke the back of 750 years of Islamic colonization. Ferdinand and Isabel consolidated Spain as a nation-state with Christianity as the official religion. In the same stroke they initiated what would eventually become a global Spanish empire through their support of Columbus' voyages of "discovery" (note 2). The powerful banner of the Christian religion united disparate groups of Spaniards under the new monarchs. The system of religious courts known as the Inquisition had begun in Aragon and Italy in the thirteenth century under papal governance from Rome. The Inquisition was introduced into Spain toward the end of the Reconquest period and came under the supervision of the crown. The removal of Muslim and Jewish religious practice along with political and scientific ideas and movements considered not officially Christian or not formally approved by the Spanish state facilitated Spain's new identity. Objectionable persons and groups did officially have the option of conversion to Christianity within the Inquisition system. Groups of these converts often simply took their religions and opinions into hiding while appearing externally to have converted fully to the Spanish Christian ideal. Others were executed or exiled for refusing to change. Succeeding popes in Rome were later to become uneasy over the workings of the Inquisition in Spain and placed restrictions on it (Herring 1968:76).

2. The terms "discovery" and "encounter" are politically loaded expressions. From an Indigenous perspective, the discovery of the Americas by Europeans implies that the geography and peoples of this continent did not exist until they fell under the gaze of these outsiders. People holding this point of view prefer the term "encounter," which makes the coming together of the peoples of Europe and America more of a meeting between equals. From a European perspective, especially

of the fifteenth century, the word "discover" describes their finding of the Americas with accuracy.

Ferdinand and Isabel conceived of their consolidation of Spain in terms of a new national identity that required exclusive adherence to ideas and lifeways considered culturally Spanish and religiously Christian. These notions of conquest allied to religious conversion plus the idea of removing or extracting those harboring distinct or opposing philosophies transferred directly to the exploration and colonization of the Americas. The Reconquest hardly ended when the voyages of exploration began. Ferdinand and Isabel needed alternative trade routes to reach the riches of Asia. Their new nation had to expand its influence to achieve power, avoiding overland trade networks controlled by Muslims and circum-African routes defended by Portugal. They could well afford to bet on Columbus. The initial investment was small, and Spanish mariners, due to their former colonial overlords, were cognizant of Arab maps conceiving of the earth as a round globe with accurate indications as to winds, ocean currents, and guiding stars. Columbus did not live to see the day the Spanish became fully aware that they had stumbled upon a completely new continent.

Once some of the new territories came under Spanish governance, the *encomienda* laws assured that lands and peoples entrusted to the care of important explorers and soldiers in royal service would be governed in an environmentally sound and humane way. The king and queen of Spain rewarded explorers, soldiers, and others who helped to expand Spanish territories in the New World with large tracts of land known as *encomiendas* ("entrustments" in the form of land and the Indigenous people living on that land). The early encomiendas were vast in size. Cortez's encomienda in Mexico occupied more than one-fourth the size of today's national territory. The encomienda laws stipulated that awardees of these entrustments be good stewards of the land and that they attend to the basic needs of the Indigenous people living on these lands, including religious conversion to the Christian faith. Unfortunately, the mentality characteristic of many *encomenderos* (awardees of encomiendas) was far from humane or environmentally conscious. The disconnect between the idealistic laws and the actual and often reprehensible behavior of encomenderos in the New World was facilitated by the great geographic distance between the Iberian Peninsula and the Americas as well as the slowness of travel and communication in that era. Encomienda landholders frequently treated the territories entrusted to them and the Indigenous peoples who lived on these lands with complete lack of care, no view toward the long term, and outright abuse and cruelty (Wolf 1959:189–191).

As a result of the immense size of their holdings and tendencies toward rebellious policies, the encomenderos became a chronic challenge to the power of the crown. This was so much the case that the central government of Spain enacted laws several times to clip the encomenderos' wings. Economic constraints periodically forced the royals to cede lost rights back to the encomiendas. The powerful plantation hacienda system was an outgrowth of the encomienda structure and the privileged social class that went with it and it became an almost invincible dreadnaught in Latin American societies ever since. The hacienda system in Peru really did not suffer a collapse until the 1970s under President Juan Velasco. Even then, a lack of adequate alternative models for development in the rural sector led to massive country-to-city migration, creating serious contemporary issues and problems.

Ideologies in Conflict

Guamán Poma's chronicle outlines the abuses in the early colonial system in words and pictures. An insider to the colonial structure, Guamán was a local governmental functionary in Ayacucho (Huamanga). He had every hope that Ferdinand and Isabel would read his impassioned plea for reform that took the shape of three large tomes outlining what he perceived to be a "good" governmental system with justice toward both Inca and Spanish populations. Key to an understanding of ideological conflict over how to treat the Indigenous and later African peoples of the New World lay in the various definitions of what constituted human nature itself. How were the Spanish to view the American Indigenes? As people equal to themselves in every way? People who could possibly be redeemed by religious and cultural conversion? People innately limited for biological reasons to smaller horizons?

The early colonial government promoted a class system based on ethnicity that is sometimes called a caste/class system because of its immobility. The structure of this system was based on ideas of physical and mental abilities many Spanish colonials believed to be immutable and inherited. The basic assumption was that the more European "blood" one inherited, the more intelligence, talent, and beauty one had as innate traits. The more

Indigenous, African, or Asian ancestry a person had, the fewer talents and capacities. It would be of no use to provide for possibilities in life such as schooling, travel, access to tools and livestock, and other benefits to these limited beings. Thus, people of pure Spanish heritage occupied the top level of society, and people of mixed descent (Mestizos) took up a middle position. The Indigenous people, who were relegated to the bottom rung of the ranking system and endured the hardships thus implied, invented coping strategies in order to survive and maintain a modicum of self-respect. These adjustment tactics took form in art, and visual statements of protest became ongoing traditions. At first the caste/class system was triangular in shape, the elites being small in number, the Mestizos greater in population, and the Indigenes constituting by far the largest of the three groups. Over time, the Mestizo group would become the most populous as intermarriage became more the norm.

Spain had begun to feel the first breezes of Renaissance thinking. Greek, Latin, and Arabic texts were studied in the universities. Some boundaries of the old medieval mental world were crossed. There were a number of Spanish intellectuals whose ideas put them in the vanguard of a new way of thinking about the world and its many different peoples. Probably the most famous of these iconoclastic thinkers was Bartolomé de las Casas. He was a churchman and holder of American encomiendas himself. After first participating in the exploitation of Indigenous and African plantation workers, de las Casas had a change of heart. He came in contact with new philosophies, and these, along with personal experience, changed him into a severe critic of those who felt free to exploit non-Europeans.

Another thinker, though less popularly known perhaps more important, was Francisco de Vitoria. He was a professor in a number of universities in France and Spain, notably at the renowned university at Salamanca. Vitoria's work, which he wrote in the early sixteenth century, formed part of serious debates of the time as to the true nature of the relationship between the Spanish and the peoples of the New World. These debates seem very contemporary in that many of the same arguments are being repeated now at the beginning of the second millennium. Vitoria's criticism and discussion of thoughts put forth by Gines de Sepulveda and defense of Bartolomé de las Casas are especially interesting in this regard. Vitoria asserted that God's approval of the Israelites' banishment of pagans from the Promised Land could not be used as a justification for maltreatment of non-European peoples (1960:549). He went on to say that the "Indians" had a right to form their own state and could not be forced to convert to

Christianity (607, 615). This statement questioned the entire colonial enterprise and its justification of religious conversion. In typical Renaissance fashion, de Vitoria employed Latin and Greek texts like those of Cicero to make his arguments. He was one of many individuals as well as schools of thought to go against the tide of negative valuation and consequent justification of abuse of Native Americans and other non-Europeans, including the enslaved Africans forcibly brought to the New World.

In the end, however, riches to be gained and power to be had by colonialists all too often tipped the scales toward injustice. Ongoing and long-term development programs put in place by some of the monastic orders such as the Dominicans, Franciscans, and Jesuits were attempts to counteract the consequences of the colonialists' greed for wealth and power at all costs. However, as mentioned before, the monastic reducciones often had unforeseen effects. In their effort to save the Indigenes by concentrating their populations in limited areas the monastic orders unwittingly accelerated the spread of disease and facilitated further governmental control. Native American populations were drastically reduced in number as a result. In Peru, African labor forces consequently replaced Native Americans particularly in coastal and mining areas of the Andes. African population numbers also show severe demographic decline shortly thereafter, particularly in the mountains where they were forced to labor in mines at very high altitudes (note 3).

3. Historical evidence shows large populations of Africans being imported into Lima in the sixteenth and seventeenth centuries. A relatively small number remained in the coastal areas working as rural and urban laborers. Today the African cultural legacy in music, cuisine, and other traditions remains notable on the coast. Coastal Peruvians count Africans as well as Europeans, Asians, and Indigenes in their complex ancestral lines. A few small African communities remain today in coastal Peru, in the department of Chincha, among others. The vast majority of the Africans brought into Lima in the sixteenth and seventeenth centuries were sent to the mountain areas as mine laborers (Bowser 1974). There they perished in large numbers due to altitude sickness and mine-related diseases. There are no African communities or concentrations of population in the mountains today. However, the African cultural legacy remains strong in coastal musical and dance styles and

Andean dance-dramas featuring *negritos* dance teams (*comparsas*). Negritos dancers often wear dark-colored masks with exaggerated features. They are elaborately dressed and often exhibit superior social standing over dancers representing Indigenous people. Evidently Africans did occupy a higher class stratum than Indigenes in colonial times.

The first wave of the Spanish conquest eventually led to the development of a caste or class system dividing Peruvian society into the levels described above. These levels were determined by ethnic identity, and they were defined in terms of biological background. This arrangement served the hacienda system well, as it justified the exploitation of Indigenes, Africans, and later other non-European groups as well as Mestizos in terms of a supposedly innate limitation on their capacity to rule themselves and determine their own destiny (Manrique 2000). The biggest danger in this conceptualization is that one's destiny in life becomes biologically determined so that there is no possibility for social mobility. For this reason students of ranking systems in societies, as mentioned before, call it a "caste" (determined by birth and thus immobile) rather than "class" (determined by achievement and therefore mobile) system. This mentality is also a direct transference from the social reality of late medieval and early Renaissance Spain. At this time Spain was a deeply stratified society and for similar biologically justified reasons. Even intellectuals like Teresa de Ávila were brought before the Inquisition because of suspected Jewish relatives, challenging her "purity of blood." Authors like Lope de Vega railed against the plight of the poor in this system. Lope stages a major peasant revolt against one hacienda owner in Spain in his famous play *Fuenteovejuna*. He jeers at the social power of wealth in his poem "Poderoso caballero es don Dinero" (Sir Moneybags Is a Powerful Knight). Not only the ethnic and phenotypic traits but also the religious beliefs, philosophical perspective, and economic level of an Iberian person were seen in terms of sixteenth-century concepts of biology. As in Peru, these states of being were immutable, with no naturally occurring possibility for change. The idea that a person could improve his or her lot in life by personal effort, luck, or any other means, according to this way of thinking, would then be impossible.

In such a system, one avenue for change and improvement for people in the lowest ranks is supernatural intervention. This is probably one reason narrations featuring saints, manifestations of the Virgin Mary, and angels working miracles on behalf of the poor and disenfranchised were so appealing to common people during this period in history. Supernatural power could surely change a person's biologically determined fate, and thus accounts of miracles had great popular appeal. A good example of this is the thirteenth-century *Milagros de Nuestra Señora* by Gonzalo de Berceo, the first-known Spanish poet. In these stories the Virgin Mary descends from heaven and rights the wrongs of society. She even covers up for people's mistakes. One story has Mary hiding the fact that a nun is pregnant. Stories like this gave hope to ordinary people that their lot in life could change through the help of holy beings acting on their behalf. Thus it is no surprise that in Spain and the New World, local patron saints as well as different manifestations of the Virgin Mary and Christ and their miraculous acts hold far greater importance in the minds of impoverished people than do the formal structures of church and government. These divine messengers gave hope, while formal organizations imposed limitations. Supernatural forces could be problematic as well as beneficial in nature. Even intellectuals of the time like de Vitoria and the chronicler Cieza de León still had roots in the fantastic mental landscape of the European Middle Ages, in which chaos ruled in the wood beyond the village and devils lurked within dark corners of the house at night. Vitoria speaks of "earlier times" when nature alone could cure or cause illness in human beings and when "devils" could be involved in either positive or negative activity (1960:1290–1291).

Many Spaniards with less learning than de Vitoria or de las Casas felt that Indigenous Andeans pertained to earlier and unenlightened periods of human development. These colonizers justified religious conversion, the changing of Andean ways to Iberian ones, the use of Indigenes as an unpaid labor force, and other activities based on such assumptions. Cieza de León, an important chronicler and relatively sympathetic Spaniard, recounts "abominable acts" that took place in Inca temples during their "devil" worship (1943:190). In this way Cieza, one of the most enlightened of the chronicle writers, sanctions the need to convert the Indigenous Andeans to Christianity.

This initial period of culture contact was followed by an era of adjustment for both civilizations. One of the mutual traditions that would aid in this adjustment was a similarity and overlap in religious artistic style. The Spanish Baroque favored great pomp and ceremony, dizzying attention to detail, and lavish displays. Similarly, Inca public ritual featured casts of thousands dancing and singing to tight choreographies in resplendent costumes, sparkling artifacts of precious metals, and finely worked textiles. Andeans would learn to use the Baroque style, so similar to their own tradition, as one of their survival techniques. The second section of this chapter will examine these developments.

Long-Term Effects of the Encounter

After the initial period of the encounters, longer-term processes were set into motion. These processes involved religious combinations and contradictions that manifested in the arts. Overarching all was the influence of the Spanish Baroque as a kind of supercharged and dramatic vision of reality.

The Incas reacted to the Spanish conversion process in varying ways. The scholar Olinda Celestino (1997, 1998) divides the Spanish religious conversion campaign into three steps: the destruction of idolatry, repression, and stabilization and combination. During the destruction of idolatry stage, the colonizers tried to destroy Inca religious imagery and ritual. The repression stage involved meting out punishment for disobeying the laws regarding religious practice. This was done, probably, to make examples of a few religious practitioners who continued in the Andean traditions and thus strike fear into the majority of their fellow believers. The stabilization and combination stage had a more complex character. Despite destruction of idolatry and repression, certain aspects of Andean tradition persisted strongly. Christian missionaries and thinking clerics soon realized that they had to cede to certain Andean traditional dogmas and practices, allowing them to coexist with Christian belief and ritual. As a result, they tolerated syncretic elements of which they were and still are today fully conscious. One example of this is the cross, which is both a symbol of Christ and the crucifixion as well as a graphic indication for the Andean four directions, or Tahuantinsuyu. During the stabilization and combination stage, followers of the Inca and Christian religions extended mutual tolerance to each other's religious ideology, each taking on some aspects of the other's system. In some ways, however, each of the two religious communities continued to interpret combined visual symbols in its own individual way.

A good example of the destruction and repression stages of the colonial regime and their consequences even into the present is Spanish policy regarding Inca painted murals. Spanish colonial governors realized that certain of the Inca visual art forms had religious and communication significance, particularly painted wall murals and textiles. The significance of textiles will be described in chapter 10, so a short presentation of the importance of murals is included here primarily drawn from Duccio Bonavia's 1985 study of this topic. The Spanish viceroy Francisco de Toledo issued an edict in the early 1570s stating that Inca figures could not be painted on public or house walls. He likewise forbade Indigenous imagery on clothing, tools, and household goods (Bonavia 1985:152). Why all the excitement about pictures? one might ask. Mural painting had been a strong Andean tradition long before the advent of the Inca culture. Some ancient sacred murals were discovered by archeologists in close to mint condition because of a custom in the region of walling over successive murals with layers of protective masonry. Different Andean cultures painted their murals in varying styles, the Inca preference being abstract and geometric. Incas tended to paint their wall art in overall patterns dividing the working surface into segments or medallions into which they would place alternating designs. Plain checkerboards were common, and experts say these are designations of social rank, perhaps of the official residing in the mural's courtyard. The designs within grids resemble tocapu symbols in weaving to a high degree, so they could probably be read with a similar level of accuracy. It was the messages of religious and cultural affirmation in these artworks and their accompanying revolutionary intent that disturbed Spanish officials so greatly. In fact, some early chroniclers were convinced that the murals were definitely a kind of writing, a code to be broken.

History was not kind to Andean murals; once they were discovered by conquering armies and even by archeologists they did not last long. Bonavia consulted a series of accounts over time about the same murals, starting from the Spanish early conquest through the twentieth century, recounting the gradual demise of what once were beautiful and impressive paintings. He describes the chronicler Cieza de León's account of a fortress in the Cañete Valley as being among the most charming and handsome in the kingdom of Peru because it was heavily adorned with paintings. The chronicler Garcilaso de la Vega described the same place later in the mid-sixteenth century, saying that the once beautiful but now ruined paintings were painful to see.

Rowe, an archeologist working in the 1940s, described a piece of Inca decoration as informative and charming (1943). Rowe says in this report that the most common pictorial motifs he saw were from nature—primarily plants and flowers, then insects, human beings, and animals such as llamas and pumas. The figures were abstract, tending toward the geometric in shape, and filled with areas of flat color. According to Bonavia, very little of what Rowe saw remained in the late twentieth century. Bonavia asserted that paintings played a very important role in Inca life, far more important than is commonly realized among scholars. The early Spanish governors, however, saw the powerful effect of this art firsthand, and that is why they took great pains to stamp it out as quickly and efficiently as possible. The extreme nature of colonial policies during the first two stages provided fertile ground for revolt in active form and in the more subtle form of millenarian movements. The last stage featured religious and artistic compromise on both Spanish and Inca sides.

The following paragraphs show how the two cultures in contact envisioned cosmological space, sacred time and yearly cycles, and divinities and supernatural beings. The continuing syncretic process brought about protests, millenarian movements, and new rituals, many of them featuring combined images and arts.

The subjects of space, time, and pantheons of divinities reflect an interesting evolutionary pattern as the colonial period progressed. Contact with Spanish Christian missionaries had a number of effects on Indigenous religious belief and practice. Since the sacred cosmologies of Christianity and the Inca religion resembled one another, the transition in spatial metaphorical terms was almost imperceptible in that area. Both cosmological systems had three levels on the vertical dimension with similar beings residing in each: divinities above, living people in this world, and problematic beings and the deceased below. More effort was needed to make the Christian and Andean calendars coalesce. One of the main reasons for this is that the Northern and Southern Hemispheres experience opposite seasonal cycles. Eventually, Indigenous believers highlighted those Christian festivals that happened to coincide with their own important celebrations in the austral calendric system. Easter and Corpus Christi are close in the calendar to Inti Raymi, so these major celebrations in the two religious systems blended seamlessly. Another example is the celebration of Natividad (the feast day for the birth of the Virgin Mary, September 8) and to a lesser extent Christmas (Navidad, December 25). These Christian feast days conflate with the Andean beginning of the rainy season, the wet "female" time of the austral year. The problem of monotheism versus polytheism found its solution by converting the myriad Christian saints into alternative identities for Andean divinities, angels into huamani—beings that can fly—and the like.

The conversion process over time was then more of a two-sided conversation and mutual adjustment than an imposition. Eventually most Andeans participated in a combined religion. The arts express this process of adjustment and its outcome.

The cosmologies of the two civilizations in contact had similarities and differences. First of all and important to keep in mind is that unlike the contemporary era, Spanish and Andean thinkers did not distinguish the religious universe, or cosmos of faith, from the scientific one. The distinction between science and religion so evident in contemporary thought categories would have been completely foreign to these two cultures during the early colonial era. In fact, the capacity that denizens of the second millennium have for compartmentalizing the spiritual realm versus the natural universe would have astounded these natives of the sixteenth century. The Spanish Christian cosmos drawn from the first books of the Judeo-Christian Bible is tripartite in nature, with heaven at the top, earth in the middle, and hell below. Purgatory and limbo do not seem to have a particular location in this spatial metaphoric scheme. Other ancient cosmologies still intruded upon Spanish religious thought of the era. The notion of "chaos" being a vast ocean containing such monsters as Leviathan (a whale) and Belial (a dragon) come from an early Hebraic cosmos featuring an ocean below the earth plus an ocean above the earth with stars at its base. The trajectory of a Spanish Christian soul would be to inhabit a body during life on earth. Good behavior in life means transport to the dimension of reward in heaven, where God, Christ, the Virgin Mary, saints, and angels reside. Bad behavior means the soul's transport to punishment in Hell below, a fiery hot place inhabited by Lucifer and other devils. Purgatory was a place where souls could expiate moderately bad behavior before transport to heaven. Limbo provided a spiritual home for the souls of unbaptized children.

Spiritual powers for good or evil could invade the world of living people and help or hinder their progress. Christianity has designated sites on earth where benevolent beings have appeared and/or performed miracles. These places often have churches or other monuments marking their importance. The particular manifestations of Christ, virgins, or saints honored, then, become special patrons of nearby communities, towns, and cities.

In brief, the two religious traditions shared the idea of a tripartite cosmos inhabited by somewhat similar natural and supernatural beings. The religions also shared the designation of sacred spaces in the natural plane of existence, an afterlife, a concept of reward and punishment, and the idea of soul or life force separate from the material body. The two thought systems differed in that Christianity is monotheistic, while the Incas are polytheists. Christians would work out their spiritual destinies on the natural (visible, human) plane and receive their eternal reward or punishment in the afterlife. By contrast, Andeans, regardless of behavior in the World of Here, would have to labor spiritually in the not-too-pleasant World of Below and later receive their reward or punishment. Andeans further had the possibility of reincarnation, an idea not found in Christian theology.

Christian missionaries and their converts came to a meeting of the minds on the monotheism/polytheism question by emphasizing Christianity's large population of saints. These holy but natural persons from the Christian perspective took on divine characteristics in the minds of Andeans. To hard-working and appropriately generous Andeans faced with more spiritual drudgery in the World of Below, the Christian paradise must have looked very attractive. Existing for eternity in heaven may well have seemed as good as or even better than natural reincarnation, given Christian saints' apparent ability to make appearances in the natural world when their help was needed, much like the traditional role of Andean deceased ancestors.

The Indigenous system of sacred lines (*ceques*) connecting holy points (*huacas*) often have become, post–Spanish conquest, the very same places where saints have appeared and performed miracles. The tripartite nature of each cosmos, powerful associations between the sea and destruction or chaos, good and evil spiritual powers, eternal reward and punishment, and the form of the cross are a few of many similarities that facilitated the coming together of these two religious traditions in ideas about space.

In terms of time, the two traditions happened to share certain overlaps about sacred points in the yearly cycle of events. Reasons for considering these dates important, however, started out being very different. The process of conquest and conversion encouraged a certain fuzziness in exact calendar days. The Mediterranean cycle of climatic events corresponds to the Northern Hemisphere and the Andean seasons to the Southern Hemisphere. The Andean calendric system was originally distinct from the Spanish one, though increasingly the Spanish names for months and other terms crept into a more and more creolized Quechua language.

Andeans divided all time into ages. At the end of each age, there would be a pachacuti, or inversion of the world. The Spanish conquest constituted a pachacuti, and various millenarian movements and revolts were attempts to create pachacutis that would set the world back as it used to be under the Andean rule. The Inca empire-building process resulted in the accretion of a number of creation stories, among them the Cuzco myth of the Hermanos Ayar and the Lake Titicaca myth. Similarly, the Spanish divided spiritual time into segments, notably before versus after the birth of Jesus Christ. The book Genesis in the Judeo-Christian Bible contains at least two creation myths, the story of the creation of the world in seven days and the story of the garden. Guamán, the great chronicler, resolved all of these ideas of origin neatly by positing several creations, some Andean and some Christian. He located these stories at different points in time and stated that the Incas had been formerly ignorant of the more important Christian dates (1988:42, 89).

The agricultural year for Andeans has distinct segments, according to Celestino (1997, 1998). The winter, from April to August, is when the most important religious events of the year take place. This has logic in part because this cold, dry season will not support agriculture and so is a time of rest for farmers and in part because the austral winter means diminished available light for growing crops. It so happens that Holy Week, Easter, and Corpus Christi, which are of high importance in the Christian calendar, occur close to this time of the year. Inti Raymi, the Southern Hemisphere's winter solstice in June, was one of the most sacred times for the Andeans and still is today for many mountain people. It corresponds to Corpus Christi (loosely according to the lunar system) in most years. Thus, Corpus Christi is celebrated today with high ceremony combining the two religious and cultural traditions. Easter, the most important of all holy days for Christians, is close enough to Corpus Christi and Inti Raymi to satisfy all parties (Dean 1999). Contemporary Catholic priests accompany a mountain procession in honor of the sun at the close of festivities near Cuzco. The clerics realize that combining forces with precolonial Andean ritual practice supports their cause and that ignoring such traditions would be detrimental to their ministries. Holy Week and Easter in the Christian calendar correspond with Andean harvest and thanksgiving ceremonies. Good Friday, a day of pachacuti because of the death of

Christ, is a time when Andean spiritual forces come out with particular power and strength.

The winter for Andean farmers is also the period when irrigation canals must be cleaned, animals branded, and water management attended. The positions of the sun, moon, planets, and constellations like the Pleiades indicate when these tasks ought to be done. Celestino (1997, 1998) characterizes these winter months as dry, dedicated to the sun, and male in nature within the Andean conceptual system of symbolic oppositions, and so male divinities receive most honor. The months from September through March or April correspond to the Andean planting and growing season. This half of the year is wet, dedicated to the moon, and a time of goddess worship.

In the Andean spring the earth is becoming fertile and pregnant again. The serpent rises in the night sky, and so does the llama. However, too much water is a constant danger. To prevent inundation, particularly from the sea, Andeans make offerings to Yacana, the black llama, using ritual sacred seashells, particularly those of serrated spondylus that populates beaches in El Niño years and the strombus conch. It is hoped, then, that she who resides as a dark space in the Milky Way will drink up enough seawater by means of the starry river that it will not flood the land. Angels, post-conquest, help Yacana in this important task. Christmas, which takes place during this time of the year, does not receive the same emphasis as it does in northern latitudes. There is more concentration on the importance of the Virgin Mary and her pregnancy than on the birth of her divine son.

Christian and Andean concepts of the divine have a direct correspondence. Celestino points out that early missionaries employed their knowledge of Inca belief to facilitate the conversion process. The Christian notion of the Trinity was presented in terms of the three related gods, Rayo (Lightning), Relámpago (Lightning Flash), and Trueno (Thunder). Just as the Incas collapsed their accreted creation myths into one, which justified their own greatness, the Spanish concentrated the meanings of Viracocha into one unseen God the Father.

Pachacamac, the coastal god acquired by the Incas, walked on water and took human shape that merged with that of Christ, who walked on the Sea of Galilee (Matthew 14:22–33). Pachacamac delights in taking the form of an old beggar and testing people's morals and ethics. He then reveals his divine reality and metes out rewards and punishments. Pachamama,

Mother Earth, merges with the Virgin Mary. Mamacha Asunta (the Assumption), celebrated on August 15 in the Christian calendar, is a presaging for the rainy "female" months of the Andean growing season. The goddess New Moon is the Virgin of Guadalupe. Saint Rose of Lima, patroness of Lima, and her goddess counterpart appear on Andean *curanderos'* (spiritual experts' and healers') ritual tables. Saint Mark, a patron of farm animals, presides over branding ceremonies. Angels are evident everywhere unusual events have taken place and serve as stand-ins for the winged huamanis. All Andean divinities and sacred beings eventually had their Christian counterparts whose appearances and miracles took place at Inca sacred sites, or huacas, in the form of apus, ceques, caves, waterfalls, and the like.

On the dark side, the devil, Lucifer (leader of the devils and himself a fallen angel), Supay, and Pishtaco resonate with one another but in complex ways. Supay is a power from the World of Inside. He is capable of helpful or destructive acts or both. Some religious and ritual specialists must make pacts with Supay in order to practice their arts. This is always a dangerous proposition, as Supay is apt to take his due in return for granting power in a kind of Faustian bargain with his human supplicants. The results can be tragic for human beings involved. The Christian devil, unlike Supay, appears to be fully destructive, a force of evil. Some readings of religious texts make this bad angel called the devil more intelligent than the good ones, however. In a way similar to Lucifer, Supay was once the good offspring of a beneficent divinity who later turned bad in a way similar to Lucifer. Lucifer for Andeans becomes linguistically and conceptually mixed with the idea of Lucero, the morning and evening star, and so for them even the Christian head of the forces of darkness is not so much evil as he is simply powerful, like Supay.

Pishtaco is a formidable though low-ranking figure who scurries about at night intent upon eating the fat (sometimes flesh and blood as well) of human beings. He formerly fed only on llamas, but postconquest he became a danger particularly to Indigenes as he is after their life force. He takes the disguise of a foreigner, once a Spanish conquistador, now an archeologist, medical worker, or tourist. Pishtaco's doings in modern times are most revealing (chapter 5).

The Spanish viewed all Inca religious practice as devil worship during Celestino's first stage of the conversion process, destruction of idols. As a result, the Andeans took within themselves the idea that their way of life was diabolic. This is so much the case that certain religious specialists are known as "devils," though this term means for them "spiritual power" rather than "evil" as it does for Christians. Such positive use of the word "devil" is a good example of the workings of inversion. This is an instance of how inversion can negate W.E.B. DuBois's worst fears about dual subjectivity.

The Spanish banished certain types of Andean power beings to mountain territories above the snow line. Such entities either reward or wreak havoc during pilgrimages to these most sacred of places. Some of the holiest pilgrimages for Andeans involve trekking up sacred apus to a level above the snow line to gather divinely imbued chunks of ice. A pilgrim who succumbs to a climbing accident might signal the need for a human sacrifice to the mountain gods even in contemporary times. Andean worship of animals, birds, fish, plants, and certain natural arrangements of the landscape generally escaped the notice of missionaries. This was because saints' appearances, miracles, and the associations between natural forms and personages in the Christian pantheon are very common in Indigenous Andean religious thought, as were the pre-Columbian concepts with which they blended.

The Indigenes reacted violently in a number of open revolts to the extreme measures taken by the early colonial regime. Some of the most dramatic protest movements in Peruvian history happened at this time. Interestingly, many of these were not political or military but religious and philosophical in nature. The Incas believed, as described previously, that the Spanish had been allowed to conquer them because they had not performed religious rituals in the proper manner. After an initial period characterized primarily by violence, most social protest went into partial hiding and took the form of millenarian movements. The shared penchant for public display between the two cultures in contact reinforced a tendency toward massive religious events with casts of hundreds and even thousands. Such large-scale worship still characterizes Andean religious ritual. Andean belief, past and present, posits that divinities expect rituals to be enacted in every way with perfection. Dance-drama teams must have beautiful and coordinated costumes. Dance steps need be performed en masse with complex choreography and precision, music played and songs sung with high art. Most important, worshippers must show great joy on their faces.

The conquest proved that the Incas had let their divinities down, and as the conversion process went forward, the huamanis, the huacas, and many of the other traditional beliefs were increasingly ignored and forgotten. Two movements of a millenarian nature, Taki Onqoy and Inkarri, illustrate two ways Andeans tried to worship their divinities once more in the strictly correct manner and thus bring back the former and, to their way of thinking, proper Andean order of things.

Taki is a traditional religious dance (*danza*). Most takis are performed by competing teams of dancers and musicians. Takis are customarily performed in October and November because they ensure a good planting and growing season. The *danza de tijeras*, the scissors dance described in chapter 5, probably descended from the pre-Columbian takis. Taki Onqoy ("dance sickness" in Quechua) was a marathon dance similar to the North American plains Ghost Dance tradition in that it arose for similar reasons of protest (note 4).

4. The Ghost Dance of the nineteenth century was an attempt by Native North Americans of several tribal origins to enlist the help of their traditional divinities against the white man's invasion of their lands. The Ghost Dancers believed their gods had abandoned them through some fault of their own as less than perfect worshippers. When they saw their traditional world collapsing around them, Ghost Dancers painted their faces and dressed in traditional or special clothing. They danced day and night to the point of exhaustion, illness, and even death in hopes of winning the support of their divinities once more. Like the Taki Onqoy, the Ghost Dance is a millenarian movement and as such apparently religious. However, such movements often have goals similar to those of political or military revolutions.

Guamán Poma served in the Spanish attempts initiated by the legal official Cristobal Albornoz to stamp out the Taki Onqoy in Ayacucho. The takis can involve mutual flagellation intended to draw blood. This blood serves to fertilize Mother Earth. They can entail other physical trials intended as evidence of dancers' worshipful attitude. During the period of the Taki Onqoy movement, in the late sixteenth and early seventeenth centuries, dancers would perform to the point of collapse and even death (again like the Ghost Dance), so great was their fervor to bring back former days through a divinely induced pachacuti.

The Inkarri myth centers around the demise of the last Inca, Tupac Amaru, who was beheaded and then drawn and quartered by the Spanish in 1781. The word *inkarri* may be a pronunciation of the Spanish title "Inka rey" (Inca emperor) using Quechua vowel forms. Though the Spanish at that time were not aware, the human head for Incas is symbolic of the idea of a plant seed, especially once it is buried in the ground. According to the Inkarri myth, Tupac Amaru's head is growing a new body within the World of Inside, gathering former body parts together from the four quarters of Tahuantinsuyu. The body is still small, but once it is grown the Inca emperor will return, the world will experience a pachacuti, and the Inca empire will reign once more. Of the Taki Onqoy and Inkarri movements, Inkarri is by far the stronger and still in evidence today, as will be seen in later discussion of a new, contemporary saint with many Inkarri-like characteristics.

Scholars in the field discuss the tendency to make negative valuations positive through "inversion." In other words, being diabolical actually

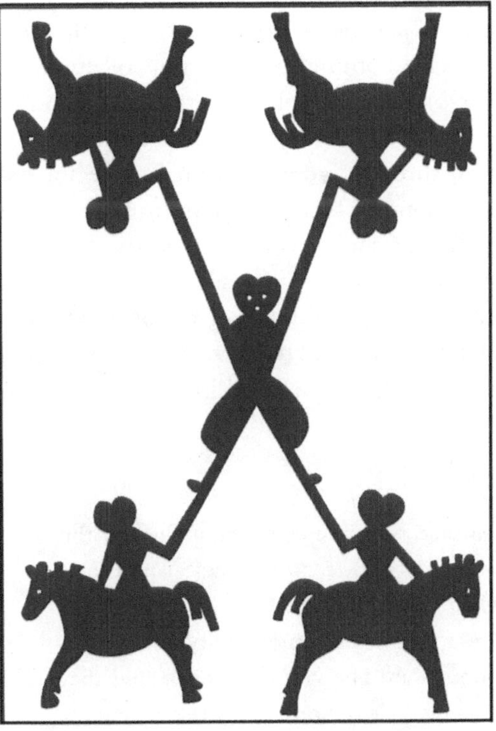

3.2 Colonial-style Inkarri motif on textile. Spanish horsemen execute the last Inca emperor, Tupac Amaru. Drawing by the author after illustration in Davies and Fini 1994:60.

becomes good, or being executed means hope for a brave new world. Deeper analysis, however, reveals that Andean tradition has an antidote for evils that may befall its people, whether assigned by outside colonizers or simply perceived from within their own group. If Andeans want to improve their world, they need to conform to the letter to classic ritual requirements. This is millenarian thinking with strong thematic elements of the hero saga. Luis Millones (2000:266) points out that even today Andean manifestations of the Virgin Mary punish those who do not perform their ritual duty. Andean divinities have always done this: clothes, artifacts, candles, songs, choreography, and emotional attitude must fulfill demanding traditional requirements. Only such impeccable religious behavior will bring about the desired inversion of the world.

There are two types of large-scale public religious events that over time became the major ways in which many Andeans express their faith. Celestino (1997) compares and contrasts the two: the patron saint festival and the pilgrimage. Millones, Timoeda, and Kato (2001) analyze contemporary examples of both types, explaining how their syncretic nature is rooted in the colonial era.

The patron-saint festival, or *fiesta patronal*, is a usually spectacular celebration oriented toward a particular community or group of communities. The festival features street parades, church processions, and other events whose purpose is to strengthen community ties. The desired community cohesiveness comes about through sacred and profane reciprocal exchanges carried out in the saint's honor. The *cargo* system (note 5), which requires more well-to-do individuals, families, craft unions, and ayllus to sponsor festival refreshments, dance troupes, music, decorations, and the like, is one example. The cargo or *encargo* (assignment of responsibility) rotates from sponsor to sponsor each year and functions as a leveler of wealth and a way to accumulate honor, respect, and political influence for those who support the fiestas.

5. The term *cargo* is somewhat a misnomer when applied to this set of customs, though it is used widely by scholars. The Spanish term *encargar* means to give or assign responsibility for an activity, person, or item. The noun form *encargo* means the responsibility itself and is probably more apt. Fiesta sponsors are known as *encargados*, and they underwrite the costs of community celebrations. The word *cargo* more correctly refers to the "cargo cults" of Pacific islanders who historically

created rituals to try to bring cargo planes loaded with desired materials to themselves as well as to the foreigners who otherwise seemed to be the only beneficiaries of airborne bounty.

Millones describes fiestas patronales in Cuzco that honor Our Lord of the Earthquakes and the Virgin of the Immaculate Conception. At these festivals, parades of dance-drama groups represent labor unions and ethnic groups from different parts of the former Tahuantinsuyu. The capac chunchus group represents people from Amazonia. They are adorned with colorful feathers, wear little clothing, and execute dance steps very different from the mountain traditions. Some of these "jungle" people join a pilgrimage associated with the festival to carry sacred glacial ice back to Cuzco on their backs from the summit of the local apu Qoyllur Riti. Behind these and other dance troupes in contemporary times, the Inca emperor is carried on a litter complete with his official royal forehead tassel and coat of arms with two snakes and a castle (note 6). Like other contemporary patron saints festivals, this celebration exhibits the coming together of two religious traditions but with emphasis on the Indigenous side of the equation.

6. The carrying of the emperor figure on a litter and other "Inca" ceremonies connected with Inti Raymi in Cuzco are recent developments though informed by respectable ethnohistorical data. They are an example of a socially useful cultural creativity on the part of contemporary Andeans. These groups wish to promote Andean influence in Peruvian society and believe it is significant to show that the former Inca capital still has a vibrant and respectable tradition different than the official one sanctioned by the nation-state's more socially powerful elements. Public dramatizations like this influence Peruvian society as a whole and function to raise consciousness and pride among Andeans of Indigenous and mixed descent.

A pilgrimage, on the other hand, is a multicommunity event. It involves travel, often to difficult places, and the formation of a new community of pilgrims focused on a common purpose. The pilgrimage period is in an outside-the-ordinary time and space. These pilgrims are temporarily in a mind set close to what literary analysts call a suspension of disbelief. There is a special and very popular pilgrimage known as Qoyllur Riti (New Star) to the apu Ausangate, a peak near Cuzco whose summit crests at 18,000 feet. Qoyllur Riti takes place at the time of Corpus Christi and its coincidence with Inti Raymi. This climb is made in honor of Our Lord of Qoyllur Riti, who is truly a manifestation of Christ and of Andean divinities at the same time. This site is so difficult to reach and many climbers so ill prepared in clothing for conditions at such an altitude that there are often accidents. If pilgrims meet their death in this way, people believe that the divine entity or divinities have required them to be sacrificed. The ultimate sacrifice of Christ on the cross clearly combines here with Indigenous thought.

The religious arts, which made up the lion's share of all colonial art produced in that era, expressed these philosophical and social processes in material form. The imagery available to the general public and to art makers derives from the arts and material cultures of the Incas, other Andean groups, and the Spanish in culturally separate and blended form. As the colonial period proceeded forward in time, clothing, architecture, paintings, statuary, church decorations, festival costumes, and in fact every type of art portrayed an Indigenous and Spanish cultural combination. Millones (2000) demonstrates that Indigenous tradition extends further back in time, even, than the Incas and that these pre-Incan roots of combined cultural forms can still be observed in contemporary Andean arts. He analyzes religious rituals on the North Coast of Peru that retain Moche elements conjoined with later Christian images. Guamán's illustrations resemble European book plates he probably saw in imported printed editions that were available during his lifetime.

Missionaries working with Indigenous languages that had no autochthonous orthography used visual methods to convert. A notable example is the small book used by the missionary Pedro de Gante in Mexico that was made up entirely of simple visual images, and another is the Andean pictographic catechism studied by Mitchell with Jaye (1996). Visual images and forms communicated in a multiethnic way impossible using culturally limited spoken and textual languages. Later Quechua, Nahuatl, and Maya "grammars" were written using Spanish phonemes, but these served only the educated and literate, that is, the missionaries themselves and few others.

During the first two stages of the conversion process, destruction of idolatry and repression and stabilization, according to Celestino (1997,

1998), the colonial government tried to obliterate Indigenous religious imagery of all sorts. There were even decrees demanding the destruction of all murals, clothing, and painted house decoration. However, by the third stage of the conversion process, with a certain tolerance for combined traditions, there seemed almost to be a conscious promotion of religious syncretic art. The paintings from the colonial Cuzco and Ayacucho schools of art are good examples. They feature Christian saints but also scenes from local daily life and Andean religious symbols. Religious images and goods were important trade items. Merchants called *arrieros* traveled over the mountains with llamas and burros carrying Christian rosaries and medals, along with Andean sacred seashells (*mullus*), carved stones, and other items for sale to religious customers over wide geographic areas.

The religious monastic orders, now settled in permanent Andean missions, began to see the local Indigenous people as the noble savages of nascent Enlightenment thinking. The many saint-related myths and miracles of Spain blended with Indigenous ones. Thus, certain manifestations of the Virgin Mary, Christ, the saints, and angels became special to local communities. Andean ancestor worship was directed to saints, and the Inca allyus became stronger as they took on the devotional functions of Spanish cofradías. Andean homes display the cross, which for them evokes both Christ and the World of Four Directions. Home altars also have saints, angels, condors, and Supay. Dancers at religious festivals wear clothing that mirrors Spanish carnival tradition and the mountain gods. Their paintings show the Virgin Mary/Pachamama assuring the growth of the corn and potato crops. The denouement of the conquest drama ends in peaceful blending. However, the arts constantly reenact all the stages of what came before.

The Baroque era in Spain encouraged and fortified a religious visual culture that was very similar to the Andean preference. Andeans and Spaniards alike promoted the projection of power, whether sacred or mundane, in the form of massive public spectacles. In the book *Dioses familiares* (2000) Millones states that the process of religious combination was tremendously facilitated by such similarities in the two cultural styles in contact. The author's chapter "Power as Spectacle" is particularly descriptive of this dovetailing. The Andeans employed animals, plants, and other particularly awe-inspiring elements of nature in their religious displays. Spectacle as a means of social control is a thing often seen in human history and discussed at length by Michel Foucault (1965) in his writings about European medieval public trials and punishments. Certainly the Mexica penchant for petrifying exhibits of human sacrifice had this purpose along with a spiritual one. The European Middle Ages displays of boiling criminals in oil, the colonial-era town-square executions of witches at Salem, Massachusetts, and similar acts were carried out to the same end.

Spain of the Baroque era shared this tradition. Millones quotes Philip II's ambassador, who suffers chiding on the part of his royal highness for giving greater attention to a ceremony than more important affairs. The ambassador shoots back:

> What do you mean forgetting all in favor of a ceremony? Your majesty is nothing if not a ceremony. (2000:70)

This statement speaks volumes about the dramatic qualities of life in Baroque Spain. Along with parades integrated into dance and dramatic production, there were bullfights, fireworks, and other events seen also in Peru during religious festivities. In his account of a contemporary conquest drama in the town of Carhuamayo, Millones shows how Indigenes of today use baroque theatrical style to recount their pro-Andean version of the conquest story (2000:84–109).

The Baroque period in Spain and in Peru was a time when society continued to dramatize issues resulting from the original conquest debates. The Church constructed enormous cathedrals, sponsored mass processions and autos da fé to support its belief system and officially sanctioned code of behavior. The Baroque was a time of the grand gesture, mass ritual events, sumptuous public parades, and effluvient architecture, perhaps culminating in the dizzying Plateresque style of the Americas and the Churrigueresque style of Europe. Some historians note that the recognitions of miracles and canonizations of saints in the seventeenth century were truly "inflationary" in number (García Cancel 2000:56). The colonial wealth engine financed excess, and excess supported the claims of inheritance for the already privileged and wealthy while denying access to the poor. In this there was little difference between Spain and its colonies in the Americas.

The folk religious art and thought of the Spanish peninsula and the Americas gave great importance to signs and portents of divine direction behind human historical events. Spanish historical accounts of the toppling of Atahuallpa and Montezuma associate the emperors' downfall with such imaginative portents as comets, magical birds with mirror eyes, and other supernatural events as much as did the Mexica codices and the histories recorded by early chroniclers in the Andes.

The Inca tradition of dancing and singing as a form of mass public, joyful prayer meshed well with the Spanish Baroque religious procession and the morality play enacted on the steps of the cathedral. Taki Onqoy and Inkarri are high theater that can impress their audiences far more than mere military or political activity alone.

The Andeans in their arts of then and now appear on the surface to identify themselves with the old-time enemies of Christian Spain: Judas, Jews, devils, and Moors. Guamán's illustration shows an image drawn from the Spanish church iconography Santiago Matamoros (Saint James the Moor Killer) mounted on a fiery steed, only this time the figure under the horse's hooves is not a Moor, but an Inca (1988:364). The Spanish transport of Reconquest ideas to the Americas and the Inca identity with another enemy, the Moor, can be seen here. In another of Guamán's images, the Incas conquer the Spanish (an inversion) when in actual fact the opposite took place (1988:400). This use of the Spanish Baroque style (disjunction) in many folk art genera of today shows how Andean contestation cleverly takes on the trappings of the mediator (dual subjectivity). This is, indeed, a most subtle disguise. Arts in the contemporary, or second, age of globalization in Peru have, interestingly, some parallel characteristics.

It seems almost contradictory but nonetheless true that while culture-contact processes like the one described here diminish culture varieties, they also create new and combined cultures. Succeeding chapters will show that artists have the capacity to keep old values and add new ones at the same time. In this way, Andean artists may not choose one tradition or another as much as embrace several ways of thinking and being at once. Similar tendencies in Andean and Spanish Baroque visual expression facilitated an artistic coming together. However, Andean artists asserted their own traditions using ploys such as disjunction, inversion, and dual subjectivity. Thus, their art was accepted and understood by different audiences who interpreted the work in very distinct and sometimes opposing ways.

CHAPTER 4

Globalization Today

The second great variation this book considers is that of the modern period from the mid-twentieth century to the first decade of the twenty-first century. This was a time of profound change among Andeans. Peru shifted from being a primarily rural to an urbanizing country. Most rural-to-urban migrants have Indigenous cultural background. Many Andeans also migrate to other countries in search of employment and have now established expatriate communities in a number of foreign lands. Technology, particularly in the area of telecommunications, changed Andeans' perceptions of their world in a fundamental way. Globalization of trade, agriculture, industry—in short, every human product and behavior—painted an entirely new portrait of life's realities and possibilities.

The Spanish Baroque, with its dynamic movement, brilliant colors, *horror vacui* (designs that fill all available space with images and forms), love of the grand gesture, and cast-of-thousands theatricality has much in common with mass visual communication systems of the present millennium. The way these communication systems capture as well as limit the public imagination is also similar. Artists continue to make use of tactics like disjunction, inversion, and dual subjectivity to assert their own pride in cultural identity even within the maelstrom now known as globalization. This chapter presents information about recent large-scale social changes in Peru brought about by internal and international migration, the activities of the Shining Path, urban squatter movements, the great influence of mass media, and other contemporary realities. There will be a discussion about how changes like these influence the arts and a section about the promotion and sale of Andean folk arts locally, globally, and over the Internet.

A World Perspective

The contemporary global age in Peru resembles the first one discussed here, the Spanish colonial era, in several ways. The actors are different in that the cultures in contact have evolved over time, and many more groups than two now confront one another in popular religious art expression. However, what remains the same is that there are similarities between contemporary times and the intensely public Baroque-inspired style of the sixteenth through eighteenth centuries and the effects of mass media and the world consumerism engines of today. In the popular mind in places in the world including Latin America, the idea of globalization often means a system that benefits the rich of the world. There are various alternatives for the poor such as socialism, the promotion of local industries and micro-enterprises, ATOs (alternative trade organizations), and the like. Some of the major globalization theorists would very much agree that it is a system that benefits the rich and further exploits the poor. Notable among these is Manuel Castells. On the other side of the fence are theorists like Hernando de Soto who assert that contemporary global systems, if left untrammeled within free-market forces, will prove to be the salvation for all, rich and poor.

For Andean art makers, globalization means that their hand-produced traditional styles and products are copied more cheaply by low-wage workers using inexpensive man-made materials and in much greater volume in modern factories located on other continents. It means that the internationally focused middlemen are more interested in quantity and low price than in quality. As a result, many artists produce shoddy work to keep afloat economically. It means that children in art-making families must seek other than traditional ways of making a living. These and many more difficulties and conundrums face Andean artists today. The world economic collapse of 2008 calls some of these global economic tendencies into question and so gives credence to the wisdom offered by Andean artists regarding their own contemporary situations and solutions for problems they encounter.

Analysts of Globalization

Manuel Castells has produced several volumes about the phenomenon of contemporary globalization. Before analyzing his point of view in contrast to that of other experts, it is useful to employ his description of the nature of this contemporary age as a baseline. Castells contends that an entirely new form of socioeconomic organization has now emerged. The state as an entity lost prominence with the collapse of the Soviet Union. For the first time, the entire globe is within the capitalist system. This form of capitalism is at the same time old and new. It depends on competition in the pursuit of profit in the familiar way. The new information and communication technologies upon which it depends make this economic process distinct in a number of areas (Castells 1998b:2). Information and communication technologies affect art profoundly, as its material nature (even in performance art) is basically that of a commodity that is now part of worldwide trade systems. Various dangers are apparent in this new reality and at the same time some encouraging and beneficial alternative possibilities.

Points of View about the World Marketplace

Several points of view are useful to this discussion. Some students of globalization believe it to be a fundamentally positive process. Others contend that global systems help the already well-off at the increasing expense of the poor and disenfranchised. Another contingent asserts that if certain pitfalls can be avoided, globalization can be beneficial if the poor as well as the rich are kept in mind.

The theorists in the scholarly and popular press who take the view that globalization is in general a positive process say that if free-market forces are left to act on their own, globalization will benefit everyone. However, there is evidence that extant market forces are far from free; in fact, they appear to be rigged in favor of the already wealthy countries. In the *New York Times* opinion piece "The Rigged Trade Game" (July 20, 2003) the writer cites Philippine agriculture as an example and shows how rich countries "stack the deck" for their own farmers by subsidizing them. Philippine farmers' far lower labor costs, then, do not help them. Dumping supplies such as agricultural products from extranationally subsidized farming systems actually drives Filipinos off farms and into overpopulated cities in their search for survival. Joining the WTO (World

Trade Organization) caused the Philippines to lose thousands of farm jobs. This situation is worse than one that produces dire need; it actually kills people because they are increasingly deprived of basic needs like food.

One billion people try to live on a dollar a day, while European cows are subsidized at two dollars a day. This tragic situation goes beyond issues of economics and health. It fuels political and religious fundamentalist movements of a violent nature. Robin Hahnel (1998:2, 4) cites studies of the Gini coefficient, a measure of income inequality, between 1975 and 1993. Studies showed a 14 percent increase in inequality of incomes among different groups of the world's peoples, with the largest drops in the lowest wage brackets worldwide. In sum, Hahnel states that the recent era of deregulation and globalization has been the best of times for a few and the worst of times for most of the globe's population. This situation affects the people of the United States as well. The middle classes (the numerical majority or middle-income classes) have less predictable employment and therefore will have fewer possibilities of serving as one of the consumer engines that fuel global commodity production. This perspective has certainly proved true in terms of how the 2008 financial crisis has affected even workers in the world's wealthy countries, forcing them into unemployment, bankruptcy, and home foreclosure.

In many countries of the "developing" world there is a suspicion that globalization is simply the newest and latest form of capitalist imperialism. The governments of Hugo Chávez in Venezuela and Evo Morales in Bolivia have drawn strength from this idea, and leaders like these enshrine themselves as being "men of the people" in traditional and some say passé Marxian socialist terms. The contemporary movement led by Evo Morales in Bolivia is typical of this view. Morales promoted himself as a socialist and coca-leaf agriculture as a way of making a living in the only terms allowed by the global economic system. Castells characterizes this option, which might be called a Jesse James or Robin Hood economic position, as one taken commonly by those disenfranchised by globalization: "Well, if you don't value me as a producer of bananas, I'll produce cocaine" (1998b:2). This underground economy amounts to $1.5 trillion worldwide, equivalent to the GDP of Britain. The enormous scale of this response is entirely new. Terrorist and religious fundamentalist movements operate from the same perspective. Enormous social class differences between and within countries strengthen this trend (note 1).

1. Coca, specifically, is a traditionally grown herb used for thousands of years in the Andean region. Its customary use in the naturally dried leaf form usually does not have serious consequences for users. Employers historically encouraged its heavy consumption by farm laborers and miners to diminish their need for food and increase their work capacity. Cocaine is a highly processed essence extracted from the coca leaf.

Manuel Castells sees a number of dangerous trends and tendencies in contemporary times. He says the new socioeconomic system operates in a way that produces inequality and social exclusion on an unprecedented planetary scale (1998b). There are a number of reasons for this. First, the information and communication technology that fuels much human activity is in the hands of the few and the privileged. Large areas of the non-Western world have little access to the Internet and few possibilities for education. The recent increase in cell phone and wireless Internet access has changed this situation to a degree (note 2).

2. Here Castells' writings have become somewhat dated. He could not have known that in less than a decade, cell phone acquisition and use would explode over the world. Neither did he know that satellite-enabled Internet use would also increase at an enormous rate. Wireless audiovisual technology access is one of the most powerful engines that has allowed formerly marginalized people to become connected to, at least in the sense of being aware of, world information networks. The filmmaker and anthropologist Jayansinjhi Jhala has said this technology, including cell phones and interactive audiovisual Internet sites, makes it possible to circumvent the need to read and write as well as the need for wire-based electricity infrastructure, giving educationally marginalized people a large boost into awareness about, though probably not full participation in, the mainstream of world events and commerce (in Strong and Wilder 2009:5).

Castells' main point about vast differences in access to the world's wealth and privilege still hold. Access does not necessarily translate into economic well-being. Even within wealthy societies are populations of poor and disenfranchised people cut off from the benefits of schooling and access to communications technology. Castells insists that there is "an undeniable tendency toward a polarized social structure, between countries and within countries" (1998b:3). The solution to these problems, he finds, is neither economic nor technological but rather social. A society must consciously decide whether participation in the information age will be "a virtuous cycle of development, or a downward spiral of underdevelopment" (ibid.).

Though everyone is affected by globalization, not everyone is included in it. Most people's concerns center on the local and the regional. The new organizational form important today is what Castells calls the "network" at national and international levels; arrangements like the European Union and NAFTA (North American Free Trade Agreement) have supplanted the state. At all levels, networks are adaptable and flexible in the extreme. Networks are also centralized and decentralized simultaneously. They can be coordinated without a center (note 3).

3. The scholar Jonathan Friedman (1994) discusses this seemingly paradoxical characteristic of contemporary network systems. He points out that this model has supplanted the older idea of "center versus periphery." The two processes definitive of the new era are decentralization and competition. These two forces fluctuate in relation to one another. At the same time as political and economic entities unify into large aggregates like the European Union and NAFTA blocs, Basques in Spain and some former Soviet Republics, using the opposite strategy, seek smaller, separate identities. Friedman relates the cohesive tendencies to order and power. He equates the separatist movements with disorder but also with invention and creativity. The options taken by a group of people choosing between these interacting poles depend on their goals, and these are often defined in terms of basic survival. Curiously enough, the work of scholars of revitalization like Wallace (1956, 1989) shows that what one may call innovations are often actually revitalizations of forms traditional to an ethnic or pan-ethnic group (Strong 1998).

What ties networks together is one goal: profit. If human beings in networks stand in the way of profit, they are jettisoned, excluded, switched off. The fastest-growing population in the world consists of people living at 50 percent of the poverty line or below (UNDP 1997). These are the waste thrown away by global networks. These excluded poor inhabit what Castells and others call a "fourth world" cut off from global system benefits. In order for globalization to benefit everyone to the fullest extent, all human beings must be empowered by education, access to technology, good health, decent housing, psychological stability, and cultural fulfillment. All of these benefits have a positive effect as well on the natural environment without which human society has no future. This means that networks must operate not on the principle of cost lowering but rather on productivity enhancing. In other words, Castells is a profound idealist asking that all human beings be equally valued. Without this as an underlying philosophy, he contends, world development will not take place. Castells seems convinced that "productivity enhancing" within his humanitarian perspective will lead, in the long run, to profit for all people.

The traditional artists of Peru are part of the fourth world within their nation and the rest of the world's countries. Their response to contemporary global forces of power and profit is appropriate, given what is discussed above. The artists' accurate grasp of messages and codes received from first-world communications technologies attests to Castells' characterization of the way networks operate. Yet these artists have shown themselves to be proactive participants in global systems. Given entrée along the lines Castells suggests—basic respect and fulfillment of fundamental human needs—they have untold potential to enrich the rest of the world, as would all other fourth-world populations.

Recent History, Globalization, and Artists in Peru

Peru shares in processes taking place in the world as a whole, and these affect Andean artists and their work. The nation itself has experienced a particularly turbulent recent history. One must take this background into account to fully understand contemporary arts.

Social theorists in Peru contend that Indigenous people and other non-elite ethnic groups there live in a mental world that is at once global and local. Various important processes have radically transformed Peruvian society since the mid-twentieth century. These include massive rural-to-urban migration and the revolutionary activities of the Shining Path movement and to a lesser extent the Tupac Amaru movement. From the middle of the twentieth century to the birth of the twenty-first, Peru has changed from a rural, agricultural country to one that is primarily urban and now experiences considerable emigration to the highly industrialized countries of the world. In the 1940s, 60 percent of the population lived in the interior mountain region. These people were primarily Indigenous and Mestizo and made their living as farmers, many as workers on large haciendas. Today, less than 40 percent of the popula-tion lives in rural areas, while more than 60 percent lives in cities, thus reversing the character of the country from rural to urban (Flindell Klarén 2000:323–358, Starn et al. 1995:254–307).

Even the meanings of the terms "Indian" and "Mestizo" have changed from biological to occupational categories. An Indian now is a rural farmer. A newer term, *cholo*, applies more readily to urban Indians and Mestizos who consider themselves occupational Mestizos in the urban context (Manrique 2000). Peru is far more complex, ethnically speaking, as it has African and Asian populations primarily in its coastal cities and a varied Indigenous population not closely related to the mountain-dwelling Quechua or Aymara in its vast Amazonian jungle region. These groups are relatively small. Though they will be mentioned from time to time, the main focus here is on the Indigenes and Mestizos of mountain origin.

Lima, Peru's capital, is a major destination of rural-to-urban migrants. Its population has grown tremendously between the mid-twentieth century and the early twenty-first century so that now it constitutes 25 percent or more of the total population of the country (Flindell Klarén 2009, Starn et al. 1995). An important flow of rural migrants settled on the outskirts of the city in shantytowns beginning in the 1940s. This flow grew into a flood beginning in the 1970s during the administration of President Juan Velasco. In its effort to dismantle the centuries-old hacienda system and replace it with land-reform initiatives, the government unfortunately did not plan for or include adequate provision for the large numbers of farmworkers liberated from peonage. They had no tools, land, water resources, or other basics they needed to farm for themselves. Rather than face starvation, these displaced people poured into the cities. In this new urban environment they were forced to compete for the same unreliable employment and hardscrabble existence in infrahuman conditions. Meanwhile, many of those who stayed in the mountains suffered from dire poverty (Dobyns and Doughty 1976, Doughty 1969, Sabogal Wiesse 1978).

The situation was ripe for revolution, and the Shining Path (Sendero Luminoso) movement gathered power (note 4). This political group, founded by university professors and students of European and Mestizo descent, did not coalesce with other socialist groups in the Peruvian political tradition. Instead, the Shining Path followed its own interpretation of the philosophy of China's chairman Mao Tse Tung. Like Mao, they built a "center of strength" in a rural area, in this case the department of Ayacucho and particularly in its capital city of Huamanga. At first, movement membership increased because of the inherent appeal of the movement's agenda and the resemblance of many Andean traditions and philosophies (though there is no historical connection) such as cooperative labor and labor exchange to socialist ones. As time went on, however, the Shining Path as well as the government forces opposing its armies began to abuse the very people they each had set out to save. Government and Sendero armies needed provisions and stole them from poor farmers. They needed young men in their ranks, so they conscripted mountain boys by threatening to kill their family members. Independent militias arose and took advantage of the chaotic situation for their own political and economic benefit. Battles took place on farmers' plots and pastures. Rural living became dangerous for many people, and the torrent of migration to the cities reached tidal wave proportions by the 1980s and 1990s (Starn, de Gregori, and Kirk 1995:304–342). When Abimael Guzman, the Shining Path leader, was captured in the mid-1990s, the siege of terror began to subside. Analysts find that the Shining Path may very well have reached its goals if its leaders had not interpreted Mao so narrowly that they ignored the ethnic diversity of Peru, particularly Indigenous philosophies and values.

4. The name Sendero Luminoso, or Shining Path, comes from Mao Tse Tung's "little red book," a collection of his quotations carried by masses of his followers and often held aloft during public demonstrations. Mao states in the book that once the revolution takes place, society will improve as it ascends a "shining path" onward and upward to the most ideal human existence possible. Mao was the leader of the People's Republic of China from 1949 to 1976; the red book was published in 1966.

The "Real" Revolution

Some theorists in Peru argue that although the Shining Path failed in an attempt at social change, Peru's urban poor have actually succeeded in doing so. In 1968 a large squatter encampment took root in Lima and introduced a new age of accelerated and massive rural migration to the capital. A supposedly unused plot of land belonging to a wealthy owner was taken over at dawn in classic squatter fashion by large groups of demonstrators. A number of people were arrested, including some religious leaders who adhered to the philosophy known as liberation theology (note 5). Eventually the city allowed the squatters to stay and the land they "liberated" for themselves to become a "new town" neighborhood called Villa El Salvador. This neighborhood has since become a globally known model for "bootstraps" development. What was once an enormous squatter settlement covered with flimsy shacks now has solidly built homes, paved streets and sidewalks, water, electricity, sanitation, and a plethora of thriving entrepreneurial associations and businesses, including arts and craft production centers. All of these came about because of the people themselves working together in the old Andean communal way in a society without the financial wherewithal to offer them the smallest social assistance (note 6).

5. Liberation theology is a set of ideas developed in Peru by the cleric Gustavo Gutiérrez (Tamayo Acosta 1989:56) as well as by Leonardo Boff in Brazil and others. According to this movement within the clergy and faithful of the Roman Catholic Church, it is the responsibility of religious institutions to see to the material as well as spiritual well-being of the poor. Followers of liberation theology often use consciousness-raising techniques promoted by Paulo Freire (2001). Many clerical and lay church members throughout Latin America became followers of this movement.

6. A number of Lima rural migrant neighborhoods, or New Towns (*pueblos nuevos*), have followed the same path toward development as Villa El Salvador. However, few have reached the technical and financial level attained by La Villa, as it is called, or enjoyed its notoriety. La Villa's success is in part due to external and even international investment brought about by a good system of public relations.

This, say de Soto, Ghersi, and Ghibellini (1987), is free enterprise operating in a totally untrammeled fashion. The end point of this evolution, they assert, will be true equality for the burgeoning cholo urban migrants (note 7). The bootstraps revolution for de Soto and his school of thought adds credence to the idea that globalization can only be beneficial in an environment of truly free enterprise. Hernando de Soto contends that the key to allowing the poor to be free and empowered to produce new wealth is licensing of property ownership. In Peru, property and business enterprises carried on by the poor are largely off the books, outside the law. For this reason a large chunk of Peru's economic potential is in the form of urban-gypsy cab companies, street vendors, craft manufacture, and the like known as informal enterprises, *los informales*. The formal economy, or property and business within the legal system or on the books, is still in the hands of the elite social classes. De Soto asserts that once the poor's property and businesses are legalized they will become wealthy, and so will the country as a whole.

7. *Cholo* and *chola* refer to an Indigenous or Mestizo person living and working outside the rural context on a full- or part-time basis. Cholos typically have taken on some urban ways and modes of dress. Traveling women market vendors and small-restaurant owners are often called cholas as well. Cholas have a particular clothing style that is basically Indigenous in form but may be expensive due to cholas' lucrative participation in the cash economy. This term is not as commonly used today as it was a generation or two in the past.

Informal business and property owners can be quite wealthy in the monetary sense and yet still see themselves as members of the lower classes because they neither are accepted as new elites nor have any governmental guarantees over the long term for the success and protection of their enterprises. De Soto's hope for "depauperization" of the informal sector has yet to be realized. His ideas are intriguing, particularly his comments about informal or criminal activity such as the *cocaleros*, growers of coca leaves for the drug trade in cocaine. If cocaleros could own their own land, de Soto offers as an example, they would soon see that growing oil palms would give them six times the income they now receive for growing coca.

What de Soto proposes seems to be a combination of legalizing heretofore illegal landholdings and business activities and then incorporating them into laissez faire free enterprise. Though the ideas sound good, they do not take scale into account or the need for capital. The informales are typically small, locally oriented concerns. They cannot compete in the national and international arena of today without organizing into larger regional businesses that have access to loans for economic development. Villa El Salvador receives adequate start-up loans and has been organized to operate on a competitive scale because good public relations have fomented an influx of national and overseas market interests as well as capital investments.

From the point of view of 2009–2010, immediately after the global economic downturn, one might speculate as to whether uninhibited globalized capitalism is even beneficial for the rich and powerful of the world. People in Peru and elsewhere, true to form, are suffering in a more immediate and profound way than those living in more economically fortunate societies. The recent world economic crisis, the "great recession" beginning in 2008, falls especially heavily on Peru's artists, as many of them have become at least partially dependent on international economic networks.

The Televised Revolution and Peru.com

Significant promoters of arts innovation along with almost all other sociocultural transformation in Peru are television and other forms of telecommunication such as cell phones and the Internet. Antennas and satellite dishes sprout even from the flapping plastic drop-cloth roofs of newly arrived rural migrants in Lima. Internet cafes staffed with new-fashioned cyber letter writers for the many marginally literate clients dot migrant neighborhoods or new towns of Lima and some rural areas as soon as cell phone towers are installed and wireless capacity provided. Many more Peruvian children and young people than in previous generations have grown up with television and other mass communications media. Cell phones are everywhere, even among the poor, though few are enabled for the Internet. The standard television set and radio receiver still exert enormous influence on viewers and listeners.

"In Peru," according to Rafo León, poet and satirist, "TV doesn't reflect the country, it is the country. The perfect example of the New Pe (the New Peruvian) is the just-arrived-to-Lima teenage peasant with a boom box blaring techno-cumbia that stimulates the most primitive impulses—that kid is Peru" (in Fuguet 2001:36). Alberto Fuguet, in his article "This Revolution Is Being Televised," goes on to explain that at that time 90 percent of Peruvian programming was locally produced and made to appeal to New Pes. This should be compared to the vast majority of programming formerly produced in the United States and Europe in the 1960s and 1970s. Interestingly, talk, game, and news shows and other locally oriented programs produced in Peru, Mexico, and other countries with heavy immigrant populations in the United States are broadcast daily over the air and cable on Spanish-language networks like Telemundo, Univision, and Telefutura that cover the entire continents of South and North America. New York City is one of the major Latin American immigrant destinations in the United States. Spanish-language programs on these networks blast from large-screen televisions thoughtfully mounted to the walls of neighborhood Laundromats, stores, and cafes. Extranational New Pes, Mexicans, Ecuadorians, and other Spanish speakers who have migrated to New York City have their eyes glued to the screen while their hands fold undershirts and towels in Laundromats, hold coffee cups in restaurants, or reach for jugs of milk in grocery stores. However, the program is from NBC, which owns the Telemundo Spanish-language network, not its Peruvian or other Latin American production centers. Thus once again, profit has slipped through Peruvian fingers. U.S. media magnates know a good thing when they see it: "Viewers don't like dubbed *I Love Lucy* any more. OK, let's give them a talk show with music in Spanish." The question of abuse of this media form for blatantly commercial ends aside, the process of globalization in communications media can take many interesting twists and turns. This example lends weight to Castells' argument in the sense that it shows how globalization benefits the already wealthy. Peruvian and other producers export shows via NBC-owned Telemundo to the United States because people like the New Pes are now an important audience and potential market in North America. The New Pes live in many countries other than Peru today because they have migrated over the globe looking for work. *El Comercio* newspaper and other news outlets in Lima give them all an Internet forum to keep up with happenings in Peru and air their concerns. In January 2010 there were articles and email statements from Peruvians living in the United States, Spain, Italy, England, France, Japan, Germany, Switzerland, Sweden, Norway, and Canada on the *El Comercio* web page for Peruvians everywhere. This media network that influences its vast international audience so profoundly has no discernible center, and there is no predictable direction for the flow of people, funds, and information, all of which must adjust course at any moment to survive in the new and unpredictable contemporary climate.

Arguedas and the Fish-Meal Factory

Far from being the romantic promoter of an extinct Andean "folklore" that he is often made out to be, the anthropologist José María Arguedas watched the beginning of the global revolution with a huamani's eagle eye in the 1960s. Arguedas felt deeply that the way to improve the future of his beloved Indigenous people would be for Peru to accept itself as a Mestizo culture. In an odd sort of way, Peru now finally sees itself as Mestizo. The old caste or class system divided the European elite at the top from a mixed-race grouping at the center, and that group in turn held a more privileged position than the pure Indigenes, Africans, and Asians at the bottom of the heap. Such a structure seems to be losing strength as a way of strictly dividing social ranks. For many people this means a denial of the Indigenous part of their mixed heritage because they wish to forget the rural and "primitive" past they have learned to devalue.

Some of Arguedas' most interesting and prescient observations appear in poetic form embedded in the novel *El zorro de arriba y el zorro de abajo* (1971). The story takes place in a fish-meal factory in Chimbote, a large Dodge City of industrial sprawl on Peru's coast, where the cold Humboldt Current delivers up a wealth of marine life. Bird droppings (*guano*) collected from the enormous marine-bird rookeries on islands near the shore and fish meal (for fertilizer, feeds, and food production) are important trade commodities on Peru's coast. The two main characters in the tale are the capitalist fish-meal factory owner and a magical trickster-figure worker who has many scissors-dancer qualities. Claudette Kemper Columbus writes (1998:170) that the factory-owner fox thinks only of the extraction of resources, manufacturing, production, and sales. He is convinced that he lives in the real world, which is exclusively that of capitalistic commerce. The trickster-worker fox opposes this worldview with the metaphoric power of humor and art that suggest an attainable even though utopian alternative universe.

This sort of opposition between the commercial and traditional beliefs expressed in art appears in contemporary versions of some of the religious philosophies discussed in Part III of this volume. This is so not only in Arguedas' fiction but also in the field notes of contemporary ethnographers. Pishtaco marauds in the Lima new towns just as he did in Andean villages, only now his desires are more complex. He goes after children for use of their organs in transplants, promotes International Monetary Fund loans with exploitive repayment schedules, and takes the shape of foreign tourists, NGO workers, and businesspeople (Celestino 1998).

These new occupations for traditional forces of evil express Andeans' correct perceptions of modern forces as being dangerous to their identity and well-being. Two examples of detrimental developments that have resulted from globalization in general and the mass media in particular are oversimplification and increased violence. Art makers learn about worldwide trends and modes through telecommunications media. Some Peruvian artists and craftspeople use traditional Andean forms to exhibit Mexican imagery because Mexico and other areas of Latin America and the Caribbean are indistinguishable in the minds of many buyers in the United States. Perhaps more dangerous than this sort of oversimplification leading to the disappearance of regional variety is an upswing in risky behavior in some of the performance arts due to the influence of television programs featuring such behavior as desirable. This increases audience expectation for greater thresholds of dangerous activity. Increasing levels of risk mean correspondingly greater illness and mortality. An article in the *New York Times Magazine* documents a contemporary performance with the same features. A young singer in the United States, though he is physically ill, must perform in accordance with his audience's expectations. The writer describes the singer's act:

> For one thing, his performance is less about singing than about the ritual giving of himself to his audience; by exhausting himself emotionally and physically—jumping, sprinting, diving off the stage into the arms of the crowd—he makes himself into an offering . . . At the end of the set, he lies down across the monitors at the front of the stage and pants like a bellows, whereupon . . . he vomits. The crowd responds adoringly. (Dee 2003)

Developments in the graphic and plastic arts show parallel aping of what presents itself in the media. Scenes from the Mexican painter Frida Kahlo's work are featured in Peruvian retablos sold on the Internet. Art forms show enhanced edginess and flamboyance as representations feature more of what arouses shock, fear, and prurience in audiences.

The second millennium vies with the Baroque Age in Europe in the high value placed on the most overwrought, almost absurd of dramatic modes of presentation. Farcical performances like the one Dee describes above and some talk shows display stereotypic images of ethnic reality and human diversity flattened to bidimensional plane. On the other hand, there are notable attempts to stem this tide of personal and collective harm. Among them is the formation of alternative trade organizations (ATOs) and non-governmental organizations (NGOs) to promote the arts.

NGOs and ATOs as Alternatives—Their Good Points and Limitations

A strong and dangerous tendency inherent in globalization is the disappearance of cultural traditions not perceived as profitable or viable by powerful commercial networks. In opposition to this tendency are the thoughts and words of Octavio Paz and José María Arguedas. The Mexican writer Octavio Paz creates a metaphor taken from the evolutionary value of biological diversity: "With every culture that disappears from the face of the earth, so does another possibility for human survival" (in Azcuy 1986).

This does not mean, for either Paz or Arguedas, that the cultures of Mexico or Peru must remain static, for they have always been dynamic and have interacted one with another. In the case of Peru, the "local" and "global" are no more opposed than "Indian" and *misti* (elite, or person of European descent), since the concepts blend. What appears real and definitely detrimental in nature is the confrontation between ethnic and other groups engaged in cultural and economic usurpation (Cornejo-Polar et al. 1998). Melis further states that Peruvian ideas of "traditional" and "new" are in a continual process of reformulation and reconsideration (1998). An interesting example of this is artistic inversion. From a postcolonial, postmodernist perspective, Peruvians "countermediate" their art in order to assert what is uniquely theirs. The process of inversion continues today in the face of globalization's excesses (De Grandis 1998:62).

One of the most interesting organized examples of the movement toward giving small-scale art producers a greater share in profits are the NGOs (note 8) and ATOs (note 9) that foster the production, distribution, and sale of Andean arts. Most of these organizations offer alternative styles within each art genre. Some of these are made exclusively for Andeans, some for sale to art specialists and connoisseurs of past traditions, some for tourists, and some for faraway markets with sparse knowledge of Andean reality. The art makers show enormous flexibility in combining elements in different ways for different audiences, all the while retaining clear distinctions between sacred and profane arts as well as between fine art versus commercial art. Making work with subtle changes for different audiences of buyers is classic dual subjectivity in action. The artists show great ability in dealing with the global marketplace. The alternative trade organizations save them from economic exploitation and total destruction of their own highly valued past.

8. "NGO" usually refers to a nonprofit or volunteer association with idealistic or humanitarian purpose like the Red Cross that are not under the aegis of a nation-state.

9. "ATO" refers usually to a voluntary or nonprofit business firm whose purpose is to advance the interests of economically poor agricultural or craft producers. ATOs try to give producers a share in profits that otherwise go exclusively to middlemen in today's multilevel marketing process.

The idea of fair trade, with its principles of equality, transparency, and long-term commitment to the development of the global South, is inherently beneficial to the world. Alternative trade organizations not only help artisans in their art making but also help to provide literacy instruction, health care, and other basic benefits. Few of the young urban migrant New Pes of Lima can realistically go back to the mountains and work in agriculture. Craftwork provides them with income along with pride in the world where they lived their childhood. The relative influence of the ATOs and NGOs is not yet strong. The traditional designs and forms of Peruvian arts are now produced en masse and more cheaply by machine in China (Norma Velásquez, personal communications; note 10).

10. Norma Velásquez is the director of MINKA, a successful nonprofit organization dedicated to the promotion and sale of Andean arts and the well-being of Indigenous craftspeople (http://minkafairtrade.com).

Non-organized or self-employed and family artists in Peru have not a ghost of a chance in the face of such competition. The character Gabriel in Arguedas' work *El sexto* makes a valuable statement with respect to this aspect of globalization:

> We desire technical know-how, the development of science, the dominion of the universe, but at the service of human beings, not to cause them to mortally confront each other, not to make their bodies and souls so uniform that they are born and raised worse than dogs and vermin, because even the vermin and the dogs have their individual difference, their voice, their buzzing, their color, their distinct size. (In Sandoval and Boschetto-Sandoval 1998a:138)

Ideally the fair trade movement will win this battle to preserve variety in human expression and human beings themselves. In the meantime, artists keep finding ingenious methods for making even adversity work in their favor.

Global/Local Imagery, the Negotiation and Interface between Global Mass Culture and Local Traditions

A general perception is that global imagery (that is, images common in mass media today, for example) and the associated ideological and behavioral baggage usually replace the local by force and storm. Research presented here shows that though this is at times the case, actual processes of interaction can be more multidirectional in nature. This was so under the Inca and Spanish empires in Peru and may be so now as well. The causal factors for replacement of past styles with new genres are compelling, among them economic and technological tendencies, changing work and living patterns, and the inexorable attraction global imagery seems to inspire.

Economic factors include the reality that world centers of wealth and power produce and distribute imagery via television, film, the Internet, print media, and other communication modes. Many producers and distributors are gigantic multinational corporations, more powerful than a good number of nation-states. The lack of telecommunication and cybernetic infrastructure in economically poor countries often means that it must be imported. The usual pattern is that along with the foreign hardware comes associated software (in other words, equally foreign ways of thinking and behaving) as a complete package.

Changing work patterns throughout the world, instigated by global economic trends, have their primary effect on the young, perhaps the age set most inclined to sociocultural change. It is also the young who benefit most in terms of income, as the trends often give them nontraditionally sanctioned power and influence over their seniors. Among important processes here are massive rural-to-urban migration with its proletarianization of the workforce and the change in emphasis from the extended to the nuclear family. Transnationalism exerts an enormous force for sociocultural change in all aspects of life. In this case, people transport themselves into the centers of fabrication for what is called global culture. Tourism accomplishes the opposite with similar effect. As tourists, the wealthy move to economically poor areas. Both processes result in equally complex changes in imagery and related values.

Artists' Observations and Recommendations

Following in summary form are a few important points made by artists during recent stages of research for this book plus further reflections about Andean artists and their work in contemporary times. Themes include the legacy of the Shining Path particularly in Huamanga (Ayacucho), trends in marketing and consumption of Andean arts; market demand and artists' responses, teaching and learning of arts traditions, and the importance of religion.

The Legacy of the Shining Path

The Shining Path movement, along with the Peruvian government's reaction to it, produced a condition of civil war for almost twenty years from the 1970s through the 1990s, an entire generation. A number of independent militias arose as well, each having its own individual agenda not necessarily related to those of the two major adversaries. This situation made normal life impossible for Peruvians in the countryside and the cities. The warring armies conscripted young men by force, ate farm animals and crops, and used terrorist bombings and assassinations to enforce their will. Their activities made physical survival, especially in many rural sectors, tenuous. As a result, part-time artists who had once been full-time farmers as well moved to cities such as Huamanga and Lima. In their new urban locations the former farmers became full-time artisans. This created a glut of craft producers in urban areas who depended totally on art to make their living.

Since Huamanga was the official capital of Shining Path operations, people living in this city and the surrounding countryside suffered most. The Sendero period in Huamanga resulted in a high number of deaths in many artists' families. The psychological effect has had an impact on adults in the form of recurring memories of wartime atrocities. Teachers speak of an entire generation of youngsters in need of psychological therapy.

The retama's bright-yellow bloom became a symbol of resistance for the people of Huamanga during the violent years of the 1970s through 1990s. The Sendero Luminoso and government forces as well as assorted wildcat militias all inflicted horrors on ordinary citizens during this period of strife that spanned a generation. The flower is featured in a *huayno*, a traditional highland folk music and dance, written by the educator Ricardo Dolorier Urbano and titled "Flor de retama" (Retama Flower). It was first performed by the Trio Huanta ("Huanta" here meaning from Huamanga, the city itself, and referring to the local Huanta Indigenous group of pre-Inca times). Dolorier wrote the song in 1969 in response to a violent incident that resulted in a number of deaths. The song was again sung by the people of Huamanga in the 1980s and 1990s in response to the terrible events of that period. An excerpt of the lyrics (translated by the author) follows:

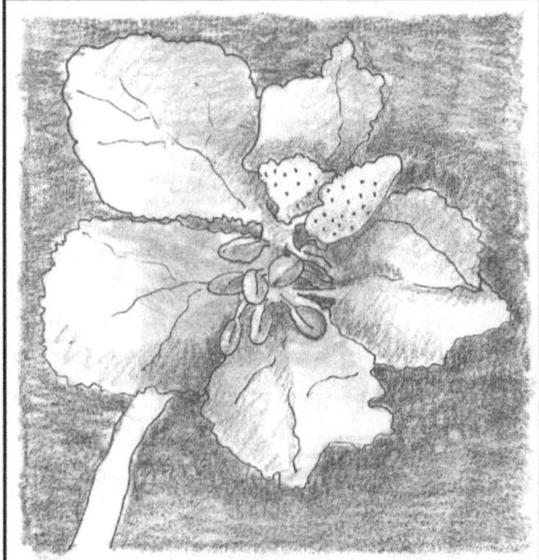

4.1 Retama flower. Drawing by the author.

Everyone come and see, let us see
In the small plaza of Huanta the yellow retama flower
Yellow, little yellow retama
Yellow, yellowing retama flower
Where the blood of the people flows

. . . they are going to kill the students, heartfelt Huantinos

. . . they are going to kill the farmers, heartfelt Huantinos

the plaza smells like jasmine, violets, geraniums

And dust and dynamite

Listeners can hear in this song the Andeans' way of likening those they esteem to flowers and their use of flower themes to hide darker messages. Artists in Huamanga continue to feel the effects of the Sendero period at the beginning of the twenty-first century.

Living conditions for artists in recent history are precarious, to say the least. The vast immigration of art workers into the small provincial city that is Huamanga has made these conditions even more difficult. Artists live where no one else wants to, such as steep inclines, the edges of cliffs, and areas of the city without amenities like water and electricity. They have little access to health care, schools, and nutritious food. In this way, they are worse off than in the countryside since there they were at least able to grow their own food and had access to water sources. Despite all of these difficulties, contemporary artists continue to produce work of extremely high quality using very simple tools.

History and Contemporary Trends

Traditional and nontraditional marketing and consumption of Andean arts naturally changes with time and conditions. Outsiders have in the past and may in the future influence the shape that Andean arts traditions eventually take. University-educated and specially trained professionals establish canons for the objects artists produce and organize them into production groups. Foreign buyers and lenders often underwrite arts production to a greater degree than do locals by means of direct purchase, investment, and technological assistance. Many of these outsiders wish to apply a model for development that may or may not be applicable to the Andean context.

Role of the Professional or Educated Middle Person in the Co-Creative Process

Professionals in anthropology, the arts, and folk traditions have had a major role in creating the forms, colors, and styles of the Andean arts in all media. Historical figures like José Sabogal, José María Arguedas, and Alicia Bustamante determined which traditional forms would survive and how they should look. They did this by promoting particular artists to a broad public, writing scholarly studies and popular articles, sponsoring exhibits, creating collections, and so forth. Some professionals not only have promoted existing folk arts to nontraditional audiences but have actually created new and successful genres. The folklorist and collector Alicia Bustamante working with the artist Joaquín López Antay changed the designation "San Marcos box" to *retablo* (home altar) and decided how its "classic" form should look (chapter 6). This was put in writing and thus became a kind of gold standard against which retablo quality was thereafter measured.

In recent years the anthropologist Pablo Macera and others working with board painters helped change the traditional *tabla* (painted board) of Sarhua into something resembling an illustration or easel painting while encouraging *costumbrista* (rural traditions) imagery (chapter 9; Strong 2003a). Under the auspices of a foreign aid organization, local tin artists were encouraged to produce decorative rather than utilitarian tin ware and paint tin pieces in colors resembling those used in retablos. All of these professionals had and have artists' best interests at heart and have indeed helped many producers in this way. The role of outsiders in creating Haitian folk paintings, Eskimo soapstone carvings and prints, and similar processes abound throughout the world. The question of whether outsider intervention sullies "pure" folk traditions appears moot for professionals like these (Graburn 1976, 1999).

Organizing Artists into Groups

Today's market forces require artists to produce their pieces in larger numbers than was traditional in small family workshops. In response to this requirement, some artists in Huamanga have organized into workshops of fifty or more families. This allows them to meet large orders for standardized items coming from urban stores and overseas marketers. For example, an arts organization received a large overseas order for Huamanga alabaster wine goblets while the writer was present. The stoneworkers' wing of the organization immediately set to work producing the cups. While such experiences motivate artists to organize, they must overcome a strong tendency to be jealous and secretive about their individual creative work. They must also guard against the tendency to make careless and shoddy work in order to meet large-scale market requirements. As of 2006 a group of weavers has found a way to coalesce to meet mass orders for standardized pieces and return to their individual and family mode of producing specialized traditional and creative work for smaller and more focused markets. Thus the group adapts well to what Castells identifies as a constantly fluctuating network, which the members have acutely observed in the course of daily interactions with their diverse buying public.

Foreign Markets

Foreigners, be they tourists, commercial buyers, or art collectors, seem to have a greater appreciation for Andean arts than do Peruvians, according to many Huamanga artists. This perception may arise when a foreign order produces a large influx of cash while domestic sales provide smaller amounts of income though in a more constant flow. Since Peruvian commercial buyers sell in part to foreign markets, further study of this phenomenon could be pursued from a financial perspective. Foreigners certainly do not have the tradition of discrimination against Indigenous people and their culture that still exists in Peru, and so they tend to welcome Andean artists and their art with open arms on foreign soil.

Art Developers' Philosophy

Some leaders and experts working in art development say that the road to success in benefiting artists lies in a classic capitalist business model. According to these ideas, artists should standardize production, work toward large-volume capacity to serve market demands, expand markets, and reduce prices. However, highly mechanized factories elsewhere do all these activities much more efficiently than organizations of Huamanga workers. Some foreign factories even produce items such as "Andean" sweaters using traditional motifs and artificial fibers. These factories have, in addition, very broad market access. An alternate path perhaps more appropriate for Andean artists may be to produce for a more select group of national and international buyers. However, these buyers must be trained to appreciate Andean arts and able to pay premium prices for them.

Exploitation among Artists

Within the group of artists themselves (often in tandem with middlemen at various levels), systems of exploitation severely inhibit the youngest, most geographically marginal, and economically poorest artists. The global marketplace has helped to create a kind of feudal system among artisans. Acknowledged "masters" of given craft forms as well as well-connected entrepreneurs receive work made by younger artists. These privileged "lords" sign their "vassals'" work, pass it off as their own, and make considerable profits from doing so. More remote communities of artists, such as in Cochas, a rural satellite of Huamanga that encompasses Cochas Chico and Cochas Grande, are compelled to join this system by supplying more urban "network-connected" artists. Some of these remotely located art producers make work of much higher quality than the "masters" who sign it. Freire saw this tendency during his research and explained that among exploited people an initial tendency is to erroneously think that they must in turn exploit others to gain self-respect and dignity (2001:45–46).

Artists with Several Lines of Production

Artists consciously produce several types of objects to meet the needs of different groups of clients. However, mass production of items with Andean motifs elsewhere in the world often trumps these efforts. Artists have a great deal of flexibility in conceiving and producing their work. They make clear distinctions between religious art, made for their own sacred purposes, and profane or worldly lines of production that they make for sale. In Huamanga, for example, all the artists who participated in this study produced several commercial lines. First are "fine arts" pieces. These are skillfully made, usually large in size, either traditional or creative and innovative. These pieces are sold to collectors, primarily people well versed in Andean traditions, who can pay premium prices. Second, political works referring to the Sendero period in Huamanga will go, as well, to a more discerning though less knowledgeable audience at prices lower than fine arts pieces. Third, happy "costumbrista" pieces showing traditional rural activities, nativity scenes with Andean details, and the like go to tourist buyers. Finally, quickly made series of products usually in small sizes are produced for tourists seeking very inexpensive souvenirs. All of these commercial lines are distinct from the religious works that artists create for their own communities, and many artists would much prefer to produce community pieces only were that economically possible.

Artists' various lines of production express the dual subjectivity they experience mentally. Many of the pieces themselves have details that communicate inversion and disjunction. Artists are quite aware in a conscious way of the difference and separation between works with religious meaning and purely secular pieces.

Andean Forms Copied Elsewhere

It is a reality that "Andean" art forms are produced very inexpensively and in great quantity in world manufacturing centers where labor is cheap, production is highly mechanized, and distribution takes place on a large scale. Not only is art being reproduced but legal rights to Andean traditional images have been copyrighted in wealthy countries. One example is the Tumi (Sicán "decapitator" divinity), which is now officially registered with a patent in France.

Contemporary Market Demand and Artists' Responses

The section above includes trends discussed from the perspective of the market. This section emphasizes the artists' point of view as creators, that is, how they respond to contemporary developments in innovative ways.

Machines Needed

The process of art making, especially for larger-scale market demand, can be speeded up considerably by providing artists' organizations with a few simple tools and implements. Loans for micro-enterprises available from humanitarian aid–oriented banking institutions like the Grameen Bank, which innovated the idea of the micro-enterprise loan in South Asia, would go far in aiding artists along these lines. For example, tinware makers would benefit greatly from a few hand-operated stamping machines.

Decorative Emphasis

Andean arts traditions have often included a large repertoire of utilitarian products with decorative features. Mass-produced utilitarian objects in synthetic materials like plastics have recently supplanted the utilitarian objects artists once made using natural materials. Art producers now place much more emphasis on purely decorative ware and the decorative aspects of items that once had practical uses. They also make use of some synthetic materials such as sealants for items made of wood and other substances that preclude the utilitarian function of their art pieces.

In the twenty-first century, artists notice that Indigenous versions of such standard vignettes as nativity scenes sell very well. Thus, the baby Jesus wears a *chullo* (Andean man's knitted hat with ear flaps), and Bethlehem shepherds care for alpacas rather than sheep. This was, of course, not always the case. During Spanish colonial times, artists needed to reproduce Renaissance versions of nativity scenes with European details. What is going on today might be described as a kind of disjunction or reverse disjunction, since the Christian concept of the nativity is not part of the pre-Columbian religious tradition. This is an example, too, of artists' subtle countermediation.

Fusion of Genera

Artists increasingly borrow from art forms other than their specialties. This creates a process of blending genre and media lines. One ceramic artist attaches Huamanga stone flowers to his bulls of Pucará as well as to his horse and llama versions. Mate artists put small plaster and wood retablos inside their decorated gourds. Retablo makers put Huamanga stone figures inside wooden retablo boxes, as was also done at times in the past. Textile artists put ceramic motifs in weavings, and ceramic makers put weaving designs on ceramics. Tinware makers attach typical flower shapes found on retablos to their pieces and paint their metal works with retablo designs. Such fusion allows for a kind of innovation based on cross-fertilization. In many inexpensive souvenir pieces, the number of crossovers in form is so great that it has made distinctions between different art traditions disappear as distinguishable types. A long historical and prehistorical view reveals that these types of media and imagery blendings have long been characteristic of the Andean region along with intercultural borrowings and combinations of materials and motifs.

Individual Innovation

While some artists use materials and images from other arts to innovate, others create new ideas based on unusual personal experiences. This has probably always been part of the process of invention. Often, however, they subject creative aspects of their work to the discipline of a recognizable tradition. Natividad (chapter 6) lived much of her life in jungle areas. She innovates by placing jungle imagery rather than the standard high-mountain motifs in her retablos. However, she remains true to the retablo form and tradition and does not introduce materials other than the wood, paints, and sculpting mixtures standard in the genre.

Shoddy Production

Artists lament tourists' inability to appreciate finely made work that has led many art producers to fall into lazy habits of shoddy production. The tourist market seems to favor producers who can turn out large amounts of sloppily made pieces to meet the needs of such indiscriminate clients. Some do this to make extra income quickly, but they seem to feel guilty about it. Many express shame for having compromised their own standards of excellence.

Evolution and Extinction of Some Forms

Artists have commented that the different kinds of arts produced in Huamanga during their lifetimes had decreased considerably in number. Carved gourds have become extinct among Huamanga art makers but are now very much alive in Huancayo, Cochas, and Junín. Tinware is very apt to follow carved gourds as an extinct production line, although painted tin pieces are now so popular that the market for them may actually increase. Alabaster carvers as well may have to look for buyer-pleasing innovations in order to preserve their art.

Spontaneous Regeneration of Art Forms

Art fairs, art contests, and museum exhibits can have a powerful effect on particular craft traditions. Many artists will copy prize-winning artists' styles. The famous Mendivil family of statue makers, for example, won awards for innovation in making long-necked human figures. As a result, many artists have taken on this long-necked style. National and international contest winners can even resuscitate historical styles. The horse and llama versions of the bull of Pucará (chapter 8) are making a comeback because of a national award winner who reproduced these styles. The Indian baby Jesus or Manuelito statue, a Spanish colonial form plus Indigenous clothing details, has reappeared in a similar manner. Many contests and museums also have a way of appropriating artists' best work without compensating them, another in a long line of injustices that artists are expected to tolerate.

Schools, Apprenticeships, and the Teaching and Learning of Art Traditions

The passing on of Andean arts traditions from older master artists to young learners of the trades traditionally took place within families. Parents passed their knowledge and skill on to their children. In the twenty-first century the teaching and learning of Andean arts has become more vital and more complex. Many members of the younger generations train in fields in which potential future income is greater than in the arts. Formal school systems impinge on traditional arts instruction in problematic ways.

One young son of a master Andean artist was being supported by a sponsor to study at the Huamanga School of Fine Arts. He felt that his training at the school was in many ways a repetition of what he had learned from his father but that formal training was nonetheless somewhat beneficial to him. On the other hand, a daughter of another master artist studied at the same school and came to a different conclusion. She found that the teachers at the formal school actually taught very little and that they discriminated against Indigenous traditions.

The two young students handled the Western idea of creativity in very different ways. They both learned certain production formulas from their parents, as is the case in many "folk" traditions. The teachers at the school no doubt refrained from formulaic teaching so their students would be "creative." The creative pieces produced by advanced students have a certain similarity, as is probably the case in any epoch dominated by particular styles. Many of these pieces produced by students who jettison Andean and family art traditions in favor of those taught in schools have a kind of bland and conformist semi-abstract modernism about them.

Several of the senior masters, or *amautas* ("wise teachers" in Quechua), in different arts and living in various places (Lima, Lurín, Huamanga) have expressed a deep desire to start schools of their own. They fear that teaching only their children will not be enough to preserve their arts. They would like to reach a wider set of young people. The amautas do not have the financial wherewithal to procure workshops and tools such that the teaching they desire to do could take place. They cannot depend on the Peruvian Ministry of Education for these facilities because it will not award teaching certificates to those without degrees from "normal schools" of education or pedagogy that award national teaching licenses to graduates. The amautas do not have the necessary secondary-level formal schooling in general studies to enter normal schools, and their ages (usually fifty or more years) would also be a handicap. Here is another area in which some flexibility in certification and small loans for space and tools could go a very long way. In conjunction with Andean arts schools, the amautas have expressed a desire to have access to illustrated books for consultation.

Master artists must overcome their preference to work alone or only with their families and apprentices. They must suppress, at least to a degree, their reluctance to share creative ideas. These barriers stand in the way of their economic success in today's marketplace and the establishment of schools for teaching broader populations of young people. The marketing compromise that the group of textile artists made, producing in groups for big orders and alone for individual small orders, is a step in a positive direction.

Generations of Artists

There are notable distinctions among different age sets of artists. Unlike artists of López Antay's generation, who were not self-conscious about such a thing as an Andean arts tradition, the senior masters of today seem much concerned with realism and what they feel is true and genuine, including proper bodily proportions for ceramic figures and genuine Huari or Paracas designs for textiles. These amautas prize classic Andean production techniques and materials. Many use all-natural dyes, wood-fired kilns, and only camellid fibers.

Although most artists in their thirties and forties have no formal fine arts training, many produce their own creative versions of traditional genres. They experiment with alternative colors, sexy female images, shocking or comical scenes, and other innovations. They try to produce more works than their elders in response to perceived market demand and are not averse to shortcuts such as the use of molds for stock figures.

Those artists in their twenties who study fine arts produce "modern" abstract versions of Andean arts. Many copy world-famous artists with a gimmick, like Botero. A good number of these artists, whether trained traditionally or in school, complain about producing for the older artists in a way that cuts them out of most of the profit and allows someone else to claim authorship of their work.

Some even younger artists as early as their teens become very skilled in traditional craft production and study fine arts formally. Others lose themselves in modern vices or switch to new careers that they expect will better pay their future living expenses. The survival of Andean arts probably depends on this generation.

The Evolution of Andean Art Production as an Occupation

The older amautas testify that in their childhood, most artists worked at their crafts part-time. The disturbances of the Sendero period and other factors pushed many of these individuals into cities where they dedicated themselves to earning a full-time living from art. The newer generations, ages thirty and under, include many art makers who earn their main incomes from urban occupations for which they have received some formal training or have served apprenticeships, for example, as cooks, construction workers, or office workers. They reserve craft production for weekends. Huamanga has been home to many full-time artists since the 1940s, and the Sendero period increased their numbers in Huamanga and Lima as well. The new tendency among younger artists, fueled by much competition and economic necessity, will likely make craftwork once more a part-time occupation. The difference between this new development and the past is that the typical full-time job in Peru is now urban rather than rural. This may mean that artists will continue to make nostalgic imagery about rural Andean life but will have less actual contact with the sources of their creative inspiration.

Study of Archeology and History

Artists find the study of history and prehistory useful to their work. "Study" often means looking at images and examining artworks from the Andean past, particularly for older artists because they may have minimal literacy skills. The amautas who want to start schools in the Andean arts as well as younger up-and-coming stars have mentioned a desire to see illustrated books or other visual media about Andean cultural traditions. Artists are greatly inspired by seeing images of their ancestors' work and hearing about archeological and historical studies. On many occasions the writer has seen artists poring over tattered volumes and integrating what they see into their art. However, public institutions like museums and libraries seem to make little effort to provide artists with such assets as reading rooms, bookmobiles, computer use, or Internet access. Lack of funds and electricity and the difficult terrain where many artists live are true barriers to the spread of much-desired knowledge. Here again, small loans might go far to help artists help themselves in this regard. One aid organization working with Huamanga artists plans to provide arts workers with access to computerized Andean arts imagery in a location near their homes but unlike their homes in that it has electricity and a phone connection allowing for Internet access. Professionals like art historians and anthropologists who have the privilege of studying in exotic locales often forget to share their knowledge with the very people who have the most right to it: the local populations.

As Huamanga weavers prepare to make carpets or tapestries, they make multiple drawings of the imagery they wish to use. Each weaver has a small collection of copies and tracings based on book and magazine illustrations. To have access to a book on Wari textiles with photographs would be for them "like paradise on earth," one textile worker said. A ten-year-old ceramics decorator, as another example, deftly painted free-hand images just as he saw them in a worn paperback travelogue about Peru. He mixed Nazca, Inca, and Paracas motifs in blissful ignorance, believing they are all of a piece. He "re-created" his past in this way (Strong 1998), and he probably continues to do so with pride into adulthood. This kind of ersatz idea of a noble Andean past is a good working roots-discovery process and a source of cultural pride. Older artists, however, know what the young people are missing and say that youth deserve access to the specific and detailed knowledge they seek.

Importance of Religion

As will be discussed in later chapters about several types of Andean arts, most genres have historical origins of a religious nature. Artists still produce for this sacred or spiritual use market, but these pieces do not constitute a large proportion of sales. In fact, artists steeply discount truly sacred work or receive in-kind payment in the form of food or labor assistance for this category of artwork that they make for their peers.

The cognoscenti of fine arts buyers, collectors, scholars, and museums look for spiritually significant art, but again this is a small market. Some demand for quasireligious themes like the recent U.S. penchant for angels, based on dramatic works about victims of AIDS, war, and other tragedies, has encouraged the production of pieces with this motif. Artists produce angels with details of Andean dress, animals, plants, and other local contextual referents. Though the fad for angels in the United States has diminished, artists continue to produce works on this theme. Fad-based demand is usually short-lived, and it would be helpful for artists to have access to knowledge about longer-lasting market-driven modes and styles.

Christmas, with its seasonal gift-giving and typical imagery such as nativity scenes, constitutes another major outlet for religious art making. The Christmas demand in Peru and overseas is constant and provides work and income to artists in a predictable way. Bethlehem scenes, Jesus in the manger, shepherds and their sheep, and other Christmas-related themes appear in all Andean arts. More secular visuals like Santa Claus, Christmas trees, and the like exist but are not produced in large quantities.

The religious belief systems of Andeans are syncretic with multiple cultural origins. Retablos may show Christian saints in a Holy Week procession, owls as harbingers of death, condors and other huamani floating in the sky, and evangelical preachers expounding on the evils of dancing and drinking all at the same time. Huamanga artists profess a number of faiths—Roman Catholic, evangelical Christian, and Mormon, to name a few. Yet these belief systems do not stop them from depicting Mamacha Asunta on the top of a mountain with fiery openings in its sides out of which fly ancient and terrible beings from the World of Below. Thus, contemporary religious belief and practice blend with what came before.

In addition to and apart from their religious work, artists have secular lines of production that they view as inferior to their religious pieces. These are filled with imagery from television, films, and current global events. Better-known and more organized individuals and groups of artists receive orders to produce large quantities of creations in modish designs. Receiving and meeting regular large-scale orders, religious and secular, is an ideal situation for artists. In this way, they can afford to spend more time making art than in other economic pursuits. They also can have the freedom to produce what many of them say is closest to their hearts: sacred pieces for their families and friends.

Andean arts reflect a complex cultural tradition and a series of socio-political events unique to the region and shared with the rest of the world. The artworks express ideas about beauty, philosophy, religion, the environment, traditional practices, and many other concepts to cultural insiders and outsiders. Artists appreciate their work in terms of esthetic excellence, as a means to reinforce ethnic identity and pride, and last but hardly least, as a way of making a living. The following chapters will present these points in detail. Art makers often must adjust to opposing sets of requirements such as the conflicts between esthetic canons or religious beliefs and patrons' or buyers' preferences. To do this they make use of creative ploys and tactics to survive in the material sense and yet simultaneously retain their values by sending different visual messages to multiple audiences. Artists need to survive practically and economically, but they should not have to do this at the expense of their identity, spiritual values, and independence. Small assistance including loans, opportunities to set up Andean art schools, and accessible sources of traditional visual information would help these productive and creative people beyond measure.

Part III

Andean Arts Today

Part I and Part II of this volume provide prehistorical and historical background for Part III, about contemporary Andean arts with an emphasis on artists now living in or originally from the Huamanga region in the department of Ayacucho of the Central Andes of Peru. The ethnohistorical perspective taken by this study is typically expressed in the arts, since they communicate some ideas that are new (variations) but most often against a constantly replaying background of what came before (themes). Part III has seven chapters, each featuring a type of art or medium and emphasizing the religious meaning in a few of the nature motifs represented within the art type under discussion. The city of Huamanga and its larger political and geographic context within the department of Ayacucho constitute the central emphasis, though also included are parts of the nearby departments of Huancavelica, Apurimac, and Junín. In addition, Huamanga natives who are temporary or permanent migrants to Cuzco, Lima, and the Lima satellite town of Lurín exchange art influences with relatives in their home region. The mental and social landscape of the contemporary Central Andes is now even larger because it includes television as well as cell phone and Internet communications and visits with relatives and friends who are living and working overseas.

In some cases Huamanga artists borrow but also make their own versions of styles from regions and times on the edges of and distant from their immediate context. The tendency of Andeans to borrow, agglomerate, and tweak forms and styles from elsewhere and to add these to their own art genera continues as an ongoing process in media-saturated contemporary times. Parallels among religious belief systems and classic artists' visual ploys aid in the process of countermediation required to produce such work.

At the time of this writing there are many Web sites on the Internet made by Andean artists and community members about the art forms in these chapters. Inexpensive digital cameras and other new and easily acquired technologies and skills make this possible. Most sites are oriented toward the artists' own in-groups, that is, people who already understand the meanings of these art forms, at least in an intuitive way. It is important that those with academic training and access to documentary and visual resources of the past collaborate with these Web pioneers to communicate the full cultural richness of Andean visual traditions to the people themselves, for whom such knowledge would mean so much.

CHAPTER 5

The Scissors Dance (La Danza de las Tijeras)

The scissors dance (*danza de las tijeras*) is one of a number of ritual dance theaters performed in the Andes today in honor of local communities' patron saints. Traditionally, elaborately costumed group dancing was the highest form of prayer to the divinities in Andean tradition. This custom combined with European carnival and auto da fé elements during colonial times. It may have arisen directly from the Taki Onqoy ("dance sickness" in Quechua), a millenarian movement that came about as a reaction against colonial religious repression of Indigenous belief and practice. Always a test of strength, a kind of physical trial or sacrifice to divine powers, this dance today requires performers at times to literally risk their lives to meet modern urban community expectations for a good performance.

The scissors dancers in their large hats and intricately decorated, gleaming, flounced costumes leap and spin to the sound of violin and harp and the constant clanging rhythm of a large pair of shears held in one hand. The origin of using scissors as rhythm instruments is obscure. Some say they were originally wool-shearing tools used by herders; others assert that they derive from the rhythm sticks traditionally used by Europeans in celebrations or the ringing bells, disks, or clacking castanets played by a number of Mediterranean peoples. Scissors rituals feature competitive performances given by two or more three-person teams, each consisting of a dancer, a violinist, and a harpist.

The dramatic dance ritual is one of the most spectacular that survives in contemporary Peru. On its surface it appears to be a phenomenon that owes most of its present-day components, such as musical instruments, costume, and occasions when it is practiced, to its Spanish European heritage. However, the danza's religious meaning reflects precolonial roots very strongly, as does the style of its accompanying music. Beginning in colonial times, the ritual traditionally took place as part of religious activities during Holy Week, particularly on Good Friday, and during patron saint celebrations. Today, in the urban and international contexts of its performance, the practice appears in temporally and spatially truncated form. Modern performance venues often have less to do with sacred space and time than with secular occasions. A disturbing aspect of contemporary danza de las tijeras performance is the increasing tendency for dancers to take dangerous physical risks. Audience exposure to mass media is one among several causes for raising the threshold of expectation for a thrilling enactment of the ritual.

Underlying Beliefs from the Deep Past

The scissors dance resulted from a combination of Indigenous and European colonial traditions. The form continues to evolve in contemporary times.

Indigenous Period

Certain aspects of Andean religious belief are particularly important in understanding the scissors dance. These include ideas about the structure of the cosmos, water, the huamanis, Supay, pachacuti, dance as a form of prayer, and the necessity to endure trials as a form of sacrifice. The Andean cosmos, with its three vertical levels, forms an important part of the ideological underpinnings for this dance. The divinities in the World of Above receive propitiation by means of music, dance, and physical trial. Costumed dance to music was one of the highest forms of prayer during Indigenous times. However, the performance takes place in the World of Here, where human beings live, and the spiritual power employed by musicians and dancers derives from the World of Inside. The actual steps and choreography of the scissors dance address each cosmic level in turn. High leaping reflects the Above level; toe dancing and stamping represent the middle Here level, with their references to agriculture; prone and sitting postures and movements mark the frontier area between the Worlds of Here and Below; and the entire trial stage of the ritual indicates spiritual power derived from the World of Below.

Perhaps the most valuable and sacred element in nature for Andeans is water. Mother Earth, Pachamama, has a circulation system made of water in the form of rivers above and below ground, lakes, waterfalls, rain, and the ocean. Water is the source of all life. The well-watered Mother Earth produces good crops and in turn healthy animals and people. Although early European viewers of the scissors dance believed it was enacted for gold, its basic purpose is to ensure a good water supply, according to scissors dancers who were interviewed for this study. On a practical level, the three Peruvian departments of the Chanca region (Ayacucho, Huancavelica, and Apurimac) are among the driest in Peru in yearly rainfall. No doubt that is one reason the scissors dance arose in this particular area and why the region even today has a high index of economic poverty and rural-to-urban migration.

The huamanis are Inca spiritual powers. These often take the form of birds, especially raptors such as condors, eagles, hawks, and falcons, and they reside in sacred places such as mountains. Scissors dancers try to call them forth as allies. The huamanis' appearance is at the same time welcome and fearsome because what they might do is unpredictable. Spiritual powers reside in other animals as well, such as pumas, foxes, and llamas. Scissors dancers for this reason often take these and other animal designations as their stage names. Supay is a powerful spiritual force who lives in the World of Inside. The name Supay derives in the Quechua language from the root *upay*, meaning "shadow" or "soul." The term means a kind of spiritual force or power that in Andean theology has neither negative nor positive valuation. It is Supay who is courted by the scissors dancers for aid in performing their spiritual cleansing function.

A pachacuti, in Quechua, is a world turned upside down. The universe inverted periodically in the Inca concept of time. To make the world right itself, renewed dedication to prayer and ritual needed to arise. At these times, strict religious observance became extremely important. For the Andeans, costumed dance with accompanying music was a vital form of prayer. The elaborately dressed dance troupes who perform in Cuzco at the time of the winter solstice (Inti Raymi) and mass displays such as the celebrations of La Candelaria in Puno are contemporary testament to the continued importance of dance as prayer. Performers take great pains to perform their intricate choreography perfectly, to maintain an attitude of happiness and joy, and to wear elaborate matching costumes. Guamán's chronicles of 1603 mention other kinds of dances, also religious, that feature small groups or individuals who compete with one another. The scissors ritual derives more closely from this latter competitive form. Celestino points out (1997, 1998) a number of worshipful dance prayers known as taki. The performance of taki involved inter-allyu regional or neighborhood competitions among teams of dancers, musicians, and singers.

The Inca religion and its predecessors gave great importance to the idea of sacrifice. Some Andean civilizations practiced human sacrifice. Though the jury is still out on whether and to what degree the Incas practiced human sacrifice, they certainly did (and do) practice animal sacrifice. There is, however, an idea of human trial and suffering in honor of divinities that is important. The water in the circulatory system of Pachamama is symbolically coterminous with the blood coursing through human veins. To assure a water supply, a good food-growing season, lack of natural calamity, and other basic human needs, blood letting and other forms of suffering are required. The logic behind this thinking is that if blood is set free from an animal or human body, there will be a corresponding increase of water in Mother Earth. More water means environmental and human health and well-being (note 1). Religious practitioners take enormous risks, engage in mutual whipping bouts, face dangerous animals unarmed, and perform other feats as prayer. Although not technically human sacrifice, pilgrims will climb to the snow line of local sacred mountains without proper shoes or warm clothing, as described previously. If a mountain takes such a climber into an ice crevasse to their death, then so be it. The loss of life was required to keep the universe in good order.

1. The idea that what is done to an animal or human being will have a parallel effect in another dimension has been called "sympathetic magic." Religious traditions whose practitioners consider themselves far removed from magical thinking have elements of this kind in contemporary ritual. Christening and baptism in Christianity are rituals in which water poured on a child's head parallels the washing away of spiritual sin. The cathartic effect of ritual requires these material stand-ins for what is going on in a larger, supernatural context. Only the most cerebral sects of world religions deemphasize acts of this kind.

Contemporary oral tradition from storytellers including Jesús Caso Arias and Juan Igas de la Cruz carries ancestors' descriptions of priest-soldiers called *layguas* or *qapac layguas* who could place themselves between good and evil and relay messages from huamanis. Although they were mortals, layguas appeared to fly from place to place, as ordered by the apus, to heal the sick by dancing. Arguedas describes one of these religious specialists in the novel *Yawar Fiesta* (1985). He is called a *layk'a* in the local postcolonial dialect of the Lucanas region of the department of Ayacucho, and it is he who magically goes out and finds the fearsome bull named Misitu by calling to him. The layk'a dies on Misitu's horns as payment to the huamanis and apus in return for the bull's capture. Arguedas' layk'a is similar to though distinct from the scissors dancer in the novel, Tankayllu. These descriptions show the magical qualities of the tijera dancers and their possible antecedents (layguas or layk'as) as well as their powerful spiritual position as intermediaries.

Colonial Period

One of the primary activities taking place during colonial times was the process of religious conversion. This often was understood to mean the stamping out (*extirpación*, "extirpation," removal as by surgical means) of Indigenous sacred belief and practice. Christian missionaries most often took an educated approach to their task, attempting to maximize emphasis in areas where Christian and Inca beliefs were similar. The existing Spanish medieval and Baroque affection for lavish public displays in religious ritual mirrored the Andean love of prayer in the form of mass dances. The tripartite cosmos, each level inhabited by different spiritual and natural beings, was also shared. The problem of transposing a polytheist tradition to monotheism was resolved by attributing the characters of Inca minor gods and powers to Christian saints, angels, and devils.

The scissors ritual, in a similar fashion, drew on sets of beliefs and practices brought to the Andes by Europeans that blended with extant traditions. Patron saint celebrations are one example. This performance form grew out of an amalgam of competitive taki dances and Spanish outdoor rituals enacted in honor of patron saints. Missionaries introduced the violin and harp, and these replaced the Indigenous flutes and drums. Costumes resembling late-medieval to early Renaissance carnival wear superseded Inca togas. The Inca idea of dance as prayer unified with the theatrical auto da fé at times during the several days of rituals when scissors dancers joined other troupes to perform dance theaters in the streets. These enactments conveyed religious, moral, and social messages.

Some experts contend that there is a more specific point of origin. Lucy Núñez Rebaza (n.d.) and other scholars say the scissors dance of today grew from the colonial millenarian movement Taki Onqoy. Andeans interpreted the pachacuti marked by the Spanish invasion as evidence that the gods were not pleased with their level of religious fervor. Specifically, the local Chanca people, whose descendants now live in Ayacucho, Huancavelica, and Apurimac, were never completely conquered by the Incas during their empire period. The rebellious nature of the Chancas probably helped to produce the scissors dance under their European overlords. The purpose of the Taki Onqoy was to reinvert the world so that it would go back to the way it was under the Indigenous rule.

Felipe Juan Guamán Poma de Ayala worked as a minor colonial employee during the time of the Taki Onqoy. Part of his job was to help colonial officials stamp out the practice, which had gained a large and potentially rebellious following among Indigenous people. Like the Plains Indians' Ghost Dance in nineteenth-century North America, Taki Onqoy rituals required physical trials, feats of strength, and dance marathons that lasted for days at a time. Many dancers did sicken and die as a result. Even today, Núñez Rebaza and other experts say that the most important calendar date for the scissors dance is Good Friday because on this day Jesus died, leaving the world open to inversion and huaca (sacred place and the spiritual power residing there), taking the reins of control from European Christians. (*Huacos*, it should be noted, are objects found in such sacred places, and they embody some of the huaca's power.)

The mythical idea of Inkarri inspired Taki Onqoy. The Inkarri myth arose at the time of the last Inca emperor's execution and fuels the fires of millenarian fervor even today. According to this tradition, although the last Inca emperor, Tupac Amaru, was beheaded and his body was drawn and quartered, he will one day return to life. The head, buried underground, is like a seed that is very slowly growing a new body. This idea relates very much to the Inca afterlife theology and its possibility of reincarnation for spiritually deserving deceased ancestors. Traditionally, the Andean dead were put in a squatting position, wrapped like plant bulbs, and buried in the World of Inside to one day sprout forth in the World of Here with renewed life. The same idea of "sprouting" recurs in Inkarri narratives and relates to the ancient belief in reincarnation. Through his second coming,

Inkarri will one day reinstitute the Inca empire according to believers in this tradition (note 2; Kato 2001).

2. Takahiro Kato (2001) describes a present-day religious cult surrounding a statue made from a child's skeleton. Little by little worshippers add pieces to the statue, making it bigger and more lifelike. Cult members recount dreams based on some tradition of common consciousness that the statue is really a manifestation of the boy Jesus, who reputedly made an original historical appearance in the local area Kato studied. The statue also has many Inkarri-like characteristics.

In Peru as well as other areas of Latin America today, Catholic worshippers have the custom of bringing dolls or statues representing the child Jesus to church at particular times during the ritual year involving the life of Jesus. During this period (December 25 until Easter Sunday), Jesus grows from infancy to adulthood. Accordingly, families bring baby dolls or real newborns to church at Christmas, then toddler dolls or real toddlers at a later date, and so on as the child spiritually grows for special blessings. Cummins (2004:12–14) discusses the clothing of Christ child statues in Inca garments during Spanish colonial times in Peru. It appears that the tradition has a good deal of historical depth and thus is not limited to contemporary *manuelitos* (baby Jesus figures) produced today by artists in Peru. For these reasons, what Kato may in fact be observing is both a manifestation of Inkarri as well as Christian belief and ritual in syncretic combination.

Other beliefs within Christianity closely resembled Andean tradition, like the idea of trial and sacrifice. The European Christian tradition also has within it a high valuation for sacrificial acts as forms of worship. Religious orders, clergy, and faithful fast and abstain from certain foods on special holy days. Monks, nuns, and holy persons of the past took this to the extreme, subsisting on minimal food and drink, sleep, and rest so that they could pray. Some religious rituals in the Christian world involve flagellation, lengthy travel in bare feet and on knees during pilgrimages, and the wearing of sack cloth or other uncomfortable clothes. Animal sacrifice existed in the ancient Middle Eastern roots of Christianity, and Christ made the ultimate self-sacrifice on the cross. Patron saint celebrations in

Spain and elsewhere often involve greater or lesser degrees of physical risk and trial, which are forms of prayer. The scissors dance combines Andean and Christian respect for prayerful trial, as the ritual can involve minor feats like headstands but can also include major risks such as lying on beds of glass.

The scissors dance continues to be very much alive in contemporary times. The ritual retains its Mestizo character inherited from the two periods and cultural traditions described above. The venue, time frame, and occasion in which the dance now takes place have taken on the character of many other aspects of modern life, as the discussion below will demonstrate.

Description of the Scissors Dance

Lucy Núñez Rebaza (1990) gives a complete verbal description complemented with her detailed graphic illustrations of the history, meaning, and enactment of the scissors dance in the rural towns of Ayacucho, Huancavelica, and Apurimac departments. She explains how it is shortened in time and adapted to the limited spatial context of the city of Lima, where many migrants from these three departments now live. José María Arguedas concentrated his ethnographic and fictional writings on the department of Ayacucho, where he spent his youth. He wrote anthropological studies of the dance (1958, for example) and several ethnographic novels in which the scissors ritual figures prominently (1962, 1971, 1985). This writer had the privilege of helping to sponsor and seeing performances in August 2000 by Arguedas' favorite violinist and his group of musicians and dancers. The group is one of the very best in Peru and was able to give a small taste of the entire weeklong rural ritual in a series of performances sixty to ninety minutes long. The performers would plan these in short discussions before making stage appearances. The following is based on participant observation and interviews and conversations with members of this group and others from Ayacucho and from Huancavelica over the past ten years in Peru and the United States, viewed against a backdrop of previous research by Núñez Rebaza, Arguedas, and others.

The Ritual of the Country and the City

Musicians and dancers apprentice with masters in their fields starting from a young age. Many are born into families of musicians and dancers and tend to realize almost from toddlerhood what their future destinies will be. The apprenticeship process takes many years, and its final stages involve not only demonstration of technical and artistic skill but more importantly the taking on of spiritual power.

The following are excerpts from the author's field notes. This scissors dance troupe consists of a violinist, a harpist, and two dancers.

(Alberto. Violinist. Place of birth, a village in department of Ayacucho. Age at interview, early sixties.) His father was a violinist. He played scissors dance music and other styles. He was away from home a lot and drank too much. When he came home, he would leave his violin out of tune so Alberto could not play it. He did not want Alberto to follow in his footsteps because he said a musician's life means constant travel, too much alcohol, and bad health. However, Alberto was so attracted to the violin he could not stay away. He memorized the music and watched his father and the other musicians play. He would practice the violin when his father was not home. Eventually, Alberto became a master violinist and went through the fearsome final rituals in special holy places and caves to acquire spiritual power. His family's economic needs, however, forced him to migrate to Lima as a young man and work as a weaver, house servant, janitor, and general laborer. He had a breakthrough as an artist when José María Arguedas discovered him. Arguedas arranged for performances, traveling presentations, and work as a music teacher. Alberto still teaches but also spends a great deal of his time working at jobs other than music. Although he refuses to compromise his art for commercial gain, he fears the coming of advanced age and what it may bring. He believes that the element of spirituality in the scissors tradition is much diminished today in comparison to the past.

(Beto. Harpist from a village in the department of Ayacucho. Age at interview, twenty-three.) Beto started learning the harp when he was fifteen years old. He did this mostly by himself, watching other harpists. He did take two lessons in how to tune the harp. The harp is his friend, he says. He very much likes traditional Andean music, though in the future he wants to be a better musician and learn more styles. Beto speaks Spanish with difficulty, and though he has lived some years in Lima as well as in his hometown, he appears to have had little contact with outsiders to his native culture. When he is not playing his harp at traditional events he works at odd jobs to make a living.

(Jaime. Dancer. Born in a village in the department of Ayacucho. Age at interview, twenty-two.) He is known by his stage name Llaspa, which means "thin man" in Quechua, *flaquito* in Spanish. (Having a slender figure is an advantage for scissors dancers because it is easier for them to perform the required acrobatic feats.) Jaime started dancing when he was fourteen, but back when he was a much younger boy he saw scissors dancers. His friends and he practiced dancing using two stones as "scissors" instruments. Later in life he learned more from good dancers. He learned to work out too, to keep his body strong. He explained that a person can only make a living as a dancer during the ritual season (winter in the Southern Hemisphere). At other times, he works in building construction. Many people, according to Jaime, do not seem to realize that scissors dancing is religious and that it is about blessing water. People and animals need water to live, and scissors dancers are the "devils" who protect the water, he explains. Jaime hopes one day to study, perhaps at the university. He points out that there are no universities in the countryside, only in the city. He does not think studying will take him away from scissors dancing.

(Eduardo. Dancer. Age at interview, thirty-two. Born in a village in Ayacucho.) Eduardo's stage name is Halcón (falcon). His grandparents were master dancers. At first they did not want him to learn because dancers suffer a great deal. They go for days without eating, and they often have to travel on foot because there are no buses. Even though they did not want him to, Eduardo learned how to dance and started when he was nine. Like Jaime, Eduardo used stones to make the scissors sound at first, and then another dancer lent him scissors. After that time, he had to migrate to find work in Lima, and this forced him to leave dancing for three years. He could not stand being away from scissors dancing and was very sad until he eventually took it up again. People in the countryside honor the scissors dance troupes and honor this ritual tradition, asserts Eduardo. They call the dancers "devils," but they smile when the troupe arrives in the village. People respect scissors dancers because they assure the presence of water. Everyone needs water, according [to] Eduardo, even in New York, where the troupe was performing. In addition to dancing, Eduardo learned to play the violin, and he feels a passion for both arts. Eduardo talked about his final initiation as a dancer in a special cave and explained how when dancers are buried it must be face down; otherwise, deceased dancers can be spiritually dangerous. Dancing requires great strength, flexibility, and a very special mental attitude, which allows Llaspa and Halcón to perform extraordinary and at times frightening feats.

The scissors dance performers in the Andean countryside travel from town to town primarily during the winter season in the Southern Hemisphere (June, July, August), when farmers have the free time to engage in elaborate rituals and festivities. Townspeople host the performers in their homes, feed them, and pay them in exchange for their special services during the weeklong or more traditional time frame. In a rural village the ritual takes place in the streets, in front of the church, and in the town's main square. This main square is often oriented so that its sides correspond to the four directions of the Andean cosmos as well as the European four cardinal points.

In the city, the scissors ritual shortens in time to fit into a weekend. Urban migrants, now working at wage labor rather than on a farming schedule cannot afford to take more than a weekend away from their jobs. The places for performance can include city streets and church patios but most often occur completely inside small, enclosed yards. City audiences pay dancers and musicians, but the pay can be very low in comparison to high urban expenses. Some scissors dance groups will perform for soccer games, store openings, political meetings, and the like and work at other jobs in addition. Scissors dancers often become circular migrants, working part of the year in the city and part in the countryside. Those who are conscientious traditionalists work hard to maintain the genuine ritual even given the truncated time and space and low wages afforded them in the City.

The choreography varies according to the occasion but invariably features a series of dances, most with movements relating to agriculture. There are generally three phases of the dance, early, propitiatory, and closing.

In the rural context each dance step corresponds to a different day in a ritual lasting more than a week. In the urban environment, all steps might be danced in an hour or two. As an example, the group interviewed above performed the following kinds of early phase steps in New York City in August 2000:

- *Entrada, pasacalle* (note 3). Here musicians and dancers parade though village streets. In the urban or international milieu, the group dances to the stage through the audience.

- *Atipanacuy*. Dancers take turns showing their skill, competing with one another.
- *Alto ensayo*. Dancers execute high leaps.
- *Pampa ensayo*. Dancers squat and kick dance in Cossack fashion and sit on the ground bouncing from feet to buttocks.
- *Zapateo*. Dancers take minuscule steps; they may stamp but do not tap dance as Spanish zapateo dancers do.
- *Patada* or *patara*. This is toe dancing.

These early phase movements of the choreography mimic the motions of farmers removing grain from corn cobs, walking like various animals including owls, grinding pepper, kicking like a vizcacha, stamping on potatoes to make *chuño* (freeze-dried potatoes), making love (conterminous symbolically with agriculture), and herding llamas. All of the beginning dance steps express natural movement in the rural context. Alan Lomax's studies of work (in Gioia 2006:1–13) and its relation to dance and music are well borne out by this tradition.

3. Patron saint festivals in Spain feature street performances and rituals with some of the same names for phases or steps common in the traditional scissors dance. The pasacalle, for example, is a period or periods in a festival taking place over several days in contemporary Spanish villages. Musicians, dancers, and people in costume parade through the streets playing music and performing. This inheritance from Spain is evidence of the European colonial side of the double origin for many aspects of the bicultural scissors dance tradition in Peru.

The second, propitiatory or sacrificial phase of the ritual involves acts of ascending levels of difficulty and risk. This second phase is the high point or most important part of the drama. Balancing upside down on the harp, bouncing full length on the floor, and similar acrobatics mark the beginning of this stage. *Pasta* is the name given to the first part of this phase. Dancers engage in minor magical acts like pulling rabbits out of hats, stick each other with cactus branches, and pin the violin to the lip and swing it. There may or may not be more difficult propitiation stages. More serious than pasta is the escalated *prueba de sangre*, in which a dancer may climb up the church spire by means of a rope. More dangerous and dramatic still is *yawar mayu*, or river of blood (note 4), in which dancers lie on glass, swallow swords, or allow themselves to be crucified. Once the dancers have reached the crescendo of the propitiation stages in which they die symbolically, marking the highest point in this phase, the remaining acts lead in the direction of a general denouement. The ritual then becomes less an exhibition of the *danzantes*' spiritual power and more oriented toward human society, nature, and agriculture again. The music and dance now return the focus to life, the environment, and the community.

4. The expression "river of blood" shows the direct parallel symbolism between the human circulatory system and the riverine "blood" in the veins and arteries of Pachamama, Mother Earth. The term is associated with risky trials performed in the scissors dance ritual such as sword swallowing, passing ropes and other items through bodily orifices or wounds made for the purpose, and other feats involving blood letting.

The *caramuza* (*karamusaq*) style of music often accompanies the final or third stage. In this last act there is general song and dance with audience participation. Sometimes this is the final step in the performance, but other stages can follow it, such as *toril* for branding cattle and *wasichacuyt* for the completion of building a new home. Huaynos, a common folk music and social dance style, may also be performed. The term *despacho* means both a goodbye song, which has a particular style, and a spiritual offering. When played at the end of scissors dance rituals, despacho can have both meanings simultaneously.

Wifala ("flag," an important symbol of Andean identity), *carnaval*, and styles relating to the cleaning of irrigation canals or the burial of children and similar melodies relating to common events in human life and the agricultural cycle may be performed in the ritual depending on local desires as well as the troupes' preferences. Núñez Rebaza includes other possible music and dance styles in her list for the Huamanga/Ayacucho region. Among these are the *marcha* (military-style march), *wallpa waquay* (when it is three o'clock in the morning and the rooster crows), *ensayo* (dragging of feet along the ground), *tipaq-tipaq* (onomatopoeia for heel-to-toe step), *huamanguina* (humorous, dancer takes on the movements of a drunkard), *payasada* (dance with eyes covered), *chunchunki* (kicking air with both feet raised), *agonía* (fainting, as if dying), and *mala vida* (goodbye, farewell, perhaps translating as the "bad side of life" because the ritual is over).

The musical style, the instruments, and the way the instruments are played reflect Andean general traditions. Some aspects of the music such as the use of dissonance and high-pitched, otherworldly sounding phrases especially on the violin, are unique to the scissors ritual. The scissors dance music, though played on European instruments, resembles East Asian musical traditions more than European ones. The minor scale and complex counterpoint is exotic to European ears, and every stage of the enactment has special musical accompaniment (Damian n.d.). The scissors held in the dancer's hand function as a percussion instrument. They produce a constant clanging sound with a mesmerizing effect. This probably serves to induce the trance state eventually exacted of dancers. Dancers say that the scissors are the sound of rushing or falling water. Spanish missionaries introduced the violin and harp to Andean peoples. The form of these instruments and a common playing style can be found throughout the Indigenous areas of the Americas. The music played, however, as noted above, has a salient pre-Columbian as well as European component. The flute and drum in various sizes and forms, the ocarina, and the conch shell are more typically Indigenous instruments, as they were played in pre-Columbian times.

After the Spanish colonial introduction of the harp and violin, an autochthonous instrument-making craft tradition arose. Andean violins and harps feature Indigenous visual decoration. The Indigenous violin is handmade and often has carvings of folk imagery on the neck and echo chamber. The violinist balances the instrument in the crook of the arm rather than under the chin. The violin is smaller than the typical Western one made today (Volinsky 2003). The Andean-made harp is similar to an early form of the European instrument attached to an echo chamber and mounted on four small feet. In addition to the strings the harpist plays the echo chamber like a drum accompaniment. This form of the harp can be found among Latin American folk performers in Mexico and elsewhere as well as in Peru. The scissors dance harpist typically carries his large instrument aloft over one shoulder rather than standing it on its legs and ties it on his body with a woven belt so he can play while walking. The dancers' scissors rhythm instrument is specially made of metal for the purpose in the shape of oversize scissors. These are held in an unusual way, somewhat like castanets, in one gloved hand so the weight of the upper blade against the lower one produces sound by flicking the wrist as well as moving the fingers.

Costume and Staging

The scissors dancer costume may have part of its Indigenous roots in costumes worn during pre-Columbian times by sacred dancers called chunchus or chunchos. The chunchu wears an elaborate tall headdress made of feathers and other accoutrements that indicate their origin in the jungle. (*Chuncho* is a term often used in a derogatory sense to indicate jungle dwellers, though chunchos are also experts in mystical and medicinal knowledge.) Dancers say their resplendent costume is much like the dramatic markings and fur of the skunk. Núñez Rebaza was surprised to hear this, though the symbolic relation to skunks may have more to do with their behavior and dancers' reports of having seen them at night wearing hats and boots (Núñez Rebaza 1990:54–57) than with their actual coloration. Skunks are said to hold all-night dance parties while wearing pieces of cow dung on their heads shaped by the animals to resemble the danzantes' large *montera* hats. The identification of dancers with skunks (*zorrinos*) and foxes (*zorros*) recognizes the social nature, intelligence, and physical grace of these small animals. In Quechua "skunk" is añas. A famous danzante quoted by Núñez Rebaza goes by the performance name Añascha, or "skunk" with a diminutive, affectionate suffix.

Under the headdress the dancer wears a close-fitting cap covered by a scarf. The cap has a long "devil's tail" that is tucked behind the upper jumper vest, belt [chumpi] and a front apron. Dancers make their own

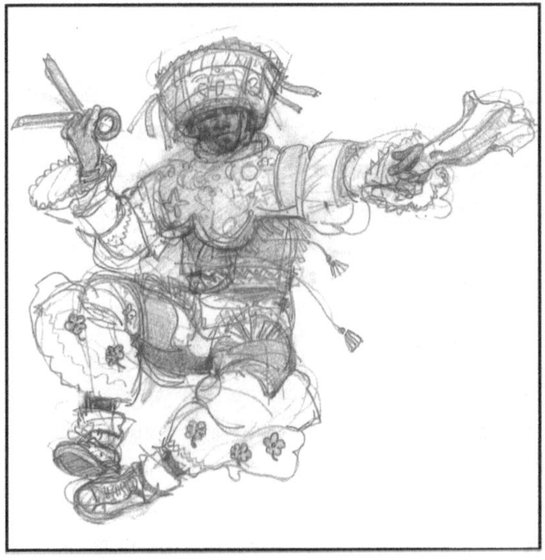

5.1 Scissors dancer performing high leap. Drawing by the author.

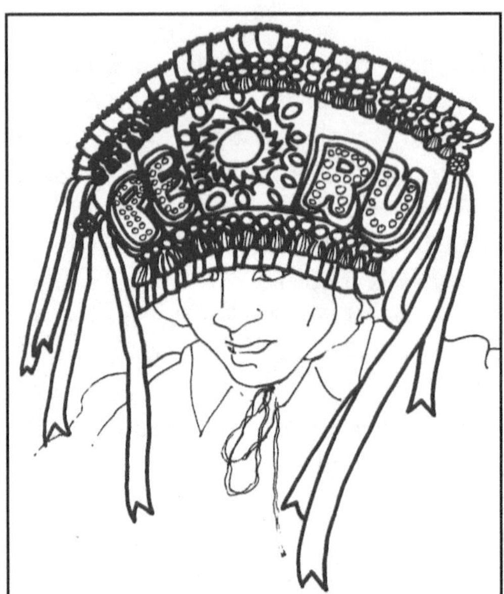

5.2 Scissors dancer's headdress. Drawing by the author.

costumes, which are multicolored, festooned with sequins and mirrors, and often bearing their embroidered performance names as well as images of Andean animals, flowers, and other elements of nature.

Under the vest and apron the Ayacucho dancer wears a shirt and pants with flounced lower arms and legs. Dancers wear heavy socks and thick-soled canvas sneakers on their feet and carry a multicolored glove on the hand that plays the scissors. From the large headdress hang festoons of ribbons, and metallic fringe in front covers the eyes and upper face from onlookers' view (note 5). The general effect of the costume resembles European, particularly Spanish, carnival wear. In fact, scissors dancers in Huancavelica are known as *galas*, a Spanish word meaning special clothing worn for community celebrations or simply one's "good clothes" worn at special times.

5. The fringe over the eyes was called a *borla* by the Spanish and was typical of pre-Columbian Inca elite dress. The Inca emperor wore a red borla. The hiding of the eyes gives the dancers a quality of mystery and otherworldliness. In Quechua the borla is called *maskay pacha*, which has two definitions and usages. Sometimes it means the eye fringe or tassel alone, and sometimes it refers to the entire Inca royal insignia in

the form of a headdress. This headdress includes a fringe hung from a headband, though at times the depictions take a quadrilateral form with horizontal bands that may be flanked by condor figures and/or surmounted by flag shapes or other extensions (Cummins 2004: note 4, figures 11, 12). In his illustrated chapter on the succession of Inca emperors, Guamán Poma shows emperors wearing fringe atop various kinds of head ornaments. He consistently names the fringe alone *maskha paycha* (1988:62–97); Guamán's spellings differ due to the time and circumstances of his writing.

Trance and the Process of Inversion

Two aspects of the scissors dance especially intrigue students and analysts of the tradition. The first is the trance state achieved by dancers, which they say helps them execute and endure the trial phase of the ritual. The second is the process of spiritual, social, and symbolic inversion that the dance represents.

Scissors dancers remark that the rhythm of the clanging scissors is in actuality the sound of water. Medical experts have found that the trance state in many cultural traditions is preceded by the sound of rushing water (Harner 1968). Health professionals interpret this as a neurological state, while scissors dancers achieve, in this way, communion with their objective: water. There is also a commonly recounted effect of moving through a long tunnel with a light at the end. Dancers describe cave experiences of this kind. People who have had near-death encounters also describe such a tunnel and light, and it should be recalled that the trial phase of the scissors ritual involves symbolic death and later rebirth of the dancers. People in trance report small animals running around on the tunnel's walls. The delight with which dancers describe the antics of skunks and other small animals fits into the pattern, as does the idea that they themselves become animals. Their apprenticeships involve conscious deprivation of food, water, and sleep, extreme physical exertion, and possibly alcohol and drug enhancement. These are among the classic means for producing the trance state not only in scissors dancers but in others as well (Williams 2002b). It is by means of trance that dancers swallow swords, recline on beds of glass, eat live toads, pierce their facial cavities and bodies, crucify themselves, and perform other feats of an extreme nature.

Núñez Rebaza, Arguedas, Celestino, and Millones, among others, have presented and analyzed ways Andeans employ symbolic inversion such that what outsiders may consider to be negative is made positive by insiders and vice versa. A further understanding of pachacuti, Supay, and the scissors dancers as vessels of power helps to explain this process of inversion. The Taki Onqoy, the probable predecessor to the scissors dance, had pachacuti as its objective. If Andean prayers were performed in the right way, then the Spanish would lose their power and the Andean way of life would once again reign supreme.

To induce the desired pachacuti, scissors dancers invoke the powers of Ukupacha (the Below world), namely Supay. There is a significant difference, as previously described, between the Spanish Christian understanding and the Indigenous concept of the devil or Supay. For Christians this being represents the power of evil. For Andeans this personage can use his great power as much for good as for evil. In fact, Andeans accept the idea that what might seem evil to mere humans may very well be good in the grand supernatural scheme of things. Spanish missionaries labeled Indigenous beliefs and practices as "diabolic" and religious specialists as "devils." Their aim, of course, was to clear the Indigenes' minds of their own religion and replace it with the Christian one. Meantime, the scissors dancers' ultimate function was to take power unto themselves in order for water to flow freely and the earth to yield her fruits. This process involved imbibing the spiritual power of Supay.

Supay resides in the World of Below or Inside in Andean cosmology. This is why final apprenticeship rituals tend to take place in caves, springs, and waterfalls where the World of Here and the World of Inside overlap. Christian missionaries glossed Supay with their idea of the devil, a demonic being who lives in the spatial and metaphorical region of hell. Hell is represented as being "below" this world, just as heaven is "above." This makes the tripartite cosmological divisions employed by the Andeans similar enough to European Christian ones to allow for the tangential creation of many syncretic beliefs related to the cosmological structure. The easy crossover involving Andean imaging of huamani as birds and the later colonial and postcolonial fascination with angels in art also were discussed previously. The belief system—such as it was understood by outsiders—behind the scissors dance made the term "devil" doubly applicable, and so even today dancers are known by fellow Andeans as "devils." They and their communities, however, view this title as positive and admirable because it denotes alliance with spiritual power that has the potential for great good.

Núñez Rebaza (n.d.) asserts that the millenarian nature of Taki Onqoy creates the phenomenon of inversion, causing the "bad" to be "good" and vice-versa. Ergo, the danzantes make pacts with the devil (Millones 2000), from whom they derive power to assure effective irrigation, good crops, and healthy animals. A close study of Supay, the Andean counterpart of the devil, amends this idea to a degree. The danzantes de tijeras derive their power from a special spiritual state they achieve through long internship with master dancers and musicians. Traditionally this meant "making a pact with the devil."

Other Andean spiritual powers such as the huamani themselves are not only helpful but at the same time quite fearsome. Where Christianity divides spiritual entities into camps of good and evil, notably angels and devils, the Andean religion blends these concepts to create a being embodying the concept of symbolic opposition in one entity.

In his chapter "Dioses y demonios de Tucume" (2000:110–219), Millones analyzes the concepts of good and evil in Andean and Christian thought. Supay inhabits the World of Inside (Uku Pacha) along with seeds and the dead. The location of Uku Pacha "below" this world made it metaphorically coterminous with hell. Millones explains that European Christianity during Spanish colonial times still carried within it the theological baggage of pre–Old Testament cosmologies in which the dragon Belial and the whale Leviathan were associated with an ancient state of chaos in which these beasts and the water where they lived had the capacity to destroy the sun, this world, and human life (169).

Scissors dancers make pacts with Supay (soul, shadow, devil). This allows them to derive Supay's power to promote the well-being of people and agriculture. However, Supay's dark power builds up within them at the same time, as he can take their lives at an early age, make them sick, or exact some other price for the use of his power. Núñez Rebaza (1990:45) recounts numbers games played by dancers to outwit Supay's designs. When a scissors dance troupe leaves a village after its ritual, no one is supposed to know it or see them, not even the village dogs, according to one scissors dancer. When dancers die, they must be buried face down, said another dancer cited earlier, because otherwise they could wreak spiritual havoc among the living. In this way, dancers are repositories of power, some constructive and some destructive. Their willingness to take on destructive power makes them trickster figures but also heroes in a deep sense. They are heroes because they pay the cosmic consequences of divine favor for all the other people in the community. This is why they are so loved and admired.

In *La agonía de Rasu Ñiti* (1962), Arguedas describes the mysterious and sudden death of a scissors dancer. When the dancer passes away, a huamani in the form of a large bird appears to mark his end. Shortly afterward, power is passed on to the deceased's young apprentice. Similarly, in his *Yawar Fiesta* (1985), scissors dancers represent the Indigenous worldview in which blood sacrifice and risk taking by human beings is required by divine powers. Andeans often use a bull with a flapping condor lashed to its shoulders (chapter 8) as their symbolic image to express such beliefs. In *Yawar Fiesta,* dancers like the novel's character Tankayllu enforce the right of the poor Indians to have their condor and bull fight in the Andean rather than the European "proper" way. This means there is no real bull ring enclosure and no *banderilleros, picadores,* or other assistants for the bullfighter. As a result, several Indigenes are killed, as must happen when the mountain gods require such a sacrifice. The scissors dancer, moving to the silvery rhythm of his clanging scissors, is a mythical figure. He is a trickster in the true sense of the term, for he playfully juggles the most serious problems of life and death. At any moment, he can fall into the abyss himself. Worse, if he is not careful he can loose the mysterious powers of the high Andes upon an unsuspecting world. Though Andean communities call dancers devils, they nonetheless honor their deep heroism as they, in a sparkle and swirl of color, dance lightly along oblivion's edge.

Perhaps the strongest and most laudatory statement Arguedas makes is when he writes in *El zorro de arriba y el zorro de abajo* of scissors dancers as defenders of Andean culture, spirituality, humor, art, and nature in the face of the crass, mechanical, rational, and logical capitalist modern world. Interestingly enough, the modern world also has its access to power, so each of the novel's two contenders (scissors dancer versus factory owner) for control of the cosmos has the name "fox," a close animal familiar of scissors dancers along with the skunk.

Comparison of Sacred Dance in Peru and Spain

There are a number of similarities between the scissors dance ritual in Peru and certain aspects of patron saint celebrations in Spain. These similarities aided and abetted the creation of the scissors dance as it is practiced today. The scissors dance may have started out as a ritual of protest, but it also bears multivalent resemblance to Iberian ritual practice. Perhaps this came about in part to better disguise the true revolutionary purpose of the scissors tradition. Scissors dancers often perform as a part of patron saint celebrations in Peru as dancers of other styles do in Spain.

The Peruvian danzantes' costumes are an almost direct transfer from European festival or carnival wear. The colors are bright and the attire replete with ribbons, flounces, bells, and rattles. The headdress even has similarity to some European styles. Spanish danzantes often make dance rhythms with castanets or double sticks. The decorative imagery covering the costumes, however, is quite different. Spanish dancers' costumes include imagery from their belief system and natural context, while Andean costumes display New World motifs. Both decoration styles do feature the florid, curvilinear horror vacui concept characteristic of the Spanish Baroque.

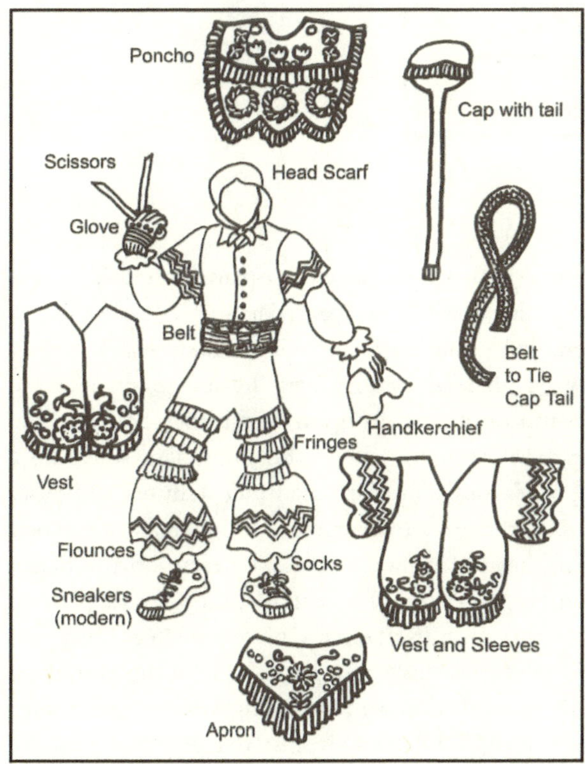

5.3 Ayacucho-style scissors dance costume. Drawing by the author after Núñez Rebaza 1990:78.

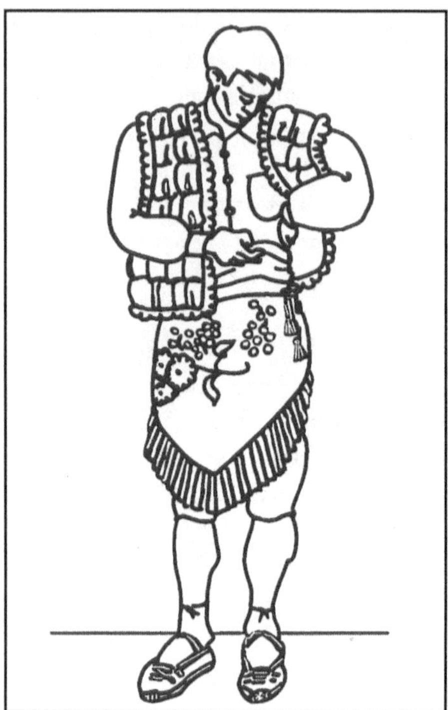

5.4 Anguiano dancer in costume with some undergarments shown. The Anguiano dancer wears a heavy skirt over this ensemble. Drawing by the author after photographs in Martínez Alesanco 2003.

Propitiation and Physical Trial

The danza of the village of Anguiano in La Rioja, Spain (note 6) provides a comparative model for the scissors dance (Martinez Alesanco 2003 gives a detailed ethnography). The Anguiano ritual takes place in July in honor of Saint Mary Magdalene. Young men dressed much like the Peruvian scissors dancers mount high stilts upon which they dance to the accompaniment of their own castanets while other musicians strike up a characteristic tune using *bandurrias* (similar to mandolins), flutes, and *gaitas* (clarinet-like instruments, in this case, or bagpipes). On change of melody the dancers begin to whirl around in rapid circles, whereupon the heavy skirts worn over their leggings expand. These skirts, they say, help them keep balance. Each dancer in turn spins in circles down a steep cobblestone street at a mad pace. The street descends precipitously from the church of the saint, located on high ground. Often these young athletes meet with injury, though the audience, which stands against the external walls of village houses like so much human padding on each side of the twisting downward path, takes pains to catch them before they fall.

6. The writer observed the danzantes of Anguiano ritual a number of times between 1978 and 2002. In recent years the small town has become inundated with tourists desirous of seeing this rite, which probably has gone on for a half-millennium or more, according to Martínez Alesanco (2003). It is the type of tradition that Spanish missionaries transported to Peru almost intact in the sixteenth and seventeenth centuries.

What is clear is a convergence of the historical and contemporary beliefs of Andeans and Spaniards. One must exhibit great skill and take considerable risk in honor of one's patron saint, who is an intermediary with the divinity. These actions also serve as penance for sin and constitute a sacrificial act, which is highly valued in both religious traditions.

Another set of beliefs seems to be similar. Just as the danzante de las tijeras performs his often frightening acts with color, humor, and grace, so does the Spanish danzante. In Spain, there is great admiration for a quality called *duende*, literally "elf" or "gnome" or "fairy," a magical capacity for dealing with life in creative ways. There is an entire literature in Spain dedicated to the tradition of the *pícaro*, a personality full of irony and humor who craftily overcomes life's obstacles. A major embodiment of these values is the bullfighter, who nimbly dances and pirouettes in his shining costume. The bull, a metaphor for fate and sometimes-cruel destiny, charges, rumbling back and forth with tremendous power and energy. Whether man or bull wins, then so be it. The loser is borne out of the ring with as much respect and honor as the winner. The Andeans tie a condor to the bull in Arguedas' *Yawar Fiesta*, unifying two similar spiritual power beings. The condor tied to the bull's shoulders usually gives its mount a very hard time as it flaps enormous wings, pecks with a sharp bill, and clutches with long claws. The condor is the Indian *torero*'s ally. The Indian bullfighter, with less protection than the Spanish one, is more likely to be taken in sacrifice at the mountain gods' bidding.

Ritual Space

The dances in Peru and Spain today take place outside the church itself, although there is a kind of extension of the church's sacred space by means of music and dance. In Peru a four-sided dance field outside the church

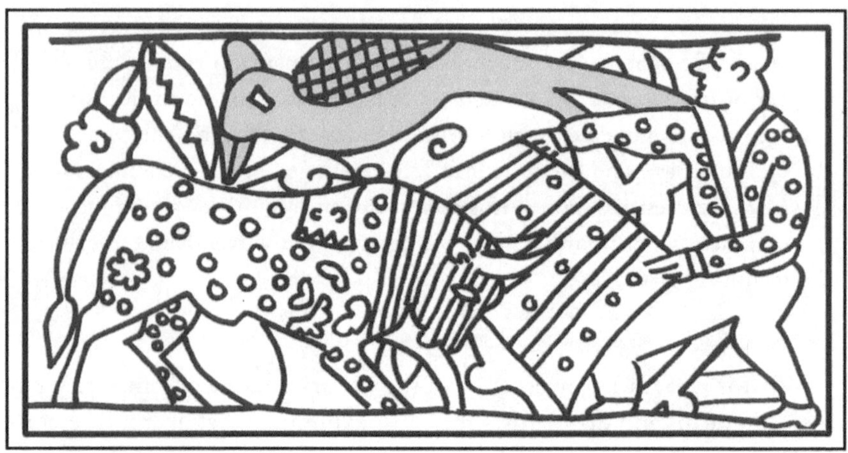

5.5 Condor and bull. An oversized condor is on the bull's shoulders, and an Indigenous bullfighter uses a poncho as a cape. Drawing by the author after Sabogal Diéguez 1949:19, figure 10.

door represents the Andean four directions. The dancer and musician teams in Peru often represent village neighborhoods standing for the four directions and the allyus living within them. The saint being honored often has two names, one Christian and one Andean, for example, Mary of the Assumption and Mamacha Asunta.

Other customs surrounding patron saint festivities often involve the primary agricultural or economic base of a particular town (sheep, pine trees, tomatoes in Spain and alpacas, potatoes, corn in Peru; note 7). Town parades in Spain feature danzantes as well as figures from the Spanish medieval and Baroque eras such as *gigantes* (giant puppets managed by several puppeteers) and *cabezudos* (costumed dancers with very large heads in the form of puppet masks mounted over their own heads). In Peru, dancers and dance troupes often wear elaborate masks and costumes as well. They perform small dramas at different points along the parade routes and at celebrations, just like cabezudos and gigantes do in Spain.

7. The idea of asking for supernatural aid to assure the health of crops and livestock is common in rural religious ritual. The farmer is at the mercy of natural forces, and a good outcome for agricultural labor is a matter of life or death. As a result, important religious rites tend to focus specifically on the agricultural specialties of particular towns. In

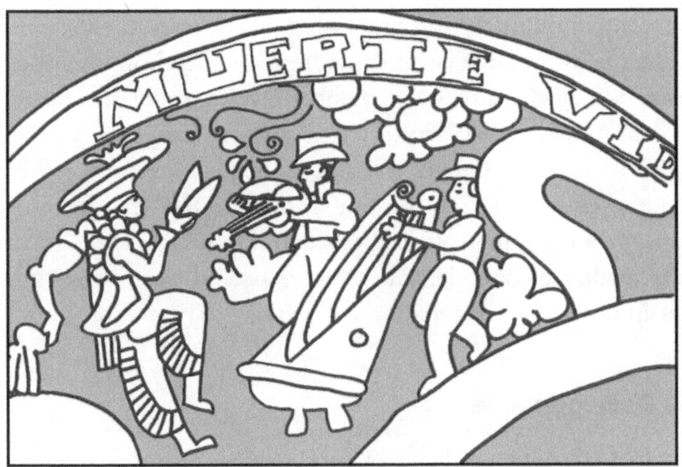

5.6 Scissors dance image after carved gourd. The carving from the late eighteenth to early nineteenth century shows a scissors dancer, violinist, and harpist. Drawing by the author after Sabogal Diéguez 1945:43, photograph.

> the high puna altitudes of Peru, herding is the only option, so danzantes concentrate on choreographies that reflect the activities of alpacas, llamas, and their herders. At lower altitudes, potato, corn, or pepper growing might be emphasized. The same specificity characterizes danzas in Spain. A town that specializes in growing tomatoes or grapes institutes those activities into ritual and features tomatoes or grapes in foods served on festival occasions.

The musical style in the tijeras sequence has a pasacalle (note 3) for the beginning musical street parade and a final *karemusa* (the Spanish use different terms for the ending parade), both of which allow for audience participation and appear as well in Spain. The phenomenon of dance-drama groups characteristic of all regions of Peru derives in part from European customs along the same lines. Originally, taki performers in the Inca era may have been ayllu-based. However, postconquest *comparsas* (performance groups) are often related to craft guilds, labor unions, and neighborhood organizations as in traditional Spain. Celestino contends (1997, 1998) that early Spanish colonizers consciously sought to, and to an extent did, break the ayllu system by refocusing celebrations toward organizing by craft guilds or religious brotherhoods (cofradías).

The Spanish contributions to this ritual are musical instruments, costumes, and the change of occasion from those honoring Andean divinities to important feast days in the Christian calendar. There is also an idea of physical trial and propitiation in Spanish rituals of this kind very similar to that of the scissors dancers. Finally, the almost magical persona of the Peruvian danzante resembles the Spanish one in many ways. The figure of the Spanish bullfighter combined with the much-admired folk tradition of the pícaro, the quality of duende, and other respected traits constitute important values in both cultures today.

Contemporary Developments

The two scholars of the scissors dance whose work stands out in their appreciation for recent developments are José María Arguedas and Lucy Núñez Rebaza. Arguedas' ethnographic novel *Zorro de arriba, zorro de abajo* pits the value system of the scissors dancer (the fox from below) against that of the capitalist fertilizer factory owner (the fox from above). Lucy Núñez Rebaza, in her illustrated ethnography *Los dansaq* (1990), studies the adaptations in the scissors dance ritual that have taken place among rural-to urban-immigrants. Both writers point out the destructive influence of commercialism, individualism, competition, the unhealthy urban environment, and rising expectations created by media influence. Lucy Núñez Rebaza speaks in detail about how city scissors rituals reduce over a week of activity to one weekend and the enormous spaces of a mountain agricultural town to a tiny city yard. To their observations this writer adds recent experience as a sponsor and guest at several scissors dance performances in New York City and in Lima.

In 2005 the author participated as a guest in urban scissors dance performances in Lima. These were sponsored by urban migrants from particular towns in Ayacucho department who were proudly celebrating their village patron saint festivals in the short period of a weekend. These celebrations featured a very shortened version of the scissors dance ritual and took place within an enclosed area where townspeople viewed two troupes competing with one another. Two feasting sessions took place during dancers' rest periods in one afternoon. As much as possible, villagers tried to follow the proper sequence of events according to tradition, though they were squeezed into a tiny space and within two days' time. Proceeds from the sale of food, drink, and souvenirs went toward building and furnishing a school in the urban migrants' home village, whose patron saint is the Holy Cross. Models and images of the cross placed on a stage at the end of the rectangular enclosure had Andean as well as Christian elements. Children dressed in scissors dance costumes proudly posed for family pictures. Sponsors of the event, who paid all expenses according to the requirements of the encargo, swelled with pride. They said there was still great interest in the scissors dance and other traditions among villagers no matter where they were located. Some participants in the festivities had come all the way from Canada and the United States to share this important occasion with fellow villagers of their native land.

New Audience Demands

The ideologies represented by city life tend to form the minds of young people referred to as New Pes in particular ways. In addition, many urban young people have little or no firsthand experience in the rural world upon which the danza de las tijeras is based. Matthiessen's assessment of the effect of the same process among the Lakota Sioux applies as well to young Andeans now living in cities like Lima: "A decline in their first hand experience in Native American customs has resulted in a reactionary mentality that poses as traditionalism . . . and a degraded 'pow wow' view of themselves" (1992:196). Scissors dancers now perform at soccer games, store openings, and similar secular occasions. Young men go to gymnasiums to strengthen their bodies so they can perform feats that to them are purely physical in nature and devoid of spiritual content. There is still a popular demand for the dance and a respect for musician dance groups. As a result, important figures in the media and others manage scissors dancers as if they were prize boxers.

Many dancers and musicians now perceive the ritual as one of several part-time jobs. This foments competition among danzantes and an individualistic orientation rather than one of community service. Managers receive large sums for booking dance groups but often pay the artists miserably. No public health care system, no community feasting or hospitality are available to help performers over rough times. As a result, many musicians and dancers fall into poor health at a young age. Mass audiences in enormous stadiums and of television viewers promote a tendency among danzantes to perform many fewer types of dance steps and to concentrate on what is most spectacular.

To summarize, what was once a religious collaboration is now an athletic competition. A formerly reciprocal exchange of goods and services between dance groups and communities is now a low-paid, part-time job. What used to be a respected life that would lead to becoming a master of the art and teacher of the young now often ends in early illness and injury. In a mass audience, many of whose members are not from the Chanca region or the mountains or even Peru, few know the meaning of the scissors dance. Thus, audiences, especially those conditioned by modern action films, computer games, and television, want acts of derring-do. The scissors groups must concentrate on pasta, prueba de sangre, and yawar mayu. If not, their audiences are disappointed. If yes, the artists risk serious injury or worse on a regular basis. The circus maximus of television has desensitized audiences to this tragic reality. According to the wife of a scissors troupe musician, it was once sufficient for a danzante to swing down from a church steeple on a rope. Now audiences demand very frightening and even life-threatening behavior. Even the costumes, she told this writer, are far too fancy.

Scissors dancers must join and compete with boxers, wrestlers, and the like as they put themselves constantly in serious danger. They do so to survive. As Núñez Rebaza points out, Lima migrants from the Chanca region are the poorest of Peru's poor. As one dancer poignantly said in Núñez Rebaza work, "Now (in the city, these days) there is no love" (1990:113).

Scissors Dancers Abroad

This writer accompanied and helped sponsor Alberto's scissors dance group in New York City during a tour of performances at a major arts center and a museum. The tour in 2000 was revealing in that it corroborated at an international level much of what Arguedas and Núñez Rebaza have said. Still, unexpected twists and turns in this experience allow for some favorable conclusions about the adjustment of the scissors dance tradition in the twenty-first century.

Folkloric performances without a doubt have become a commodity in the national and international media market and stage circuit. The museum and performance center that invited the dancers attempted to collaborate with the Peruvian diplomatic missions in the city to arrange for travel documents and amenities for the group. There were many bureaucratic entanglements, and in the end, the artists had to crowd in with New York migrant relatives living in a dilapidated Brooklyn building. Their pay was spent on airfare, and as a result they barely broke even financially. The cultural institutions and diplomatic mission did quite well as a result of the danzantes' work, both politically and economically. It appears that international touring is no better than performing in Lima, as described by Núñez Rebaza, in terms of income.

The group is quite special in that its members include some of the artists Arguedas once sponsored on national and international tours as well as dancers and musicians in their early twenties. Though all reside part-time in Lima, all were also born in mountain villages where they learned their art, and they customarily return to the countryside for lengthy periods.

The general audiences at the performances had no background on what they were seeing save a paragraph or two in handouts and fliers. They appreciated the leaping steps and colors and were intrigued as well as appalled by the physical trial steps presented. At one point announcers cautioned children "not to try any of this at home." This writer was told that there would be "no time for you to explain the ritual to audiences," much to the artists' consternation. The artists decided upon exactly how they would perform in the five minutes before they went on stage. Basically, they were asked to truncate over a week of rituals into one hour. They did this good-naturedly. They were also required to perform three acts in succession with short rests in between during which they collapsed backstage. They asked this writer a number of times why no one wanted to know what the ritual meant. The audiences no doubt perceived the danza as a kind of athletic circus act and showed a good deal of appreciation for it. The Huamanga natives among the Peruvian immigrants in the audience reacted to the performance as they would to a church ritual. However, when asked what it meant, few really knew much more than it "was something our grandparents thought was very important . . . part of our tradition . . . our folklore." Elite Peruvians in the audience did not show much more knowledge than their economically poor countrymen.

The dance group toured around the city for a day or two before returning home. The members stayed close to one another and drowned out the sounds and music of Gotham with small tape recorders of Andean music clapped close to their ears. They were curious about New York but commented on its similarities to Lima and especially its rivers and the ocean, saying "water, very important." They kept up a constant humorous repartee, commenting on what they saw in mountain village terms and passing jibes back and forth among themselves. At one point they visited the World Trade Center and climbed to its top. A year later they would commiserate with this writer in letters about the tragic events of September 11. One got the impression that these international travelers, unpaid for their labor, as usual, and treated, as always, like "Indians" are very sure of and proud of who they are. Who they are combines a full awareness of all that is new in today's world and at the same time all that is valuable and unchanging in their own tradition. They are "transnationals" in the truest sense, able to jump high, spin, pirouette, perform magic in time and space as scissors dancers always have done.

Final Thoughts

The scissors dance started out as a millenarian movement whose purpose was to put the Indigenous Andeans back in charge and be rid of Spanish colonial power. Today, the dance retains this meaning of the word "inversion," but it also inverts the modern world philosophically by performing the Andean cosmos and sense of time. This is a statement that contradicts the ruling worldwide ideologies of today, even reduced as it is to short periods of time and small spaces. Of course, many modern viewers have little inkling of these messages, for in the tradition of the arts of inversion, they are meant for insiders only.

It might be said with some authority that the scissors dancers and their ritual suffer when under the control of those who do not understand or care about the spiritual meaning of the tradition. Close association with the group that came to New York and observation of village-sponsored rituals in Lima show a different side to this story. People who inherit these traditions cherish them and appear to have no intention of letting them change beyond recognition or disappear.

CHAPTER 6

Home Altars (Retablos)

Retablos are small, portable altars that have the shape of a box with doors that can be tied in a closed position. Inside are one or more shelves replete with small figures of people and animals, some sacred and some profane, as well as painted background scenery. The box is a miniature of a large altarpiece and the two doors plus shelf or shelves that echo the church altar triptychs of the Spanish colonials. The idea of a portable altar was almost certainly a Spanish one, though Andean seers, prophets, and the holy persons carried and still carry portable items (seashells such as the strombus and spondylus, stones, *illas*, carvings, plaster statues, and the like) that serve similar purposes (note 1). The retablo has transformed in size, shape, and function a number of times. The altars, however, have always contained in their tiniest of scenes tales of social protest and praise of Andean traditional culture. These details are represented in a way undetectable to the average non-Andean viewer. Today, retablo makers serve a global and Internet market, producing figures for their boxes that reflect market misperceptions as often as they do Andean realities. Despite such constraints, artists express their pride in traditional lifeways for those who can read the disguised messages in their retablos.

1. Illas are small stones slightly carved into the shapes of llamas, alpacas, or sheep. Andeans say they are regurgitated by llamas and/

or struck by lightning. Both of these origins for the stones attest to their sacred nature. Illas bring good fortune, and they may be worn as amulets.

Retablos are primarily Spanish colonial in external appearance. However, as movable holy objects that can create sacred spaces wherever they are placed, retablos have Indigenous forebears as well. The structure of the box mirrors both colonial church altars and the Andean cosmos. Artists make home altars according to generally accepted canons. Within these requirements there is much variety in size, theme, figure-modeling techniques, color, and other aspects of construction.

History and Use

The use of sacred objects that religious specialists could transport from one place to another characterizes Indigenous, colonial, and contemporary historical periods. The home altar, or retablo, is a religious art form of this kind.

Before the coming of Europeans, Indigenous Andeans employed portable objects such as stone religious plaques with carvings on them, slightly incised stone figures called *illas*, and metal figurines, some dressed in elaborate textiles, along with other holy objects they used for religious purposes. Archeologists still find plaques and stone figures, some made to hold offerings, in ancient ritual spaces, in huacas or sacred burial grounds, and at the bottom of lakes and riverbeds where they were once thrown. Metal figurines of people and animals, some very well arrayed in fine textiles, accompany the dead in burials. Indigenous religious and medical practitioners sometimes still carry small stone illas, stone plaques, and other objects along with retablos inside blankets wrapped around all the items as well as curative materials of many kinds that they employ in their vocation of priests and healers. Tomoeda (2001:199–200) describes a *mesaqepi*, in "Quechuañol" (mixed Quechua and Spanish), a blanket or shawl used as a makeshift table. Women and even men use work-a-day shawls to carry babies, groceries, and other items on their backs. The idea of the table refers to the way religious specialists spread their objects on blankets often placed on the ground, the most common "table" used. Small, portable altars can be wrapped in such blankets along with other ritual objects and materials such as special cups (keros), coca leaves, incense, and seashells. The tendency to employ portable objects for open-air religious ceremonies meshed well with Spanish Christian practices of the same kind.

Spanish missionaries brought with them portable statues of saints and small, movable altars. These statues and altars represented larger versions of the same objects in churches. Portable saints and altars allowed missionaries to create an environment like a church wherever they happened to be. This idea dovetails with previous Indigenous concepts along the same lines. An exhibition catalogue offers an example of a portable altar (Phipps 2004:261) made in the Peruvian altiplano in the seventeenth century that shows the likely beginnings of this meshing of Indigenous and Christian holy and movable objects. The image is of a portable retablo in triptych form. The side pieces can close over the central image for transport. The images of the Virgin, angels, and saints are three-dimensional and formed of polychrome maguey, or American agave plant, a source of leaf fiber for paper and molding material as well as some wood and gesso (note 2). The central image in a large round-arched niche, the Virgin of Copacabana, is an alternate manifestation of La Candelaria, or Virgin of the Lake, who is highly honored in the Lake Titicaca region. Surrounding her are smaller niches containing images of archangels, saints, and the Virgin herself, who is pictured at different stages in her life. These types of altars never exceeded about three feet in height to facilitate their portability. A burro or mule loaded with one or two of these inspirational and instructional works often followed a seventeenth-century Christian missionary from town to town in the Andean highlands.

2. The maguey plant is of the agave family. It has a rosette of tall, sword-shaped leaves with thorns on their edges. A few times during its long life of ten or fifteen years, the plant grows a woody stalk with a large flower at the top, the ensemble resembling a spear in shape. Indigenous peoples have long used the maguey for multiple practical purposes. Its fibrous leaves produce paper and cloth, the juicy pulp makes soap, the end thorn can be peeled back from the tip to form a needle and thread, and juices produce soft or hard drinks. Peoples living in dry and not so heavily wooded areas like those at middle to high Andean altitudes near or above the tree line also produce planks of

pressed "wood" from maguey fibers combined with a natural adhesive. Historically, Andean artists used maguey wood to construct the cabinet part of Saint Mark's boxes, and artists today still use it as a support for paintings and as raw material for making sculptures and musical instruments. Contemporary craftspeople use maguey wood for surfboards, planters, small boxes, and other items.

Another example of a portable altar with closing doors is one made primarily of Peruvian silver and sent as a gift in 1749 to Ynes María Manso y Torres, abbess of the Convent of Santa Clara in Nájera, Spain, by her brother the Most Excellent Señor Don Joseph Manso Belasco y Torres, Knight of the Order of Saint James, Lieutenant General of the Royal Armies of His Majesty, Viscount of Puente Tapia, Count of Superunda, and Viceroy of Peru. This small but elaborately made altar was on display in 2005 in a special exhibit about the Church of Santa María la Real in Nájera. It usually resides hidden behind the cloister of the Sisters of Saint Clare, who now live in the convent of Santa Elena. Again, the central round arch shows the Virgin of Copacabana. She wears a tall crown and carries her infant son, also wearing a crown. Interestingly, the virgin's figure with its flared and flowing hair and wide skirts resembles a mountain. The Indigenous and Mestizo artisans who made the figure were no doubt thinking of Pachamama, the earth mother, as well as of Mother Mary. This work is a classic example of the phenomenon of dual subjectivity. The figure is surrounded by high Baroque designs of great complexity. Figures of Christ, religious leaders, and saints occupy other niches flanking the central one. The insides of the closing doors portray angels, Christ, and Mary at other stages in her life. In contrast to the gold-covered silver interior, when the doors are closed the altar presents its fantastic profusion of figures and designs in silver relief (Instituto de Estudios Riojanos 2005:197).

The custom of making and using portable altars containing figures of religious personages like saints and angels and other symbols continues in Spain to this day. Plaster saint figures in wooden boxes with doors make regular rounds from home to home within neighborhoods. The family who has the saint prays with the special help of the spiritual intermediary represented inside the box. Many of the boxes and statues today are made by professionals and/or in series. Older people remember making saint figures from mixtures of flour and plaster in a way similar to that described below for the construction of figures by artists in Peru. It is likely that Spanish colonial missionaries taught their converts this method of altar making by using readily available, humble materials. Specialized and more highly trained artists made altars for the elites out of materials such as gold and silver (notes 3, 4).

3. The exhibition catalogue that includes the silver portable altar sent to Nájera, Spain, from Peru has a general section devoted to gifts sent from the Americas to the Rioja region, where Nájera is located. Rioja received a number of such sumptuous gifts, and many of these had the Virgin Mary as a theme. Religious images from the Americas provided new models for the artists of Spain, who up until seeing these gifts were totally steeped in the Romanesque and early Renaissance visual templates that surrounded them. Instituto de Estudios Riojanos 2005:194.

4. In 2010, in Brooklyn, New York, the Latin American immigrant faithful in the author's neighborhood church regularly passed a doored box containing a statue of the Virgin Mary from family to family for the purpose of home worship. The box is handmade by a local carver, and the statue is mass-produced in painted plaster. From this it appears that Latin American migrants have brought esteemed customs related to portable altars with them to far-flung areas where they have traveled in search of employment.

By the early part of the twentieth century, Andeans made and used retablos for their own religious and practical purposes. These more recent works still bore the stamp of the Baroque style passed on by the Spanish but no longer had rich silver ornamentation or gold-leaf painted decoration. Maguey wood still served as material for the box, but elaborate round-arched niches for saints changed into simple shelves. The most common saint figures became those of the patrons and patronesses of livestock. Saint Mark is the patron of cattle and, sometimes, sheep, llamas, and/or alpacas, depending on farming region. Saint Mark figures are the most common of the major saints represented in retablos. During a good part of the postcolonial era, traveling muleteers (*arrieros*) carried what they called *cajones de San Marcos*, or Saint Mark's boxes, as an important item among the trade goods they would take from one farming community to another. Artisans who made these boxes could derive a decent part-time income to supplement farming.

Retablos accompanied the important yearly event of animal branding or marking. The boxes sat on the cut pieces from animals' ears (one traditional way of branding). Figures of Saint Mark in these small altars show him holding a book. Though some students of Andean art assert that Saint Mark reads sacred texts or prayers from this book, in actuality it is an account ledger he holds in his hands. Saint Mark thus officiates over farmers' stewardship of Mother Earth's bounty in its animal forms. Saint John the Baptist similarly is the patron of sheep, Saint Agnes of goats, and Saint Anthony of horses. Pedro, a retablo maker of Huamanga, stated that Saint Agnes is patron of female goats, Saint Mark of sheep and cattle, Saint Luke of llamas and alpacas, and Saint John of male goats. Though there is some difference of opinion, Saint Mark invariably comes up as a major figure. These other saints often flank Saint Mark on the upper floor of retablos from past eras as well as today. Retablos also play important roles in other yearly agricultural events such as springtime clearing of irrigation canals and blessing of waterways. Some observers of these rites recount that participants throw Saint Mark's boxes into the water to increase the water's sacred power. People appear to throw retablos just as their ancestors once threw natural and manmade objects into waterways for similar purifying and preserving reasons to protect this most vital resource.

In the early 1940s Alicia Bustamante, an Andean arts expert, ventured forth from Lima into the mountain hinterlands of her country in search of Indigenous arts. She traveled to the Andean interior several times beginning in the late 1930s. In the early 1940s she met master artist Joaquín López Antay, a retablo maker, in Huamanga. López regularly made Saint Mark's boxes for local use in the Huamanga region, though arrieros carried them as far away as Puno and beyond. His altars contained all five patron saints of domestic animals on their top shelves as well as scenes from local traditional life such as harvesting, house building, herding, and festivals on a lower shelf. Alicia Bustamante's influence went far to make this two-shelved retablo a standard or "classic" form. She required that the lower shelf have a costumbrista, or local traditional scene. The top shelf of a typical classic San Marcos retablo has one or more saints arranged side by side sitting in chairs or standing. Other Christian and Indigenous religious figures like angels, condors, and flowers may accompany them.

The lower shelf features such scenes as dances, cockfights, nativities, a hat maker's shop, animal herding, and crop harvesting. López Antay's retablos divide this lower shelf into a "passion" (*pasión*) scene of human suffering on the left and a happy scene of celebration or resolution called a *reunión* on the right.

It is interesting that in many of the world's arts, negative ideas appear on the left and positive notions on the right (Hertz 1973:3–32). The Spanish language, like English, must be read from left to right. "Reading" of imagery seems to work in similar ways. Thus, López Antay's "reunion" scene makes a kind of happy ending that is satisfying to viewers of his work. Adorno wrote a study (1979, 2000) of Guamán's drawings in terms of right/left symbolic oppositions. She found that to understand the right/left significance of Guamán's illustrations the viewer must see himself as inside the picture looking out. Thus "right" and "left" change places in arts with heavier Indigenous influence. López Antay, particularly under the influence of Bustamante, took on the European way of presenting the negative left/positive right symbolic opposition with the viewer on the outside of his retablos looking into them.

The painter José Sabogal Diéguez suggested the Huancavelica jail as a passion scene to López. Arguedas' study of Mestizo arts (1958) shows an illustration of a López retablo containing this jail scene. Anthropologist José María Arguedas remarked on mixtures of imagery such as Indigenous condors occupying parts of reunión figures along with more contemporary Mestizo costumbrista materials. The influence of Bustamante, Sabogal Diéguez, and Arguedas over the evolution of retablos illustrates how well-educated professionals can shape a "folk" tradition (Strong 2003a). Bustamante's ability to buy these retablos made to her specifications for sale in Lima went far in the process of making this particular style of Saint Mark's box a classic retablo form. In fact, Bustamante gave the name *retablo* (altar or altar piece) to these small cabinets, and this term replaced *cajón de San Marcos* (Saint Mark's box). The professional experts' suggestions also aided in increasing general sales of retablos in urban areas. Bustamante, Sabogal Diéguez, and Arguedas not only studied the home altar as an art form but also had a strong hand in creating the standard retablo design seen today. These professionals created what now is considered a classic cultural form. There are a number of examples of this phenomenon throughout the world, such as Eskimo soapstone carvings and prints, Haitian folk paintings, and many other "folk" and "traditional" forms of art instigated by highly trained outsiders with the best of intentions. Nelson Graburn (1976, 1999) has collected a number of histories describing this process in other areas of the world.

The art expert Francisco Stastny notes that the original models for the Huamanga retablos were church altars made from alabaster and stucco.

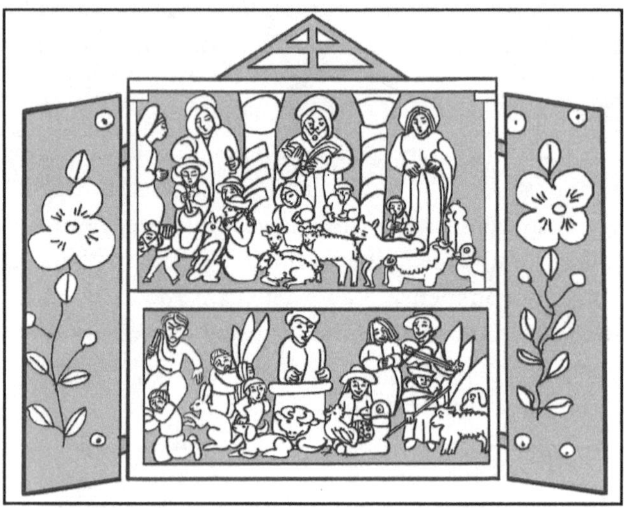

6.1 "Classic" retablo by Joaquín López Antay. This figure shows the design plan for the complete work. Drawing by the author after Arguedas 1958:351, photograph.

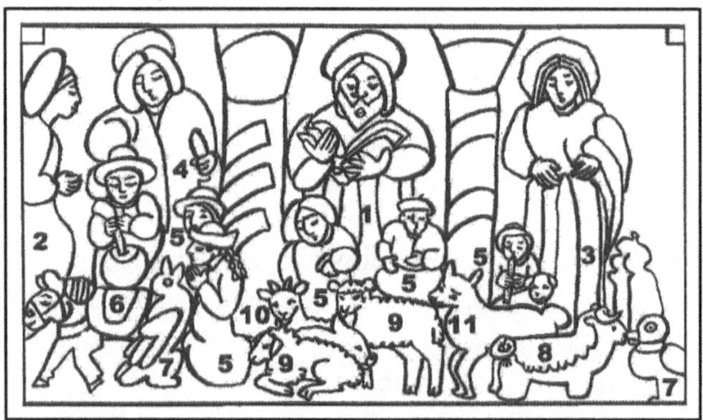

6.2 Top-shelf details in figure 6.1. 1. Saint Mark with account book. 2–4. Patron saints of animals. 5. Rural people praying and carrying on everyday activities. 6. Horse. 7. Condors. 8. Bull. 9. Sheep. 10. Goat. 11. Llama. Drawing by the author after Arguedas 1958:351, photograph.

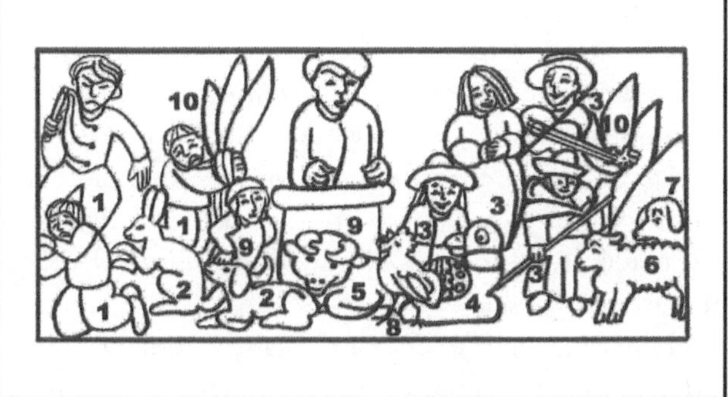

6.3 Bottom-shelf details in figure 6.1. 1. Rural workers being flogged by supervisor, passion scene on left. 2. Solicitous vizcacha and dog. 3. Rural people enjoying music, reunion scene on right. 4. Condor. 5. Bull. 6. Sheep. 7. Dog. 8. Rooster. 9. Judge. Drawing by the author after photograph in Arguedas 1958:351.

These probably morphed into the portable maguey-based type carried by missionaries, and this evolved into the classic San Marcos retablo of today. Retablos were originally used by shepherds and farmers of the Ayacucho area only. For this reason they are still considered an original Huamanga art form, though artists in other regions now make them. Famous Huamanga craftspeople and their families developed the religious, traditional, and historical or realistic retablo types as recognizable genres.

Massive rural-to-urban migration in recent times has reduced the demand for some kinds of retablos and raised the demand for other types. The violence and chaos that characterized the Sendero era urbanized many artisans who once made only a part-time living from retablos as a supplement to farming. Now, many town-dwelling artists find themselves supporting their families on art production alone. The demand for traditional San Marcos boxes still exists and forms a smaller part of crafts families' clientele. However, tourism, export trade, and the Internet make ever-changing demands on artists even to the point that they must keep abreast of changing market desires based on an oversimplified, stereotypical, or mistaken market-driven idea of Andean customs.

Two contemporary realities that strongly shape retablos of today are tourism, the global and Internet market, and to a lesser degree fine arts collectors. The collectors have an effect only on a few highly talented individual artists. The tourist trade, both national and international, is an important part of the Peruvian economy. Tourists want their souvenirs to be small, appealing, low-priced, and available in quantity. Retablo makers have organized themselves into groups to facilitate rapid mass production to meet this demand. As a result of poor materials employed to keep the price low and of too-rapid fabrication, much work made for tourists is of low quality. Retablos sized to fit into a shopping bag sell best, and bland scenes of idealized "country life" please buyers most. There is a more specialized tourist market made up of travelers educated in Andean tradition, but this forms a small part of total sales.

Some retablo makers have taken the idea of miniaturization and made it into a specialty, and within these small parameters they produce high-quality work. Pedro and his family of Huamanga make a good example of this resolution of the size dilemma. He produces finely made retablos using matchboxes and slightly larger wooden containers. He complains, however, of having to let other artists (those more successful in marketing their products) sign his work as if it were their own. The family supplements its tourist art income with occasional contracts to build giant retablos for local public spaces as symbols of regional culture. Some retablo makers specialize in these giant works for museums, public buildings, and fine arts collectors. Both in Peru and abroad these artists are usually very well known and have won national and international awards.

Though most tourist buyers prefer bland and happy costumbrista scenes in their small retablos, a smaller group will purchase work with angry political imagery. Tomás and his family of Huamanga make retablos with this kind of imagery. Many of his boxes have scenes from the time when Huamanga was Sendero Luminoso's capital of operations and many people of all political persuasions suffered greatly. He often surmounts his scenes of criticism and civil war devastation with hanging figures of condors suspended from the roof of the top shelf or cunning and diabolic Supay images on the bottom shelf. Here he is referring to Andean cosmology and its supernatural denizens. Some grounding in Andean tradition precludes an understanding of Tomás' work. His art serves an educated-traveler clientele at the higher end pole of fine art buyers. He also must produce more standard tourist and commercial fare. For example, he received an order to make retablos featuring cute kittens and puppies for a store in the United States. He planned to meet this order to support his family.

Tomás talks about the kitten and puppy orders with humor. He would much prefer to spend most of his time on the scathing and ironic political pieces that are his trademark. His dark visual metaphors make heavy use of inversion and disjunction. Andean peasants win out over heavily armed government forces in his scenes. He presents historical events in the guise of the present day and vice-versa, forcing the viewer to see a panorama of social patterns with little change. In the tradition of reunion scenes, Tomás' work offers a bright note of hope (Toledo Bruckmann 2003). Tomás innovates also in his way of constructing retablo figures. His work is unlike that of most of his contemporaries who make, among other figures, people in the rather wooden poses that adhere to clients' conceptions of "folk" art. Tomás' political commentary figures, in contrast, are in full movement with clothing blown by the wind and strong facial expressions (figure 6.11).

The wider, globalized world of buyers comes to Andean retablo makers through the minds and hands of many intermediaries. This long path between producer and buyer promotes stereotyping, gross overgeneralization, and good profits only at the point of final sale. The point of final sale usually means wealthy buyers in the United States, Asia, or Europe. These buyers apparently do not know very much about Andean cultures but believe they do. Artists, then, must feed a stereotypical market demand for some sort of generalized "Latin America" that exists in the minds of such buyers. True to what they have learned from Hollywood, television, and the popular press, this Latin America has Mexican and Caribbean overtones. Thus, Peruvian retablos feature images of Frida Kahlo, Mexican Day of the Dead figures, Carmen Miranda, men in Mexican charro hats, and the like.

Some artists, with the help of savvy intermediaries, lock into the U.S. "outsider art" market. They might depict a sculptural version of the 1946 "Wounded Deer" surrealist painting by Frida Kahlo with her face mounted on a deer's body topped with antlers and running through a boreal forest as well as other images that come directly from Kahlo's paintings. An artist totally dedicated to this market would have little use for his or her own native traditions.

Global destinations and Internet sites abound in more or less bland and pleasing rural scenes for which buyers do not need much background to appreciate. The Internet, above all, seems a two-edged sword. It markets not only to the middle-ground buyer by presenting benign rural scenes but also to the wider extremes. The Internet simultaneously can reach audiences interested in totally transformed "outsider" styles and those aware of highly specialized local traditions. The knowing retablo producer can and does make different sorts of work for all types of potential buyers: mass market, art world outsider audiences, and those somewhat to very familiar with Andean culture, thus ensuring economic survival while not sacrificing cherished traditions.

There exists a group of art buyers who have profound knowledge of Andean traditions, appreciation for well-made work, and deep pockets. Art museums, collectors, fine arts marketers, and public institutions make up this sector. Neither money nor space places limitations on the work, and the artist has the luxury of time to produce a well-made piece. The Huamanga city airport, though small, has two enormous retablos decorating the passenger waiting area. These works, emblematic of the region's wealth of artistic tradition, exhibit the local government's pride of place and people. Artists and families known to produce very high-quality work receive commissions from fine arts buyers to produce pieces of this type. Since the 1960s there have been yearly Andean folk arts competitions and national as well as international prizes. These contests help to establish and solidify the reputations of older artists as well as to highlight new and shining stars among younger crafts workers. Unfortunately, the artists still do not receive adequate recompense for their pieces. Museums and individuals often snap up fine works without paying one sol (about thirty to fifty U.S. cents) to the artists. The competitions facilitate such abuse. In this way, even unusually talented artists remain impoverished. The fine arts market at its best, without such exploitation, is a small one. Though there are a lucky few who do well as fine artists, most retablo makers must produce for the other, larger groups of buyers.

How Retablos Are Made

The wood used for the retablo box was traditionally maguey, though today craftspeople may use other readily available woods such as eucalyptus. The artist forms the box with small planks of wood, joining them together with tacks or nails. More traditional retablos have a triangle affixed with nails or glue to the front like the peak of an altarpiece. The artist cuts small pieces of wood for the doors and glues in one or more shelves, at times with the aid of grooves and tacks. The box receives a base coat of white paint, and the craftsman paints the edges of the box and shelves with usually red or other colored margin lines. The *retablero* then paints arabesques and flower designs into each of the squares formed by the sides of the box and both sides of the doors, surrounding these with red borders. The triangular peak gets a cross or X design symbolizing the Christian cross and the land of four directions. Common colors for these box decorations are dark purple, green, blue, red, and yellow. Most retablos conform to certain conventions in the shape of central flowers and radiating petals and leaves in the exterior designs. The flowers are abstracted and conventionalized representations of typical Andean blooms such as the cantuta, retama, and sunflower. Backgrounds within the box are abstract lines, dots, and so forth. Retablo makers in Joaquín López' time used natural dyes, aniline dyes, oil-based paints, and handmade brushes of chewed sticks, for example, for this work. Today, craftspeople use latex paints and commercially made brushes that facilitate drawing and painting with much greater precision. A good number of artists have learned to finish their works with sealants that preserves more recent retablos, preventing the kind of age-related and insect-produced degradation characteristic of older pieces.

The artists make the figures for internal scenes separately. They use potato-flour paste, plaster, apricot seed, glued cloth, and other materials for the figures. The artist starts by rolling out a cylinder of sculpting material for the main body of a human or animal figure. She then uses toothpicks, pencils, matches, and other instruments to shape the figure and incise designs. Limbs and head can be shaped from the main cylinder or added. The craftsperson can also press the sculpting materials into handmade molds to produce stock figures like chickens or tree foliage. More elaborate main figures have a unique character and may be given clothes made of custom-shaped, starched fabric prepared previously by the artist. Makers of miniature retablos often work only with toothpicks or match sticks, fashioning all their figures from tiny cylinders of molding material and these miniscule instruments. Large retablo figures can be shaped with the fingers. After the figures dry well, the artist paints them in bright colors over a dried base coat of white, allows another drying, and then adds small features like facial details for a person and harness pieces for a horse or ox. After the box and figures dry fully, the artist glues the figures in place. Taller figures like trees and people go into the back of the shelves, and small figures like ducks, flowers, and dogs get placed in the front.

The artist may attach the box's doors before or after adding the figures. Small squares of leather or other tough material tacked to the box and doors serve as hinges. A small hole drilled or punched through the front of each door allows the artist to pass a colored ribbon through the holes and close the box for travel.

Today's retablo artist gets a precise response from her commercially made brush and latex paints that was impossible for retableros of past generations to achieve. The style of most retablo figures still has an unmistakable resemblance to the Baroque statues and portable altars that served as original models for this genre centuries ago. Dynamic design, bold and varied color, and crowded imagery represent a few of the design hallmarks.

Meaning in Retablos

Retablos create sacred spaces wherever they happen to be placed, but they are in themselves spiritually powerful objects, or huacas (Macera 1977, Mendizabal Losack 1964, Stastny 1981). The structure of retablos reiterates, perhaps better said, iterates the Andean cosmological structure. The classic

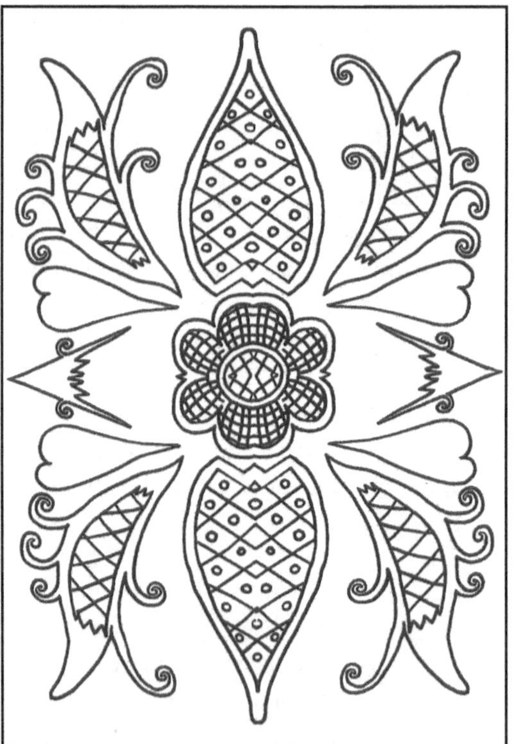

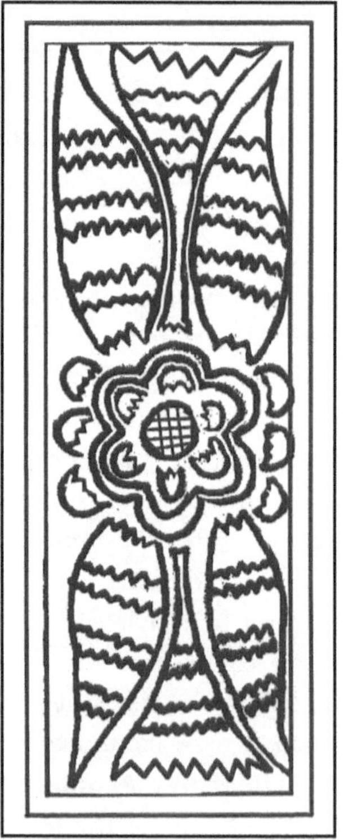

6.4 Flower design for retablo door. Drawing by the author after retablos in her personal collection.

6.5 Flower design for retablo door. Drawing by the author after retablos in her personal collection.

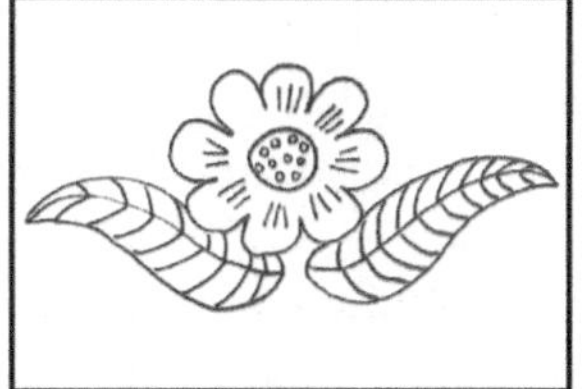

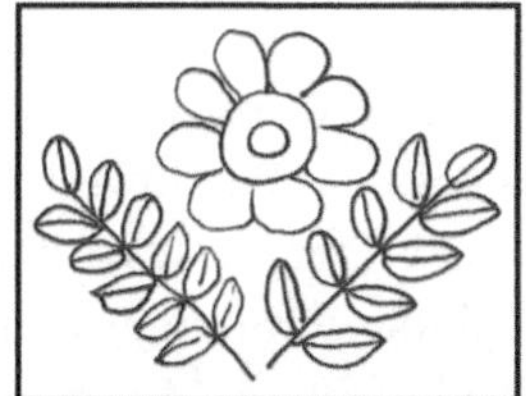

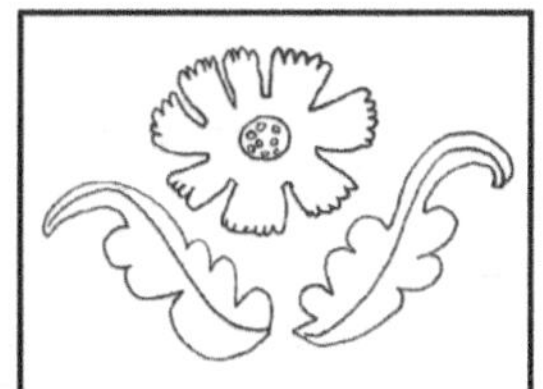

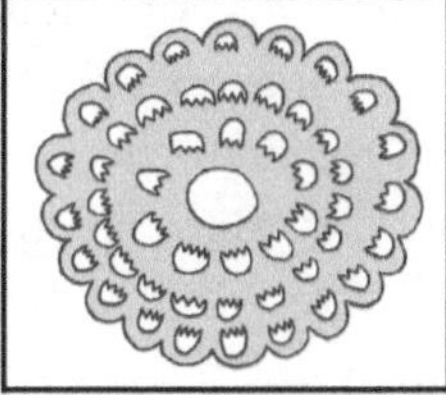

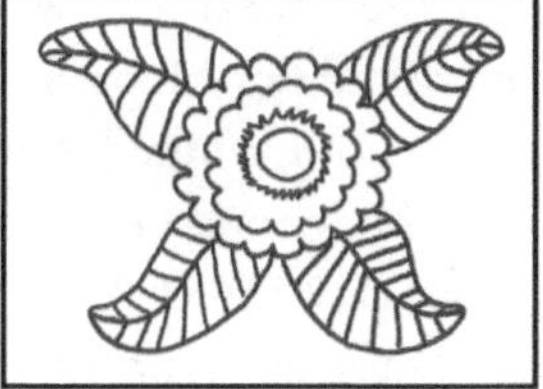

6.6 Flower design for carnation (*clavelito*). Drawing by the author after retablos in her personal collection.

6.7 Flower design for dahlia (*dalia*). Drawing by the author after retablos in her personal collection.

6.8 Flower design for daisy (*margarita*). Drawing by the author after retablos in her personal collection.

6.9 Flower design for sunflower (*girasol*). Drawing by the author after retablos in her personal collection.

6. 10 Flower design for sumac (*sumaq*). Drawing by the author after retablos in her personal collection.

San Marcos retablo has two shelves. The upper shelf containing saints and the divinities stands for Hanan Pacha, or World of Above, the upper world. The lower shelf represents Kay Pacha, the World of Here, this life, the middle world in which people live. The lower shelf of a San Marcos with a passion scene of suffering on the left has its complement of a reunión scene of happiness and celebration on the right. Arguedas (1958) analyzes a retablo by Joaquín López Antay showing a *pasión* in which a poor, Indigenous peasant is flogged by a cruel, Mestizo overseer. On the right, in the reunión scene, happy people sing and dance. Arguedas points out a glaring condor that presides over this scene of resolution, implying the victory of Indigenous spirituality over social difficulties. The scholarly literature on the symbolic opposition discussed earlier, of right (positive meaning) and left (negative meaning), applies here.

Millones speaks also of devil and Supay images in retablos (2000:194). Some more recent retablos have three floors to accommodate all levels of the Andean and Christian cosmos. The lowest floor with diabolical images and lost souls or the deceased refers to Uku Pacha, the World of Inside, or hell. Retablos with fewer floors sometimes contain devil or Supay figures on the lower level, or World of Here. Millones describes the devil figures as goat-men jumping about on their hind legs with long claws on their hands and feet. Scenes in the retablo describe battles between these figures and angels. The devils and angels, both winged, stand in for the huamani, often manifested as birds. The Indigenous believer, then, is more apt to interpret these battles not so much as between "good" and "evil" but more as a way of achieving a balance between opposite spiritual forces. Recent retablos feature a large, flying condor suspended from the roof of the upper floor in spatial and metaphorical testimony to pro-Indigenous political movements.

In their role as free-standing emanators of sacred power, retablos also serve in medical consultations, as offerings or sacrifices, for assurance of a good water supply, and in promoting the health of herd animals, among other purposes. Celestino describes some of these uses, especially in relation to the Andean belief that water is most precious as the source of life. All water, whether from the sea, mountain lakes, rivers, subterranean streams, or rain, is Yucumama, Mother Water. She is the life principle and vital force. This force is masculine when it pours down from mountains and into rivers and fertilizes the land, giving life to growing things. Water is feminine when it is still and contained in lakes. Water relates to ancestors and their place of origin. Local apus, ancestors, and Pachamama herself control water (Celestino 1998:16).

Human beings can make acts of propitiation to these powers through special ceremonies. These involve *mesas*, or sacred tables, a common variation of which is the blanket or shawl *mesaqepi* described earlier. A retablo often occupies a special place on this table among other, now more numerous than ever before, objects such as illas, bottles of *aguardiente* (strong liquor), wine, chicha or aja (corn beer), coca leaves, and strombus and spondylus shells (known as *mullu*), animal fat, llama fetuses, fine examples of crop plants or fruits, clothing, blood of sacrificed animals, ashes, aromatic herbs, incense, crucifixes, volcanic rocks, Buddha statues, and more. The mullu, or seashells, are almost always present. Their ritual use dates from early Indigenous times. They figure strongly in Andean religion because the sea, Mamacocha ("mother of lakes" in Quechua) has seashells acting as

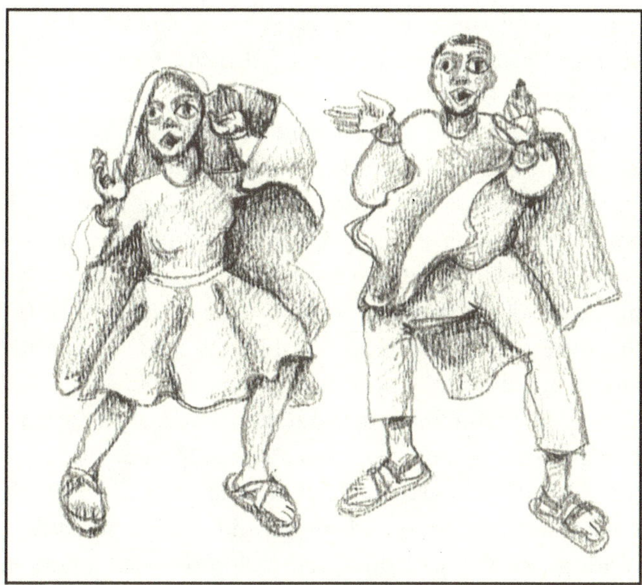

6.11 Retablo figures. The dramatic facial expressions, angular movement, and flowing garments characterize Tomas' political work. Drawing by the author after figures made by Tomás and given to her.

intermediaries between her great waters and those used for irrigation. The sea, important lakes, and springs are especially sacred *pacarinas*, or origin places of the ancestors. Postcolonial traveling muleteers, arrieros, carried on a brisk business in sales of mullus along with Christian saint statuettes, medals, and Mestizo retablos as they traveled between Peru's seacoast and mountains.

Retablos still preside over rituals attached to the cleaning and repair of irrigation canals at the beginning of the second stage in the agricultural cycle, the season for planting and growth of crops. Retablos officiate as well at the time of llama, alpaca, cattle, sheep, and goat branding and marking ceremonies. Retablos made and used today acquired their embedded symbolic meaning over several stages of historical time. The retablos' form, structure, and imagery illustrate a kind of fusion between Indigenous and Spanish Christian religious ideas especially in areas where the belief systems ran parallel. Arguedas certainly promoted this idea. Macera, Mendizabal Losack, and others argue that since the retablo itself is a huaca that emanates power, it is principally of Indigenous spiritual tradition. Those differing opinions being as they may, there are features in the history of Huamanga and the trajectory of Peruvian intellectual life that influenced the meaning and production of this art form (Toledo Bruckmann 2003a:18–19).

Huamanga, the site of the retablo-making tradition, was a place of impressive agricultural and mining production in the seventeenth and eighteenth centuries. This financial success promoted Huamanga as a prime place of residence for the Spanish aristocracy. Churches, convents, and residences were constantly under construction to satisfy the elite influx. The edifices required furniture, decorative elements, paintings, carpets, tableware, and other necessities. Spanish artisans established workshops with Indigenous and Mestizo apprentices to make such items as statuary, paintings, and home furnishings. In the seventeenth century, artisans began to produce nativity scenes from Huamanga stone, a readily available local alabaster. These were placed in boxes much like those used for the San Marcos retablos. Retablos at that time had several different forms: stone, stone and wood, paintings on wood, plaques, and sculptures made of other materials in various sizes—small for transportation in mule trains and large for permanent installation in city buildings.

As part of the "Indigenist" intellectual movement, the folklorist Alicia Bustamante and the painter José Sabogal Diéguez visited Huamanga beginning in 1941. They were concerned with two trends. First, they found that the traditional San Marcos box was beginning, or so they thought, to become an extinct form. It was for this reason that Bustamante and Sabogal Diéguez suggested the idea of including everyday events like agricultural activities, dances, cockfights, religious rituals, hat making, and similar scenes in the retablos. These intellectuals probably also saw that the customs they wished to see depicted in retablos were also disappearing. General exmigrations of retablo makers from the countryside to Huamanga and Lima seemed to make the retablos increasingly "folkloric" and less religious in nature due to market demand from outside the artists' own communities for the next thirty years.

Between the 1970s and 1990s the predominance of the Sendero Luminoso in Huamanga as its capital actually fomented a return to Indigenous and Mestizo religious and cultural imagery. However, new political consciousness as well as increasing violence created more rural-to-urban migration, along with a developing retablo style driven by political and cultural identity. Increased economic pressures on retablo makers came about because they could no longer make one part-time living from farming and another from retablos. This was particularly true of craftspeople who went to Lima as strife between the Sendero and government forces escalated in the 1980s and 1990s.

In the twenty-first century so far, a relatively peaceful time for retableros seems to have allowed them to come up with practical solutions for their multiple sets of clients. They make religious retablos for traditional use that they believe are imbued with spiritual power as they have always been. They make secular boxes for tourists, wholesale buyers, and fine art collectors. Artists view these as nonspiritual objects that they make for sale alone. Though an artist may give great care to a piece made for a contest or fine arts collector, it is not the same as the awe felt for a religious retablo. It is a solution that both satisfies artists spiritually and at the same time allows for their economic survival in today's complex world.

Retablo Artists and Their Work

The following descriptions illustrate varying types of retablos observable at the time of this writing. First, the differing works of older and younger generations in Ronaldo's family show a temporal stylistic trajectory. Second, the work of Pedro's and Tomás' families demonstrates how artists produce for multiple audiences. The description of Diana and her art shows a craftsperson's adaptations to large-scale commercial demands.

Ronaldo's Family and the Classic San Marcos Retablo in Transition

Ronaldo's work in the mid-twentieth century already shows transition from the "classic" San Marcos box. The writer spoke with him in the late 1960s and received a small retablo from him at one of the first folk-art fairs ever to take place in Peru. The retablo measures about 6" x 4" x 4". The external decorations are simplified because of Ronaldo's homemade tools and older paint types that allowed for little precision at this small scale. The box has two shelves with Saint Mark and farmers plus a few small animals on the top shelf. On the bottom shelf are scenes of harvesting on one side and musicians on the other. This small box made for sale at the fair represents a kind of watered-down version of a more classic cajón de San Marcos such as those in Segundo's workshop that were made by his father, Ronaldo. In these, livestock such as horses, cattle, and sheep as well as other domesticates and their species' patron saints flank a figure of Saint Mark. The animals recline in front, with farmer figures in the middle and saints in the rear. The bottom shelves contain pasión and reunión scenes as described by the folklorists and anthropologists in the mid-twentieth century (López Antay n.d.).

Ronaldo's children and grandchildren make retablos of high quality, in part because they have access to modern, commercially made brushes, paints, and other materials. However, the typical imagery they choose reflects a major change. Ronaldo's descendants sell fine-quality signed or stamped retablos from their workshop. A typical second- or third-generation retablo has a nativity scene at the top. These sell well at Christmas, the most important commercial season. The bottom shelf features a pleasing standard scene such as cactus-fruit harvesting, a hat shop, or animal herding. The precise tools, modern paints, and more anatomic proportions utilized by Ronaldo's children make their retablos more appreciated by a wider audience.

Segundo, Ronaldo's son, and Natividad, Segundo's wife, have blended an understanding of the urban world of fine arts with the Indigenous tradition of arts apprenticeship in their tiny home and work space. Segundo and Natividad are husband and wife. Between them they maintain a miniature museum and studio that pays homage to Ronaldo but also passes the craft to new generations with interesting innovations. Segundo, now a grandfather, no longer makes retablos but teaches students the meaning of retablo imagery. Natividad is an Indigenous person born and brought up in the jungle area of Peru. She makes one-floored retablos replete with the jaguars, monkeys, snakes, parrots, lush vegetation, and rivers of Amazonia. Her colors and subject matter are completely unique, but her boxes carry on the tradition of creating sacred spaces that are in themselves spiritually powerful as well. Though Natividad has removed her retablos from their mountain roots, she has retained their religious intensity.

Pedro and His Family: High Craftsmanship for Some Audiences, Sales for Others

Pedro and his family, kin to another retablo-making dynasty, consciously adapt to producing different kinds of work for varying types of clients. Pedro, his wife, and their older daughter, who was seven or eight years of age when the writer first visited the family workshop in 2004, work together making retablos. They produce for two markets, "traditional" and "modern." They make Saint Mark's boxes for farmers, and they produce two kinds of modern works. One consists of commissions to make very large retablos for public spaces. They also put retablo figures on full-sized mirrors, furniture, and other decorative and utilitarian pieces. For these commissions, Pedro's family produces traditional retablo imagery such as Andean wild and domestic animals and plants, saints and angels, bull-fighters, nativity scenes, and agricultural activities. The other kind of modern work involves miniature retablos made in tiny wooden boxes the size of a pack of cigarettes and even in matchboxes. The family produces these miniatures in series. Miniature imagery includes Mexican Day of the Dead skulls and skeletons, Valentine's Day vignettes, and similar scenes exotic to the Andean world. The miniatures ultimately have foreign destinations after passing through the hands of many brokers. The family's survival, especially as it grows, depends on the miniatures produced in series, although the artists prefer to make sacred retablos for farmers and works for commissions from more traditionally minded clients.

Tomás: Political and Art-World Influences

While the work of Ronaldo's and Pedro's families exemplify dual subjectivity, Tomás' art, as explained earlier, shows a strong element of inversion, particularly in the political dimension. Tomás courageously innovates in color and design to convey his critical messages to local and more educated urban and foreign viewers and buyers. His use of contemporary, elongated anatomy and modern dress for his human figures is a disjunctive departure from the generally baroque design sense that retablos most often exhibit. As a young man like Pedro, Tomás was moved deeply by the long period of unrest in Ayacucho caused by the Sendero movement and its conflicts among various wildcat militias and government forces. Like many retablo makers, he has lost close family members who died during this violent time. His retablos show the ideal socialist agenda of the Sendero and how it was originally promoted to improve the lives of Indigenous people. The new utopian society proposed in these scenes would provide the poor with land, education, health care, and other basic needs. Later retablos show the cruel reality of the many-sided civil war as it escalated.

Tomás still makes traditional boxes as well as retablos showing abstract and metaphorical work based on influences from the global art world. However, this kind of work has a very small set of buyers. Tomás' bread and butter, or rather potatoes and corn, come from retablos that are completely costumbrista or commissions for series in totally exotic subjects. His "agricultural life" retablos show standard scenes like harvesting potatoes, bands and musical instruments, and the like, while his figures and colors are his own innovation. Rather than the standard red as a base color, he may use tangerine orange or mauve. Figures of people are anatomically realistic, even to the point of having fashion-model proportions, and take dramatic poses in flowing raiment (figure 6.11). Even better for the pocketbook are commissions from stores to make retablos with baby animals, hearts and flowers, and other motifs.

Diana: Mass Production with Pride

At the time of this study, Diana was in her twenties and labored in a group workshop providing retablos to large-scale urban distribution centers. She adapts to the huge scale of demand by mass-producing in an incipient way. However, she remains very proud and aware of the Indigenous cultural and spiritual meaning of the work she produces. Diana is a transplanted Huamanga artist who lives in Lurín, a town close to the capital city of Lima. She works with a group of retablo makers to produce small pieces in great numbers in response to large orders. Proximity to Lima gives artists like her access to city commercial establishments as well as export businesses. Her work table is covered with small pieces, all of similar kind so that she can make a few variations on a costumbrista scene in series. The table has piles of llamas, cactus plants, human figures, condors, and similar stock figures Diana has sculpted. On one side of her space is a group of small prepared and painted boxes with doors waiting to be filled with the glued-in figures. As long as Diana and her workshop partners keep producing with some quality control, they can survive at a basic level. The craft association members have direct access to good-quality raw materials from the city, and this adds greatly to the finished look, precision, and attraction of their work. Diana's fingers do not stop moving as she talks, explaining with great pride the rural Andean traditional customs upon which her retablos are based.

Final Thoughts

The above presents a wide-angle view over time and space of some of the different survival needs and preferences of retablo makers today. Young people in retablo-making families—ages ten to twenty—learn their trade in childhood and have a high degree of skill by the time they are teenagers. They face conflicts that include the siren call of the modern world and the fact that training in other, more highly paid vocations might assure

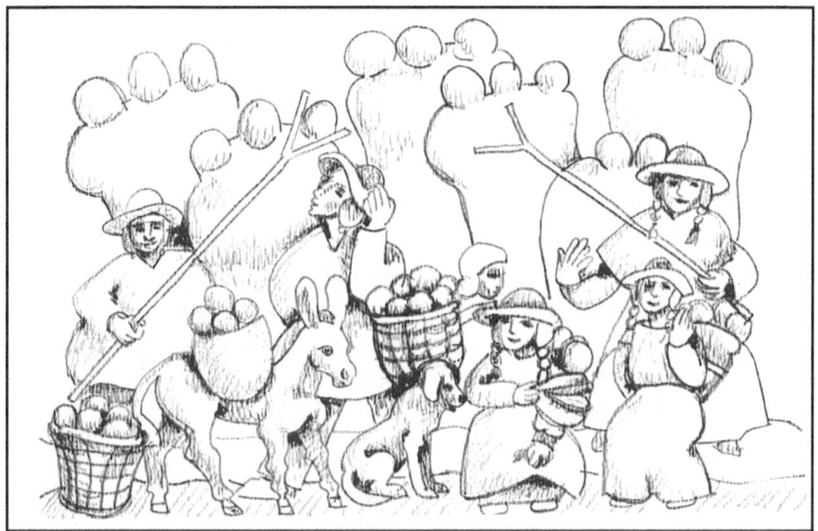

6.12 Costumbrista scene showing harvest of cactus fruit. Drawing by the author after retablo in her personal collection.

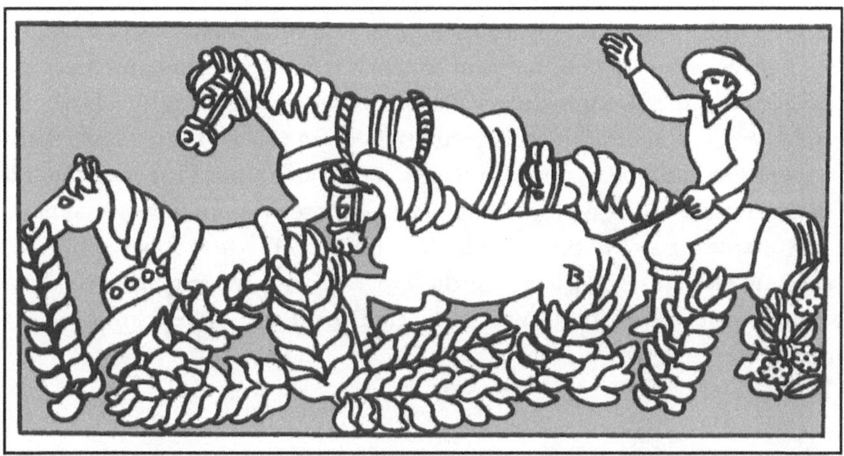

6.13 Costumbrista scene of winnowing with horses in retablo by Joaquín López Antay. Drawing by the author after photograph in Arguedas 1958:105, figure 28.

them a better and more constantly predictable livelihood than does art making. It may very well be that retablo making will return to its role as a part-time pursuit to supplement a first income permitted by vocational education for urban employment now available to some young people. Youthful artists expressed this desire in conversations and insisted that they had great respect and love for their family's art-making traditions. For many others whose vocational education still takes place primarily in the home, economic survival will depend on increased access to wider distribution and marketing networks. For now, retablos continue to inspire awe in rituals, delight travelers, and command the respect and interest of artists and collectors.

Retablos descend from a combination of Indigenous and Spanish Christian holy objects that, once moved to a particular space, could make that space sacred. The Incas used illa stones, mullus, and other objects to create and extend sacred spaces, and this custom-blended with the Spanish use of portable altars. The triptych as a genre in European art history echoes the form of a church altar with movable doors, called a retablo in Spanish.

The standardized two-floor Saint Mark's box promoted by academic experts as well as the three-floor and one-floor variations express details and the whole of the Andean cosmos. The box and figures with painted doors on each side recalls Spanish Christian church altars. Figures inside the boxes include saints and condors, the devil and Supay, as well as domestic and wild animals and plants. Bland folk and rural traditions or costumbrista pieces stand in counterpoint to satirical depictions of contemporary political and social commentary. Probably the ploy used most clearly by retablo artists is that of dual subjectivity because the art form allows them to represent multiple figures and scenes at the same time. However, the still very prevalent Baroque style template illustrates disjunction. Placement, for example, of a condor at the highest point in the box above Christian religious referents and changing the cross (Christ, the crucifixion) form to an X shape (Tahuantinsuyu's four directions) are subtle expressions of inversion.

CHAPTER 7

Carved Gourds (Mates)

Dried and decorated gourds called *mates* appear everywhere in Peruvian craft markets. The word *mate* comes from the Quechua *mati*, meaning gourd. *Mate* is also a term referring to certain kinds of herbal tea that were traditionally prepared and drunk from gourds in some areas of Latin America. Mates have various sizes and shapes, from a round, long-necked pear to a golf ball. Some remain closed with dry seeds rattling inside, and others are hollow with removable lids. Artists carve and paint the skins of some of these fruits to resemble people or animals, and others have simple or ornate carved scenes from daily life, sacred symbols, and writing. Decoration consists of pyroengraved, incised, or acid-induced outlines as well as carved negative and positive space. Pyroengraving, burnishing and burning with or without adding paints, dyes, and pitch heighten the basic carving with tones and colors.

Gourd carving is one of the very oldest Andean arts. With the exception of stone carving, it predates ceramics and work in other sculptural media. Ceramics made at much later dates gave decorative homage to this ancestral creative as well as utilitarian medium. Gourds are vegetables and so ephemeral by nature. They grow in one season, and unless preserved, they will disintegrate in a short time, taking the beauty and wisdom invested in them away from view.

History

The history, or rather prehistory of cultivating, transforming, and using gourds began in the distant past. The colonial period brought new uses and designs for mates. Migration among gourd crafters plus new buyer demands has changed the places of production and the look of mates made today. Andean peoples have created mates for sacred and profane purposes for thousands of years. Moseley states (1992:85–86) that early inhabitants of Guitarrero Cave in the Andes at about 10,000 feet of altitude cultivated the bottle gourd 10,000 years ago and those on the northwest coast of Peru 7,000 to 8,000 years ago. People used undecorated gourds as containers and fishing floats. Archeologists classify the carving and decorating of gourds as a "preceramic" technology. Junius Bird found some of the first decorated mates at the Huaca Prieta site on the North Coast of Peru and dated their manufacture at 4,000 BP (2000 BCE). Of the 10,770 gourds Bird excavated, 13 were decorated with cultural and sacred symbols (Bird and Hyslop 1985). Morris and Von Hagen (1993:34) present a large photograph of one of these pyroengraved gourds. McDonald Boyer (1976) explains that the people of the Paracas culture carved gourds with images of spiritual beings. Burger (1992) shows that the northern Andean Chavín civilization extended its stylistic influence to a number of coastal cultures, including Huaca Prieta and Paracas, as evidenced by Chavín-derived imagery on carved gourds made by these and other coastal peoples. For this reason, the Chavín may have been one of the first Andean civilizations to decorate gourds. On the North Coast, Moche and their Chimú descendants who coexisted in time with the Incas and were their rivals were also consummate ceramics artists. The artist-ethnographer José Sabogal Diéguez recounts how the Mochica-Chimú, as these peoples are sometimes called, made some of their famed ceramic pieces in the shapes of pumpkins and gourds. The ceramic gourds paid homage to and served the same purposes as their vegetable ancestors (Sabogal Diéguez 1945:16).

In the Central and South Andes archeologists have found carved gourds of the Huari culture (Huamanga area) that date to between 550 and 1,100 years ago. Primary documents written by Spanish chroniclers in the sixteenth century speak of an Inca colonizing (*mitimae*) community centers in Matipampa ("savannah of mates" in Quechua) in the area of Huancavelica and Ayacucho departments today. This suggests that good agricultural conditions for gourd cultivation and/or carved gourd production made this particular region a natural microniche for the gourd-carving arts to develop and flourish during the Inca empire period and

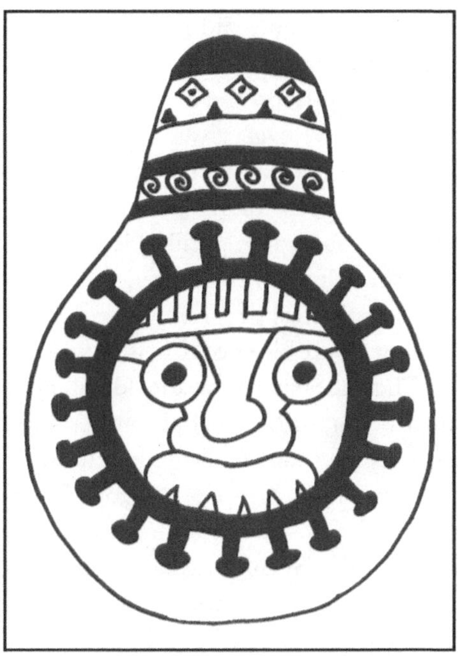

7.1. Huari carved gourd showing humanoid face. Drawing by the author after gourd in the collection of the Museum of Popular Art of Ayacucho. Museo de Arte Popular de Ayacucho 2002.

the European colonial era that was to follow it. Most gourds grow best in dry tropical conditions and have been traditionally imported from the North Coast of Peru. Huamanga and its environs have a relatively mild and dry climate. It is just over the mountains from a jungle area, which has a softening influence on what would otherwise be colder temperatures. The Indigenous Andeans carved numerous gourds and used them in decorated as well as undecorated form for many different purposes. The early Spanish chronicler Bernabé Cobo wrote in 1653 about the Inca use of gourds, saying that the Indians used all kinds of dry pumpkins for crockery (1956). The smaller ones served as dishes and the larger ones as tubs, troughs, and water containers used in travel. The smallest became tumblers for drinks.

Like the Chavín and Huari before them, the Inca designed carved gourds. Their design preference for abstraction, the geometric, and the lineal led them to divide the gourd into registers much like the lines of latitude drawn on a world globe. Within these registers they carved processional scenes featuring people, plants, and animals. Other Inca arts, such as large ceremonial cups or keros (Rowe 1961), sashes, skirts, tunics, and headbands had designs encased in parallel zones. Each panel featured processional scenes different from those above and below. The Incas used mates as a dishware but also as musical instruments and for religious and ceremonial purposes like carrying ritual chicha (corn beer). The Incas favored a two-color scheme with a white background and black design. The figures take a very simplified or abstract form. Imagery was arranged with high sophistication in a horizontal/vertical design balance that communicates visual harmony and tranquility. The pre-Columbian Andean tendency to divide round and pillow-shaped gourds into parallel "latitudes" is employed by contemporary gourd carvers, along with syncretic additions to refer to and celebrate the Andean cosmological structure.

The Spanish chroniclers recount their impressions of beliefs connected with mates and their practical uses. They speak of how the "devil" (this must mean a pre-Columbian spiritual being) attracts people to perdition by making a mate dance on a lake's surface. Bernabé Cobo, in his chronicle of 1653, describes how Indigenous people used mates netted together as flotation devices for water transport and for aids in swimming, much like life jackets, inner tubes, and "floaties" of today. Spanish explorers and missionaries brought the florid Baroque esthetic to mate production as well as new uses for carved mates. Colonial art styles changed the dignified Inca registers to curving partitions and rondelles.

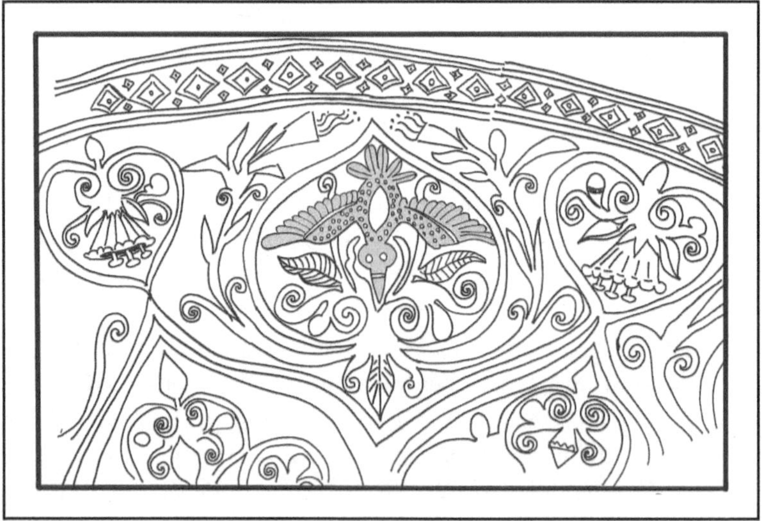

7.2 Detail of contemporary gourd carved in colonial motif by anonymous artist in Cochas. Heart-shaped rondelles with botanical flourishes encase a hummingbird and truncated cantuta flowers, in a design grid typical of colonial style. Drawing by the author after photograph by Antonio Vásquez.

Both Indigenous and Spanish types of design grids allow the viewer to "read" the gourd by rotating it using the stem as an axis, but the colonial design leads the eye up and down as well as horizontally across the sphere. Spanish or Moorish canons organize designs into curves and rondelles. These, rather than geometric divisions, became the basic design grid. The copious use of the curve and the diagonal as design elements conveys a feeling of movement and excitement.

Some very fine colonial pieces reveal tiny, almost microscopic attention to detail that recalls the ornate woodwork of Islamic Spain. However, Mediterranean imagery gave way to mixtures with Indigenous or other mixed forms in the hands of Andean artists. Lions change to pumas, condors float over scenes of Christian ritual in place of crosses, and suns and moons reign in the upper registers. The floral element introduced by Spanish artists became a mixed Quechua-Spanish *tica maceta*, or "flower pot," a term used to designate mates with flower decoration (Sabogal Diéguez 1945:98). In areas outside important colonial cities such as Huamanga, mates retained a good deal of their Inca traditional form. Within Huamanga, Europeans introduced new techniques for pyroengraving and encouraged multiple natural tones as well as painting and dyeing of mates for polychrome effects. Colonial mates can have silver and other metallic decorations attached to them. For example, the *azucarero*, or sugar bowl, classic colonial mate type can have silver feet, handle, or lid clasp. Some azucareros are lined with silver leaf.

Mates of this period also display writing. Some are poetic references to their owners, replete with names, dates, and uses such as holding chicha for the owner to drink: "My destiny is to hold chicha. My goal is to be loyal to my owner, Don Eduardo Marroquin" (in Jiménez Borja 1948).

Colonials used mates to send messages to each other, including romantic messages like this one: *Amores tengo de sobra como las flores del campo. Lloraré porque te quiero. No será porque te falte* [My love is greater than all the flowers in the countryside. I will cry because I love you. Not because I would miss you] (in Stastny 1981:139).

Along with religious images and traditional customs, colonial mates have morality tales, fables, and historical events in visual and text form incised into them. This custom, which continues today, makes mates important sources of biographical, historical, and cultural information in both visual and written form (López Albujar 1937).

From republican times to the mid-twentieth century, mate carving was concentrated in two adjacent areas in the Central and South Andes. Until the 1950s the Huanta area on the one hand, including the Mantaro region, particularly Mayocc, and the city of Huamanga, and to a lesser degree on the other hand Huancas, or towns near the city of Huancayo, made up the main centers for carved gourd production. The Huanta and Huanca areas correspond to two different subcultures eventually conquered by the Incas.

The Huanta (Huamanga, Mayocc) mates and the Huanca (Huancayo and nearby towns) mates of today exhibit different degrees of Spanish influence over artistic style, in addition to having origins that correspond to two local Indigenous subcultures. The Huanta people came under heavy Spanish subjugation and cultural influence. Their capital, Huamanga ("place of the condors"), became Ayacucho ("place of the dead") under Spanish rule as an important colonial center. Huanta mates have many more Mediterranean design elements and images than those made by the Huanca. Huanta-style work exhibits more script, more colonial flowers, bullfights, people in colonial dress and other *criollo* (bicultural) touches.

The Huancas, on the other hand, were renowned for never being totally subdued by either Incas or Spaniards. The Huancas helped foment the Taki Onqoy millenarian movement. They continued making mates with Andean design elements and images. Thus, their mates have no writing and few curves, spirals, and diagonals. Representations of today tend toward costumbrista scenes, or daily activities of rural people such as plowing, herding, and religious festivals. These scenes appear in parallel registers and have a processional format following in the Andean tradition. However free they may have been from European colonial influence, *materos* (gourd carvers) have responded to contemporary events with interesting innovations. Airplanes, trains, rocket ships, and other new technologies appear in mates, as well as portraits of presidents, important events like the death of Tupac Amaru, and a war with Chile. The Huancayo-area artists specialize also in using the form of the calabash to represent a person or animal.

In the 1950s these kinds of regional differentiations began to blur. Most of the Huantas and Ayacucho mate makers moved to Lima or Huancayo, where the market for their work was better. The Huancayo contingent of migrants from Huantas and Mayocc taught their art to the people of Cochas Chico and Cochas Grande, two towns near Huancayo in Junín. There remains only one mate maker in Huancas, Gerónimo, who at the time of this study was in his eighties. He primarily farmed, grew his own gourds on small *chacra* (farm) in the district of Mayocc, and worked daily in the outdoor patio of his house when farm chores were finished. His mate designs represent folk customs in rural life, for example, a celebration called *tirajarros* ("jar throwing"), carnival, bullfights, house construction, festivals, marriage celebrations, winnowing, animal herding, plowing with a yoke of oxen, and many more rural village themes as well as Christian religious topics such as the birth of Jesus.

The mate makers in Cochas today produce work in a style that is strongly Spanish colonial. This is the logical outgrowth of having learned the Huanta style from teachers of that tradition in the 1950s. Cochas materos live a life much like Gerónimo's. Farming is their major occupation and gourd carving a part-time occupation to earn extra income. The most important art produced in Cochas is weaving, so there are even more weavers than mate makers. In the twenty-first century, Cochas materos feel subjugated to conditions that have produced a chain of middlemen who deal in decorated gourds. Tourism also has a major influence on Cochas art makers because it has increased demand in terms of numbers of products and at the same time reduced the quality of many artisans' workmanship due to bulk orders with short deadlines, price-point limitations, and other factors.

How Mates Are Made

The basic raw materials are gourds or calabashes of different varieties, shapes, and sizes. These give rise to varied uses and types of decoration. Artists employ a small repertoire of tools and materials to prepare and decorate mates. When good craftspeople take their time, they produce small jewels of very high quality. However, the basic materials are by their nature fragile and perishable. The most preferred gourd for mate carving is the common gourd *lagenaria vulgaris*. Other varieties used include *crescencia*, known simply as "the gourd," which is cheaper, and *lagenaria sicararia*, which is softer and easier to carve. A warm, dry climate favors gourd cultivation, and they grow well along the entire Peruvian coastal area, especially in the north. They also grow very well in the mountain microclimate of Mayocc, Huancavelica, which in part explains its prevalence as a gourd-carving center. Gourd plants take up a lot of space with their extended creeping vines, so farmers tend to plant them on the borders of fields in August. The plants flower in January and fruit thereafter.

Among the three basic categories of gourds—*poros*, *morochos*, and *almidones*—carvers prefer the yellow, round *morochos* and *almidones*. Morochos produce the best mates because their hard skin makes the designs stand out, but they are difficult to work. Almidones are white, round, and soft, making them easy to engrave, but their very softness makes good results difficult to achieve. Different shapes of gourds have distinctive final uses. *Pucos* (round) or azucareros (slightly flattened and round) are the most typical carved gourds that can be used as lidded containers. *Buros* and *huiros* have pear shapes with necks. These can become containers or human or animal shapes. A large, round gourd can be bisected to form deep-dish plates or bowls. (Museo del Arte Popular de Ayacucho 2002 and the museum archive present details on gourd agriculture and species.)

Mate makers use cutting and burnishing tools and simple drawing implements for the basic decoration. Different types of pyroengraving enhance the basic design, and some artists use, in addition, colored dyes. The following tools and materials are typical.

- Cutting points (burins). A local blacksmith makes these steel points in various shapes and thicknesses. The points are embedded in quinal wood or corncob handles. Corncob handles do not slip in the hands, making the artists' precision work easier.

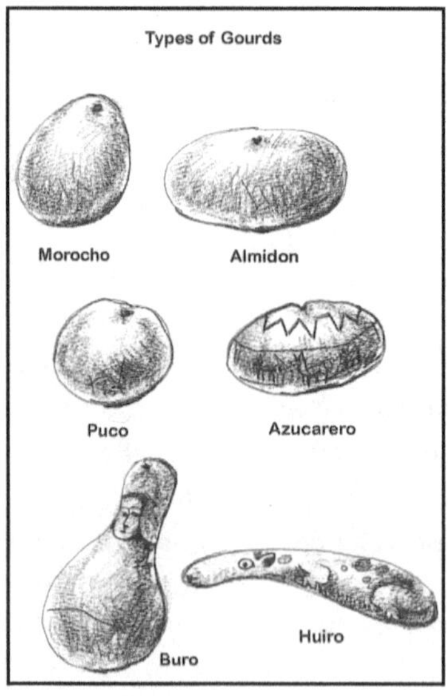

7.3 Types of gourds. Drawing by the author based on archival material of the Museum of Popular Art of Ayacucho, particularly Morales Chávez 1981.

- Brushes. Artists use very small, pointed brushes for painting with aniline dyes.
- Wood. Quinal wood with a burned carved tip is used for pyroengraving.
- Stones. Materos use stones for filing cutting points and blades.
- Knives. These are used for removing gourd lids and for gouging.
- Compass and pencil. Materos use these implements for making the design sketches, circles, registers, and arcs defining design areas.

After they carve the gourds, materos use these materials to finish the pieces: aniline dyes, or manufactured colors; cooking or linseed oil; ichu or barley grass or stubble for making ash; pig lard; rags; and containers.

The production process involves various stages of preparing the gourds for working, drawing, and carving. Then the artist engraves, dyes, and finishes the piece. After being harvested from the vines, the gourds are left out to dry. Gourds destined to be plates are cut in half right away and cleaned of pulp and seeds. The artist sands the outside and leaves the shells to dry in the sun for about eight days. For azucareros and other decorative ware, the gourds dry in the sun as is for twenty days or so. After the gourds have dried, carvers clean them with water and mud from good earth along with a little sand to softly polish the surface. Some carvers wash the gourds and then cover them with cooking or linseed oil to achieve a smooth surface.

There are two basic production traditions. The Huancayo style is practiced today in Cochas Chico, Cochas Grande, and Mayocc. The second is the Ayacucho or Huanta style, once characteristic of the city but now extinct there. Artists in Cochas Chico and Cochas Grande produce work in both styles, plus a third style described below.

Craft makers working in the Huancayo style proceed along the following lines.

1. First, the artist draws the design with a pencil or other pointed instrument. Some carvers avoid this stage, especially for designs they produce often.
2. Then the artist deepens and widens the lines with cutting blades and points.
3. The engraver takes the red-hot tip of a burning piece of quinal wood and scorches the gourd skin to the desired color (tan, brown, black).

The longer the hot wood tip touches the gourd surface, the darker the color will be.

4. Next the carver removes the background area by chiseling and gouging with various burins and the knife. She works carefully in parallel strokes. This natural background is white; the addition of calcium carbonate rubbed into the background enhances the white color if desired.
5. If the artist wants a lid, she uses a knife to cut through the top around the stem as a center point. The lid usually has a simple zigzag edge already worked into the design.

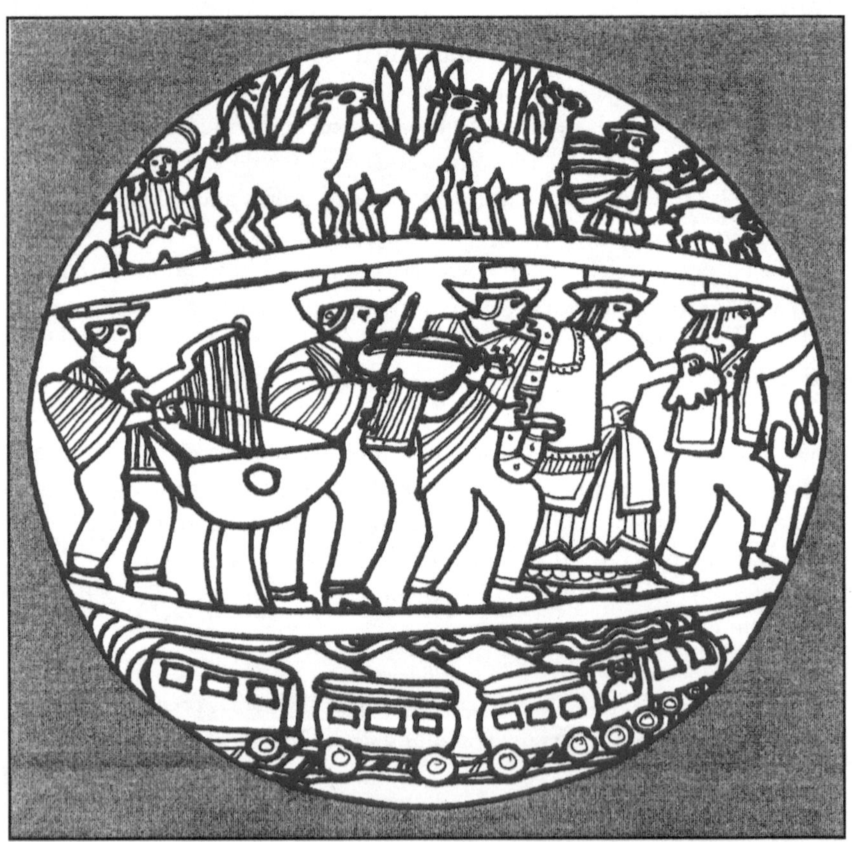

7.4 Huanca-style mate showing scenes of daily life: herding llamas (top), festival parade (center), and train (bottom). Parallel parades of images divided by latitudinal lines characterize Indigenous style. Drawing by the author after carved gourd in her collection.

6. Finally, the carver removes the seeds and sands the edges of the lid with sandpaper.

The Ayacucho-style mates look different from those of Huancayo style, and the artist uses a distinct production process. Gourds in the Ayacucho style have a black background rather than a white one, and they tend to be bicolor with a black background and natural foreground. Steps for producing the Ayacucho style are as follows.

1. The engraver makes a sketch with a pencil or other pointed tool if he wishes.
2. He enhances the outline with one or more burins.
3. With burins and/or knife, the artist carves out the background.
4. The engraver then mixes the ashes of burned ichu, a high-altitude grass and one of the foods llamas and alpacas favor most, with lard, usually pig fat. He heats the fat and ash together to form a liquid. He then rubs this liquid onto the gourd. Some artists use barley grass or stubble in place of ichu and shoe polish instead of the ash and fat mixture.
5. The artist washes the gourd, and the cream or gold design foreground comes clean, leaving the black background.
6. The artist may desire to do additional engraving in white at this point for contrast or for a multitoned effect.
7. If he wishes, the artist cuts a lid.

A third style, involving aniline dyes available at hardware stores, is sometimes combined with the Huancayo or Ayacucho style, or it can be used alone. The carvers of Cochas Chico and Cochas Grande know and use all three of these techniques. For this third style the artist dips the fruit into a dye bath of red, purple, green, or any color. The gourd dries. The carver incises a design with a very fine burin and then cuts out wider spaces. (This technique using aniline dyes works well for tree gourds from the jungle area.) The mate maker may cover the finished work with a coating of oil for shine.

In contemporary times, gourds imported from areas such as coastal Lambayeque come with a design already on them. They are most often overall geometric or floral patterns as well as written mottos. Lambayeque artisans use acids such as silver nitrate or sulphuric acid to create these patterns. When Cochas carvers receive such semi-prepared gourds, they

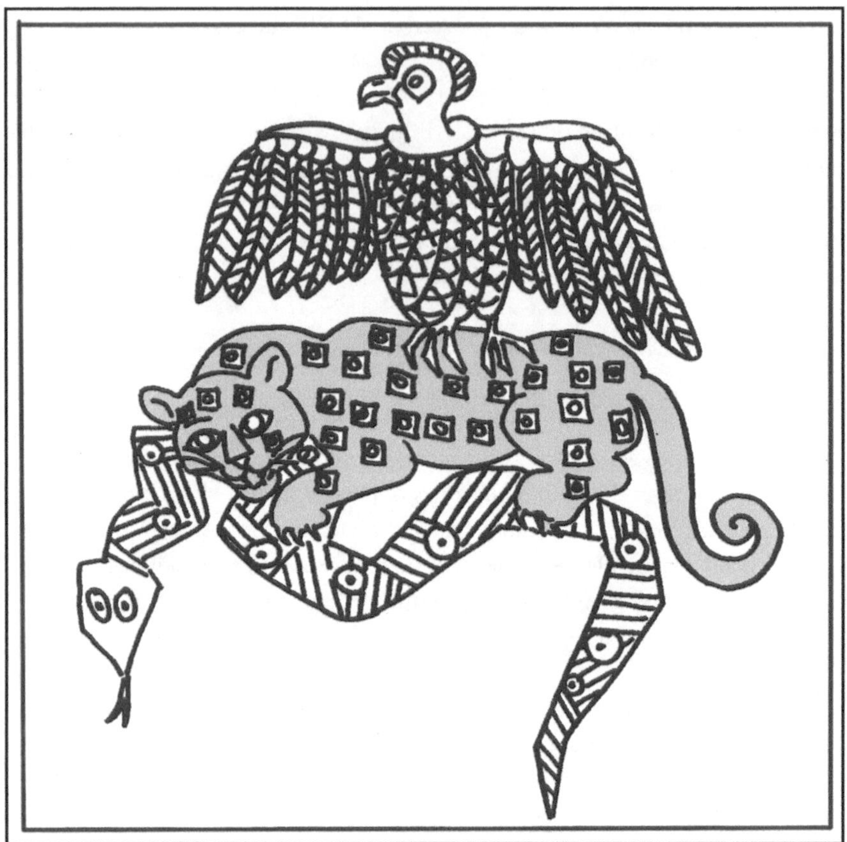

7.5 Detail from Huanta-style mate. The condor, jaguar or puma, and serpent are Andean versions of animal divinities found in Indigenous religions throughout the Americas. Drawing by the author after mate in her collection.

simply put their own bold designs on top of the relatively faint acid production. They hope that the acid designs will not show through too much. (CIAP n.d. provides more detail on production techniques.)

Meaning in Carved Gourds

Mate designs have meaning that may be historical, cultural, and/or spiritual. The forms and uses of utilitarian decorated gourds take roles in their meaning, or artists can make mates with purely commercial forms and motifs. Mates serve as community and individual histories and diaries, and they may function to strengthen religious belief and a sense of the sacred.

The carved and embellished mates often serve practical purposes similar to plainer dried gourds. They are most often used for serving, eating, and storing food. The decorated gourds provide makers and users with a visual account of villagers' daily life in the rural context as well. These gourds feature scenes of domestic and agricultural activity such as weaving and spinning, plowing with a yoke of oxen, herding animals to pasture, going to market, harvesting potatoes, and similar activities. Mates also might show scenes unique to a particular person's life such as a trip to the jungle or the capital city or a temporary job with a mining company. Some mates show unusual events such as a plane crash or a famous visitor to the town. These mates constitute family histories and community records. They visually celebrate a people and a way of life.

The tendency of mates to display celebrations traditional to Andean communities makes many of them religious objects as well as graphic documents because most celebrations tend to be basically religious in nature, though they also have profane elements in them. Religious aspects of celebrations show syncretism between Andean sacred tradition and that of Christianity. Gourds depicting town patron saint festivities show holy processions and the village church alongside bullfights, feasts, and dances. Births of babies conflate visually with Bethlehem scenes carved beside them. Angels fly with condors. The Andean sun and moon overarch figures of saints and virgins. Thus spiritual concepts in mates reflect the muddy complexity of human nature and the mixed ethnic and religious past shared by Andean communities.

Meanings and uses for mates have changed and evolved over time. Like biological species, gourd decoration traditions in some areas have gone extinct only to rise up in other geographic regions. As mates are plant fruits, the material preservation as well as artistic promotion of decorated gourds is particularly important if the art form is to survive. From precolonial times to the present, carved gourds have served different purposes: utilitarian, religious, ceremonial, and purely decorative. Gourds are fragile, and during the Indigenous and colonial periods and on into the present they have coexisted with pottery and metal and recently with plastics as well. Pottery and metal have much greater strength than mates, which is why archeologists observe pottery items replacing gourds once pottery is invented. In contemporary times plastics supplant even pottery and to some extent metals because of their light weight and ability to withstand abuse without breakage. For these reasons, it may be the decorative qualities of carved mates that have made them appealing over hundreds of years despite the competition of similar products made in more resistant materials. However, there seems always to have been a population so poor that gourds, which they could grow themselves, proved more economical than purchasing pots, metal, or plastic items in the market. This population still exists.

Mates evolved over time and changed according to the demands of each new set of circumstances. The sparse literature on materos and their work in the colonial era and early twentieth century concentrates on mate production in Huamanga or Ayacucho primarily and Huancayo secondarily (Arguedas 1958, Jiménez Borja 1941, Sabogal Diéguez 1945, Stastny 1981). Evidently during colonial times and periods up until the mid-twentieth century, a small number of skilled artists could make almost a full-time living by producing mates. Thus materos who made fine art–quality decorated gourds could maintain permanent houses in Huamanga. During the 1950s an enormous change took place. Mate makers in Huamanga and its surroundings began to migrate to Lima and in the process taught other artists their techniques. These newly taught materos settled in Cochas Grande and Cochas Chico in Junín, where they have close proximity to the large Sunday crafts market in the town of Huancayo. The two groups of materos, in Lima and Cochas, now produce all the styles once considered characteristic of particular subregions.

To use biological terms, Ayacucho-style mates became "extinct" in their place of origin but sprang to new life in Cochas and Lima with the addition of fortifying "genes" added in their new production centers that gave them enough "hybrid vigor" to flourish once more. Folk arts experts decry the extinction of the Ayacucho style in its place of origin. However, more important is the way mates represent an entire genre of folk production that may disappear altogether even in Cochas and Lima along with other traditions such as *hojalatería*, or tinworking (chapter 11). Carved mates in the twenty-first century have market value purely as decorative items and are by nature ephemeral. Mates are dried vegetables, and without very specialized production and care they succumb to insects and naturally disintegrate with time. Besides their physical fragility, mates have few local admiring audiences. Aside from the artists themselves and their own communities, few potential local buyers know or care enough about Andean rural life to appreciate mates. Indigenous people and their lifeways are objects of discrimination and derision on the part of their wealthier and ethnically different "betters" in Peruvian society. In the Huancayo markets materos and mate wholesalers sell directly to tourists and to other wholesalers bound for Lima and international destinations. There is numerically a very limited fine arts market in Huancayo, Lima, and internationally. Faced with this reality, wholesalers prefer to buy large quantities of quickly and poorly made items for urban tourist sales. Tourists often do not discriminate between crudely produced and finely made work because they have little background knowledge. They want items that represent the "exotic" locale they are visiting and small enough to pack into suitcases. One artisan lamented that the exporters take advantage of this situation, and as a result many artists have fallen into the trap of making things of not very high quality to meet such demands (note 1).

1. The information in these paragraphs is based on interviews with mate makers by Antonio Vasquez, an art development worker. The interviews took place in 2004 in Cochas and were shared with the author.

Some jobbers and wholesalers have learned that signed art has a kind of fine arts cachet and so force artisans to produce unsigned work. The wholesaler then signs his or her own name and becomes an instant celebrity. Several high-quality mate makers give in to this corrupt scheme in order to survive. One artist commented that if she signs her work the wholesalers will not buy from her. They have her trapped in this way because she cannot leave her home and family for long periods to sell the work herself (note 1).

Fine arts materos and even those who make work of fair to middling quality feel frustration with a new global reality that favors more quantity in less time for lower prices. These requirements for vast numbers of goods made at lightning speed and sold for practically nothing benefits grand-scale business enterprises and undermine creative work of quality simultaneously. A fine arts matero can spend several weeks working five or six hours per day on one masterpiece. The artist often takes care of a family and maintains a small farm that provides a basic living for the domestic unit. For this reason, those artists who do good work cannot produce mates in great quantity (note 1).

Materos correctly see the eventual doom of well-made work that gives them pride as creators, sustains the value of Andean culture, and supplements their family incomes. If decorated mates cease to exist, so will pride and knowledge about everything that has meaning for Andean people.

External help is greatly needed, especially for artists of forms like mates that are in danger of disappearing.

Mate Artists and Their Work

To give some idea of mates and what they are like, the following descriptions serve as concrete examples.

Huancayo-Style Azucareco

Purchased at the Sunday market in Huancayo in the late 1960s, this mate by an unknown artist is a round azucarero with a lid. It is approximately five inches tall and five inches in diameter and of medium quality. Its colors are primarily two: the white of the background (the pulp under the outer skin) and the natural tan skin color of the gourd in the foreground. Some foreground areas have been burned slightly to achieve a golden brown, and aniline dyes in red, green, and purple have been added to some figures. The design follows the Indigenous design grid in that the carver made a series of latitudinal lines circling the fruit at different vertical distances from one another. The top three registers have geometric forms and patterns. The bottom three registers are simple circles. These top and bottom registers are relatively narrow. One wide central register features figures and a two-story Andean home. Marching on either side of the home are men and women in Indigenous dress carrying burdens on their backs. Llamas, also with packs on their backs, parade between the human figures. In the background are two smaller human figures, a man and woman, who are bent over as if working in a field and carry perhaps a harvested crop in their hands. The artist carved vegetation in the form of large leaves and flowers into the background as well.

Ayacucho-Style Bowl

The second mate is a bowl about 7 1/2" in diameter and about 2 1/2" deep made in the Ayacucho style. it was purchased in the 1960s at a folk art fair, one of the very first to take place in recognition of Indigenous art traditions, in Lima. The work on the bowl is finer than that of the sugar bowl described above.

The piece has two colors only, the black background typical of Ayacucho ware and a burnished red-brown foreground. The bowl's overall design plan is essentially Indigenous. This design scheme is atypical of Ayacucho mates, which are traditionally based on colonial curves and rondelles. Here one sees the mixing of styles that had begun to take place in the 1950s. The design is divided into three wide registers and a parade of figures in all three parades proceeding from left to right within each section. The top register shows a parade of llamas with an Indigenous man bringing up the rear in a striped poncho. Leading the parade is a dog followed by a woman in a fedora, a wide skirt (*pollera*), and a shawl (*lliclla*) over her back. In the background are hints of vegetation, maguey leaves at the top and slightly arabesque leaves and flowers. At the bottom the man bringing up the rear waves a herding lasso, and his mouth is open as if calling and whistling to keep the llamas on the move.

The middle section is the widest and shows a line of musicians playing traditional instruments. At the end is an Andean harp player, before him a violinist, in front of him a saxophone player, then a clarinet player. All of these musicians are men, and they wear striped ponchos and fedoras. In front of the clarinet player walks an elaborately attired woman dancer. She is wearing several shawls, the outer one with shoulder patches and fringe. Her several flounced and patterned skirts (*polleras*) are layered one atop the other. She waves a handkerchief, which is an important prop for dancers when performing the *marinera* and some huaynos (traditional folk dance styles). The first person in the parade is a man who carries a staff, or *vara*, and wears a suit jacket rather than a poncho. Diagonally across his chest is a sash decorated with figures. He is the *alferez*, the sponsor or man in charge of a community festival. The woman following him may be his wife. This parade represents an important community festival. The background consists of a few leaf designs plus a cactus carved in the space in front of the alferez. The bottom register is the second largest and shows a train with a steam engine, such as are still in use today. Only the engineer shows though the window of the engine; all other windows are blank. The background consists of smoke from the engine, hills, and suggestions of vegetation. The introduction of the register depicting the train shows how mates evolve over time. They include new technologies, historical events, and similar imagery that changes as time passes.

Pear-Shaped Mate without Lid, Ayacucho Style

This is a very small gourd, 2 1/2 inches high, made and signed by Elena in Cochas Chico, twenty-first century. The bottom of the gourd, the widest part, is only about 1 3/4 inches in diameter. The mate has two colors, natural golden tan foreground and black background. It is a very fine, highly detailed piece of artwork.

The basic design divisions are an upper area (small end of pear shape) delineated by a curvilinear zigzag with two rondelles, conforming to the Spanish colonial style of a curvilinear, diagonal, rondelle design grid. There is a flower shape at the top. The bottom area below the curved zigzag has scenes separated by angled zigzag lines and a simple bottom consisting of two lined registers. The overall visual effect recalls Spanish colonial period pieces. Multiple figures and grounds in every square inch of the main design areas fill to bursting with miniscule but well-executed details in the Baroque horror vacui tradition. The top area above the zigzags encloses the sun in one rondelle and the moon and stars in the other, recalling Andean worship of these astral bodies. A large condor perches atop a jaguar or puma that in turn grasps a large serpent. These Andean divinities show their superior religious importance, in the artist's perspective, by occupying higher sections in the design scheme, toward the top of the fruit. Another large figure has what appears to be a doorway with two ladder shapes on either side, each with three rungs at this same high level. Two llamas recline between the ladders. The ladder shapes may represent the three Andean cosmic worlds, and the llamas pose as stand-ins for human beings, as they do in Indigenous theology. Archeologists have found representations like this design, called ushnu, in excavations. They say the ladder or series of three steps represents doorways between the cosmological levels (Hoopes 2009, Yaeger 2004:17).

Other figures in the top area include drums, flutes, and the Andean harp all nestled in elaborate twisting and curling representations of background foliage consisting of leaves and flowers. The area below the zigzag encloses several large, complicated scenes "read" by rotating the gourd. First, there is a church with a cross and a bell tower. In front of this is a religious procession and onlookers. In the foreground are an ice cream cart labeled *helados* and intricately represented vegetation including maguey and penca cactus and cantuta flowers. To the right of the church as the gourd rotates are village buildings, a bullfight, and scenes of dancing, drinking, and general merriment. This is a village festival.

A thin, vertical, jagged line serves as a scene break, and the new vignette is one of grazing llamas feasting on tree leaves alongside a field hut, a bird, and people working in a field. To the right a scene break forms a mountain shape upon which llamas or alpacas graze. The scene to the right of this shows field huts, people working in fields, llama grazing, and fish being trapped. In the next scene people plow with a yoke of oxen and llamas and people go to market. Succeeding these images is another mountain with grazing llamas and the church scene again.

This small mate shows different aspects of typical agricultural village life with mixed religious influences. On the surface the decorations are of the pleasing costumbrista type. Only Andeans and well-trained outsiders, however, can read the meanings in the purely Indigenous religious referents. In this way, the art work demonstrates dual subjectivity. The placement of Andean religious symbols near the top area of the gourd expresses the phenomenon of inversion. The artist here indicates plainly her preference for Indigenous religious references over those introduced by outsiders, since she places these at lower latitudes in her design scheme.

Small, Round Mate

The last example, also of Ayacucho style, is a small, round gourd about 3 inches in diameter and about 2 1/2 inches high, probably made by Elena because it shows her unique style and fine workmanship, but it is not signed by her. The top of the gourd is divided into a round register and has figures almost equal to those in the previous example. Then there is a series of zigzags and narrow registers filled with geometric shapes and botanical arabesques.

A wide parallel register runs around the width of the gourd and is divided into square panels. At the top of each panel a short text explains the scene below it. It is the story of the romance, engagement, and eventual marriage of a young couple. They meet in a field where the girl tends sheep and go through the formalities of announcing their intentions to both sets of parents. Things are not right, however, until they are married in church, getting God's approval. The bride in this scene wears a Western bridal outfit. In the end, the happy couple moves to their own home, where they are pictured at a meal with their two children. Their small corral of animals and storage houses figure in the background.

This tiny gourd's romantic story masks a demonstration of dual subjectivity and inversion. Andean courting customs are such that a young couple traditionally decides to marry even after sexual intimacy and having children. They then may inform the two sets of parents that they plan to marry. The church wedding, a colonial introduction, is a kind of ex post facto nod to the reigning religious stricture. Similarly, Western dress for this event is an acknowledgement of international and urban society. Like the previous example, there is more to this work of art than what first appears on the surface. The Andean symbols at the top of the gourd correspond to the upper world of the cosmos and indicate superior importance. Thus the artist shows that what takes place in the middle narrative portion of the gourd is secondary since it corresponds to the World of Here. The gourd is a globe-shaped model, then, of the Andean cosmos with the understood spatially based valuations and interpretations thus implied.

Change and Innovation

The contemporary mates described in some detail above illustrate the great value of these small objects as cultural documents that not only preserve tradition but also strengthen it for succeeding generations. The gourds serve as repositories of culturally mixed design elements and imagery styles while still allowing for individual creativity and innovation. Carved gourds, first, have high value as cultural and historical documents. They contain information about the natural environment, traditional customs, and religion and include written texts. Second, the design and style of the imagery itself illustrate important thought processes.

Mates document traditional life and contemporary change visually and verbally. Examples in the following paragraphs show how mates perform this role within four categories of information: the environment, traditional customs, texts, and religious beliefs.

Environmental scenes on mates show characteristic Andean physical features, plants, animals, and architecture. Plants, particularly of the cactus family like maguey and penca and cactus fruits and flowers, abound in dry highland scenes. The sacred cantuta flower appears often. Palm fronds grace subtropical scenes at lower altitudes. Ichu grass, so important as food to herd animals, also finds its place. Trees form background patterns for many scenes. Llamas, alpacas, sheep, dogs, donkeys, horses, and cattle, especially bulls, figure strongly in mate scenes. These are animals that live with farmers. Sometimes materos depict chickens, ducks, turkeys, cats, and guinea pigs as well. Wild creatures like fish, birds, foxes, wolves, and pumas make appearances. Many of these have religious significance and appear associated with sacred imagery. Mountains, rivers, waterfalls, hills, valleys, clouds, farmers' fields, and other grand-scale physical features form a backdrop for village homes, storehouses, churches, field huts, corrals, cobblestone streets, and similar features of the Andean manmade environment.

Mates show Andean Indigenous people going about their daily lives of agricultural and craft work, rest, play, and family life. Scenes of plowing, harvesting, winnowing, herding, weaving, pot making, cooking, and the like show these activities' accompanying tool kits in great detail. Human figures wear traditional clothing: men have ponchos, fedoras, and sandals, and women wear pollera skirts, lliclla shawls, fedoras, and sandals and sport braided hair. These items of clothing symbolize Indigenous culture. Materos carve the trajectory of people's lives marked by important rites of passage: birth, marriage, children, and death. Celebrations with their sacred processions and church rites counterbalance the dancing, eating, drinking, courting, and excesses characteristic of parties the world over. The mate carver achieves a balance between the two aspects of village celebrations with understanding and humor.

Texts generally appear in simplified Spanish that employs Quechua sentence structure and partial vocabulary. Many people speak this combined language, sometimes called Quechuañol, with a greater or lesser degree of skill. Women usually have less command of Spanish than men. Quechua, originally a spoken language only, was written down using Spanish orthography by early European missionaries. However, written Quechua belongs to the world of scholars. For Andeans, it is usually an oral language, and Spanish is used in writing. The combination of text with images on mates dating from the colonial period and after is unusual in the arts of the Andes. Text and imagery act in tandem to illuminate meaning. This allows students of Andean belief systems to learn more from mates than from some Indigenous art forms without text.

Many mates document the syncretic nature of Andean religious beliefs by placing Inca divinities and sacred symbols in juxtaposition with Christian ones. Some artists, like Elena, place the two sets of religious imagery in different registers, with the sun, moon, stars, condors, pumas or jaguars, and snakes in upper registers and churches, crosses, processions, and church marriage ceremonies with priests in middle registers. Certain symbols permeate Indigenous and European belief systems. The cantuta, for example, serves as colorful foliage in front of a church, but it is also an Andean sacred flower. Llamas inhabit the doorways to Andean sacred mountains as spiritual stand-ins for human beings, but they also graze in farmers' pastures and carry goods for sale to the market in their role as domestic animals. Bullfights form part of community celebrations, and the artist makes bullring scenes as large as church scenes, attesting to their mystic importance. Bullfights with condors on the bulls' shoulders are common images. The tale of the young couple's engagement attests to the way youth may practice the Andean tradition of trial marriage but in the end must have the Christian blessing of the marriage ceremony as well in order to live happily ever after in a combined cultural world. This story of romance illustrates graphically the position of Christian belief that coexists with Indigenous spirituality. The two religions converge, for example in Elena's design band devoted to the World of Here, and yet the purely Indigenous occupants of the Above world inhabit a superior space.

Mates likewise can illustrate the continuation of some Indigenous design strategies into the present. The idea of registers and parading figures, common in the Huancayo region previous to 1950, still is seen in contemporary mates. The Spanish Baroque horror vacui, arabesques, attention to miniscule detail, and the curve, diagonal, and spiral also abound. In fact, both those traditions can be exhibited often in the same carved gourd. It is not only Huancayo and Ayacucho coloring and finishing techniques that contemporary Cochas and Lima materos have combined but also overall approaches to design. Images show the stiffness and inclination toward simplification and abstraction attributed to Indigenous visual tradition. In part this is due to the requirements of a low-relief sculptural medium. Some artists, however, achieve rounded and curved shapes despite the medium's limitation and even today make mates rivaling those produced during the colonial era in this style. There is a tendency on the part of art critics to value colonial-style mates over primarily Indigenous styles. Contemporary Andean artists' skilled use of combined styles makes this valuation increasingly hard to discern.

The mixing of these styles as well as of regional production techniques has left the door wide open to innovators. Today's materos combine elements from the past with injections of more recent ideas. New technologies, world events, and mass communication are depicted on mates in heretofore unseen images such as space satellites and cell phones. Artists imbibe design principles from televised advertising, films, and print publications. These new ideas fold into the old ones to that the past interweaves tranquilly into the present and the future. Mates, in their fragile vulnerability, are like small pocket libraries of paperback books that contain and reinforce a wealth of cultural information. In a certain way, carved gourds illustrate the realities of contemporary rural life better than other art forms. This is because many materos are still farmers as well, another reason the transitory medium deserves special care and conservation.

Dried gourds, or calabashes, are a renewable resource that has provided economical dishware to people in the Andes since prehistoric times. They are light in weight and relatively resilient, and they hold liquid and dry ingredients well. They can be capped, stoppered, or lidded for travel. Though gourds are highly practical and useful, their delicate charm and great value lie as well in their decorations. These almost throw-away little cups and dishes wear a people's history on their outer skins. As such, mates are treasures to be kept and appreciated.

CHAPTER 8
Ceramics (Cerámica)

Ceramic arts are a complex tradition in the Andes. For this reason, the chapter concentrates on one type of object, a jar in the shape of an animal; this evolved over time and developed regional variations. Inca and pre-Inca civilizations are famous for the great quality and variety of ceramic ware that they created. All aspects of human life and the natural world found shape in ceramic form. This chapter focuses on a particular type of figure that may have been started as a stone libation vessel in Indigenous times and transformed into a ceramic house-guardian figure during the Spanish colonial period. Its form changed from that of a llama or alpaca to a bull or horse that in contemporary times can morph into an airplane, train, or other technological wonder while retaining meanings embodied in previous forms. The surface decorations, which symbolize divine powers in nature, and some elements of the objects' general shape are small in scale. Small size is a far from insignificant assertion of continuity in the Andean way of thought and life, even in the face of profound social and economic change. Smallness and subtlety are ways of hiding messages that might be otherwise disturbing to some audiences.

Ceramic making is a very old and highly respected art form in the Andes. Some of the pre-Inca cultures like the Moche, Nazca, and Huari developed impressive pottery traditions. Clayware can be either utilitarian, decorative, or both at the same time. This chapter presents only a few themes from this most complex and beautiful range of regional art traditions in clay.

History and Use

The ceramic tradition in the Andean region spans thousands of years. The following sections about work in this material through the ages give a brief idea of how the craft developed during pre-Colombian history. The work of Michael Moseley (1992), Richard Burger (1992), and Craig Morris and Adriana Von Hagen (1993) are helpful background sources for detailed information about prehistoric periods.

Several pre-Inca civilizations developed in different regions of Peru whose work in ceramics stands out. The Incas copied some of what they saw as their empire expanded and engulfed other civilizations. The technical and esthetic quality of Andean ceramics rivaled that of their own fine weaving tradition. Impressive ceramic styles later introduced by the Spanish added to the high quality of Andean clayware. Before the invention of ceramics, Andeans made utilitarian, religious, and decorative items using stone, gourds, and basketry, among other materials. Later ceramic versions of these creations often bear the stamp of their pre-ceramic forbears in form or decoration. The earliest ceramics came into being between 2,000 and 1,000 BCE in most subregions.

The Chavín people produced a ceramics repertoire the forms of which mirrored those of their masterful stone carvings. Some of this stone art still adorns the remains of their capital city, Chavín de Huantar in the northern Andes. Chavín clayware exhibits patterns that would influence later cultural traditions; among these are the stirrup-spouted vessel form and the idea of making pottery in plant, animal, human, architectural, and other shapes. Chavín ceramics have an unmistakable stylistic character. Pottery makers skillfully blended angular and rounded shapes and applied designs to produce a kind of geometrized realism much like the Art Deco movement in twentieth-century Western art, as previously noted. This design style also marked their work in other media.

The Huari, who resided near what is now Huamanga, produced distinctive pottery of remarkable color and design as well as resilient high-fire production methods. The contemporary potters of Huamanga and the nearby town of Quinua are direct descendants of the Huari civilization. For this reason, they would like to learn Huari techniques for producing porcelain and complex glazing effects and are hoping that archeologists will discover what kinds of kilns, fuels, and pottery materials the Huari once used.

The Pucará culture near Lake Titicaca gives its name to the town of Pucará. This area was and still is a ceramics center today. Probably the most mysterious and intriguing ancient culture of this region, the Tiahanacu made pottery using distinct and ornate design devices that mimicked their stonework. The Tiahuanacu people created enormous stone towers covered with low-relief images made up of complex iconography. Design elements called "kennings" figured strongly in such depictions, and these appear in the pottery work of this and other Andean traditions.

Paracas ceramics are almost as distinctive as the masterful textiles made by that culture. The Nazca inherited much knowledge about clayware from their Paracas parent tradition. Nazca ceramics feature marine motifs, mirroring the coastal environment. The Nazca did make ceramic pieces in animal, human, and other sculptural forms, but they are better known for the illustrations they placed on the surfaces of their pots. Nazca two-dimensional painted designs on clayware have a unique beauty. The Nazca used an abstracted naturalism that recalls ancient Greek pottery painting but combined this with extremely vivid polychrome coloring. The Nazca were masters of brightly colored glazes. Rather than making pots with unique shapes, they used common forms as canvases upon which to paint their striking multicolored designs. Potters depicted animal divinities, plant forms, and human activities.

It was the art traditions of the North Coast cultures that perhaps influenced Inca work most. The Moche produced pots that depicted almost every aspect of Andean life—religion, household activities, agriculture, buildings, animals, and plants. The list of themes is almost infinite. Moche pots exhibit high skill in sculptural form. Colors tend to be those of the natural clays with some contrasting slips of earth tones.

In a way almost opposite the Nazca, Moche artists concentrated on the form of their pots rather than on surface decoration. Moche pottery is highly realistic, and the repertoire encompasses portraits of political leaders and representations of agricultural, ritual, craft activity, animals, plants, insects, topography, and more. For this reason Moche pottery constitutes a very valuable and encyclopedically detailed visual history of this cultural tradition.

The Sicán and Chimú traditions are Moche offspring in which pottery continues as a major art form. The Chimú's grand capital of Chan Chan is itself a wonder created from earth materials: clay and adobe were formed into complex patterns and shapes. The walls around Chan Chan and on its major buildings have clay geometric patterns of great variety sculptured in high relief.

The Inca vied with the Chimú for regional hegemony and eventually won exclusive control. One of their first state programs involved the importation of Chimú ceramicists to the Inca capital of Cuzco. The Incas created utilitarian clayware in standard shapes, though it was covered with their own distinctive geometric decoration. They did take on some Chimú and Nazca styles and forms as well as work based on models they found at Pachacamac, Tiahuanacu, and other ancient cultural centers for which they felt special admiration as their empire expanded.

Throughout the Indigenous period in Andean history certain common processes were taking place. One of these was a sharing and crossing over of design motifs of cultures and art materials. Cultures in particular regions passed designs and techniques through time to descendants but also across space by means of trade and religious pilgrimages facilitated by interregional empires like the Chavín, the Huari, and the Inca. There was also a crossing over of designs of arts made in different media. Many of the two-dimensional images and abstract figures found in textiles, for example, also appeared in ceramics. These blending processes from the deep Andean past still take place in contemporary times.

The coming of Europeans to the Andes introduced new ceramic tools, production materials, imagery, forms, and symbolic meanings to the region. The Spanish colonial art schools in important centers like Cuzco and Huamanga trained Indigenous and Mestizo artisans to produce pottery for European clients, just as they trained students in painting, textiles, carving, and other arts. One of the pottery techniques the Spanish introduced is majolica ware. A short history of majolica's origins and introduction into the Andes serves as an example of general processes that took place during the European colonial era.

In the tenth century, the caliph of Persia received a gift of two thousand pieces of porcelain from the emperor of China. Persian artisans could not determine how the Chinese produced these beautiful pieces, so they invented their own methods for creating facsimiles. Persian potters then exported their fine clayware over the entire North African area. Many of these artists themselves migrated to Morocco and then on to the Moorish-controlled Spain. The Spanish city of Talavera de la Reina became a major center of majolica production, and from there the style spread to Italy, where it was named *faenza*. The French called it *faience* when they learned the techniques. The craft then diffused to Holland, where the style was called *delft*, and to Germany, where its name was Dresden.

The name majolica may refer to the island of Mallorca or the city of Malaga, from which majolica was first exported to European countries outside Spain. Between 1550 and 1570 majolica arrived in Puebla, Mexico, and in the Andean region at about the same time.

The artisan forms majolica on a wheel or by using a mold. The pottery wheel did not exist in the Americas before the Europeans introduced it. After the potter shapes the clay, it is dried and fired once. This once-fired bisque ware cools and then gets a covering of a white glaze made of lead and tin oxide. Once this underglaze dries, the artist paints colored glazes on top of the white base coat and fires the piece again.

The artist can paint the decorations freehand using a brush or by making a stencil from parchment, poking the design with pin pricks, and fluffing charcoal through these to make guidelines for painting the design. Before firing, the colored glazes appear to be dull gray and blue. After firing, majolica pottery has brilliant coloring, oftentimes blue and white only but multicolored as well. The designs reflect the tradition's long intercontinental history through Asian, Islamic, and Mediterranean lands and into the Americas, where Indigenous admixtures further enriched it. The sixteenth- and seventeenth-century designs that appear on majolica ware made in Peru combine Islamic abstraction, Spanish religious imagery, and European and Asian flora and fauna with all the pre-Columbian ceramic styles that existed in the Andean region until that time. This global combination of influences in majolica ware received another dose from Asia particularly in the coastal Andean region as a result of Spain's trade networks with the Far East. Llamas and condors cavort with European deer and African lions, Islamic arabesques in plant form twine around the borders, and Chinese motifs surrounded with curly Central Asian clouds coexist in typical Andean combined pieces. Similar processes took place for objects made according to traditions that entered the Andean region along with majolica (Karmason with Stacke 2002, Lister 2003).

Stastny asserts (1981:99) that there is no art in which viewers perceive the best of Andean artistic creativity, technical skill, and sense of play as much as in pottery. However, he does point out as well that a colonial-era prejudice against "dirty" work reduced pottery making to a low-prestige occupation. For this reason, the art form has struggled through historical periods in which it was held in low esteem. Today, potters make utilitarian pieces for kitchen use, for example, that have very little decoration. Cups, plates, trays, baking dishes, and pots for plants still have wide use, though plastic ware competes with them. Items that are both utilitarian and decorative have a double clientele. Local householders and tourists alike are apt to buy them, for different reasons. The form and decorative design elements in this type of pottery exhibit colonial combinations of styles, mimic Indigenous techniques, and/or reflect individual creativity. Other items include hastily made reproductions of exotic forms the artist may have observed in the mass media as well as high-quality, innovative pieces. The same pottery workshop can have all of these types of work on its sale shelves, perhaps a majolica figurine of a saint or a Pucará bull, a *canopa* (jar) in llama form, a figure of Elvis Presley, and a large fine art representation of a huamani or devil inhabiting the local apu. The workshop shelves may also display pottery musical instruments, angels in Andean dress, flowerpots, movie stars, characters from folktales, a menagerie of animals, and local, foreign, mythical, and comical groups of characters. Groups of gossipy women (Las Chismosas) or tipsy chicha-drinking men (Los Borrachos) represent stock pieces for sale to the urban and tourist trade.

How Pottery Is Made

The most important raw material is clay. Pottery centers like Quinua near Huamanga and Pucará near Puno generally have substantial clay deposits nearby. Much of Peru has characteristic red clay. An artist first combines calcium-containing materials, sand, and baked pottery shards with the clay. The jungle-dwelling Shipibo believe that the ash of the apacharama tree gives the clay greater resistance in the firing process. There are similar local beliefs in other areas that change the recipe for the basic clay mixture from region to region. The potter removes impurities from the clay and adds water. Then, with the clay now formed into small blocks, it dries on shallow, recessed beds made of red bricks and sometimes topped with plastic coverings. This process allows the wet mixture to dry slightly and become pliable. Then the potter removes air bubbles either by hand or by using a simple tool.

Modeling is the next step. Forming a long cylinder or "snake" of clay is the most ancient technique. Pre-Columbian potters made all their work this way and turned their pots by sliding two clay disks mounted one on top of the other onto a stone platform. Another technique used in some regions, especially in northern Peru, entails forming pots by beating the clay with flat wooden sticks. First the artist makes the basic form with clay cylinders. Then she places a smooth stone on the inside of the piece while beating the outside with the flat stick until she produces the desired form.

For figures, the artist takes prepared clay and models by hand, sometimes using an interior armature for structural support. The artist uses fingers and wooden tools for this work. Molds work well for utilitarian items. She makes these of plaster. One kind of mold allows the potter to press clay into it. Another kind is closed but for a hole through which the potter pours liquid clay. The clay for use in poured molds has high water content. The artist pours the liquid through an opening at the top of the mold and lets a thin coating dry inside. Later, she pours successive thin layers until the piece inside the mold has walls of the desired thickness. The artist separates the clay piece from the two halves of the mold once the poured liquid inside has dried sufficiently. Artists use the wheel for making round pieces. Throughout the Andes they use the wheel, though in places like Rachi near Cuzco potters still use the pre-Columbian method of disks and stone platform for turning their pieces.

When the pieces become partially dry, the artist goes over them with a sponge or smoothing tool to remove imperfections. For decorative figures, artists add incised details and designs at this time. The pieces then dry completely and go through one or more firings. The artists dip the pieces in glazes or paint them on during this firing process. The best work has single-fired or multiple-fired glazes. Some modern potters fall into the lazy habit of applying designs with enamels or other paints after all firing and cooling to save trouble and time.

Many ceramists still use the old-style Indigenous kiln made of movable stones or bricks and wood fuel. Artisans recommend particular woods to achieve desired effects. Some workshops have pooled resources and now use gas-powered kilns to elicit more predictable outcomes. Much work results from firing at low temperatures, and so it is brittle and less desirable. For this reason, Huamanga and Quinua artists of today have great curiosity about rediscovering the ancient techniques of the Huari, from whom they trace their own ancestry. The Huari produced excellent, resilient pottery. This was somehow fired at high temperatures without, of course, the aid of such work-saving devices as gas kilns and modern commercial glazes. Huari surface designs resemble the woven tapestries of that culture, with their bright, jewel-like colors in rich patterns. Figures in Huari ware often represent divinities in shapes and forms uniquely theirs.

Meaning in Ceramics

A pottery piece can be purely decorative, completely for ritual use, exclusively for adornment, or totally utilitarian. However, most pottery pieces serve more than one purpose.

The tradition of making useful objects that also had cultural and spiritual meaning probably reached its high point in Moche and Nazca pottery. A clay bottle for holding liquid might have the form of a pile of potatoes, an owl as a symbol of impending doom, an ear of corn, or a domestic or agricultural scene complete with buildings and animal and human figurines. If this pot had a double spout and a particular structure, it would whistle when liquid was poured out. European clayware also had a multivalent purpose. When the two traditions were combined, the idea of multiple yet simultaneous uses was expressed in a strong and continuing manner. Stastny presents a photograph (1981:115) of a combined pot, showing six small jars joined into one, each having a llama head. This pot, a contemporary work, represents the spirit being called a *jarjacho*, or llama with six heads, the form taken by people after death who have committed the great sin of incest. Jarjachos, needless to say, are very evil spirits. This jar, though it has such shocking symbolic import, also serves as a container for a variety of foods or condiments that can be served all at the same time.

The chronological trajectory of another jar or container figure, this one with the external form of a series of mystical animals, can be traced over time, culminating in some of today's technological wonders. A visitor to Huamanga, and especially to Quinua, a nearby town known for its ceramics, immediately sees a number of small clay figures perched on the main spines of house roofs. Some are animal forms—alpacas, llamas, bulls, and horses. Some are statuettes of churches. The animal shapes, on closer inspection, prove to be hollow with openings in their backs. Both churches and animals have similar sculptured and glazed decorations in the forms of flowers, spirals, scallops, and zigzags. Pottery workshops may have all these forms on their shelves for sale, plus ceramic buses, airplanes, trains, and other modern accoutrements painted with the same designs. The roof figures serve as guardians against evil forces, protecting the home and the family within it. These were placed on the roof for spiritual defense when the house was built (chapter 9). The *iglesias de Quinua* (Quinua churches) are emblematic of the town and its famed ceramics artists. Yet there are just as many camellid and taurine jars sitting on the roofs, plus a few horses. Sometimes filigree metal crosses overlaid with symbols of Christ's crucifixion stand between pairs of flanking ceramic figures.

Ceramics, like weaving, is an ancient and regionally complex art in the Andes. The bull-shaped house guardian is an example of how ceramic forms have evolved from pre-Columbian times, when the figures were originally stone and then ceramic camellids, to the present. The church figures have a less obvious connection to pre-Columbian forms. The bulls are called *toros de Pucará*, (bulls of Pucará) after the town near Puno most famous for producing them. Today, artists make them and they grace the house roofs of many other Andean towns as well, including Huamanga and Quinua.

The piece as it is made today consists of a squat and rounded clay figure of a bull with a hole in its back. The hole makes the figure a hollow jar, and it serves as a drinking vessel on some occasions such as wedding celebrations as well as a container for burning offerings during rituals. Europeans introduced cattle to the Andean region. Before the colonial period, llamas and alpacas were the only large animals domesticated by Indigenous Andeans. The native llamas and alpacas from pre-Columbian times that archeologists have found may be the symbolic ancestors of the bull of Pucará. An animal figure with a hole in its back and at times a hollow interior is an *ulti* (sacred object or container) or *canopa* (probably related to *canope* in Spanish and "canopic jar" in English, both of which refer to cups found in tombs of ancient Egyptians to hold the viscera of mummies). Ultis are figures made of stone, and if they are special—regurgitated by llamas or struck by lightning—they are lightly carved and called *illa*. Canopas can be of stone but also of wood or ceramic. Canopas or ultis and illas are objects with sacred potentialities. The bull of Pucará is a kind of canopa or ulti. Its oldest ancestor was probably a llama or alpaca made of stone and used during pre-Inca times.

Stone alpacas and llamas, usually carved in abstract style, had holes carved in their backs to hold spiritual offerings. Religious practitioners placed mixtures of animal fat and blood in these openings as offerings to spiritual powers. Canopas planted in pastures assured the fertility of herd animals. Archeologists have found such stone vessels that contain ashes. These finds indicate that faithful worshippers burned llama fat and blood or other mixtures (including coca leaves, for example) as an aspect of worship. The llama or alpaca form expresses the great importance of these aboriginal animals as suppliers of wool, meat, and labor, in ritual as sacrificial victims, and as spiritual intermediaries between humans and divine powers.

Animals, plants, and other natural elements both contain and express spiritual power in the Andean religion. This power, by itself, can be negative or positive. Human ritual intervention can enhance beneficent aspects of these forces. The llama is an autochthonous animal, very important in Inca life and religion. Representations of llamas over time in Inca ethnohistory serve as examples here. Llamas, as discussed earlier, are symbolically

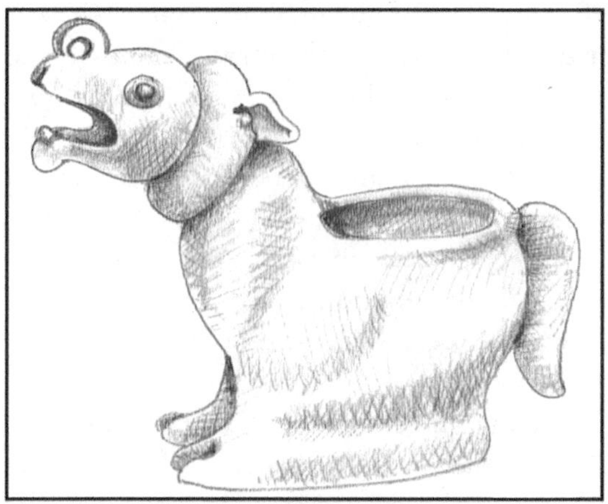

8.1 Llama ceramic canopa, Tiahuanacu style. Drawing by the author after photograph in Morris and Von Hagen 1993:107, figure 97.

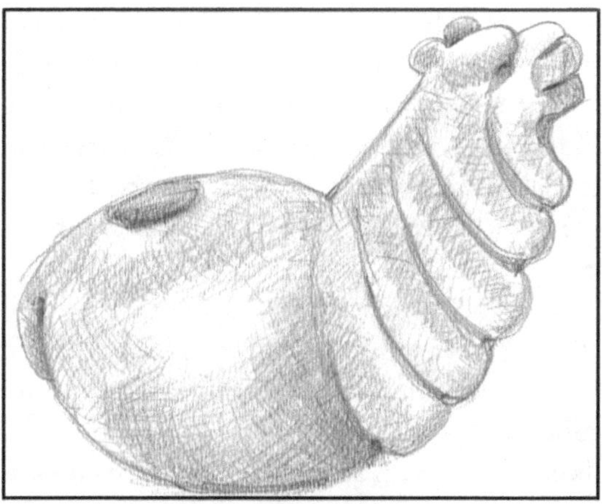

8.2 Alpaca stone canopa, Inca and modern style. Drawing by the author after photograph in Morris and Von Hagen 1993:172, figure 160.

coterminous with human beings. They talk to people in Inca myth. Llama babies are like human babies, and mothers of both species have pain giving birth to them. Llamas are sacrificed in place of people. Folk dances and dance-dramas feature people galloping about like llamas, complete with pelts and bells, or walking like llama herders. Llamas, two of them, form part of Peru's national crest.

Sometimes canopas or illas carved in llama shape could be sacrificed in convenient replacement for the actual animal. Some canopas have a large hollow, indicating their use as libation vessels. These would serve as receptacles for chicha (aja, aha) or other drinks taken by the faithful during rituals.

With the coming of the first Europeans and particularly as a result of strong influence from early missionaries, religious traditions of the two continents began to blend. Religious stories that fired the imaginations of Andean visual artists provided fertile ground for the symbolic mixing process. The universal flood story is a worldwide phenomenon in human mythology. The Andean version described previously features a talking llama who warns its herder of a coming inundation. After a shabby response (the herder throws a corncob at the llama), the herder is finally convinced to seek safety with his family and a collection of animals at the pinnacle of a high mountain until the waters subside. Parallels with the Bible story of Noah's ark did not escape the notice of Christian missionaries. They employed this myth in a conscious promotion of the syncretic process as a means of conversion. Less-educated clerics and settlers brought ancient and medieval Mediterranean notions of sea monsters and other forces associated with the sea, water, floods, and a primal state of cosmic chaos. The Inca flood story, the Bible flood story, and the medieval Mediterranean ideas about bodies of water, animals, and people all became mixed in the minds of Andeans during the early colonial era. Artists expressed these mixtures of ideas in their creative work.

As the colonial system became more established, Europeans imported their own domestic animals. Cattle, sheep, horses, goats, and chickens came to the Andes and in some places supplanted local animals. The powerful and mysterious ancient Mediterranean bull replaced the llama to some degree in Andean art. The bull embodied many of the same qualities as the llama. Incas and their predecessor civilizations had combined llamas, birds, serpents, and pumas mythically in their overlapping powers. For this reason, several animals could be combined into the same composite image or serve as mutual stand-ins for similar activities. Now the figure of the bull joined this cast of constantly morphing creatures. The contemporary and colonial folk form known as the bull of Pucará is an example. This is a ceramic jar in a bull shape that serves as a house guardian. They are usually mounted on rooftops (not only in Quinua, as described before, but in many other Andean towns) and are symbolically interchangeable with pottery llama figures and clay churches. Many of these ceramic figures bear the ochre fertility symbols once placed on living llamas and later bulls at designated times during the yearly agricultural and ritual cycle.

José Sabogal Diéguez (1949: 21) recounts that patron-saint festivities in Andean towns involve dedicating young bulls (*novillos*) to the saint. The bulls receive Christian names usually given only to human beings as well as a kind of baptism complete with godparents. The stance, form, and decoration of the bull of Pucará ceramic figure overlaps directly with the llama-shaped forms of previous eras. The clay taurine figure comes in various sizes and depicts a small, brave bull standing at attention. A hole in the bull's back indicates the figure's use as a jar. The figure's color most often is natural terra cotta with brown, white, and green curved lines and spirals glazed on it. Applied ceramic flowers appear on its shoulders and flanks. Decorative ridges and curls are applied to the neck and head. The body is thick and strong with an arched neck. The head is held high and proud. Many colonial bulls were of majolica style, some finished in shiny green or gold-colored glaze. These also had longer legs and lighter bodies than contemporary figures. All Pucará bulls have a rigid stance, the tongue extended over the nose and the tail curled across the rump. Sabogal Diéguez explains the figure's design as based on a fall agricultural ceremony (1949:12).

The ceremony takes place on May 3, Day of the Cross. Every neighborhood (ayllu) or village chooses a bull, ties its feet, and places it on top of a poncho. They paint the animal with drawings in zigzag, straight, wavy, and spiral forms using red ochre. The participants place ashes in small cuts above the bull's eye, nose, and soft part of the chest. The ritualists then throw blood from the cuts in the four sacred cardinal points in honor of Pachamama. Finally, the bull receives a little alcohol on the nose and ground hot pepper under the tail. Participants then set the animal free to run and jump (in response to the alcohol and pepper). The bull thus initiates a dance in which the people form lines in the same shapes as the red markings on the bull's body, which represent water, lightning, and other vital natural elements and forces. Thirty years later (1978), Joseph Bastien described his personal observation of a similar ritual in which a llama was

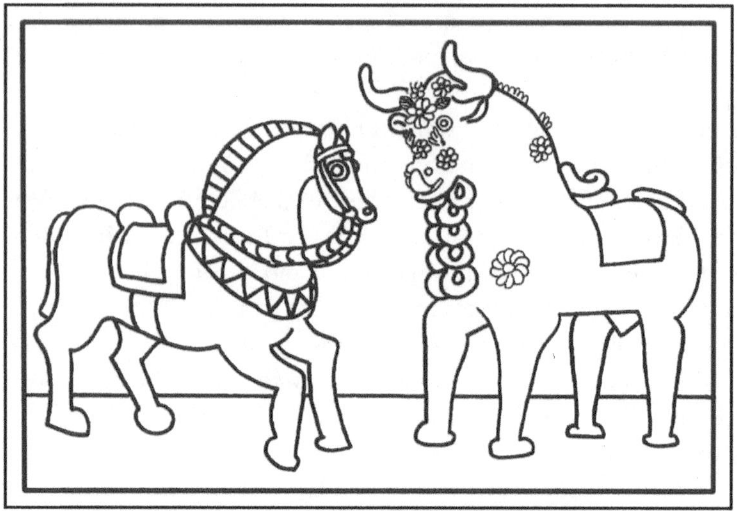

8.3 Colonial-period ceramic bull and horse. Drawing by the author from photographs in Stastny 1981:105, figure 99 (bull); 63, figure 56 (horse).

the prime animal actor. Sabogal Diéguez asserts that the ritual and the clay bull figures made to express its importance had their origin in the region of Checca. In 2003 the ceramic artist Carlos Runcie studied the origin of Pucará bulls in the community of Checca, district of Pupuja, in the region near Pucará. This helped him in his work of aiding contemporary producers of bulls and related figures to make a good living without sacrificing artistic quality (Trivelli 2003b).

The ceramic bull's tongue wipes its nose because of the alcohol. The tail curves across the back because of the hot pepper. The hole in its back and hollow interior serve to hold grease or resin to start a sacrificial fire for a llama or bull offered to divine powers in return for healthy herd animals. The hollow form also allowed the ceramic bulls, like the pottery llamas, to be used as ritual chicha jars at important festivals like marriage ceremonies. The tradition of the bull as a mystical being both beneficent and dangerous shared many qualities with Andean traditional concepts of spiritual powers. This similarity facilitated the symbolic transition from llama to bull.

Another reason bulls supplanted llamas was a legal one. In the 1780s several genres of Indigenous art became illegal in the colonies. Spanish politicians and religious leaders were anything but ignorant of its significance. As a response, Indigenous artisans began to employ disjunction and inversion so they could continue expressing traditional religious ideas to believers. One coping strategy in response to these laws may well have been making canopas in bull form rather than in the shape of llamas or alpacas. This process shows how dual subjectivity can change over time into disjunction as succeeding generations of artists forget original forms and images. In the nineteenth century, with the coming of the republican era upon Peru's independence from Spain, the llama population collapsed biologically in the Andean countryside. In part this was due to preference by Indigenous Andeans for horses, sheep, and cattle, which had been denied them by law in colonial times. These introduced creatures possessed the cachet of the forbidden and association with elite classes. Llamas, correspondingly, also disappeared in art. Shortly thereafter, however, they nostalgically reappeared in art.

In the twentieth century the rural llama population experienced a boom in both the biological and artistic sense. Llamas, now a desired and exotic commodity, appeared everywhere in Andean arts, particularly those made for the urban and international tourist markets in the contemporary period. During the transition from colonial to republican times, bull canopas shared the stage with horse canopas. Llama jars painted like bulls of Pucará increased in number along with the animals they represented only in recent history. The parallel trajectories in relative numbers of bulls and llamas in art closely follow their demographic patterns in life over time. These shifts express changes in the ideological climate. At the same time, the way the two animals (plus, to some degree, the horse) as well as their clay representations now share the same mystique in the modern era signals the fruiting of a long cultural combination process.

The Indigenist movement in Peru and later developments in anthropology and folklore studies lead to interest in preserving traditional "folk" arts. Several famous anthropologists, artists, and collectors intervened by offering an income to increasingly impoverished Andean craftsmen. These patrons have a desire for "genuine" work made according to these same outsiders' specifications. Now, Andean ceramics makers use the time-honored ploy of double consciousness, which is another way of saying dual subjectivity. Thus they meet the double demands of economic survival and maintaining their own cultural identity in the same stroke. Among images in most demand is that of the llama. Both the animal and its artful representations are everywhere in evidence. Llamas and their alpaca cousins have migrated in body and image over seas and lands. They now serve the needs of foreign mountain backpackers, collectors, and decorators. Highly mechanized factories in the industrial world process their wool, and their

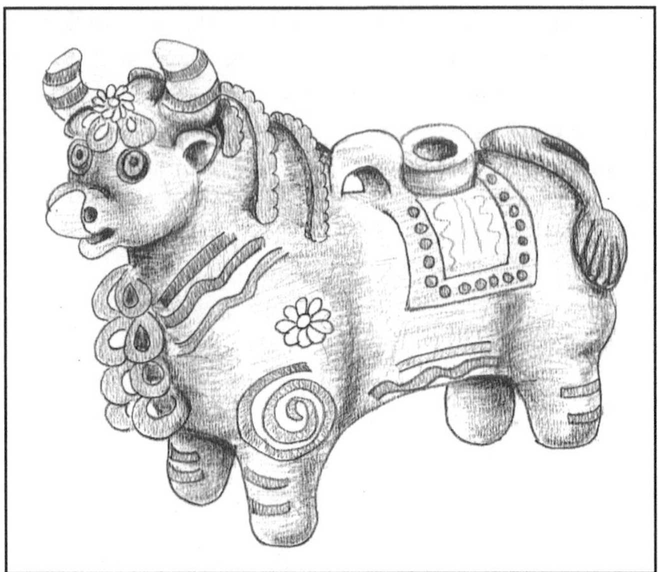

8.4 Modern bull of Pucará. Drawing by the author from piece in her personal collection.

forms and representations fit into the corners of many a traveler's suitcase. Meanwhile, the llamas' human counterparts labor in the nether economies of places like United States and Europe in a migrant labor force without face or name. Today, pottery figures of trains, airplanes, rocket ships, and cell phones bear the distinctive marks of the llamas and bulls of Pucará that stand beside them on store shelves. Once again, the form changes, but the spirit within it remains the same (Stastny 1981).

Ceramic Artists and Their Work Today

The three short accounts below give an idea of the reality within which modern Huamanga ceramics makers live. The first two ceramic artists described fall more into a traditionalist category. They strive to preserve the historical legacy of Andean arts. The third produces several different lines of work, allowing for a wider market and more daring innovation.

Rafael

Rafael left his village of origin to come to Huamanga in the time of Sendero unrest. The family suffered a great deal of terrible strife during this time.

Family members found the city of Huamanga to be a place where at least they could work together and live close enough to each other to present a united front against the constant violence. Rafael's workshop on the edge of the city is in a compound of several small, simple structures where his extended family members live and work. They make plates, bowls, cups, Quinua churches, bulls of Pucará, mythological figures, lamps, flowerpots, and candleholders. The workshop floor has stacks of handmade molds into which they press or pour some of the utilitarian ware. They use a pottery wheel for some items and build others by hand. Their style is a simplified "classic" repertoire of Andean forms. They use natural glazes such as green and ochre and a brick kiln fired with eucalyptus wood.

Rafael sells more bulls of Pucará and flower pots than anything else; he adapts some canopa forms for this purpose or as candleholders. Within traditional parameters, he innovates. For example, he resuscitates the llama and horse versions of the bull of Pucará as well as the longer legs and majolica glazes of these historical styles. He explores mixed-media production by attaching Huamanga stone (local alabaster) flowers to his horses' and bulls' shoulders rather than putting them on in glazed ceramic form. He would like also to investigate integrating hojalatería (tinware) with ceramics in some way. His market is a mixture of tourist, export, and fine arts customers, all of whom must have at least a basic knowledge of Andean crafts and cultures to appreciate what he does.

Rafael and his son José presented the writer with a small horse figure in the style of the bull of Pucará. The horse is about ten inches high and twelve inches long. It has a rounded form, gracefully arched neck, bulging eyes, and curved tail. The legs are longer than the usual modern canopa form, echoing work from the nineteenth and early twentieth centuries. There is no hole or handle on the back, though there is a sculpted saddle such as many bulls of Pucará have on their backs. Rather than using glaze, Rafael has incised forms of daisylike flowers and leaves where he affixes these forms in Huamanga stone on the shoulders, necks, and croups of some horses. The horse has a deep red terra cotta slip glaze over the whole figure. Some brown terra cotta and white is used for the saddle, eyes, nostrils, and ears.

On his workshop floor Rafael has figures of bulls with condors on their backs, more standard bulls of Pucará, Quinua churches, and horses and llamas that resemble this particular horse in shape and decoration. These other figures have a more traditional look, the horse being oriented more toward the nonlocal market. José continues in his father's tradition.

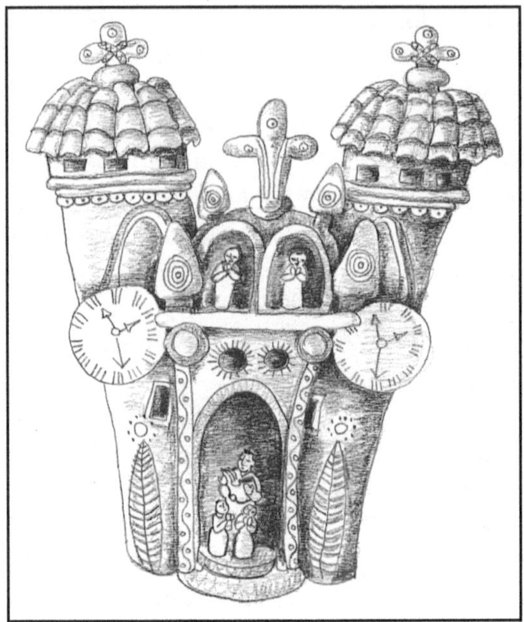

8.5 Modern Quinua church. Drawing by the author after a piece in her personal collection.

Roberto

Roberto and his family work in Lurín, a small town close to Lima and famous for the ruins of the ancient city of Pachacamac. He was born in the ceramic center of Quinua to a family of artists. The family produced more classical items like Quinua churches and *chismosos* (groups of gossips) as well as practical ceramic housewares. Like many artisan families, Roberto's parents specialized in a second art, weaving. His father, a muleteer (arriero), or itinerant peddler, traded ceramic ware for vegetable and animal foods for his family.

Roberto tries very hard to maintain older, traditional ceramic techniques because in this way he consistently produces work of high quality. He moved to Lima and then Lurín in the early 1970s and observes that urban artists' main objective is to mass-produce in order to make profits. The quality of their work suffers in this process. The exigencies of the world market can be odd indeed. For example, sales to the United States depend on size, he says. Ceramics have to be twenty inches or smaller in length. European, U.S., and Japanese buyers look for styles and fads that may be in vogue. These styles have such a short life span that by the time craftworkers produce enough to satisfy a fad-driven order, it may already be out of style.

Roberto avoids producing to satisfy such short-term trends. He glazes his work with natural colors like Rafael does, and he fires the work after glazing it. The family used to work with a brick and eucalyptus kiln and now has a small gas kiln. Rafael feeds a market in which figurative Bethlehem scenes and other biblical representations are popular and marketable. Conscious of longer-term market demands, Roberto knows that today the idea of "Andeanizing" biblical figures (disjunction) is pleasing to buyers. Ergo, he makes biblical flights into Egypt with human figures in Andean dress plus Andean plants and animals on an Inca *totora* boat, the lobed-reed vessels used by Indigenous Andeans for freshwater and sea travel. Noah's arks have a similar menagerie on an oceangoing totora craft. Baby Jesus in the manger wears a chullo, or knitted hat, and Mary and Joseph wear Indigenous Andean clothes. In front of the stable mixed with the sheep are llamas and alpacas, and a condor may roost on the roof. Roberto innovates with details that demonstrate his excellent production skills and historical knowledge. In the clay representations of textiles in his figures' clothing and in the small ceramic pieces in his scenes, the artist glazes minuscule reproductions of complex weaving and pottery designs from Inca and pre-Inca times. For Roberto, disjunction sells.

Roberto's son Ángel was already an accomplished ceramic artist at age eighteen. He was the first in his family to study art in school, and he has taken fine arts courses in Huamanga. Ángel kept quiet in the classes as other students struggled with techniques he learned from his father. Ángel said the experience was valuable nonetheless and that formal titles and degrees are necessary in the modern world. The school anatomy classes helped Ángel produce figures that have more accurate proportions while they still retain their "folk art" charm. Although his father taught ceramics in Lima and as a result left a legacy among many younger craft workers, Ángel lamented that there is no formal "paper" recognition of Roberto's high level of skill and creativity.

A small ceramic work of the Last Supper illustrates a typical piece coming out of Roberto's workshop. Jesus and the apostles sit around a log table on rustic benches. Jesus wears the kind of clothes seen in Bible illustrations, long hair, and a halo. The apostles wear chullos or felt fedoras on their heads and the sweaters and pants commonly worn by modern Andean men and carry ponchos rolled over one shoulder. Their clothes bear glazed weaving designs. On the table sit platters of Huamanga-style flat bread, Andean river fish, and jars of chicha. Larger Last Suppers have roasted guinea pigs and ears of corn as part of the repast. The jars have ceramic design glazes with the natural terra cotta backgrounds typical of utilitarian ware. This piece is an example of a type that Roberto sells to local and tourist buyers. His larger religious and secular scenes are primarily on order to a fine arts and foreign clientele.

Luis

Luis and his family live on the edge of the city of Huamanga. He works with his wife, Ana, and their children to produce several lines of work for various markets: fine arts, tourist and export, and local. Fine arts works are typically quite large and based on traditional ideas but innovative and imaginative. One figure reaches almost three feet in height and represents a demon from the World of Below. It sports a long mane of rippling hair, horns, and claws and seems to be blowing around in a vortex, tornado-fashion. It will receive a plain terra cotta glaze. For local use, the family makes utilitarian items, religious scenes, and fanciful figures from the modern world that include Elvis Presley and Michael Jackson. The pieces Luis and his family make for the tourist and export market primarily are small—under eight inches high—religious and utilitarian figurines with some Andean flavor. Bethlehem scenes, Noah's arks, and Halloween, Valentine's Day, Easter, and other seasonal figural motifs, some oriented exclusively toward a foreign clientele.

The local and tourist and international lines have bright colors, most of them paints added after firing rather than glazes baked into the ceramic. This technical shortcut allows the family to produce in volume for commercial lines. The family artists preserve traditional glazing for their fine arts pieces. Luis uses a brick kiln and eucalyptus wood for all firing. He finds the mobility of the brick walls to be a great advantage in firing different types of ceramics. Luis' family members have interesting views about formal education and passing on arts and crafts traditions. One of his daughters, Anita, like Roberto's son Ángel, studied fine arts at a local institute. She came away from the experience with mixed views. On the one hand, she appreciates having learned about correct human anatomical proportions, perspective, and the like. On the other hand, she resents the purely academic focus of many professors. The university imposes European ideas rather than allowing for creativity within the local Andean framework. Thus the school produces teachers rather than artists, she said.

Luis, like Roberto, is a highly regarded expert in this field, but he does not have teaching credentials. Without these papers he cannot teach within the formal educational system. He has a deep need, however, to pass knowledge of his craft on to young people in addition to his children. He notes that Huamanga formerly had thirty craft specialties and now has only seventeen. Basket weaving and mate carving have become extinct in the region. He wonders how long it will be before all the Andean art traditions disappear. In order to start a school, there are many obstacles to overcome. First, expert artists guard their secrets jealously and so are very reluctant to cooperate with each other. Second, political forces represented by local elites would attempt to stop the organization of such a school. Luis persists in his dream of the school regardless of these difficulties.

An example of Luis's work is an Andean angel figure for export. A decade or more before this writing, the U.S. market created a demand for angel figures and images of all sorts. The AIDS crisis, the play *Angels in America*, and other converging events helped to create this fad. Luis' workshop still produces angel figurines in large numbers, perhaps too large for the now reduced demand. However, the figures still sell fairly well to the Christmas market overseas. This figurine is of a young child with wings. He wears a chullo, poncho, knee pants, and *ojotas* (sandals made from truck tires). He plays a pan pipe and drum, pre-Columbian instruments. By his side are a cactus with flowers and the sacred cantuta flower. The figure combines Inca religious and cultural imagery with the Christian concept of the angel. The child has a large head and very large eyes, making its "cuteness index" fairly high but not intolerable to sophisticated buyers. Colors painted on after firing consist of traditional earth tones of various terra cotta shades, dark green and blue, and white. The child's facial features, hands, and feet are sculpted and incised. There is much attention to precise detail in form and painted decoration. For example, the angel's chullo bears a typical simplified textile motif. Scalloped lines delineate his wing feathers. The rounded and angular features of the face stand out clearly, and the cactus sports its typical ridges. This figure shows how a good artist can combine the demands of the market with her or his own integrity as a craftsperson who produces works of quality.

Final Thoughts

This short study shows how canopas evolved from alpaca and llama shapes to bulls and horses. Later in history, artists made cars, trucks, airplanes, and trains and then came around to alpacas and llamas again. This narrative about morphing forms in the clay medium illustrates the great flexibility in Andean art and belief. The continuation of certain elements of shape and decoration show ways the meaning embedded in such changing external forms often remains constant over time. The artist families' testimonies express the varying strategies they use to negotiate contemporary art-market demands while still maintaining creativity, quality, and pride in their cultural traditions.

The humble origin of all ceramics is clay, a kind of elastic mud, and potters spend their lives up to their elbows and sometimes knees in mud. For this reason, a good number of cultures do not hold ceramics craftspeople in very high regard. However, these mundane objects made of lowly soil have much to reveal. It seems that the llama, bull, and horse guardian figures on Andean rooftops can tell much about people and their religious beliefs, art, and animals over time and distance. Similarly, the global development of majolica illustrates much about human migration and trade over a large area and through the rise and fall of several empires. The morphing animal figures, along with other ceramic genera over time, express the phenomena of dual subjectivity, inversion, and disjunction. Small objects made from mud teach a great deal about how Andean artists adjust to new realities as they remain true to their own values.

CHAPTER 9

Painted Boards (Tablas de Sarhua)

Painted boards, or *tablas*, were traditionally long planks divided by painted lines into rectangular sections containing typical designs and scenes. Each section featured painted portraits of the homeowners' families and friends as well as images of religious symbols. The long plank shape was meant to fit on the ceiling of a family home under the main roof beam. The tradition of painting such boards and affixing them on the underside of house beams originated in Sarhua, a small town in the department of Ayacucho. Sarhuans install these works of art in their homes in recognition of their spiritual beliefs and in homage to the homeowners' family and friends, many of whom collaborate in constructing the house for a newly married couple.

Pictured on the beams were family members of the newlywed householders engaged in typical activities. Each family member was assigned a rectangular area within the painting. When political unrest forced many Sarhuans to migrate to urban areas, the house beams became cut boards usually cut between the places where the original family members' individual painted spaces once had been. The more traditional long boards depicted family members and friends engaged in activities characteristic of them as individuals, along with standard locations, scenes, divinities, and other motifs. Scenes of Andean country life typical of groups were painted on the new, partitioned tablas for sale to an urban clientele and later to tourists. Bland nostalgia, however, is far from the only subject matter.

Contemporary boards have now become an outlet for Goyaesque political commentary and criticism.

Most painted boards of Sarhua are now made and sold in Lima or overseas. The works come in all sizes and usually feature charming scenes of Andean rural life painted with commercial pigments and brushes on readily available easel-size, thin wooden boards. The esthetic, in terms of imagery, seems drawn from the instruction book *Where There Is No Artist* (Rohr-Rouendaal 1997). Figures have a standard look resembling those in many children's book illustrations. Colors are pleasingly bright, the figures are few and large, and the designs tend more toward the static than the dynamic end of the continuum. In these ways, Sarhua painted boards resemble other highly salable folk art genres in the general global marketplace. However, the boards have a specific story of origin rooted in this particular small town. Some board painters incorporate aspects of the original tradition into their work; others combine the crowd-pleasing effects of the commercial style with depictions of the complexity of Andean traditional belief and custom. There are also boards that show commentary on current political and social events and other innovative themes.

History and Use

The tabla tradition has strong roots. Indigenous and Mestizo Andeans painted religious and social imagery on their homes and public buildings throughout their history and prehistory. There is evidently a very long tradition of painting, particularly wall painting, during the pre-Columbian period. Duccio Bonavia's study *Mural Painting in Ancient Peru* (1985) traces this history from preceramic times through the age of the Inca empire. The earliest houses made of clay and other materials had painted walls. Homes at the site of El Paraiso, for example, had four-color murals. Chavín stone carving and incised-relief images served as models for later use of color on wall murals. Their mountain capital of Chavín de Huantar had numerous painted clay and plaster pieces done in relief. Birds, fish, felines, serpents, human beings, spiritual entities, geometric designs, and many other images appeared in these early paintings.

The earliest and most prolific evidence of painting and painted sculpture that experts have found is on Peru's coast. This coastal concentration is probably an artifact of the dry climate. The desert preserves remains, even feather capes and similarly fragile art works, in almost perfect condition. Bonavia as well as the famous anthropologists Alfred Kroeber and

Julio C. Tello have posited that the mountain areas also had a strong mural tradition, though relatively few of these paintings remain today due to the colder temperatures and higher humidity characteristic of the climate at increased altitudes. Of pre-Inca cultures, the Moche are best known as painters. Tello studied Moche murals in the Nepeña Valley (1933a,b,c) and Kroeber in 1925 at Huaca de la Luna in the Moche Valley (1930) based on earlier work by Seler (1923).

Kroeber made numerous drawings and technical descriptions of these works. According to Kroeber, the Moche began by preparing their walls with a layer of white plaster. While the plaster was wet, they made indentations that indicated the outlines for their images. They filled these indentations with black color made from wood ash. This kept the outlines from bleeding into the color, which was added later. Then the artists applied color: black, white, red, yellow, light blue, and pink. Brown came from leaving adobes under the plaster bare. The indentations probably derived from relief techniques handed down from earlier cultures. The colors themselves came largely from earth-derived materials except for a plant-based green (perhaps from the molle tree) and possibly a cochineal-based red. Light blue and pink resulted from mixing black and red, respectively, with the wet white plaster. This mixing process led Kroeber to call the process "fresco," like the mural technique used in Europe. Bonavia disputes this (1985), saying that the Indigenes painted on dry plaster and then sealed their work with a gel they derived from a particular kind of cactus to protect it from the elements. The Moche's painted images resembled those in their own ceramic tradition, both in form and meaning.

The Incas drew from the Moche-Chimú, Pachacamac, and other painting traditions as they formed their composite imperial identity. Inca public buildings, courtyards, and family homes had wall paintings. Common painting imagery included tocapu designs, the same as those in Andean weaving. The fact that tocapus contained readable messages that had socio-political and religious import was not lost on Spanish colonial governors during the late colonial era, and they reacted by passing a law in 1782 ordering that all murals be destroyed. Evidently, clandestine visual communications had been regularly sent to the mural viewing public for 250 years, so sure were most Europeans that the Indigenous Andeans had no system for sending graphic messages. The murals incited rebellion among the Indigenes with their communications about the greatness and perhaps imminent return of the Inca empire. These murals are an example of the processes of inversion and dual subjectivity at work.

The tocapus, encased as they are in a rectangular medallion-shaped frame, resemble to some extent the earlier tile-like coastal murals that formed checkerboards from two or more alternating design types. The Inca checkerboard wall design made from flat squares in red and/or black and white was probably a social ranking as well as military designation. This red and white pattern appeared on the clothing of high military officers appointed by the Inca emperor as well as the emperor's tunic (*uncu*). The design also appears on homes and courtyard walls in large scale. Other tocapu designs indicate additional societal or military ranks, land tenure, cultivation status of fields, season of the year, place of origin, the movements of astral bodies, numerical calculations, and many other concepts. Painted tocapus' natural referents such as stars indicate that murals probably had a ritual function. Of all the colors, red was obviously the one of those most associated with the sacred. Tocapus are an especially finely wrought version of patterns, symbols or designs called *pallai* or *pallay* (chapter 10), and they appear in Andean weaving, particularly the highly regarded cumbi textiles.

Bonavia cites several archeologists who found evidence that pre-Columbian Andeans protected their murals from the weather in two ways, by covering them with a roof and by applying a final coat of varnish made from the *aguacolla quizca* cactus. This extra care attests to a high value attributed to these paintings. Another indication of high value is the new paintings on the same wall did not mean destruction of the old painting first. A new covering of plaster between the new and old paintings preserved sometimes a whole series of superimposed works over time (1985:181–183). Along with paintings on clay and plaster walls, there is evidence of painting on wood in the pre-Hispanic period. Eventually painting on wood may have replaced murals, particularly after large public works became illegal. There is a need for further research in this area.

During the colonial period, the schools of painting founded in Cuzco, Huamanga, and elsewhere channeled Indigenous artists to produce work in the European style. Accordingly, painters made saints and religious scenes for churches, portraits for the homes of wealthy families, and mural art. The paintings express mixtures of cultural traditions and belief systems, though they seem superficially to be primarily European. A good example of this process is in a painting called "The Virgin of the Mountain" shown in 2004 at an exhibit of Andean colonial art in New York. The painting portrays the figure of the Virgin Mary subsumed within the shape of Potosí

Mountain in Bolivia. The mountain has trees and flowers and paths upon which people, horses, and llamas travel. Above the virgin, God the Father and Jesus Christ hold a crown over her head. They are flanked by angels, and the sun and moon symbols sit to the right and left of the mountain. At the base stand earthly rulers—the pope and clerics on her right and the Spanish emperor and governors on her left. The Virgin Mary, Pachamama, and sacred apu concepts blend in this painting. In the background behind the pope is a small but richly dressed Inca emperor (Phipps, Hecht, and Esteras Martín 2004:260). In fact, many of the virgins painted during this period resemble mountains with massive inverted U-shaped or Roman arch–shaped figures. A painting of La Candelaria, patroness of Puno (ibid.: 265), carries flowers and has many flower adornments. Several species of flowers have sacred significance in Andean tradition, among them the cantuta, as does the *mallqui* (sometimes translated as "the ancestors"), a bouquet of many flower species traditionally planted in a seeded corn field. The mallqui represents or has some relation to ancestors and is an offering to Pachamama asking for her help in making the planted fields produce fertile crops. At La Candelaria's feet is the red forehead fringe (borla, or mascay pacha) worn by the Inca emperor. These apparently benign and subtle symbols in colonial paintings speak volumes to Indigenous viewers about traditional belief, pride in ethnic identity, and other ideas. At the same time, non-Indigenous viewers most likely see only pleasant floral decoration. Painters have thus managed to communicate distinct messages to their two different audiences of viewers through the use of ambiguous imagery. In this way, painters express an inversion of the status quo (Strong 1998).

Indigenous and Mestizo painters learned European, Renaissance, and Baroque traditions and styles, and the use of new tools and materials along with new imagery. Eventually they began to produce unique motifs in mixed styles of their own creation. This came about in part because along with a European clientele, painters produced for the descendants of the Inca elites. These upper-crust Indigenes wanted images of themselves like the famous portraits of the Incas made during early colonial times. These early mixed-culture paintings portrayed the emperors with neo-European dress, armor, weapons, and other non-authentic details. (The Brooklyn Museum has some of these paintings in its permanent collection.) This is classic disjunction. During later colonial times and into the modern era, paintings appear on cloth other than canvas (for example, on serge). These are poor-man's versions of church art, and many of them serve sacred functions. Painting on wood also continued both large in scale for official institutions and small for domestic decoration.

Tablas de Sarhua, or Sarhuan boards, descend directly from these earlier painting traditions. They are on wood but also serve as house adornments as in Indigenous times. They contain religious and kin-based imagery from both pre- and post-Columbian eras. The town of Sarhua and Sarhuan migrants in Huamanga and Lima constitute one community that preserves the Andean tradition of painting on wood wherever they may live. In a way, Sarhuans hark back to the Andean custom of painting on walls because, as Sarhuans say in their oral tradition, Inca works on wood were at one time incorporated into the interior roofs of family homes. Archeologists do say that the Inca used wood as roofing on many of their stone buildings, though it is difficult to know whether this wood was painted due to climatic disintegration.

The original Sarhuan boards or beams were hand-hewn wood planks about six to ten feet long. The earliest dated Sarhuan boards were made as early as 1600. In 1876 there is evidence of a continuation of the board-painting custom, and Sarhuans have kept painting the boards from the early twentieth century to the present. Artists painted images on these early works in black or dark sepia outlines only until the 1930s and 1940s. Black came from firewood carbon and brown from earth. Images included Christian and Andean religious figures as well as portraits of the friends and relatives of the homeowning couple as well as the household members themselves. The board had divisions painted in the form of flower or abstract borders, and the types of images had to conform to a certain order of presentation. Each image occupied one of a long line of squares marked by the borders.

The long boards contain images in a traditional sequence. In the first square (reading the board from the extreme left end and proceeding to the right) appears a short written dedication by the house's owners. In the next square is the Virgin of the Assumption, patroness of Sarhua. Some boards have alternate virgins, but the Assumption is most common. Then the next square has drawings of the homeowners in typical clothes and activities. The succeeding squares show close relatives and friends and then more distant relations. The last squares depict the girls who sang and served chicha at the house-raising, the sun (inti), the moon (killa), and the local apu. Each square separation or border consists of flower, zigzag, star, llama-track (*llamapa chakin*), or other typical border designs.

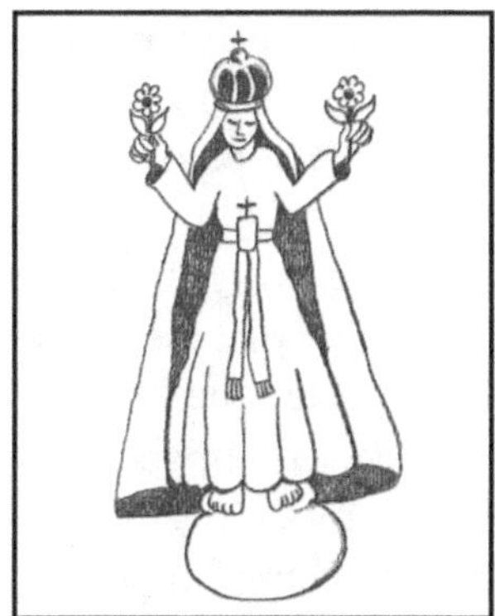

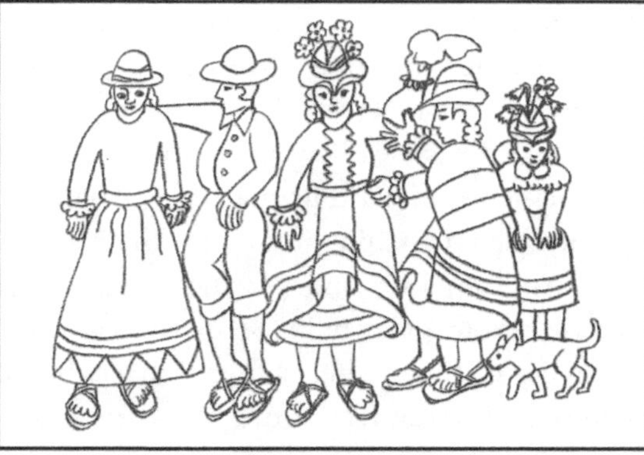

9.1 Virgin of the Assumption, typical motif in tablas of Sarhua. Drawing by the author after Berrocal in Macera and Andázabal 1999:202, figure 126.

9.2 Family group, Sarhua board illustration style. Drawing by the author after Berrocal in Macera and Andázabal 1999:203, figure 128.

After the introduction of aniline dyes in the 1930s, artists painted their boards in color. Following custom, the long board still was hung from the main beam of one of the rooms in the home. Its painting and hanging continued to take place as an integral part of the several days of ritual surrounding communal building of a new home for a recently married couple. When the violence associated with the Sendero movement began and the activities of Sendero members, government forces, and militias made survival in the village precarious, many Sarhuans exmigrated to the cities of Huamanga and Lima. Migrant painters found little market for their long boards, and so they began to paint scenes on cut square sections, finding that these sold well. Rather than religious and family imagery, transplanted Sarhuans found ready buyers for nostalgic images of rural life like plowing and herding and a smaller, intellectual market for boards with violent and political scenes depicting the Sendero era, such as firing squads and battle themes. The drawing style for these boards painted canvas-style changed from a kind of colonial primitive type of imagery to a more standardized, simplified, cartoon-type, folk style.

How Tablas Are Made

Once eucalyptus wood became available, it was most preferred for the older boards. Painters also use *lambras* (*alizo*), *pati* (*níspero*, medlar tree), or *mayu* (*sauce*, *arbol llorón*, weeping willow) woods, which are more traditional, and split maguey, the original material used. Now, some village painters make use of factory-prepared planks from Huamanga, but this is still a great luxury. The first step in the production process is to make plaster (*isku*) from boiled cow leather and burned *pachas rumi* (a type of stone). These two elements mixed together make a white paste for covering the board and producing a white ground for the images. It is notable that the plaster ground recalls Inca and pre-Inca mural preparation techniques. Willow tree or broom plant branches burned at one end make good pencils for doing the sketches. Then the artist makes black paint by mixing agave juice with *qitva* (carboniferous fire black from the kitchen ceiling) or burned material from the bottom of cooking pots. Stones of different kinds provide colors. *Muki* stones make white, yellow, and pink. However, these days even people in small villages have access to aniline dyes, which they can purchase in local markets. Painters make brushes for applying paint from the broom plant and some kinds of ichu (mountain grasses). Painting the board can take anywhere from twenty-four hours to four days, depending on how many people are involved and the general schedule. The artists try to capture their human models in typical poses surreptitiously because house owners are not supposed to know who does the painting until the end of the house-building ritual (Evanán Poma, Quispe, and Palomino Flores 1994).

Meaning in Tablas

Sarhuan boards originally had several layers of meaning. The boards and the house-building ritual of which they form a part have to do with kinship, reciprocal labor, communalism, and religion. After Sarhuans fled to cities, the urban boards still retained some of this complex, layered meaning. Painting the boards certainly does promote continued valuation of traditional rural life but in a much more general sense than before the 1970s, when exmigration from the village began. Primitivo Evanán Poma, one of the most famous of the Sarhuan board painters, provided insights into the changes and continuities of symbolic import in Sarhuan tablas in a series of interviews with the author in 2003 and 2006 and in written form (Evanán Poma, Quispe, and Palomino Flores 1994). The discussion here of the history of meaning is largely based on a translated summary of his spoken and written words.

Traditionally, house construction in Sarhua took place in the austral winter. August, in particular, has symbolic importance because it marks the end of the dry season, or *chiraw*, in which "the winds blow strong with tornadoes and lightning." August sits as seasonal and symbolic opposite to February—*loco killa*, "crazy month" or literally "crazy moon"—when there are torrential rains. Both these months are holy because they are times when the "earth opens" and the Huamani come out of the mountains demanding offerings. For this reason, lesser animals like sheep and llamas are branded most often in February and more important (bigger) animals like cattle in August. Both of these months are *pina killa*, *meses bravos*, or "wild months." House construction in August makes practical sense because little agricultural work can be done at this time. The animals are close to home, harvests have been taken in, food is abundant, and therefore it is a time of festivities when people practice reciprocal labor (*ayni*) and communal or group projects (*minka*).

Family relationships have a great deal to do with how the community divides responsibility for working on the house being constructed. The Incas' bilateral lineage designation called *ayllu* still exists in many communities. The ayllu is a very large family unit, and a marriage joins two of these exogamous groups. Sarhua has two major ayllus. Building houses must be done communally, and the custom of ayni demands that close and more distant relatives perform major reciprocal labor on the project. Close relatives (*hichpa ayllu*), such as parents and siblings and ceremonial parents such as *padrinos* (godparents) and *compadres* (co-parents), must play major house-building roles (note 1). Some of these relatives assist in painted board construction, or *tabla apakuykuy*.

1. Both blood and fictive relatives acquire the titles of "co-parent" (*compadre, comadre*) or "godparent" (*padrino, madrina*) for a number of reasons. People can become co-parents in several ways: they were promised to children of families friendly with their parents as co-parents while still children; an adult couple with a child becomes co-parents through mutual agreement with other adults; or two couples become co-parents through the baptism ceremony because they decide to build a relationship in addition to the acquisition of the title "godparents" for children that they attain through this ritual. The title "co-parent" is not a religious one. Becoming a co-parent is by agreement, and the title entails rights and responsibilities of a more practical nature.

The title "godparent," on the other hand, is a religious designation and requires both an agreement and a sacred ritual to attain. Godparents (padrinos, madrinas) are an extra set of parents for the ritually baptized child in case the natural parents cannot meet their obligations. Biological parents and godparents may decide to become co-parents as well, though this additional decision is not part of the Christian baptism ritual. Godparenthood can also take place through emergency baptism, for example, when there is no priest present or there is danger of death to an infant. Ritual co-parenthood can happen through the baptism without official clerical sanction of material items and animals. The baptism of bulls is described in chapter 8 and the baptism of an oven in the ethnography *Tambo* (Meyerson 1990).

Co-parents and godparents and those with both titles maintain close friendships with the child's parents, ideally for life. They also have special obligations throughout the child's life, such as giving him gifts or clothing and educating her. These arrangements help assure the care of children and collaboration among groups of adults for mutual benefit.

These relatives, determined through blood and ritual, also bring their own wide web of relatives into the project. In this way, building a house can involve a large part of the town's population. In addition, anyone wandering through the street can be conscripted to join in on the work for the project. The process of such conscription is called *kuyaq*.

Everyone who wants to build a house in August needs to sign up with the town mayor's office. The office then makes up a building schedule designating consecutive dates to each house. The actual owners of the house must have nothing to do with its construction. During house building, the owners become ritual strangers (*forasteros*) in the town. They supposedly have come on a visit from the fictive village of Huancarucina (the root *huanca* refers to the pre-Incaic Huanca people who rebelled fairly constantly against both Inca and Spanish rule). The owners, besides being "strangers," take on the roles of being "mute," "silly," and "paralytic." Their most preferred relative becomes the "owner" of the house for the interim. This relative supervises the construction while the real owners feed and constantly offer drink to visitors and work crews. They can only express their desires with respect to the house through an intermediary.

When the owners establish their first day for house building, they appear at three o'clock in the morning at possible collaborators' homes to offer coca leaves to chew and drinks of hot *trago* (cane liquor). In exchange, women collaborators will later appear at the construction site with food for the home's larder, first with a large bundle (*qipi*, woman's carrying shawl) of broad beans, oats, wheat, quinua, or potatoes weighing about twenty pounds. Later, women bring small offerings of salt, pepper, aji (very spicy pepper), aromatic herbs, and the like. Men bring fiber for making rope, wood, stones for cementing the walls, or ichu grass or tiles, depending on the owners' preference, for the roof. A newlywed couple whom the community holds in high esteem will probably receive more of these gifts than they can use. By the same token, couples who do not live up to community standards will be sanctioned by not receiving enough for fulfillment of their basic needs.

Villagers make adobes and roof tiles before constructing the house. *Wasi cimentay* (cementing the house) involves wall construction but also the embedding of small objects into the house to strengthen it and make it a home. For example, small clay pots ensure that the house will always have grain stores for food. Coins, old or new, ensure wealth in the home. *Coca kintu* (special, sacred coca leaves), trago (cane liquor), and holy water protect the house from evil. The roof is the ceremonial center of the home. At this point a special, previously designated "inspector" supervises the construction. There are certain townsmen known for their ability to guarantee solid roofs and at the same time keep the male construction crew and female cooking team happy and hardworking. The designee is usually one of these individuals. The inspector carries a staff of office, and he can use this to punish laggard workers. The inspector conscripts extra workers off the streets as they are needed. A number of relatives approach the homeowners to donate the painted board. This takes place at four o'clock in the morning several days after the house building has begun. The house owners accept this favor of the donated board from those to whom they can reasonably return the ayni (reciprocal labor service) obligation.

The designated artists are supposed to paint the boards in secret. In reality there is much spying back and forth, especially near finishing time so that everyone can prepare for the customary celebration in time for the presentation. When the board is ready, compadres parade it through the streets. Women bring food and drink, and men carry ichu grass for a straw roof or tiles for a tile roof. Along with the painted board, men carry two other boards, called *maman quiru*, to go on either side of the main one. A loose translation of *maman quiru* is "mother of symbols." The red and white boards hark back to the Inca royal red and white murals and to red as a most sacred color. White and red colors are derived from muki stones. The paraders set off firecrackers as they walk. A horn player with a helix-shaped wind instrument made of stacked cattle horns (*qui wayllu* or *waq'rapuku*) plays special tunes. This musician has been on site during the house raising, and at certain points in the construction he has played traditional airs.

The people on parade deliver the board very dramatically. Then follows a serious critique session. People whose images appear on the board express approval or disapproval. One young woman, a relative of painter Carmelón Berrocal Evanán (Macera and Andázabal 1999), complained that she appeared on a horse, though she always did her work as a shepherd on foot. Some people express their anger at the homeowner family or the compadres by scratching the board. Others are upset that they do not appear at all on the board, and they walk off in a huff. Most disputes get resolved by means of a traditional supplication ceremony mediated by wise community counselors.

Every house has three components: a *hatun wasi* ("big house"), a hallway, and a patio. The hatun wasi is rectangular and serves as a storage area for food and valuables. A small window (perhaps "niche" is better translation) on the back wall of this room usually has within it a wooden cross, a statue of the Virgin Mary, and retablos or San Marcos boxes. These items serve in the rituals surrounding animal branding and marking.

The next step in the process is the installation of the red and white boards (maman qiru) on either side of the tabla or board painted with images. The tabla board goes on the underside of the roof spine in the center of the ceiling beginning at the top of the window. The painted board does not form part of the supporting roof structure but is attached to it. After installation, every time the family salutes the saints they see from the corridor, they kneel also in front of the board. This shows that the cross, statues, boxes, and board all have spiritual power that their group location in the heart of the home strengthens and concentrates.

After placing the board on the inside of the roof, young men walk through the rafters and jump down holding onto ropes attached to roof poles. They do this to music and singing. Some jump head first. The serious purpose of this circus acrobat-like behavior is to make sure the roof is solidly in place. From the outside of the roof, if it is of straw, men hang rope and straw figures of llamas, people, foxes, horses, musical instruments, and the like. If the roof is tile, the roofers place small metal crosses or small ceramic bulls of Pucará. These small objects serve as talismans of well-being in various aspects of life and in conjunction with larger more important figures act as guardians protecting the house from evil forces.

The spine of the roof is its most spiritual element, the center of the home. Thus the two large ceramic bulls of Pucará (major guardian figures) sit on either side of the spine if not directly on the major beam of the roof's outside. A pair of bulls may have a metal cross placed between them. After installing the guardian figures great and small, there is more feasting and dancing with crazy costumes made of animal parts hung from strings. Finally, the next day, the "travelers" revert to their real position of homeowners through a ceremony called "farewell to the strangers" (*muqu avio*). More dancing and feasting follow, and all eventually return to their own homes.

Tabla Art and Artists Today

Today, many former Sarhua residents live in the *pueblos jóvenes* (new towns, immigrant neighborhoods) of Lima. Since 1981 the Sarhuan board painters have formed ADAPS, Asociación de Artistas Populares de Sarhua (Association of Sarhuan Folk Artists), to preserve and promote their painting traditions (note 2). The violence that caused the exmigrations from the village of Sarhua to cities now forms part of the imagery found on the new canvas-sized tablas de Sarhua. There is a small and more highly specialized audience for these. Representations of myths, legends, and rural traditions have a much larger audience.

2. For further information on tablas and tabla making see websites relating to ADAPS such as *http://www.convida.org/adaps.html.*

Francisco began painting small boards because of this new market demand. The smaller size plus happy scenes of customs such as religious festivals and processions, planting and harvesting have large numbers of buyers both at home and abroad. Francisco mentioned Luis Millones and Mary Louise Pratt's small book about Sarhua boards called *El amor brujo* (1990) during one conversation to illustrate how fickle market forces can be. He was not looking at the book so much as an academic study (which it is) as an indication of many buyers' inordinate interest in romantic themes. At this point, Francisco and Soledad, a folk musician and artist also from this region, talked about the importance of external visual symbols and places of learning for young people in order to preserve Andean tradition.

When people change clothes and start using material things from another culture they change identity, the two older artists asserted. They discussed the history of change in dress from Indigenous times through the Spanish colonial period to the present. They felt strongly that television and other influences were killing Andean customs. Francisco asserted that forming artist associations and schools could counteract this trend by allowing masters of the different arts to pass on what they know to the young.

Francisco and his children have in their Lima shop some of the older, long, traditional boards in monochromatic black or brown and white, some newer long boards executed in a few colors, and some recent works in full color. The majority of their paintings, however, are on square, easel-size boards in different dimensions. The paintings' colors are very dense and bright and the figures simplified and toylike. Landscapes have flattened perspective. There is enormous detail in some imagery such as in representations of traditional textiles and extreme simplicity in others such as in imaged peoples' faces. The paintings of a Sarhuan relative of Francisco who passed away tragically have been published in a book. Pablo Macera, a noted scholar of Andean folk tradition, and Rosaura Andázabal compiled the work (1999), which is like a museum exhibit catalogue of Carmelón Berrocal Evanán's work. The book presents charming and revealing pictures of plants, animals, villages, maps, calendars, and scenes from folk tales and myths.

Short descriptions of two of the works in the book illustrates what they are like. The first one is "Trucha" (79). In the picture is an anatomically correct but double-headed trout. This is a terrifying spirit being in Andean lore. The actual trout is a species introduced from Canada that has beat the native trout out of the environment. The picture is beautifully composed, with the trout forming a graceful curve in water and aquatic plants in the background. Nested within this curve is what at first looks like a piece of land but when looked at closely is a rather frightening human face. The artist has imbued this piece with multiple layers of meaning having to do with traditional ideas about nature being full of hidden spiritual power and modern fears about environmental and cultural change.

An image from a traditional tale shows a spotted bull holding a bleeding, prone figure at bay while two Andean men hide behind rocks (182). The prone figure is a dreaded Pishtaco or evil spirit disguised as a foreigner—he has light-colored hair and an ample beard, while the Andeans depicted have jet-black hair. (If Indigenous men have facial hair, it is usually sparse.) The bull, a guardian figure, dominates the evil spirit who is known to kill people by eating their fat. On the cave walls and surrounding mountains grow many tufts of native ichu grass, an important element and resource in the highland environment. The drawings have all figures outlined in black and filled with flat colors. Berrocal gives shaded dimension only to caves, mountains, and rocks, which are especially sacred earth forms. The Macera and Andazabal book presents written descriptions of some of the zoological and botanical paintings in Carmelón Berrocal's mixed Spanish and Quechua speaking style. This helps audiences gain some insight into the complexity of his world. A non-native viewer attempting to understand the folk-tale images would need as a prerequisite much more detailed verbal as well as visual background.

Berrocal's paintings exhibit the processes of inversion and dual subjectivity. They contain multiple and subtle references and span lengthy historical periods. Yet, many of the pictures are so charming that they would sell on that quality alone. His work also shows how a modern Sarhuan painter can take the best of his village tradition and expand upon it in such a way as to communicate with larger audiences about culturally broader themes.

Final Thoughts

The painters of Sarhua hope that the meaning of what they do will somehow stay intact despite all of the difficulties that must be overcome. Recognized master artists of this craft have combined elements of the simplified commercial esthetic with a presentation of the complex system of belief and behavior underlying this genre. The process of recognition for such a master often involves making contact with an educated patron or sponsor. These sponsors have a complex appreciation of the art tradition and help the master artist present a degree of this complexity to a more well-prepared, "high end" consumer such as a university, museum, cultural center, or individual professional buyer (Strong 2003a).

Andrea Heckman makes the interesting proposition that from her perspective, based on long-term study of Andean weavings, modern times do not require that local people give up their culture, as many are wont to assert. Instead, she states, "foreign introductions end up promoting traditional concepts" (Heckman 2003: x). Visual modes of communication, much more important to Andeans than verbal ones, facilitate this process. The illustration comes first, and the explanatory words are adjunct to it (39). This emphasis is directly opposite to the standard modes used by the industrialized world. While the word specifies, the image—tied as it is to natural referents—is wonderfully vague and general, open to a number of interpretations at once. The image can be placed anywhere in any size and in any depth of field in a two- or three- or four-dimensional format. This makes images almost infinitely flexible. Thus painted folk arts can perform very difficult high-wire acts such as maintaining an intact tradition even given modern commercial constraints in the context of globalization.

Evidently, precolonial Andeans made numerous wall paintings, and painting was an important art among them. Many of these paintings were on the walls of homes. The long roof boards of Sarhua descend from this tradition, though imagery on the boards combines Indigenous and colonial elements. Sarhua boards are arts of the family, community, and home. They recount family history and assert community values.

Tablas have a very strong sacred dimension as well. They show the Andean deities of the sun and moon and the Christian Virgin of the Assumption, patroness of Sarhua. Villagers place the boards in a sacred area accompanied by crosses and retablos, and the family prays there. Migrant Sarhuans in the city continue to make the imagery required by the original boards. They also cut the boards into squares and paint nostalgic images of rural life as well as criticism of the political regime or the violence of the Shining Path and government forces. The traditional long boards represent dual subjectivity. Nostalgic rural costumbrista scenes done on cut boards by urbanites have disjunctive qualities. Political scenes make liberal use of ironic inversion. Recent easel-size boards of both types retain spiritual meaning as well, since such themes are nourished by migrants' constant visits to their town of origin.

CHAPTER 10

Weavings (Textiles)

Weavings, and to a slightly lesser degree ceramics, constitute the most highly prized of the Andean arts. Art historians and archeologists have produced an enormous and detailed literature that presents Andean textiles in their great beauty and variety. These fine works rank with the best in the world. The Spanish chronicler Cobo remarks (in Morris and Von Hagen 1993:198) on the brilliancy of the colored dyes and the impressive concentrations of finely spun threads per unit area (112 threads per square centimeter). Though the Incas and their predecessors had gold and silver in abundance, they prized fine textiles above the shiny metals. Excavations have uncovered well-made cloth that dates from preceramic times. From that early period to the present, Andean peoples have made prodigious amounts of clothing, blankets, rugs, tapestries, bags, and cords with an expert eye for color and design. Textile designs visually express personal identity, family history, social rank, science, religion, and other important ideologies to viewers. The same symbols found in cloth art often grace ceramics, painted murals, stonework, and other genres as well. Archeologists find expertly made textiles among Andean peoples beginning in very early prehistorical times. Cloth made in recent periods also exhibits very high skill in construction and design. Colonial and modern introductions of new materials and tools have influenced production methods, resulting in combined approaches to fabric manufacture.

History and Use

The history of weaving in the Andes is uneven for climatic reasons. Cultures that arose in the desert coastal areas left complete repertoires of textiles in burials and the remains of social centers. Even elaborate capes made of fragile tropical bird feathers emerge from excavations in almost new condition along with the well-preserved mummies of those who wore them. Archeologists working in highland or jungle areas where there is rain and humidity fare less well since moisture tends to destroy cloth over time. The fine art of Andean textiles developed both regionally and chronologically, each local repertoire changing as time progressed. Because of constant empire building as well as wide economic and religious networks, Andean cultures have steadily traded motifs and production techniques with other groups through time, adding these borrowings to their own inventions. Several root traditions made major contributions to the superb fabrics produced today. Following is a short overview of some of the major textile-producing cultures.

Chavín motif innovations include double-headed animals, especially birds, and figures that combine elements from one or more animals and/or humanoid beings (Burger 1992:32–35). Burger (201) agrees with the textile expert William Conklin, who lists Chavín innovations in terms of weaving types and decorating techniques: use of camellid hair in cotton textiles; textile painting; supplemental and discontinuous warps, including several types of tapestry; dyeing camellid hair; warp wrapping; and "negative" or resist painting techniques as in tie dye and batik. Because of their extensive sphere of influence and trade networks, the Chavín were able to spread these motifs, weaving types, and decorative methods throughout the Andean region. The Huari would eventually create simplified and highly colored imagery in fine tapestries based on some of the Chavín models and methods. Huamanga weavers of today express this inheritance in their textiles.

Many experts consider Paracas weavings to be among the finest ever produced. Paracas textile workers made very detailed fabrics, incorporating complex, multicolored imagery. They worked in locally grown cotton and in camellid wool produced by mountain peoples who sold the fiber to Paracas already dyed in rich hues (Moseley 1992:47, 60–62). The Brooklyn Museum has one of these works on display, simply labeled "the Paracas Textile." It is a large weaving made up of tiny, densely colored plant and humanoid and animal combined figures. Hanging from the edges of the work is a fringe of such figures in cut-out shape with sculptural dimensions.

Nazca fine textiles grew out of the Paracas cloth-making traditions. Nazca textile imagery and techniques were in turn borrowed by the Huari in what was called the "Okros" style (Moseley 1992:219) that was adopted by the Huari and passed through time to Huamanga weavers of today. The Nazca produced plain weave, double weave, gauze, embroidery, and brocade textiles. Like the Nazca's painted ceramics, their textiles featured marine creatures as well as religious motifs.

The Tiahuanacu empire had broad influence. The striking images carved into the stone monuments at the site of the capital at Lake Titicaca also appear in the other arts of Tiahuanacu, including textiles. The Huari adapted Tiahuanacu imagery to their own purposes, expanding and contracting proportions and dimensions in much the same way as is now easily possible using computer software (Moseley 1992: figure 103). Such images of ornate staff-bearing gods and other Tiahuanacu motifs appear in Huamanga textiles today, including split-body forms of animals arranged mirror-fashion on either side of their heads in frontal view or repetitious forms called kennings. These images, however, are closer visually to the interpretations of the local Huari ancestors than they are to the Tiahuanacu originals.

The Moche and its descendant Chimú culture had a wealth of textile traditions. Many of the same images that characterized the ceramics for which these civilizations were perhaps more famous appeared, as well, in their cloth arts. The trading of designs among media worked in many directions. For example, the intricate, abstract designs in the adobe walls of the Chimú capital, Chan Chan, resemble those in their textiles. The Inca removal of Chan Chan artists to Cuzco influenced Inca textiles, and these in turn affected Huamanga area weavers during the Inca regime.

The Huari influenced Huamanga traditions probably more then any other Indigenous group. In their constantly expanding religious colonizing efforts, the Huari concentrated on the portable arts of ceramics and textiles. Huari techniques such as their brilliantly hued tapestry style and their distinctive graphic imagery had a lasting effect in the Huamanga/Ayacucho region. At the same time, the Huari invention and spread of warp patterning was to influence the Inca, and it became the major pan-highland technique, as it is still today. The prevalence of tapestry production in Huamanga over the more common pan-Andean warp patterning may have its explanation in the local inheritance of Huari tapestry techniques along with Spanish colonial emphasis on tapestry as a method of production in their Huamanga art schools and *obrajes* (weaving factories). This perhaps gave the tapestry tradition a double dose of influence in the region.

Spanish impact on the Huamanga region is more important than in some other Andean areas because the colonial government singled out its

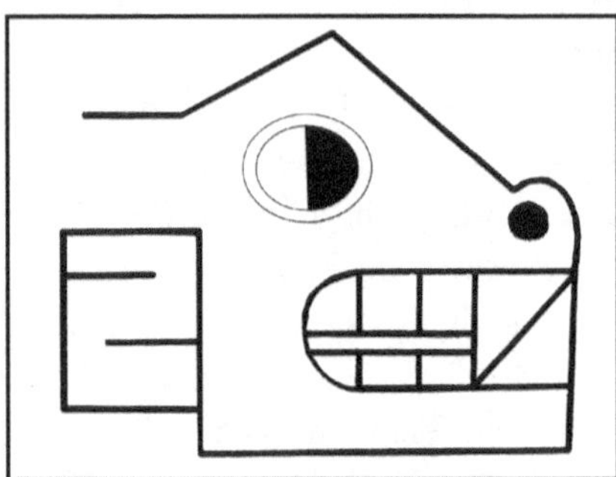

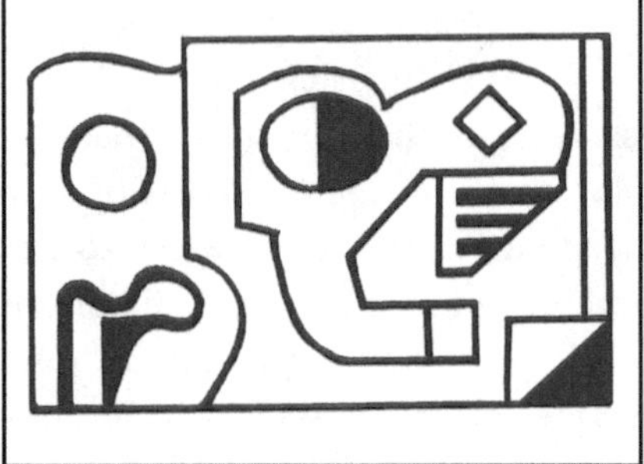

10.1 Tapestry detail of Huari cat head with typical side-staring eye and the overlapping eyeteeth of feline predators. Drawing by the author after detail in Moseley 1993:220, figure 105.

10.2 Huari bird head with stylistic eye shape and raptor beak. A smaller bird head with a diamond-shaped eye inset into the image in the original weaving is characteristic of Huari-style superimpositions. Huari designs often have lateral repetitions of complex forms as well. Drawing by the author after detail in Moseley 1993:218, figure 103.

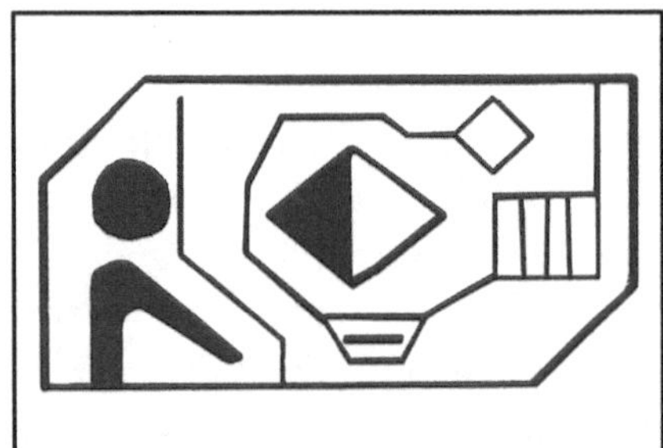

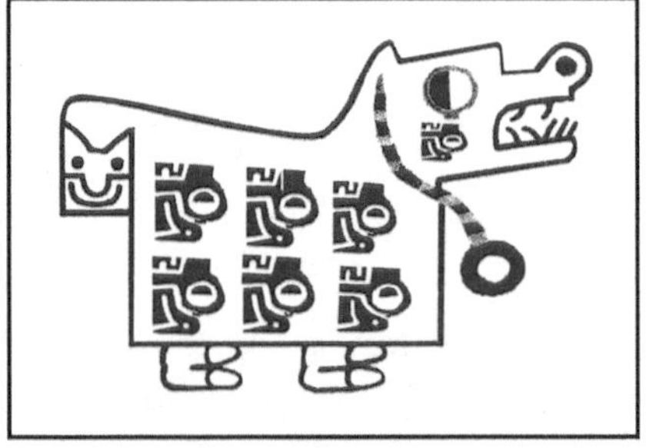

10.3 Huari bird head with diamond-shaped eye and raptor beak. Drawing by the author after detail in Moseley 1993:218, figure 103.

10.4 Huari llama figure with cat face in tail and bird heads in body. References to several spiritual beings in one figure or contiguous figures are characteristic of Andean art, especially of Tiahuanacu and Huari cultures. Drawing by Rafael Domingo after detail in a kero, a ceremonial wooden cup, in Boone 1996, 1:165.

pleasant climate and convenient location for the site of a major political and manufacturing center. During the colonial era the Spanish eventually caught on that weavings communicated important messages to Andean viewers and for this reason tried to suppress the designs. The new European conquerors attempted several times to destroy such images through legislation against their use in textiles, ceramics, painted murals, and other arts (chapters 1, 2; Bonavia 1985). Inca clothing exhibited information about the wearer's regional origin, social status, religious concepts, and other important data. This "billboard" aspect, as Heckman puts it (2003), of Andean raiment simplifies social understanding and customs in what was and is a culturally complex region. The Spanish did appreciate the great skill exhibited by Inca weavers for esthetic as well as commercial reasons. Colonial textiles show a mixing of technologies, types of fibers used, and techniques, along with imagery that had origins in both the Andean and European traditions. As the Spanish empire expanded to global dimensions, Andean weavers incorporated Asian and Middle Eastern motifs along with European and Indigenous ones into their work. Elena Phipps (2004:72–100) elaborates on these themes in her writing on colonial period weaving.

The Incas and their predecessors traditionally used alpaca wool for fine weaving. The inner hair of these animals is soft and resilient, and spinners could produce a thin, even thread from it. To a lesser extent, very fine, luxury-grade weavings from vicuña wool, coarse materials like rope from llama hair, and a sizable cotton textile industry in coastal areas formed part of the repertoire. The Spanish introduced sheep wool, which was fluffier and less resilient and elastic than alpaca fiber. European textile production methods had been adapted to the qualities of sheep wool, and the Spanish taught these techniques to Andean weavers for use in this medium. As a result, for a time the alpaca and llama population declined, since the early colonial regime valued them more for meat than wool and did not bother to preserve a breeding herd. Colonialists eventually appreciated the special character of camellid wool, such as its softness, lightweight warmth, and workability.

Inca fine weavers worked on looms set in an upright, vertical position, according to Phipps. Their techniques for warp-oriented designs and difficult interlocking weave for color changes were adapted to manufacturing work in this position. On the other hand, the Spanish designs were oriented horizontally, and European-style looms allowed for working on a flat or slanted surface. Spanish weavers used the easier methods of dovetailing

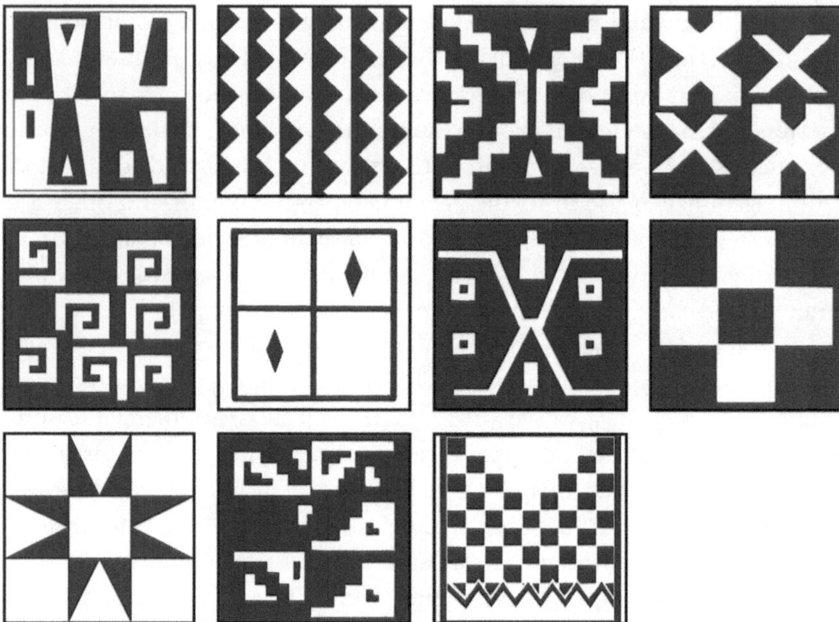

10.5 (upper left) Inca tocapu design on a blanket-size tapestry woven by Mariano in 2006 in green, yellow, cream, and brown colors. Drawing by Rafael Domingo after detail of photograph in Phipps, Hecht, and Esteras Martín 2004: catalogue figure 18.

10.6–10.15 Inca tocapu designs. Drawing by Rafael Domingo after details in photograph in Phipps, Hecht, and Esteras Martín 2004: catalogue figure 18.

or slit tapestry joining rather than the more tedious and time-consuming interlocking method. The Spanish also imported and taught the use of treadle looms. The imposition of this new technology implied both a different working posture and distinct weaving techniques for Andean workers. Europeans utilized fully executed drawings (cartoons) as a basis for their textile designs. Andeans, by contrast, used memory techniques (Phipps 2004:73). This writer observed weavers reciting numbers sequences while they worked and master weavers quizzing younger apprentices on these sequences.

Callao, port of Lima, was a major entry point for Spanish as well as global styles, fashions, printed books with illustrations, technologies, and finished pieces relevant to textile production. The Andes received objects and information very quickly from Europe, the Middle East, and elsewhere.

Phipps recounts (81) the unintended result of a sixteenth-century Spanish law forbidding the importation or manufacture of silks, satins, or silver and gold brocades from any place of origin but Spain. The logic behind this legislation was to preserve the Spanish corner on manufacture and marketing of these luxury items. As early as 1572, despite the laws, fully executed Asian textiles were coming into Lima from China and the Philippines in the guise of packing material. As a result, Andeans began to incorporate Asian imagery into their work along with Mediterranean and Middle Eastern motifs. Some of the new images were of scroll work, floral vases, artichokes, and pomegranates along with arabesque designs and color combination originating in Turkey (Anatolia) and images of spirit beings from China (81–83, 86–87). New dye colors and much-prized metallic fibers accompanied the plethora of images constantly arriving on the ships.

Cultural mixtures occurred in every area: fibers, working styles, techniques, and technologies. Weavers mixed alpaca and sheep wool, for example, for some kinds of pieces. The Andean way of leaving warp loops intact when removing a tapestry from the loom combined with the European method of cutting warp yarns by maintaining the lower-edge warp loops while cutting the upper warp threads. This made the process of finishing faster and easier. Rather than the tedious Andean single interlock technique, weavers began to use dovetailing, which also worked better to achieve European curvilinear designs (86–87).

The colonial government took advantage of the best weavers. Chroniclers including Guamán Poma speak of weavers being locked in workshops where they were forced to produce until they became ill from exhaustion. Guamán contrasts this bad treatment of artists under the colonialists with the way in which weavers were highly honored and compensated in Inca times. Later, as appreciation for their art grew, more humane working conditions became the rule for Indigenous craftspeople. Some of the descendants of these elite masters (*cumbi camayocs*) still weave at the sites of their forebears' old colonial workshops in areas including Lake Titicaca, Cuzco, and Huamanga. For average- to medium-quality textile manufacture, the Spanish instituted factories, or obrajes, for mass production. It was for use in the obrajes that the Spanish introduced the treadle loom to Andeans. Both very fine-quality and obraje weavings expressed the multicultural syncretism characteristic of the colonial age in every aspect of production as well as in finished form.

Though European occupation introduced profound changes in the Andean textile tradition, many Indigenous images and techniques survive today alongside culturally mixed and purely European introductions. Phipps points out (2004:96) that the cloth made by today's weavers expresses the colonial blending process in some ways and exhibits purely Indigenous styles in others. The warp-patterned Inca lexicon often mixes with European weft-faced patterns within a single work. While in Huamanga its influence was significant, in other areas the colonial period seems to have had little impact. One example of this is Andeans' continued fabrication of warp-patterned textiles for their own personal use in many regions outside Huamanga. Europeans changed the style of clothing worn by Indigenous people particularly in areas of higher population density. Together with changes, though, women and men still wear *chumpi* sashes replete with complex and meaningful imagery, and artists incorporate tocapu designs into tapestries. Alongside these Indigenous elements, weavers blend curvilinear Baroque arabesques, European animals, Christian religious symbols, and the like. The modern era has introduced new fibers, dyes, and images as well.

According to Stastny (1981:28) one of the reasons textiles continue to be important is that they are one of the only luxury items mountain people can afford to own. The weavers of Huamanga have inherited many aspects of the prized Huari tradition along with techniques and motifs found throughout the Andes. These artists produce high-quality textiles for themselves as well as pieces of varying caliber for multiple audiences and markets, local, national, tourist, and international.

Along with preserving tradition, today's artists incorporate innovation into their work. Weavers study and reproduce modern global imagery and design trends. They follow the flitting butterfly of international fashion. At the same time, they study the intricate production methods and religious meanings of ancient textiles. When asked if they could reproduce a Paracas textile, the unwavering response of Huamanga weavers in 2004–2006 was "yes." This assertion is not idle boasting because nearby looms held work of such very great merit based on serious and detailed studies weavers of today make of archeological textiles.

The raw materials of the modern era have also influenced contemporary weavers. Sheep wool can replace llama and low-grade alpaca wool for some textile types, though it weighs more and is less resilient against the weather than camellid wool. Synthetic fibers are now making a strong appearance, and rural buyers succumb to their low prices and easy care qualities as much as any urban and international population.

How Weavings Are Made

Various raw materials are used for weaving, some of which were discovered in ancient times. The materials include plant and animal fibers, some autochthonous and others imported. Cotton and furcrea plant-based textiles coincide with earliest human habitation. Furcrea are large succulents in the agave family and have pointed, fibrous leaves that can produce cloth.

The Peruvian coast has produced cotton in several natural colors in conjunction with the beginning of settled human habitation. Cotton colors include white, cream, tan, green, and rose. These colors grow naturally without the addition of dye. Coastal peoples wove cotton cloth of various kinds and added dyed fibers in bright colors, as well as feathers, and paint. Coastal peoples produced cotton cloth but also traded for camellid wool from mountain residents.

Locally domesticated animals like llamas and alpacas plus their wild cousins the vicuña and guanaco provided wool during Indigenous times. Llama wool and low-grade alpaca hair produce rough thread that is good for ropes, cords, and work clothing. High-grade alpaca wool and the hair of the tiny vicuña produce fine cloth, some so lightweight and close-woven that it resembles silk. This animal wool can be used in its natural colors in various intensities of white, cream, red-brown, brown, gray, and black. For dyeing, white alpaca or llama wool is best. In fact, there is some worry that modern market forces promote the breeding of white camellids to the exclusion of animals with wool in other colors. Market demand also precludes multicolor animals because this wool is difficult to use for a predictable color scheme. Some alpaca specialists say that spotted, pied, or variegated animals need to be culled from herds.

Alpaca Shearing in Huancavelica

The following descriptions are based on parts of films that the writer participated in making in 2004–2006 (Biella et al. 2006 b,c) about alpaca herders in Huancavelica department and the textile production process in Huamanga (note 1). Because these herders live near Huamanga, they supply weavers with wool, which is the basic raw material and first step in the textile-making process.

1. The series of three films made in 2006 by Biella, Wolowic, Strong, and Domingo has as its purpose continuous showings at international arts and crafts fairs to help Huamanga and Quinua artist groups sell their work to wholesale buyers. The film team worked with the support of the humanitarian aid organization Belgian Technical Assistance, San Francisco State University, and friends of the author in Peru.

Highland people are careful to shear their herds in a way that will allow their hair grow back so that it will protect them from the cold during the winter. *Alpaqueros* (alpaca herders) from the Huamanga and Huancavelica regions prefer shearing their animals in March and April because the end of the rainy season at high elevations provides these grazers with rich pasture at this time. Thus fortified, the sheared animals can regrow their heavy coats in time for the cold and dry winter in June, July, and August. The people who raise llamas and alpacas live at high altitude and so are among the most marginalized in Andean society. The economic poverty of the alpaqueros is extreme in highland Huancavelica who are major suppliers of wool to textile workers in Huamanga. In 2006 an NGO provided some of these herders with metal hand shears and introduced techniques for safely removing the hair of the animal while it is tied on top of a ground tarp. These introductions helped both alpacas and people. The alpacas escaped the agony of being shaved with shards of broken glass while they kicked in fear at the increasingly bruised humans wrestling with them. The new techniques and shears save both animals and people from needless injury and assure a better harvest of wool for the community. The tarp and temporary immobilization of the animal allow shearers to separate the valuable soft, inner hair from the coarse and often dusty outer hair and to roll the two types of wool into separate "packages" for cleaning.

Camellid Fabric Production in Huamanga Today

Once sheared and gathered, the wool must be cleaned and prepared for the next stage, which is spinning. Since most Huamanga weavers work with

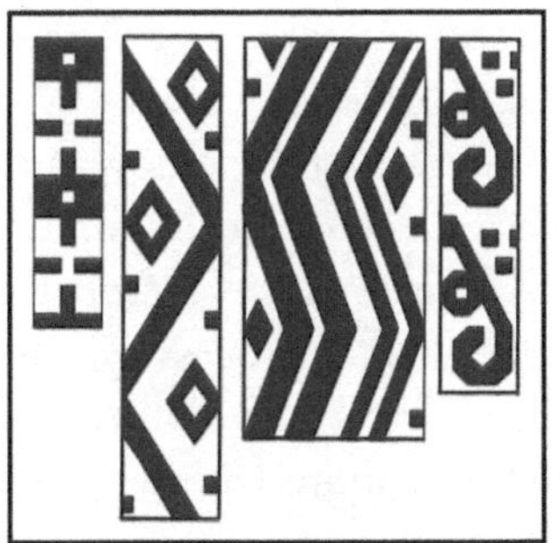

10.16 Training patterns by young girls learning to weave. Drawing by Rafael Domingo after Franquemont 2004:85, figure 6.3.

alpaca or sheep wool, the following descriptions of stages in the general weaving process concentrate on wool as the prime ingredient. One of the films mentioned earlier (2006b) depicts thread making by hand, without the use of a spinning wheel. In this method, the spinner takes a wad of cleaned wool and twists the hairs, snapping and smoothing them as she goes. She attaches the formed thread to a heavy spool on the ground. Clockwise twisting produces S-twined thread, and counterclockwise twisting produces Z-twined thread (Morris and Von Hagen 1993:94). Reversing the usual direction of spin that is traditional for a particular kind of textile can give thread special spiritual power.

Although some spinners use spinning wheels of varying complexity, skilled men and women can walk at a normal pace over fields spinning by hand and talking as they go. Their bobbins of thread hop along the ground at their sides as they fill with more and more fine and even thread. The hand-spun thread, then, gets gradually unwound from the spindle and formed into balls. The spinners may twist two or more threads together to form balls of thick or special-use threads. The thread, now wound into new balls, gets unwound again on a homemade and hand-operated circular carousel to form skeins. The wheel spins as the artist plays out the thread to a circle of movable pegs inserted into it. Weavers remove the skein from the circular frame after tying the loops at one end. The wool is now ready to dye.

Today, Andeans use both natural and synthetic dyes. Among natural dyes is cochineal, which produces various shades of red. Cochineal insects attack a common flat-leafed cactus plant, forming a kind of white rust. When rubbed between the fingers it produces brilliant red. Earths of different kinds make yellow ochres and sepias, carbon ash makes grays and blacks, calcium carbonate makes white, marine shells purple, indigo makes blue, and molle tree leaves produce various green and greenish-yellow shades. The walnut tree alone provides seven to eight different colors. Other bright colors come from wild plants such as the retama for yellow and from local mineral deposits. Mordants that make the dyes fix to or embed in fibers include urine and lemon or lime juice as well as more modern materials introduced in contemporary times. The dyeing process usually involves heating the dye materials and mordant in water and immersing the skein of thread. The weaver lifts the skein from the liquid with wooden paddles from time to time to check the intensity of the hue and to allow air to aid in making the color adhere. Aniline synthetic dyes are now readily available in local markets, as are newer dye compounds.

The artist hangs the dyed skein to dry, and the wool is now ready to use; but first the warp threads need to be set up on the loom. Sometimes the artist uses undyed and other times dyed thread, depending on the desired effect. The method of looping the warp threads involves walking back and forth between two stakes set apart the length of the piece the artist wants to weave. The artist unwinds the skein of continuous thread, making loops between the two stakes sufficient for the width and warp density of the piece. The writer observed Huamanga weavers still using this Andean-style looping technique. When finished, the artist saves the loops in an elaborate braid to prevent tangling. He then sets up the warp by deftly placing the collection of loops from one end of his braid at the desired intervals separated by tacks on the loom. He unwinds the warp braid on a long, square bar of wood until he reaches the loops at the other end for placing.

The weaver consults the design she has prepared ahead of time and makes small skeins of the appropriate colors, setting them up for passing horizontally (weft threads) through the warp. She looks at her design, hung from a top bar on the loom, as she works. For some patterns she will recite number sequences to herself, and she may shift gears from time to time, including embroidery or other decoration into her work. Indigenous looms were either upright of varying sizes or of the four-stake type or the backstrap type. The four-stake loom has a frame built parallel to the ground supported by four upright posts. Some four-stake looms can sit in an upright position. The backstrap loom is attached to the weaver's waist on one end and a post or frame at the other. These looms can accommodate complex weaves by means of various tools inserted between the warp threads as well as the weaver's own intricate handwork. Europeans introduced the treadle loom. Artists use all of these types of looms today.

Many weavers in centers like Huamanga most commonly use the treadle loom for historical reasons rooted in the European colonial period and because it accommodates the large tapestries and carpets for which they are famous.

The Andean traditional repertoire includes a very large number of weaving techniques. "Plain" weave refers to simple over-under threading between warp and weft. "Two-thread" weaves have two warp threads twisted together for strength. Three-thread weaves are much more difficult and rare and require the weaver to loop the thread and do needle-and-thread weaving. The high Andes Q'ero communities in the Cuzco area are among the few groups of weavers skilled in three-thread weaves. Cloths that exhibit images in reverse colors on both sides result from three-thread weaves that the Q'eros call Q'ero Pallay, or Q'eros patterns (Silverman 1998). The Q'eros consider their own patterns to be close to Inca techniques and superior to *qeswa pallay*, or lowland patterns. Q'ero weavers concentrate on warp patterning. Huamanga weavers produce more works using tapestry weave, though there are some textile workers who employ warp patterning as well as Q'ero-like designs. These individuals travel often to the Cuzco area for family and religious reasons.

The ancient pre-heddle Chavín ways of intertwining and looping weft yarns around warps still yield excellent cloth today. Other production methods such as double-cloth and triple-cloth weaves that combine several complete weavings together, as well as netting, gauze, brocade, and waterproof cloth techniques still survive from Indigenous times. Embroidery, appliqué, and attaching beads, metallic pieces, feathers, fringes, and tassels show both continuity and change as new decorative materials become available. The idea of innovation in attaching decorative material is not at all new. Morris and Von Hagen (1993:193) show an illustration of a feather tunic from Chan Chan covered with golden and pink feathers. Evidently, artists learned to pluck the natural green parrot feathers from the bird. By rubbing the parrot's skin with a toad secretion, artists could make new feathers grow in the desired colors.

Modern weavers look for design inspiration within their local traditions of the past and present. Huamanga artists favor Huari imagery and attempt to study it actively, using whatever archeological information they can find. At the same time, however, these artists may incorporate Paracas weaves, Greek keys, Baroque curves and flowers, Asian nature motifs, and the latest animated hit shown at the local cinema on market day. Artists mix design elements from across time and space as their ancestors did. They also create and innovate and do not feel averse to purloining a good idea from a neighbor if it suits them and sells well.

Meaning in Textiles

The symbolic imagery in textiles of the Andes makes them more than artifacts of their times and places. Cloth constitutes a system of communication. As clothing, textile images advertise a person's individual rank and prestige as well as his family history. Images in tapestries, clothing, and other pieces explain important aspects of astronomy, the agricultural cycle, topography, and plants and animals of a particular locale in addition to some symbols and general principles exhibited in textiles that are pan-Andean in nature. Images also express ideas about cosmology and about religious mythology. Millenarian movements like Inkarri can form part of this mythology. The Spanish were quite correct in their perception that the designs in cloth were powerful means of asserting and strengthening Andean belief and practice. The symbol systems today serve as practical plans for sustainable use of the environment, which for Andeans is based in their idea of proper spirituality.

Contemporary Andean people think in a way that uses spatial metaphors rooted in traditional cosmology and the environment. They employ symbols from Indigenous times and combine them with their later colonial and more recent heritage. Innovation, always part of this weaving tradition, still continues strongly. Textiles include so many images that scholars usually limit themselves to researching only a few of them. Three interesting studies of this type are Heckman's study (2003) of the lake symbol, Silverman's study of the symbols for Inti (the sun) and Chunchu (man with feather headdress), and Zorn's work on Taquile Island. The discussion that follows will look briefly at these analyses and then at some examples of Huamanga textile work.

Andrea Heckman, herself a weaver, conducted anthropological studies of weaving motifs in the Ausangate region near Cuzco. She focused on a diamond-shaped motif which refers, in that area, to the concept "lake." Lakes are important in the Andes, being part of Mother Earth's circulatory system of water. Weavers add shiny sequins and colored beads to their lakes because they "shimmer like light off lake water" (Heckman 2003:25). Heckman shows how textile designs manifest the environment, people, and spiritual beliefs of a specific local area. Inca warp patterning, inherited from the Huari, as well as other Indigenous design elements are very much in evidence in Heckman's study. She also examines the composite designs innovated by the Chavín, inherited by the Inca, and still in use among Ausangate weavers. The zigzag, or quenquo, and other geometric forms are common as well. Color symbolism related to gender (red for male and green for female, with yellow as a separation) apply as often to contemporary designs as to past symbolic categories.

Gail Silverman's work (1998) focuses on a number of design motifs, concentrating on the sun symbol, Inti, and the "jungle native" symbol, Chunchu. There is also an examination of striped (*lista*) motifs. Silverman studied at length with the Q'ero, who live in the high Andes remote from modern influences. The Spanish colonial period had little impact on the Q'ero, so little that their towns often have no church, central square, or government buildings. Once the Spanish did conquer the general area around the Q'ero communities, the Inca law against common knowledge about and wearing of royal cumbi designs lost its power. For this reason, square tocapu symbols and the color red were taken over by the masses. The masses now had access to the visual symbology formerly reserved only to the Inca elite. The Spanish takeover left a power vacuum in terms of visual design. The Spanish did not understand the political consequences of their ignorance of this process until much later. Commoners now felt free to incorporate cumbi designs, square tocapu symbols, and other formerly verboten elements into their personal dress, gradually creating revolutionary messages carried like banners on the clothes they wore every day. The Q'ero of today are descendants of those masses. Drawing on Zuidema's studies of ceques and tocapu (1964, 1990), Silverman shows how today's designs in cloth have similar social and religious meaning.

The rhomboidal (diamond-shaped) forms for the Q'ero are signs for Inti with respect to the layout of the four directions and have a particular topography marked by local mountains. The three worlds, Above, Here, and Below, are traversed by the sun and moon as they move in a circular path, at times going through the all-important water. The Q'ero area's specific local environmental positions of sunrise and sunset at particular times of the year (especially the equinoxes and solstices) signal important activities like planting and harvesting. These positions, calculated using local mountain peaks and other natural features, tell people how to live well in their particular econiche. A vertical bisecting line in design units indicates the zenith point crossing the sun's path. "Morning" signs show the sun's rays on one side of this zenith line, and "afternoon" (on the

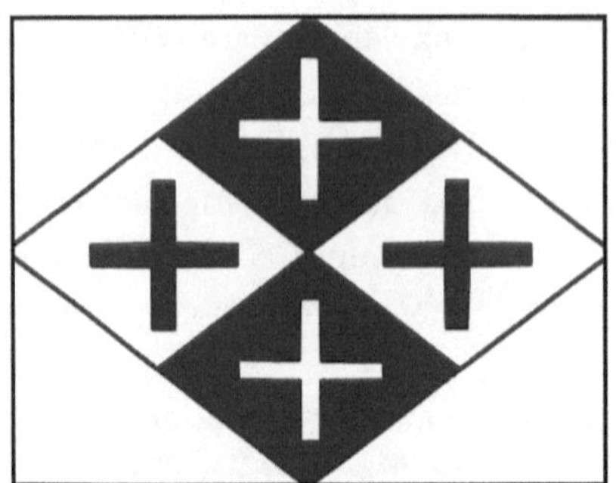

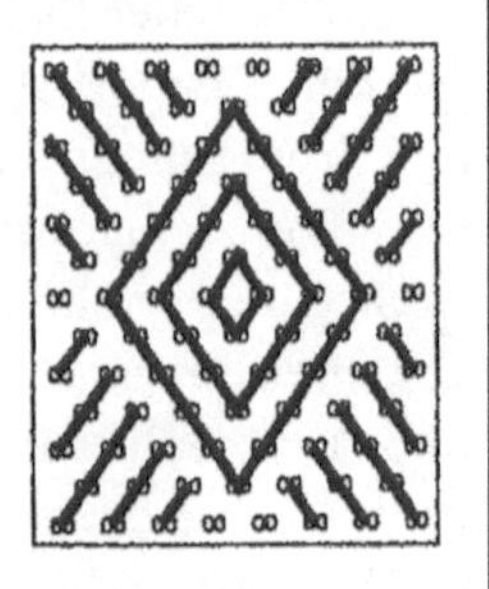

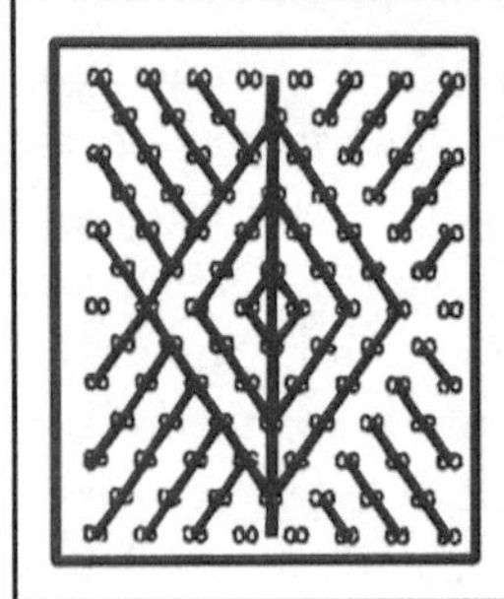

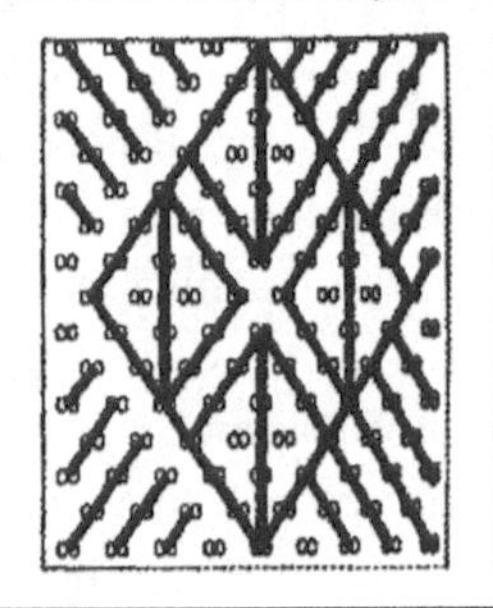

10.17 Q'eros motif "field with potato flowers." Drawing by Rafael Domingo after Silverman 1998:190–191.

10.18 Q'eros motif "sunrise." Drawing by Rafael Domingo after Silverman 1998:189, figure 1.

10.19 Q'ueros motif "noon." Drawing by Rafael Domingo after Silverman 1998:190, figure 3.

10.20 Q'ueros motif "sunset," embedded with concepts of sunrise, noon, sunset, and midnight. Drawing by Rafael Domingo after Silverman 1998:191, figure 4.

opposite side of the cloth) shows rays on the other side of the zenith line. The astronomer Aveni points out (1981) that calculating sunrise and sunset involves very small position changes in the tropic zone. Yet predicting these changes is all-important to agriculturalists. The chronicle by Guamán at the turn of the seventeenth century shows the sun with flowing whiskers during planting time (1988). People describe this "planting" sun today as having roots and shoots like a green plant. These radiating whiskers, for so they are called in Andean verbal lore, resemble the abstract growing season sun's rays in Q'ero designs. Guamán's winter sun has no beard in winter, when, of course, plants do not grow.

Silverman studied the chunchu symbol in some detail as well. This is a human stick figure with a spiked headdress that resembles the feather head decorations of today's chunchu dancers at festivals. The chunchus are said to be jungle people from Antisuyu, primitive and with no manners, according to a friend of the writer in Cuzco. This description is similar to those from the Inca era in which chunchus were thought to be ugly, primitive, and crazy, their formidable territory not even worth conquering—though this may be a way of justifying Inca reluctance to attempt such an adventure. People of the colonial period continued in this vein, calling chunchus unbaptized, uncivilized folk who did not eat salt or wear clothes (Garcilaso de la Vega 1960, 1961; Guamán Poma de Ayala 1988). Silverman delves deeper and notes that the chunchu symbol represents a mythical giver of all knowledge who indeed did come from the eastern part of the Inca empire, the jungle. Evidently, he married a primitive jungle woman, but it is to him that the Incas owe their civilization.

Somehow this chunchu knowledge giver of myth became associated with the last of the Inca emperors, Tupac Amaru, who was beheaded by the Spanish. Textile motifs often show chunchu figures with their heads and bodies separated. Sometimes a chunchu's body has two divisions and three different parts. The Inkarri myth comes into play because weavers say that the chunchu's or Inkarri's head is sending out shoots and roots and will one day grow back. When the regrowth is complete, pachacuti will occur and the Incas will reign over their world once more. President Velasco (in office 1968–1975) knew about the strength of this myth and the power of the woven symbol and promoted the weaving of the three-part chunchu to symbolize the return of Tupac Amaru (Silverman 1998:172–173). Such use

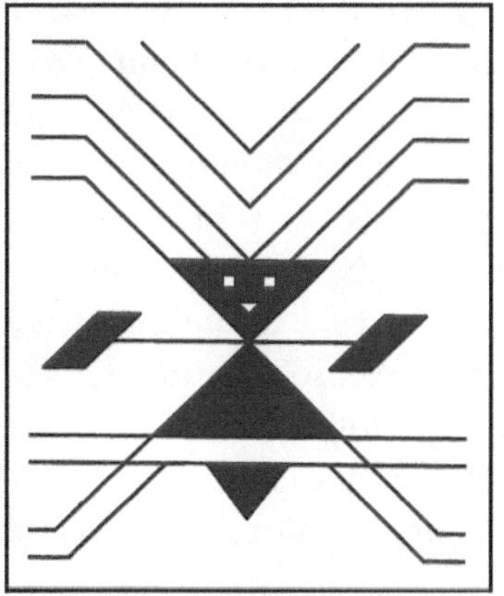

Figure 10.21 Inkarri or chunchu image. Drawing by Rafael Domingo after Silverman 1998:193, figure 9.

of colonial millenarian imagery in the twentieth and twenty-first centuries suggests that the processes of inversion and dual subjectivity continue to serve as ploys for artists to make political and cultural statements. These messages are carefully directed at a culturally savvy in-group, and in this subtle way they continue to assert the power and importance of traditional Andean values.

Silverman examined the meaning of multicolor striped motifs and connected these to the Andean penchant to classify by color. She analyzes a drawing by an informant, for example, that classifies llamas into thirty or more categories by color and mentions similar color categories for lakes (as does Heckman), planting fields, and corn. The Sarhua artist Berrocal classifies beans, stones, and potatoes in this way, by color (Macera and Andázabal 1999). Silverman suggests that different-colored woven stripes in distinct widths correspond to percentages of llamas, planting fields, lakes, and the like, classified in terms of different hues with number perhaps indicated by stripe width. She goes on to state that these stripe designs, or *listas* (lists), correspond to modern bar codes. Silverman shows other symbols for different types of plowed fields, raised beds, and other agricultural concepts.

Taquile Island on Lake Titicaca is one of the places where the Spanish colonial government attempted to preserve the highest-quality Indigenous weaving techniques. Zorn (1979, 1987) and others have studied the meanings of symbols used by weavers on Taquile, which, like Q'ero, is well known for its fine textiles. Taquile designs most often occupy squares with horizontal or vertical bands above or beside them separating chains of bands. Common symbols relate to agriculture, such as a six-sided rhomboid indicating an agricultural field. These can be divided into triangles having one or more ovals in them, indicating that the field is cultivated. Another common motif is a large mother bird followed by a number of baby birds, indicating fertility and prosperity. There is a symbol showing various plants with leaves and flowers, symbolizing the month of harvest. The morning and evening star, Lucero (the planet Venus), is shown with a bright center and extended rays. A square with an X within it represents earth, workable fields, the four directions, and the path of the sun at the solstice and equinox in a way similar to what Silverman describes for the Q'ero. Taquileños are of the Qolla subgroup (of Qollasuyu or Collasuyu, the southern part of the Inca empire) but retain the Inca custom of weaving history and identity into their wide and intricate sashes and knitted hats. These symbols very often recount the history of individuals and families as they lived through a particular agricultural year.

Huamanga weavers incorporate imagery and techniques such as those described by Heckman, Silverman, and Zorn from the Cuzco and Puno or Lake Titicaca regions. The Huamanga weavers differ from the others in that they continue the time-honored Andean custom of borrowing and combining regardless of period, region, or cultural origin. While the Cuzco and Lake Titicaca weavers preserve local traditions to a high degree, the Huamanga weavers add and borrow as much as they honor their own regional motifs and designs.

Artists and Their Art

Two of the Andean centers noted for fine weaving other than Cuzco and its environs, including Q'eros, are Taquile and Huamanga. The weaving tradition of Taquile exemplifies an area still characterized by precolonial designs and techniques. Huamanga's textile heritage, by contrast, exhibits a substantial European colonial contribution in styles produced there, though the work of some Huamanga artists resembles that of the Cuzco and Taquile weavers. The comparison is basically one between Taquile chosen as an example of a center of preservation and Huamanga as a center of borrowing and combination.

Taquile Island sits in the oceanlike Lake Titicaca. Visitors may reach it by taking a five-hour voyage in a fishing boat across the deep blue waters from Puno. The author came to know the Taquileños through her work with an NGO that sent humanitarian aid to support educational, health, and vocational efforts initiated by islanders. Like the Q'ero, Taquileños' relative isolation from the rest of the world has promoted the preservation of Indigenous weaving techniques and motifs, notably in the traditions of the Tiahuanacu and Inca cultures.

During late colonial times, the Spanish grew to appreciate traditional Indigenous textiles. Accordingly, the colonial government supported workshops for the cumbi camayocs, or excellent cumbi-pattern weavers, who lived in areas like Taquile. This reinforced the retention of precolonial motifs and weaving methods that today's Taquileño artists still employ. As a result, fine woven textiles from the island feature warp patterning and imagery much like that of the Cuzco area. Taquileños speak Quechua rather than the Aymara of close-by Bolivia. Islanders do not, however, identify closely with Cuzco, proudly calling themselves *qollas*, or natives of Qollasuyu (Collasuyu), the southern quadrant of Tahuantinsuyu. Until recent times, Taquile natives have been able to live on fishing and island agriculture. These two activities occupied most of their time, and they created textiles on a part-time basis. Recent growth in population has led Taquileños to rely increasingly on fabric-arts production in conjunction with their own small folk-tourism industry. They carry tourists to the island on their fishing boats for day and overnight visits. The travelers can eat, purchase weavings, observe festivals, and be hosted in local homes for sleepovers at a very small fee. Angry tourist-industry owners in the city of Puno responded to these upstarts by enacting legislation to limit the islanders' homegrown business attempts. Artists now spend more time on cloth production to acquire needed cash and less time on farming and fishing. The very fine work of islanders, often not much appreciated by unprepared and uneducated tourists, that is, visitors unfamiliar with Taquile iconography, gives way little by little to items made quickly and with less care. The best artists still make textiles of extremely high quality. Taquileños generously gave the author some very fine examples of their textile art in exchange (ayni) for her help to them (note 2).

2. The author went to Taquile Island to assist in the delivery of humanitarian aid in the form of health and school supplies as well as craft and household tools. She worked with the support of the NGOs MINKA, Mission of Love, and Pueblo to People and with friends in Peru.

There is little need on Taquile, at least in the immediate present, to resort to the kinds of plays on ambiguity Huamanga artists must employ to laud and preserve their identity. This situation can easily change with a tip of the knife edge upon which islanders' economic survival depends.

The following descriptions come directly from the film about the textiles in Huamanga mentioned earlier in which the author participated (Biella et al. 2006c). What follows is from the latter part of the film, showing finished work.

The weavers of villages within the department of Ayacucho, like those in Q'ero and Taquile, count themselves among the best textile artists in

Peru. Huamanga particularly was a major production center in Spanish colonial times where artists made utilitarian and decorative items for the homes of its wealthy residents. The city still boasts one of the largest concentrations of arts and crafts workers in Peru. The historical legacy of the colonial period is one contributing factor, but migration due to unrest during the Sendero period and the contemporary general trends toward urbanization in the nation as a whole have just as much importance in explaining the high concentrations of artists in the city of Huamanga. The causes and effects of migration constitute significant factors influencing the work and lives of these crafts producers. Many of the department's former village weavers find themselves living in the capital city of Huamanga today. Changes taking place in the rural sector have made it untenable to remain in small villages where weavers earn a living primarily from farming and only secondarily from weaving. As Huamanga city dwellers, they must live exclusively from weaving. The local and global markets for textiles encourage formerly solo artists to form associations in order to meet large orders. These associations adapt designs in such a way as to meet the needs of modern consumers who know little of Peruvian arts traditions.

Another group of migrants has had to leave the department of Ayacucho, including its capital city, altogether. A primary place of settlement for this group is Lurín, a town outside Lima near the ruins of the city of Pachacamac. The Lurín weavers make a better living than their peers residing in the provincial capital. Being near the large international metropolis gives foreign and domestic textile buyers easy access to Lurín textile producers. Lurín's economic advantage may be due, above all, to its location. However, Lurín weavers must often adapt and change their techniques and designs far more radically than their provincial brethren.

Weavers Who Remain in Huamanga

The weavers of Huamanga who live there now reside in small dwellings that almost dangle from the steep hills on one edge of the city. Access to their homes and workshops requires hiking up a long and steep incline, slippery from dust in the dry season and mud during the rains. Dwellings are makeshift, made of odd bits of stone, metal, and wood. Ceilings have gaping holes, through which views of the sky appear, and the tiny homes themselves huddle in a jumble of steep upgrades and downgrades with access by means of rickety stairways, planks facing precipitous drops, and ancient ladders. Artists use all sorts of looms, weaving techniques, and design styles. They produced the sample pieces described below on homemade treadle looms.

Though some Huamanga textile producers create designs like those studied by Heckman, Silverman, and Zorn, many concentrate on the tapestry weaves for which their city and department are most famous. These textiles exhibit clearly delineated designs with hard-edged transitions between colors, giving many of the more colorful pieces a jewel-like quality, in contrast to the gradual transitions that characterize warp-based styles. Many Huamanga motifs are pictorial, including recognizable shapes rooted in the natural world along with or instead of abstract images. However, Huamanga techniques are far from simple and include embroidery integrated into woven pieces, dimensional (low-relief) designs, appended materials like beads and fringes, and Escher-like designs employing natural or abstract images to create optical illusions and varying visual dimensions. The following examples give a small idea of the richness in the Huamanga repertoire.

The first example is an adaptation of an ancient coastal design featuring a repeated geometric pelican motif. Colors are cream, white, rose, brown, and orange. This work involves complicated multilayering techniques that cause the white borders around the birds to be thicker than the rest of the work. Here, the artist, Isaac, has chosen a design from an illustration in a book about a pre-Inca coastal civilization, and he adds his own creative input in graphic appearance and technique.

A second piece, an anonymous tapestry, contains a large number of colors and is divided into sections somewhat similar to the Huari and later Inca tocapu technique. It is completely geometric. One of its prime motifs is the cross symbolizing both Christianity and the four directions. The piece has cut-out areas woven into the design, and its colors are bright orange, black, and white.

A third example (anonymous) takes abstract Huari-Inca images and forms them into a scroll design that loops forward and back in space. A similar creative approach in another piece forms traditional motifs of lake flamingos into a stairstep design. The optical effect of these innovative creations rivals works by the artist Escher and graphic pieces made in the global art world. A fourth piece has a similar design that includes back views of abstracted Andean women in many colors. The rows of women appear to visually vibrate from side to side on the diagonal. These textiles employ traditional motifs designed in contemporary ways. Artists made these three weavings for sale to a national and international audience with some appreciation for Andean culture but also attracted by art makers' contemporary take in terms of design.

Some weavers still use tried and true techniques that may be thousands of years old. Andrés showed the filmmakers that weavers in his family still employ the Inca method of continuously looping a strand of thread to form the warp rather than resorting to the European tactic of cutting and tying.

Daniel and his family demonstrated wool washing, spinning, and forming a skein. Spinning still resembles chroniclers' illustrations and descriptions from Indigenous times as well. Women and men deftly form long, even threads from soft masses of raw wool. Their winding spindles dance along at their sides as they walk and chat with one another, even as they climb stairs. Daniel forms a skein by winding the balled thread on a simple circular apparatus with movable pegs to hold the thread in skeins of different sizes.

Alejandro takes a prepared skein of white wool and shows how he produces a delicate green tint from molle leaves taken from a tree in his small patio. He also describes the seven to eight shades he can derive from the walnut tree.

Felipe is a self-taught weaver who studies the illustrations in archeological books. He uses mirrors to make intricate pre-Columbian designs for his work. He has become interested in computers as well and rents one by the hour in a computer cafe to turn out some of his more complex mathematical design plans. Felipe is recognized by the other weavers as a consummate textile designer. He consciously studies and produces Huari-style tapestries. Felipe's awareness of how modern technology can help him in his work as well as his expertise in older methods are typical of the younger weavers. Felipe works on a tapestry in the film that shows a large raptor bird image in the Huari style with its eye characteristically staring to the side executed in multiple colors. Truncated birds and abstract lines mirroring the larger bird images appear on the margins of the piece as they do in Huari cloth arts. Felipe adds his own creative input by increasing the attenuation of the images and their repetitions beyond the usual Huari templates. He does all this with a school compass with its attached pencil, a small ruler, and a hand mirror. Watching him work, the writer could only imagine what Felipe might do if trained in the full use of computer design software.

Mariano and his wife, Petra, with Pablo and Ronaldo sit at looms placed in a row in a simple weaving shelter. Their looms hold modern, abstract motifs, Huari, Paracas, and combined designs of their own creation. In the film Mariano is in his twenties. He has taken one tocapu design unit to from an archeological illustration of an Inca emperor's uncu (tunic) and made it the only design in a large blanket-size weaving. The beauty of the design writ large attests to both the inventers of tocapu and this young artist's flare for innovation. The tocapu design is abstract and appears quite modern and contemporary. Knowledge about the Inca tocapus and their meaning is not necessary to appreciate the work because it stands out for the value of its visual design alone. This is naturally Mariano's objective because he is making the work for urban and overseas sale (figure 10.5).

Petra stands off to one side showing her embroidered wall hangings, which she makes for sale at the local city crafts market. Her images are costumbrista scenes showing people engaged in traditional rural tasks. Few women weave large pieces in Huamanga. Asunta (below) is an exception to the general rule, though in some families women weavers are common.

Pablo is a teenager and like his family member Mariano has chosen to blow up a tocapu design to blanket size. His work is a very simple checkerboard and so like Mariano's piece would probably not even need to be recognized as a tocapu by its potential buyer.

Ronaldo's tapestry of a classic pre-Columbian coastal design, is of such quality that it will go to Lima as an exhibit in a national craft fair. Ronaldo combines intricate weaving with fine embroidery to achieve a rich dimensional look replete with colorful imagery.

Guillermo and Asunta, his wife, show how they add elaborate embroidery work to weavings both during and after production of a plain-weave main piece. The large blanket-size weaving in the film section on embroidery shows local flora and fauna. Included are the molle tree with its purple fruits and various herbs and flowers used for dyes and medicinal purposes. Asunta proudly points to the many bright-yellow retama flowers pictured, emphasizing their importance as a symbol of resistance in Huamanga during the violence of the Sendero years. She explains the medicinal uses of mint and chamomile along with other herbs pictured. The design of the piece is Spanish colonial in style.

Armando and his large family of weavers have relatives in Cuzco, so he goes every year to participate in the pilgrimage of Qoyllur Riti there. He produces work in the warp-weave Cuzco-area style, fine copies of Paracas flying divinities blown up in size, and Huamanga-style tapestries.

This short sketch of some of the major stages in textile production plus brief descriptions of some types of finished pieces illustrates the vast range of work being made by Huamanga weavers of today. Artists are anything but preservers of local traditions. Instead, they borrow and combine as well as add their own creative input. Their repertoire spans the time dimension from the pre-Inca era to the computer age and space that encompasses the design motifs and imagery from all of Peru's regions and of other continents. Hanging outside some of these weavers' huts were large pieces in sheep wool emblazoned with Bambi, the Little Mermaid, Mickey Mouse, and figures from recent computer games. Some artists like Felipe consciously cultivate the major local culture of antiquity, the Huari. Other artists unconsciously employ Huari and Spanish tapestry techniques, or Inca motifs, just as some unconsciously use the Inca method of continuous looping when they set up their warp threads. All the artists, however, know they are doing work related to their deep identity and pride. At times this is hard to see in the most commercial lines of work, but it is there for those who take the trouble.

Weavers Who Migrated to Lurín

The artists of Lurín produce work similar to that of their Huamanga relatives and countrymen, but they must also meet orders from urban textile marketers in and outside Peru. When given a design, they produce it. Looms in Lurín held ikat weaving, patchwork pieces, painted designs, and combinations of these. The motifs include styles rooted in contemporary or historical Western tradition: pop art, art deco, art nouveau, Scandinavian interior design, and the like. Along with this work, Lurín weavers construct complex traditional pieces for museum stores and high-end interior design marketing, because in order to buy this kind of work purchasers must possess some degree of knowledge about Andean art traditions. Lurín weavers work and live in adobe structures, many with the roof open to the sky or partially covered with wood or bamboo. Since it rarely rains on the Peruvian coast, this does not cause too much of a problem.

Lurín artists have a local market as well, consisting of Lima residents for whom the town is a sunny escape from the city. During the austral winter, Lima resembles a dusty London covered in heavy fog. Lurín's location favors the artists, then, in terms of both local and international markets. However, the demand for their very high-quality traditional techniques and imagery is so specialized that it is relatively low in terms of volume.

The Lurín artists in various workshops displayed their textiles proudly as they wove. They were making many more pieces for a strictly mass commercial clientele than did their relatives in Huamanga. For example, place mats for a European department store chain had a standard fruit motif one might find anywhere in the world. Some of the looms held more traditional Andean pieces and combined designs. The artists collaborate to meet demand for bigger orders.

During the Indigenous period, textile workers preserved long-standing and pan-Andean traditions (themes), but they also borrowed and incorporated new ideas from other peoples (variations). Communities of today seem to emphasize either one or the other of the two processes. The artists of Taquile Island and the Q'ero communities on the one hand and Huamanga and Lurín on the other show how the policy of the Spanish colonial system contributed to preservation of Indigenous traditions versus the tendency to borrow and incorporate new ideas, respectively. The work of these two types of artist communities today represents different points on a continuum of separation and connection with the urban globalized market system.

The isolated Q'ero communities and remote Taquile Island are places where Indigenous techniques, imagery, and textiles are best preserved. In the more acculturated areas like Huamanga, adjustment techniques with relation to past colonialism and the present world are more in evidence. Huamanga weavers combine older methods with newer ones, for example, Inca warp thread looping and Spanish Baroque designs. Here also, artists demonstrate dual subjectivity in their combinations of Indigenous and European imagery. Insistence on dominating their overall design plans with Inca, Huari, or Paracas imagery shows inversion on the weavers' part. Though few Huamanga weavers wear traditional dress, they still depict themselves in colonial-style ponchos and chullos for men and polleras (wide skirts), lliclIas (shawls), and hats for women. By doing this artists express a kind of nostalgic and reverse disjunction. It is also in places like Huamanga and Lurín where multiple influences help create a stage for new and creative designs and techniques. This creativity (and some say, all creativity) consists of juxtaposing and combining several older traditions in new and innovative ways, such as in the Escher-like stairsteps and twisting ribbon designs some Huamanga weavers make using Inca tocapu symbols or Paracas pictograms as design units.

CHAPTER 11

Tinware (Hojalatería) and Huamanga Stone Carving (Piedra de Huamanga)

Hojalatería, or tinware, and *piedra de Huamanga*, or alabaster carving, are two arts of Ayacucho that are in danger of disappearing despite their great beauty and venerable history in Andean arts traditions. These two contemporary arts represent the complex legacies of metalworking and stone-working in the Andean past. This chapter includes the two genres in separate sections, first tinware and second Huamanga stonework.

Tinware (*Hojalatería*)

Tinworking artists of today face the disappearance of buyers for their utilitarian pieces due to factory-made metal and plastic items that now flood the market. As a response, artists focus on innovations aimed at promoting their decorative repertoire.

Tinwork, "the poor man's silver," has historical roots in the Andes as well as other areas of Latin America and in Spain. The appearance of plastics and items made through mass production in other materials have endangered the future existence of a large repertoire of pieces once made of plain or decorated tin. Hojalatería includes utilitarian tin items such as kitchen sieves, watering cans, pots, buckets, and the like. Artisans still make these by hand, though they encounter a great deal of competition from plastic and metal factory-made items. Decorative tin pieces in the shapes of Christian crosses, candlesticks, mirror and picture frames, toys, and figurines also abound. Artists leave some of these pieces in the natural metal color, though they burnish it and treat it against rust. Other pieces are brightly colored in addition to having the pressed, snipped, curled, and punched designs they share with nonpainted works. Tin crosses grace the roofs of many Andean homes to bless and guard them against evil. Tin candelabras resemble those found on church altars and like them bear designs of flowers, birds, and animals as well as religious figures such as angels and saints.

History of Andean Metalworking

Archeologists have unearthed metalwork in gold, silver, tin, bronze, copper-tin, and other pure and combined materials. Andeans perfected various complex metalworking techniques, including filigree styles that served both scientific and artistic purposes. This discussion derives primarily from archeological studies including Burger 1992, Morris and Von Hagen 1993, and Moseley 1992. Metallurgy shares with textiles and ceramics a venerable and complex past in the Andean region. Archeologists found gold foil as early as 1900–1500 BCE among pre-Chavín civilizations and copperwork before 1000 BCE (3000 BP). By 500 BCE (2500 BP) the early Chavín people were forging and annealing gold. The tradition of joining pieces of preshaped metal sheeting came about at this time as well as soldering and sweat-welding techniques. Repoussé (metal relief) decoration and the making of silver and gold alloys were also in evidence.

While in the northern Andes people had access to copper-arsenic ores and practiced gold and silver working, in the southern Andes crafts workers used copper and tin and produced bronze. There were copper-smelting sites at Tiahuanacu between 1200 and 800 BCE (3200–1800 BP).

Moche smiths worked with all metals but tin-bronze. Moche metallurgy rivaled that culture's own ceramic tradition. Moche artists worked with sheets over molds but also made cast metal with the lost-wax method. They employed hammering, annealing, soldering, welding, crimping, stapling, and attaching interlocking slabs and produced delicate filigree work. Moche ear spools, necklaces, rattles, plaques, masks, nose ornaments, headdresses, and armor abound in burial sites such as that of the Lord of Sipán. One example of this is an ornate necklace featuring medallions made up of spiders sitting on intricate webs. The Moche perfected electroplating by chemical means and techniques for making copper look like pure silver or gold. Other Peruvian coastal cultures also developed flourishing metallurgical traditions. The Nazca were making hammered-gold religious figures of combined animals like those pictured in their pottery.

The Incas brought North Coast Chimú metalworkers to Cuzco after conquering their civilization, which, in turn, had inherited and improved upon the Moche traditions. From the Lake Titicaca region the Incas brought architects to work on Cuzco buildings as well as their technique for joining stone blocks with copper clamps. The Incas borrowed the tin-bronze tradition from the Titicaca region and perfected a technique of cold hammering that made tin-bronze (copper-tin) into a metal harder than iron. The Incas may have used this hard metal for dressing stone, though it is certain that they used it for tools and for military weapons. The Inca version of tin-bronze aided their imperial expansion in the military sense and marked their increasing influence since conquered people readily took it on as a metalworking tradition. (The Spanish could resist Inca metal arms because they had perfected steelmaking technology.) Inca metallurgy also served medical purposes. Surgeons successfully repaired soldiers' head fractures with gold plates. Inca dentists filled teeth and did bridgework and tooth replacements with gold and silver and made replacement teeth with resistant stone materials such as quartz.

In 1572 the viceroy of Toledo (*virrey*, the Spanish king's representative in Toledo) allowed Indigenous people to be metalworkers after a period during which the Spanish did not allow them to practice this craft or to possess such items as Toledo steel swords. Though the Spanish taught their own techniques, Inca-trained workers already had a complex local technical tradition in their own right. Electroplating, which was unknown in Europe at that time, is an example. The Spanish set metal craftspeople to work on local raw materials rather than promoting grand-scale iron and steel technology into the Americas although these stronger, more resilient metals had aided the Spanish immensely in their conquest of the region. Accordingly, Andean artisans used their own production methods to make items in precious metals for their Spanish clientele such as the Church, and less costly metals like tin and copper for the common people.

Indigenous and Mestizo metalworkers took on Spanish Baroque decorative elements in a major way, adding a few details from their own visual tradition in the process. There was cultural blending in the technical sense. Spanish metal filigree work had developed out of a technology originating in Damascus. This Middle Eastern technique blended with the Andean styles to produce very fine and unique metal filigree pieces. Silver incense burners were common household items in the shapes of turkeys or other birds or animals; their purpose was to freshen the air in homes and patios. Baroque horror vacui design in the twirling forms of flowers plants and leaves often cover the animal figure. In addition to these European touches, the artisan might give the general shape of an Old World lion some New World puma characteristics. By the same token, a New World turkey might take on some Old World peacock elements. Elaborate and lacy filigree might form part of the decoration for these burners as well.

Probably it was in the churches where the metalworkers' art was most remarkable and where the designs most difficult to produce and elaborate appeared. The great lode of silver found in Potosí (a mountain in present-day Bolivia) as well as precious ore taken from other mines allowed silver church ornamentation on a grand scale to become relatively common. Altars often had ornamental silver plaques called *mayas* whose complex designs were created to reflect light. An altar with these mayas would glitter like a cut diamond. The Italian baroque tradition of "grotesques" is a common design element in silver mayas, church decorations, and door frames. Grotesques are animal and human figures whose bodies or limbs resemble plant branches and leaves. Some elements in these images derive from the Islamic injunction against the making of certain kinds of representations, which influenced the arts of Spain and Italy during Moorish (Islamic) colonization. Other roots of grotesques derive from mythological lore perhaps present in the ancient Mediterranean. One of these is the "green man" image, which shows a face with leaves and flowers radiating from it. Green man tales remain in the folklore of many European nations. Such imagery formed part of the Andean colonial visual repertoire. Another example of this process is the way the European winged serpent, or basilisk, became the divinity Amaru in Andean metalwork shops.

Portable altars during colonial times often had silver on the outside of the wooden retablo box that held figures of wood, Huamanga stone, or maguey paste on the inside. The silver in such an altar for the poor was replaced by tin. Colonial tinware mimicked silverwork. Tin was the poor man's silver and in many ways remains so today.

How Tin Art Is Made

There are two kinds of basic raw materials tin artists use. Found objects like cans and other metal containers cost nothing in terms of money, a great advantage. Artists can easily flatten these by cutting and hammering. *Hojalateros* also buy ready-made sheets of tin, and all need to find or purchase soldering material in the form of rods and wires. Extra items like abrasives for burnishing, rust-resistant paints, and colored enamels sit on workshop shelves as well.

Tools include measuring implements such as rulers, hand compasses, pencils and paper for design plans, metal clippers, punches, hammers, and forms for shaping three-dimensional motifs. There is a small fire burning for heating the metal rods of soldering materials and the soldering hammer if they use this traditional method. If artists have access to electricity, they use an electric soldering iron.

Artists begin the process by consulting the designs they have prepared on paper for the different parts of the pieces they desire to make. They then trace the appropriate shapes onto their metal sheets and prepare the parts by cutting, punching, and shaping them with a form and hammer or rolling and soldering them.

An artist can burnish, rust-treat, and/or paint individual parts before assembling the work as a whole. The basic support structure of some objects, such as crosses and candleholders, consists of rolled and soldered cylinders and a base form in cone shape with a circular bottom. This cone-shaped base is much like the construction of old-fashioned oil cans that tinworkers once made in quantity for their traditional clientele.

Artists solder the cylinders together to construct the support skeleton. After doing this, they affix the cutout rolled and curled added parts by lightly soldering them to the skeleton. Once completing the work, hojalateros correct small details, and some may add a coat of protective material to the fully assembled object.

Tinworking Artists and Their Art Today

Tinware today draws upon the Andean traditions of working with sheets of metal, pressing the sheets on forms to produce shapes, cutting, punching, repoussé, hanging moving parts from the main piece, and the like. Artists produce utilitarian and decorative items in the same workshop. Tin crosses illustrate the breadth of regional and individual variation that each type of product can have. Tin crosses are decorative and religious at the same time. Tourists and folk collectors buy them to adorn their homes, and villagers buy them to mount on the tops of their homes as a protection from evil forces. These crosses can have a simple filigree or botanical decoration, or they can have small symbols of the crucifixion (rooster, heart, spear, ladder, hammer, tunic, pliers, nails) placed on the cross pieces in an interesting design. The cross itself expresses belief in Christ and the four directions at the same time. The ends of the crosses' poles often terminate in sacred cantu flowers. The national flag of Peru might adorn the vertical beam. In the Callejón de Huaylas, the crosses tend to be silver in color with filigree decorations only. In Apurimac they are black. In Junín the crosses are painted in polychrome colors with all the crucifixion symbols intact. Antonio Vásquez, working in arts and crafts development and promotion, encouraged metalworkers of Huamanga to produce crosses in the Junín polychrome style for tourist and overseas sale (personal communication, 2004).

A common tin object that is utilitarian and decorative is the candleholder. Candleholders in full color with flower decorations like those used on retablo boxes (an innovation by Abrahán, a famous Huamanga tinware artist) now sell very well. Candlestick models are named for their flower decorations, such as *margarita*, "carnation," "sumaq," "sunflower," *esicha*, and "dahlia." Multiple tin candlesticks, or candelabras, hark back to the colonial silver candlestick tradition. Six or more silver candlesticks were placed in cathedrals or high churches. Tin workers call their large candelabras "cathedrals" (*catedrales*), and these may hold seven or more candles. The hojalatería tradition in general is in the process of disappearing from Huamanga and other arts centers as gourd carving already did. Only a few families still practice the craft. The acknowledged master of tinworking in Huamanga, Moisés, gave it up in 1990. There was simply too much competition from plastic and aluminum pieces available in the marketplace. Moisés' sons have since opened a shop again, and they do fairly well selling kitchen utensils and decorative pieces to local and foreign buyers.

Besides competitions from plastics, other factors make economic survival on the basis of arts production alone difficult. Multigenerational conversations with Jesús and his children reveal some of these factors. Jesús, the patriarch, was born in the early 1940s in a tiny village. Early in his life he suffered an accident that would keep him forever unable to walk. Fortunately, he learned to produce tinware from his uncle. He then moved from his small hometown to Huamanga, where he maintained a good business making tin crosses from old butter and alcohol cans as well as fabricating utilitarian ware from found or discarded items. He learned how to make candelabras from Moisés, and during the violent Sendero years he suffered a robbery in which he lost everything. Undaunted, he started working again and received invitations to show his creations in Lima in the 1990s. Early in the twenty-first century he began to make polychrome work that incorporated retablo designs and his sales improved dramatically.

Jesús works in his shop proudly alongside his wife and seven children. One of his sons, Noé, studied at the local college. He was in his early twenties at the time, and he talked about the special situation of young people of today in artisan families. Parents, he said, want their children to learn a profession in order to make a good living. Studies and professional work occupy the time once spent producing crafts. For this reason, hojalatería is only a weekend occupation for Noé. With understanding gained from his studies, Noé knows that his father's shop could do quite well with the addition of a few key tools and machines to make production physically easier and more efficient. In addition, the local and tourist markets for decorative items needs close study for the family to make products that match buyers' desires. It appears that craft production may return to being the part-time occupation it once was when Jesús and his generation lived on farms. Farm labor provided the family its main sustenance, while crafts served as a supplement. Noé's primary source of family income may come from his college training while crafts become an adjunct source of revenue.

Two pieces from Jesús' workshop will serve here as examples of contemporary tin art. The first is a metal cross. It is about one foot in height, indicating that it was made for display inside the home rather than outside on the roof, in which case it would be two or three times bigger. The cross itself consists of sheets of tin rolled into tubes. The side pieces join perpendicularly with the vertical by means of V-shaped cuts on the ends. The vertical tube fits over a closed cone shape at the bottom, oil-can fashion. In this way, the cross stands on its own. All of the metal is painted in intense colors: green, red, yellow-gold, white, black, and three shades of blue. Decorations are cut-out pieces attached to the cross and to each other in layers. These decorative pieces have a flat background color and overlay details in contrasting hues. Most of the attached shapes symbolize ideas and events surrounding the crucifixion of Christ. A black and blue tunic at the base of the cross represents Christ's clothes. Extending upward in two increasing angles attached to the base and horizontal arms of the cross are two spears, recalling the Roman soldiers and Christ's side wound. There is also a sponge on a pole in memory of the drink of gall and a ladder used to remove the body. A hammer and pliers attached at the base of these items stands for the nailing procedure. Above the tunic on the main shaft is a chalice and host, a representation of the round wafer taken in communion in some Christian rituals (the mass ritual recalls the crucifixion) and above that the heart of Christ with another cross painted on it. To the left and right of the chalice are two hands with partial sleeves representing perhaps the idea of prayer and sacrifice, or the body of Christ hanging on the cross. At the pinnacle of the cross sits a white rooster crowing in memory of Peter's denial. The decorations painted on top of the symbols are the same used in retablos in both style and form. The cross at first seems a completely Christian piece. However, there are large cantu flowers extending from the cross' horizontal arms. Flags project from the spears, and cross-timbers recall the decorations appearing in the arts of Spanish colonial times on the Inca emperor's headdress. Flags, or wifala, are identity markers for Andeans. They project from woven motifs and wave in the hands of comparsa (dance-drama troupe) leaders. The famous singer Jaime Guardia, who accompanied a scissors dance group in New York with the writer, much enjoys singing folk melodies that feature the flag symbol.

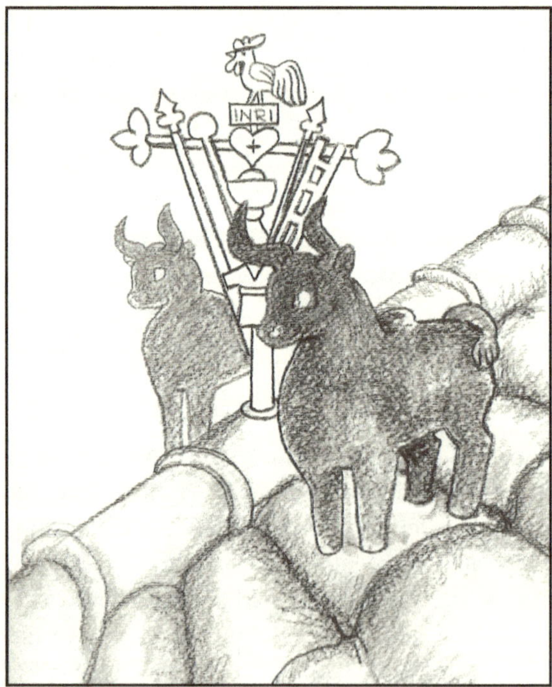

11.1 Tin cross between bulls of Pucará on roof in town of Quinua. Drawing by the author.

The second piece is a brightly painted candelabrum that holds three candles. Its basic structure resembles the cross described above except that its base is square. Where the cross-pieces of the candelabra join is a large, flat, tin cut-out painted in the sunflower design used on retablos, and at the points of the cross-pieces is the sumaq flower design. Extending up in a graceful curve joining the base and cross-pieces with a diagonal are leaf designs. Colors include three shades of blue, orange, yellow, red, white, black, and green. Jesús' workshop still produces these kinds of pieces in plain burnished tin as well as in color, with the decoration delineated by repoussé and snipping techniques.

The Andean tinware tradition is the common people's metal art, yet its beauty rivals that of pieces executed in expensive gold and silver. This genre, like carved gourds, is a fragile one. Modern plastics, other synthetic materials, and factory-made metal items fill markets for local, national, and international clients, and some of the items resemble pieces made by traditional crafts workers. If the buying public does not support the original versions of these delicate works of art, they may become extinct. Noé and other young metalworkers provide a counterforce for their continued existence, and perhaps their energetic efforts will lead them to success.

Some of the first Andean tin artists to gain recognition used recycled metal, as many still do, like other artists in economically poor areas of the world who make satchels from soda cans and decorative animal figures from cracker tins. Metalworkers who paint their pieces and, for example, use flower designs more typical of retablo doors represent a trend toward crossing between traditional genres. The artists' coping tactics, such as the dual subjectivity evidenced in the cross described above, appear in tin as much as in the other arts.

Huamanga Stone Carving (Piedra de Huamanga)

Though stone carving is an ancient and highly developed Andean art, the local alabaster of Ayacucho began to be worked in quantity beginning with the Spanish colonial period. This was in part due to Ayacucho's (Huamanga's) prominence in the colonial governmental system. Today, Huamanga stone carvers make a wide variety of objects.

Piedra de Huamanga is a kind of alabaster native to the environs of the city of Ayacucho (Huamanga). Artisans today make small and large objects from this stone, including works of fine art, nativity scenes, statues both religious and nonreligious, and utilitarian items like goblets, ashtrays, and candleholders. Though some experts say that carving in Huamanga stone is a purely colonial and contemporary phenomenon, general stoneworking in the Andes is a very old tradition.

History of Stoneworking

Andeans made stone tools and buildings by 10000 BCE (12000 BP). Carvers produced this extraordinary work at first without the aid of metal tools. They used other stones to peck their work into shape and sand and water to wear away rough areas. There are two kinds of carvings aside from the stone architecture at Chavín de Huantar. First, three-dimensional heads of people and animals hang from the walls by means of extensions or tenons embedded into fissures within the walls. These heads portray people, jaguars, serpents, predatory birds, and other beings. Second, flat granite blocks form the surface for other carving. Sculptors incised grooves and produced bas relief in these painstakingly smoothed stones. Images include animal deities and complex combined figures. Among the Chavín stone motifs, Burger comments (1992:220) on a prevalence of checkered crosses. The cross image and checkering would later become important in Inca and Spanish colonial art.

Carvers had to use sand and water to create the flat stone surfaces to be incised. They then employed percussion and pecking with hard stones to form images on these flattened supports. Different grades of sand provided for polishing. In their large carvings the Chavín used an idealized style with complex details such as picturing hair in the form of snakes, double images, split perspectives, and many other characteristic devices. They also made small items out of stone such as drinking vessels and snuff spoons.

The civilization ofTiahuanacu likewise produced extraordinary carving on stone plaques and enormous statuary in incised and bas relief styles that artists incorporated into the architecture. The Huari inherited Tiahuanacu designs and incorporated them into their own stonework. The Huarpa and Huari cultures of the ancient Huamanga region used Huamanga stone in their art and may have dyed some of their work with materials available in the local natural environment, as contemporary people do. The Huanca, Huanta, and Chanca cultures inherited this alabaster-working tradition. When they in turn became part of the Inca empire the tradition passed on to this new dominant culture.

Inca stone-carving motifs grew out of the Chavín, Tiahuanacu, and Huari traditions combined. The important stone image known as the "gateway god" studied by archeologists at Tiahuanacu became Illapa, the lightning god of the Incas. Illapa's visual characteristics and divine character resembled that of the gateway god. Similarly, Huari images of the sun and moon and other supernaturals bear resemblance to Tiahuanacu as well as Inca representations of these divinities. Inca stone images reveal some of the visual and symbolic complexity of the ancient Chavín ancestors as well. Specialists in the Inca cultural tradition, particularly the material repertoire, often say that stonework might be the Incas' most original and important art form. Inca architectural stonework at sites like Sacsayhuaman, Coricancha, and Macchu Picchu show great engineering skill as well as artistry.

Small-scale Inca stonework shows the same respect for the original form of the stone along with a very sleek and modern-looking finish as do large-scale architectural works. The stone canopa figures, illas, and other small artifacts used in rituals illustrate the Inca approach to working with this very difficult material. Stastny finds that the sacred "lake stones" that evidently were honored in the Tiahuanacu tradition are made of the same alabaster that is called Huamanga stone today. He adds that for the Incas and their ancestors, stone is a sacred material. The mountain gods, or apus, are of stone. Small stones are the apus' children. Special stones like illas, carved or uncarved stone canopas, or ultis, and stone plaques incised with symbols for making prophecy have special power among stones. Andean religious specialists still carry such items today in their blanket-covered bundles, or qepi (Stastny 1981:167, 178). Stones at particularly holy places in the landscape can become huacas, or holy sites. These sites tend to be located along lines of sacred force called ceques that cover the old Tahuantinsuyu in a grid of interlocking wheels. Trees, hills, and other natural features can become huacas by reason of such location as well. Andeans dress these stones in finely woven male and female clothing and pray near them, sometimes offering fine clothing as a burned sacrifice (Phipps 2004:3–35).

During colonial times, baby Jesus figures called manuelitos and carved in stone or made from other materials took over this role of huaca. These figures often wear intricately woven Andean clothing and take important roles in Christian rituals. The early Spanish colonists used Huamanga stone as a material for windows and skylights because of its translucent qualities. Romanesque-era churches in Europe have windows paned with alabaster, and ships directed light from the deck into the hold using this material. Huamanga stone, the local alabaster, was at first called *belenguela* by Spanish colonists. It was one of the major materials used for making utilitarian pieces such as mortars and bowls in colonial Huamanga. The early colonial institution of the School of Sculptural Arts in this city helped to make it a major center for Huamanga stone construction. The first quarry came into use as early as 1586, and the first decorative ware produced consisted of details for buildings. In this Indigenous school of sculpture students carved pumas, serpents, and other Andean motifs into colonial doorways, columns, and pillars made of alabaster. Although the stone comes naturally in different textures and colors, colonial carvers colored it with natural dyes as a finish for some of their work. The first smaller pieces in alabaster during colonial times served the needs of traveling missionaries. Sculptors carved small figures of saints, Christ, and religious scenes that priests and friars could carry on muleback. These appear in the beginning of the seventeenth century.

As time moved forward, alabaster carvers worked less for religious clients and more for everyday use. Finally in the nineteenth century, alabaster carving spread into the countryside and was taken up by rural artisans. In the twentieth and twenty-first centuries, Huamanga stone became almost entirely a "folk" and "tourist art" form. The tradition seemed to lose its connection with fine arts entirely. These changes are in part due to economic transitions. Just as important, however, is the role of Indigenist intellectuals, a kind of sanctioning body for folk art traditions. Between the seventeenth and nineteenth centuries, alabaster carvers met the demands of their clients by making work that conformed to European fine arts traditions.

This trend changed by the middle of the nineteenth century, when more highly prized materials like imported marble and bronze replaced Huamanga stone as preferred building materials. Simultaneously, the city of Arequipa, a great buyer of Huamanga stonework, became impoverished. Thus, Huamanga stonework suddenly lost its marketability. As a result, many artisans changed occupation or moved to the city of Lima. A common career change was working as tombstone carvers, but with marble rather than alabaster. Neither José María Arguedas nor José Sabogal Diéguez, important members of the Indigenist movement, gave their official imprimatur to Huamanga stone as a respectable folk tradition. These and other Indigenist intellectuals tended to pass it off as purely "colonial" art and thus foreign to the Indigenous and Mestizo national identity of Peru. Finally in the 1960s, the essayist Mercedes Gallagher de Parks completed a study of Huamanga stone, giving it validity as an Andean art form. Her son continued his mother's efforts by publishing the essay "La talla popular de Piedra de Huamanga" in 1967 (Bayona 1999).

How Huamanga Stone Is Carved

Techniques for working the various kinds of stone used by carvers in Peru are somewhat similar. Stonecraft traditions today are regional: Huamanga stone in Huamanga, granite building blocks in Arequipa, marble in Pucasmayo, and colored stone in Cajamarca. In Lima, carvers work with onyx, quartz, obsidian, and Peruvian turquoise. Huamanga stone comes naturally in different varieties and colors, and artists can add dyes to enhance or change stones' colors. Some of the natural colors are shades of white and pale tones of beige, gray, pink, and peach. Carvers' tools include hand saws, engravers, punches, rasps, chisels, knives, electric saws, sanding materials, drills, and augers. Huamanga stone can be worked by hand, so many artisans in Ayacucho carve without power tools. Artists do use power tools to carve harder and semi-precious stones.

The first stage involves cutting the stone into rectangular or cube-shaped pieces in the appropriate size for the final work the carver has in mind. Then, he starts removing big pieces of stone with larger tools. The artist produces several modules when the final work requires separate carvings to be combined in the completed piece. For example, the stable for a nativity scene starts out as a block separate from saint and animal figures. As the carver begins to work on small details in the figures, he uses smaller and smaller tools. He sharpens corners and makes folds of clothing, fingers, toes, and facial features, for example, with needles, small knives, and in some cases specialized electric tools. He smoothes and shines the work with files, sandpaper, and abrasive pastes such as rouge. When it is time to put the parts of a complex figure together, the artist places the figures on supports or inside frames he has prepared for this purpose and makes the join permanent with silicone or other adhesives. After the glue dries he removes imperfections and makes final corrections. Some artists add dyes at this point or before gluing to enhance color. The last stage involves covering the figure with a transparent varnish to seal and protect the piece (CIAP n.d.).

Alabaster Carvers and Their Work Today

The following pair of artists and their work reflect two important aspects within the tradition of alabaster stoneworking. María is a young woman just starting out as a carver. Her ideas and work show the shape of things to come for people in her generation. Román is an older male and an established, famous carver. Though he is self-taught, his work is of global fine arts quality. His ideas and creations reflect the past into present periods of history for carvers in Huamanga stone.

María sits at work in a small stall at a center for arts and crafts production and sale in Huamanga underwritten by a foreign foundation. She wears a heavy apron and carves a small figure of an Indigenous woman with a hand chisel. Around her arranged on shelves for sale are some of her other carvings: nativity scenes, saints, angels, animals, lamps, tourist sites, candleholders, ashtrays, bowls, and some allegorical and mythical "fine arts" figures. By the time she was twenty-four years old María had two children. A single mother, she desperately needed to make a living for her family. She tried alabaster carving. The first figure she sold was a comic statuette of a drunken man. After that, she sold more work and was eventually able to make a living from her carving to survive economically.

She said it is good to make a wide variety of different kinds of carvings as a shield against the fickle nature of fads, styles, and other market trends. She felt strongly that innovative pieces like her very modern lamps are just as important as tried-and-true motifs like nativity scenes. María posed for a photograph with her large, innovative pieces. One sculpture shows a rape scene, another depicts a traditionally shaped angel with elaborate wings, and a third piece is a lamp base in a sleek ovoid shape. These works, she said, symbolize her feelings about women's rights, the importance of religious faith and a positive attitude, and finally the need to be brave enough as an artist to innovate. All of these values, she said, are necessary for success as a young carver. Though she is not yet well known, María's point of view reflects that of many artists under the age of forty who may be the future stars in this craft.

Román is a very well-known artist who has won many awards, both national and international. His work could stand with carvings in the world's major museums, yet his origins resemble those of many other artists in this craft. Román was the son of an extremely impoverished single mother. He began carving Huamanga stone with a kitchen knife at a very young age and immediately began to sell his work. Encouraged by this, he carved at first in exchange for food and sundries for the family and later for cash. He carved plates, pots, nativity scenes, and statues. In the 1960s and 1970s he received a prize in a hotel crafts contest and later got a job in a local village teaching stone carving. In 1980 he won a national art prize in

Peru and four more awards in the following two years. He quit the teaching job, which he said in hindsight would have prevented him from going further in his field. Within the next few years he won several international awards in Latin America and was sent to Ecuador to participate in a business development course.

In the 1980s and 1990s the prices for Román's work went up. He began to make unique and original fine arts pieces. Some of these works are symbolic in the more traditional Andean sense, while others are metaphoric and even allegorical in a more universal way. Along with the fine arts pieces he still makes alabaster retablos, figures of Saint Martin and Saint Anthony, angels, and folkloric pieces. His large workshop and garage showroom have tables showing pieces in many styles and sizes. Colonial figures with Baroque designs of saints sit on one table, while modern statuettes sit on another. One display holds trays and trays of small, egg-shaped nativity scenes for the tourist market. The artist's six children also carve. One son, Timoteo, studied fine arts and business at the college level. His carvings are extremely simplified, smooth, and modern. He has clearly taken on a contemporary esthetic, while his father produces diverse kinds of work. Besides the diversity in types of styles, images, and themes in alabaster, Román makes ceramics, cement figures, and woodcarvings.

In one portrait photographed by the writer, Román stands next to a table full of Baroque-style carvings of saints and angels. The figures of angels are in white alabaster, and the saints—Virgin Mary and child and Saint Michael the archangel—are in wood that is painted in bright colors with gold metallic details. These wooden figures are very much in the Baroque colonial style. He holds in his hands a symbolic piece made of alabaster about two and a half feet high that shows Andean figures standing in for Mediterranean classical characters. A modern-day Inca man in country dress hefts the world on his back Atlas-fashion, and smaller figures at his feet are of Andean women and children at their daily travails.

In another portrait Román stands beside a large, multifigured work in alabaster almost three feet in height. It shows the children of all the world's continents struggling for peace, justice, equality, and their basic human rights. He spends some time talking about details on the Latin America side of this last piece. Small scenes on the base show children in agricultural labor, craft work, and other typical regional occupations. Larger figures representing American Indigenous children support a victorious condor with its wings extended on their upraised hands. The other sides of the sculpture portray Asia and Africa in similar ways. Román's style is a simplified realism characteristic of many artists who work with stone. His proportions, details, sense of design, and command of subject matter make his work stand head and shoulders above the rest. He values diversity, creativity, and risk taking. Like María, he maintains a large repertoire of traditional production lines at the same time. He is a fine artist who easily fits into a "world class" category, but he is at the same time realistic about what it takes to assure his family's well-being. In his original fine arts pieces, Román expresses inversion very clearly. His special status as a recognized artist gives him the freedom to do this in a more obvious way rather than in a completely hidden or ambiguous manner.

Lastly, two small Huamanga stone figures by an anonymous artist stand as examples of carefully made work that has a broad buying public. The figures are about three and a half inches high and of natural white stone color. One is a man and the other a woman, both in traditional Andean dress and playing local musical instruments. The woman wears a fedora hat and braided hair. Over her shoulders is a lliclla, or shawl, with a tiny incised border design. She holds a drum in her left hand hanging from a strap and beats it with a drumstick held in her right hand. Her full pollera skirt has many folds carved into it and a detailed border at the bottom. Her tiny face, hands, and feet have precise carving of details such as eyebrows and fingers. On his head the man wears a chullo, a knitted hat with ear pieces, tassels, and incised designs. His cheeks bulge as he blows on a traditional spiral-shaped trumpet (*waq'rapuku*) made of stacked cow horns. He wears a plain poncho and pants with ojotas, or truck-tire sandals. The feet on this figure are outsized and elongated, as are the feet on many such carvings. It is hard to tell whether this is a structural necessity or merely a visual convention. The overall proportions are fairly accurate, though the head-to-body ratio is more like that of a child, increasing the figure's "charm factor," which, no doubt, appeals to buyers.

Final Thoughts

Huamanga stone carving as a genre was not helped by criticism on the part of intellectuals who did not approve of craft forms they felt lacked Indigenous as well as colonial roots. However, many very beautiful arts traditions arose as a result of interventions from professional or even foreign groups and individuals. In all of these cases, an outsider helped local craftspeople elaborate on a limited genre already in their repertoire

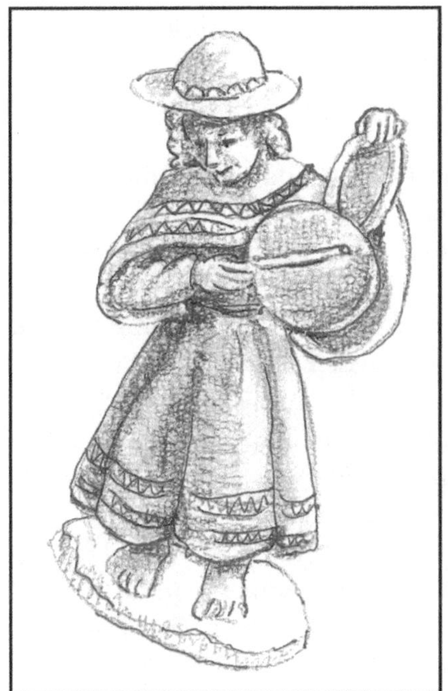

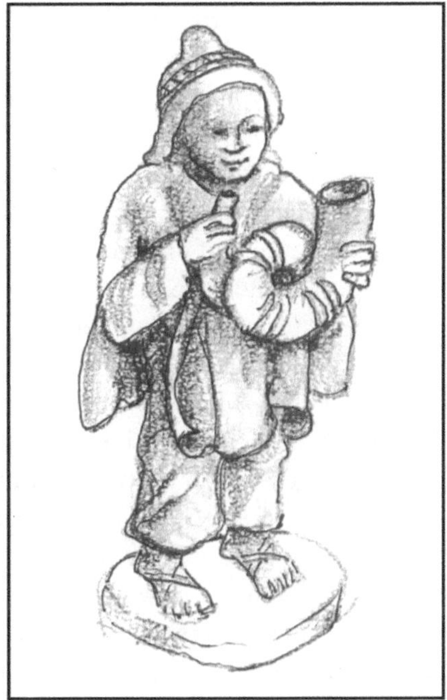

11.2 Huamanga stone figure of woman playing drum. Drawing by the author after anonymous piece in her personal collection.

11.3 Huamanga stone figure of man playing waq'rapuku musical instrument made of stacked cow horns. Drawing by the author after small anonymous piece in her personal collection.

and aided them to produce for a wider market of buyers. In the case of alabaster carving in Huamanga, there was a substantial Indigenous tradition of working in the medium before the Spanish colonial period of which the Indigenists were not aware. Western-educated appreciators of art value creativity, and such spontaneous generations of new forms are the stuff of which creativity is made.

Contemporary carving in Huamanga alabaster has begun to combine with other genres. One of the ceramics artists interviewed here applies alabaster flowers to the shoulders of his Pucará bulls. Looking at this from another angle, some of the earliest (seventeenth century) portable altars (retablos) as well as some of the very newest ones have alabaster rather than plaster or potato-flour paste figures in them. Young Huamanga stone carvers exposed to formal art training have added an abstract and modern sleekness to their figures. Whether these will sell like hot cakes, as do similarly "modern" Seri ironwood carvings in Mexico, or be looked upon as stereotypical by the art market remains to be seen (Graburn 1976, 1999).

This trend toward a kind of standardized "modernism" in all of the Andean arts constitutes a certain stylistic and esthetic disjunction. More standard examples of disjunction, such as nativity figures dressed in Andean clothing, are much more common.

The examples of art presented here show a broad range of styles: the work of a talented beginner and that of a master craftsman and fine artist and small items of good quality for mass sale. Huamanga stone carving, like tinware, has fewer and fewer specialists in the genre with each passing generation. There is a need for both market cultivation and the training of young artists to keep these endangered traditions alive. Huamanga stone carving represents one of the last remaining stone arts still connected to the Indigenous and colonial history of the Andes. Artists continue to work with the material to produce a wide range of styles for utilitarian and decorative ends. In this way, they hedge their bets in the face of unpredictable market forces and at the same time assure incomes for their families.

Conclusion

This book is about how Andean people of the past and present create meaning in their lives and assert their self-worth using images and forms as communicative media. The specific natural forms, living beings, and processes taking place in their life-sustaining and sacred mountain environment provide the raw materials for art motifs. Similar images appear over broad geographic areas as well as multiple time periods. Andean thinking about time, space, and the place of human beings in the universe are thus expressed. Verbal language contains a glimmer of what art describes to Andeans. Visual metaphors used by Westerners as illustrations or by scientists to explain such complex ideas as relativity and string theory are Andeans' everyday parlance. Andean art has a political and social dimension as well. It tells of a people long accustomed to survival in a demanding environment and who constantly assert their identity and self-worth in the face of a succession of conquerors and colonizers, be they religious, military, or economic. Andean artists draw much of their strength from the sacred that is manifest in their art. Their cosmovision is one and the same as the concrete and awe-inspiring world of nature surrounding them.

The twenty-first century, with its World Wide Web, cellular telephone networks, and air travel, destroys the historical and geographic boundaries that defined research contexts for students of Andean arts in the past. This study has different boundaries, perhaps more relevant to today's world reality. It concentrates on the arts and artists in the city of Huamanga and its surrounding area. However, what is defined as Humanguino (people and customs native to Huamanga) has been enlarged by the Internet and similar tools plus national and international labor migration to include locations throughout the globe plus all imaginable periods in history. New and not so new media as well as visits and communication with relatives and neighbors working elsewhere in Peru and abroad allow Huamanga artists to travel through time and space in an unprecedented way. Artists of today thus borrow and combine new ideas with old in the time-honored tradition of Andeans since the advent of the first urban civilizations in the region, though now with enormous reach through space and at immense speed. The much-discussed contemporary issue of "appropriation" in the visual arts, "copyright infringement," and other associated problematics have not much bothered Andean artists either now or in the past. Rather, they adhere to a common definition of creativity as the combination of existing forms made new through innovative elements born of their own imaginations.

For those first peoples who eventually founded urban civilizations in the Andes, the difficult and often unpredictable natural environment required periodic travel and migration in the constant quest for water, food, and other scarce resources. In these lives shaped and inspired by mobility, Andeans encountered, traded with, and sometimes colonized other peoples. At nodes of encounter, such as trade sites and religious shrines, the many cultures of the Andean coast, mountains, and jungle exchanged goods and ideas, especially those that visually represented religious concepts rooted in nature. The elements of nature, both animate and inanimate, that allow Andeans to thrive in their struggles for survival may just as easily cause them harm. Such powers demand constant propitiation and respect.

Andean peoples did not have the kind of writing that is familiar to readers of this book. Instead, they employed a communication system of images and forms. In this way they expressed a metaphor for space and time conceived as circular-accumulative or, perhaps better, spiral-shaped, that is hardly expressible within the linear linguistic model of European and Western thought. Andeans experience cycles that repeat (called "themes" in this study) and have the capacity to incorporate new concepts (called "variations" in this study) as they arise. These curved space-time dimensions derive from the rhythms and cycles of nature—the rising and setting of the nurturing and blinding sun, the blue shimmer of steep and slippery ice crags on mountain pinnacles, the flow of streams over a thirsty land and the mad floods of rivers in the rainy season, the opening of flowers, the rise of tender green grass blades and their incineration under lava flows, the flick of a llama's ears, the flash of fang and amber gaze of a puma. Elements of nature for Andeans were and are sacred and thus inspire deeply religious thoughts and feelings.

Andeans of today continue to think and communicate by visual means. Images and forms have a number of advantages over the words in this text. They have a certain all-at-onceness that permits viewers to "read" them in multiple ways. Groups of viewers who are more sensitive and sympathetic to artists' culture and values are better able to discern art makers' creative intent. However, artists must live with and sell their work to populations that discriminate against and repress all that Andeans hold dear. Under these adverse conditions, art makers must be clever enough to protect themselves and yet reserve their most intimate communications for a chosen few cultural insiders. The images and forms made under this paradoxical situation deliberately mislead a majority of viewers in order to please or at least not trouble them while still expressing specific messages (often critical of the said majority) to those in the know.

For Andeans, art images and forms not only stand for what they represent but also stand in for their symbolic referents (Jackson 2008, Salomon 2004b). That is, pictures and objects that artists create actually become dynamic and potent spiritual entities.

These qualities of picture-communication were particularly empowering to Andeans in the fifteenth century when conquest cultures arrived from abroad. In a way similar to the composition of a musical piece with recurrent themes made interesting by well-wrought variations, artists responded to these conquerors and other difficult outside influences that arrived later in their history. The art makers continued to reiterate and thus assert themes from their own cultural repertoire while adding variations drawn from Spanish colonial impositions and those of subsequent cultural, political, and economic systems that invaded their homeland. Artists represented and continue to represent these themes and variations in ways that disguise as much as they reveal. They use the ploys of inversion, disjunction, and dual subjectivity to communicate varying messages to multiple audiences.

Inversion refers to two ideas in this study: the traditional notion of periodic cosmic reversals in the Andean notion of time and ways artists in many places have made supposed bad into good, poor into rich, and respectable into unseemly (and the reverse) through their work. Two of the several scholars who deal with this phenomenon at length are Celestino

(1997, 1998) and Millones (2000). Stastny (1981) and many art historians analyze how artists employ disjunction, for example, to clothe figures in a nativity scene in Andean dress covered with tocapu symbols. Some viewers of this scene see a European Christian image with charming folk touches, while others see severe criticism against social discrimination in the same artwork. Perhaps the most complex of all ploys is W.E.B. DuBois's 1903 concept of dual subjectivity (1994), for here lies the motivation for the other two. A person living in a society that discriminates against her culture must maintain a balancing act to shore herself and her people up while avoiding the pitfall of self-discrimination into which many such people fall. Cleverly made art supports this vital endeavor.

The several audiences for Andean art often have widely differing or even opposite expectations, yet artists strive to please all and offend none. Cultural insiders, the most favored of audiences, have their ways of discerning the artists' most profoundly felt intentions lurking beneath the strategies and ploys they use with such skill.

In these ways, Andean artists maintain themselves in their own philosophical atmosphere, called a "mythical age" by Eliade (1954) and "communitas" by Turner (1969), a state of being where all people are equal. Thus, the artists practice a kind of "blow-back" against the oppression and discrimination they often experience at the hands of outsiders but in a way so subtle that the oppressors never feel it as such.

Today as in the past, artists successfully borrow the idiom of outsiders who may wield superior power in some ways and are often ignorant about or demeaning toward Andeans. Ironically, these same outsiders assume the role of experts and thus mediators who co-opt Andean culture. In subtle retaliation, artists respond by superficially employing the mediators' own co-opted visual idiom in their work. Hidden in this disguise like a wolf in sheep's clothing, artists speak safely, assertively, and with pride about themselves as a spiritually powerful people. This process prevails wherever artists from Huamanga find themselves.

The first half of this book presents a general ethnohistory of the Andes in Peru with a concentration on art. The first chapter gives readers a view of some of the major pre-Columbian Andean civilizations through their art making, culminating with the Incas. Chapter 2 presents Andean religious beliefs and their expression in visual motifs related to nature, many with multivalent symbolic referents. Chapter 3 describes the coming of the Spanish to the Andean region and the Indigenous reaction to their colonizing efforts. It is in chapter 3 that readers first see the strategies artists use to maintain their own cultural traditions in the face of an onslaught from outside their world. Chapter 4 continues in the same vein as chapter 3, describing how contemporary Andeans and their art survive and even prosper in the turmoil of a twenty-year civil war, national and international labor migration, cell phones, the Internet, and the vicissitudes of globalization.

In the second half of the book, an exploration of seven genres of Central Andean art in the twenty-first century shows how artists deal with complex issues with respect to the cultural meaning, esthetics, politics, and economics of art production today. Each of these seven sections presents prehistoric and historic information about the art form, its meaning in terms of religion, the environment, and relevant sociopolitical processes, and how it is constructed or performed by today's artists. There is also a final piece about representative twenty-first century artists and their work.

The two media most highly prized by Andeans are textiles and ceramics. The chapters in this book about these forms deal with limited aspects of the monumental history of work created in the two materials. The two genera span the entire history and geographic spread of Andean civilization. Each time-space context has left a legacy in clay and cloth still made by artists today. The study in the ceramics chapter illustrates the continuation of themes and morphing of variations in the llama, bull, and horse guardian figures that adorn the roofs of family homes today. Huamanguinos who produce these clay figures borrow from a tradition whose origin is in another geographic area, Pucará, also known for its clay deposits. The chapter about textiles contrasts the historic reasons for the tendency in isolated areas to preserve ancient traditions with the Huamanga penchant for borrowing, combination, and innovation. This chapter also illustrates ways today's artists show great interest in and a creative take on their own regional prehistory, in this case the legacy of the Huari civilization.

The chapters about gourd carving, tinware, and Huamanga stone represent village-centered and home-based versions of great traditions in these media, be they Indigenous, European, or contemporary, that are now in danger of extinction. The chapter on gourd carving explains why the danger of extinction is in part due to the very fragile nature and low economic value of the gourds themselves. However, the Andean addition of writing to images starting in the European colonial period and through to the present make carved gourds uniquely rich sources for understanding Andean culture. Tin art has to compete with modern materials such as plastic and mass-manufactured goods in other materials that have taken over the utilitarian uses once common for this art form. In response to this dilemma, tin artists attempt to promote decorative rather than practical aspects of their work in this medium. Huamanga stoneworkers felt the impact of Indigenist intellectuals' mistaken opinions that the medium had no Native American roots. Today stone artists struggle to promote their work in new ways, for example by combining stone with other materials and by producing for a range of different buyer tastes.

The scissors dance and home altars appear superficially to be exclusively European colonial introductions. The deeper metaphysical import of these two arts is as much due to Indigenous influence as to acculturative processes from without. The dance appears in the colonial era as an art associated with carnival or patron-saint festivities but also as a millennial ritual used to invert the world back to a time of Indigenous hegemony. Altars depict Christian saints, but among them are Andean deities. The two or three shelves of many altars illustrate the tripartite Christian cosmos with a cross surmounting all, but they also depict the Andean universe topped by the X, indicating the four parts of Tahuantinsuyu. The cosmology seen in these two genera depends on what viewers—Andean, Christian, and those who practice both creeds—prefer or expect to observe. Artists make these pieces in full awareness of the advantages inherent in the ambiguous nature of visual images and forms.

The last chapters include material oriented to each type of art form or medium first introduced in chapter 4 about contemporary art makers' desires and concerns. Artists weave skillfully between providing for a tourist market in inexpensive, small, and mass-produced items, higher-end buyers with pieces rich in political or esthetic sophistication, and their own as well as friends' and neighbors' traditional and spiritual needs and requirements. Artists do this by developing several distinct product lines in the finest corporate style.

The writer shares this information for a number of reasons. The sheer beauty of the art and the great skill of its makers begs to be expressed. The artists, far from being isolated preservers of ancient forms, are very much alive and aware of processes in the larger world and engaged with the potentialities of new technologies. They are anything but common stereotypes of "folk" artists, often represented as somehow frozen in time and space and unable or unwilling to change or even explore the prehistoric past or the other side of the world for inspiration. In fact, history and archeology show that this flexibility and creativity have long been traditional among Andeans, and for compelling reasons.

People from many walks of life can be of great assistance to these artists (and others in the world sharing similar life circumstances) by gifts of knowledge and even small amounts of tools and materials. Scholars among the readers can contribute their understandings about the Andean past and present directly to artists. Without such help, it is much easier for these very talented people to appear caught in a bubble of marginality and isolation. Even the World Wide Web often presents Andean artists using a skewed or even cartoon image of their own culture and value.

To know Andeans one must look at their art. They are a people of the eye and hand rather than the written word. They live closely with the rhythms of nature surrounding them, and it is in nature's forms and movements that they see and feel the sacred.

Empires and outside influences come and go in Andean art history. Artists borrow and incorporate what is new, what interests them, and what is necessary to survive, but they keep what to them has always been important.

They take others' low opinions and make them good. They dress their work in the costumes of those in power, but under the clothes it is still their work. They make art that lives in multiple worlds at the same time, sending messages to each. Yet, they keep their own counsel.

Andean artists perform this delicate balancing act, this performance of the reality in their mind's eye, with grace, humor, and skill. True to form, they continue to assert their identity proudly and resist opposition. They do this not with guns, harangues, pamphlets, or demonstrations but with the subtle and gentle weapon of art.

Bibliography

ADORNO, ROLENA

1979. "Paradigms Lost: A Peruvian Indian Surveys Spanish Colonial Society." *Anthropology of Visual Communication* 5:78–96. 2000. *Guaman Poma: Writing and Resistance in Colonial Peru.* Austin: University of Texas Press.

ARGUEDAS, JOSÉ MARÍA

1958. "Notas elementales sobre el arte religioso y la cultura mestiza." (Lima) *Revista del Museo Nacional* 27:140–194. 1961. *El sexto.* Lima: Librería Mejia Baca y Tip. Santa Rosa. 1962. *La agonía de Rasu Ñiti.* Lima: Taller de Artes Gráficas Icaro. 1971. *El zorro de arriba y el zorro de abajo.* Buenos Aires: Losada.1985. *Yawar Fiesta.* Austin: University of Texas Press. 1989. *Indios, mestizos, y señores.* Lima: Editorial Horizonte.

ASOCIACIÓN DE ARTISTAS POPULARES DE SARHUA (ADAPS)

N.d. *http://www.convida.org/adaps.html.*

AVENI, ANTHONY

2000. *Between the Lines: The Mystery of the Giant Drawings of Ancient Nazca, Peru.* Austin: University of Texas Press.

AZCUY, EDUARDO A.

1986. *Identidad cultural y cambio tecnológico en América Latina.* Buenos Aires: Editorial Fundación Ross.

BAILEY, GAUVIN A.

2010. *The Andean Hybrid Baroque: Convergent Cultures in the Churches of Colonial Peru.* Notre Dame, IN: Notre Dame University Press.

BASTIEN, JOSEPH W.

1978. *The Mountain of the Condor.* Monograph no. 64, American Ethnological Society. San Francisco: West.

BAUER, BRIAN S.

1998. *The Sacred Landscape of the Inca: The Cuzco Ceque System.* Austin: University of Texas Press.

BAYONA, CLAUDIA

1999. "La escultura en piedra de Huamanga." March. Organización de Estados Iberamericanos (OEI). *http://oei.org.co/sii/entrega10/arto6.htm.*

BERENGUER, JOSÉ, AND JOSÉ LUIS MARTÍNEZ

1989. "Camellids in the Andes: Rock Art, Environment, and Myths." In *Animals in Art*, ed. Howard Morphy, 390–416. London: Unwin Hyman.

BIELLA, PETER, JENNIFER WOLOWIC, MARY STRONG, AND RAFAEL DOMINGO

2006a. *Ceramics of Quinua.* Video. Produced with support from Belgian Technical Assistance and San Francisco State University.

2006b. *Embroidery of Ayacucho.* Video. Produced with support from Belgian Technical Assistance and San Francisco State University.

2006c. *Textiles of Ayacucho.* Video. Produced with support from Belgian Technical Assistance and San Francisco State University.

BIRD, JUNIUS B., AND JOHN HYSLOP

1985. "The Preceramic Excavations at Huaca Prieta Chicama Valley Peru." *Anthropological Papers of the American Museum of Natural History* 62, part 1.

BONAVIA, DUCCIO

1985. *Mural Painting of Ancient Peru.* Bloomington: Indiana University Press.

BOONE, ELIZABETH HILL, EDITOR

1996. *Andean Art at Dumbarton Oaks*, vols. 1 and 2. Washington, DC: Dumbarton Research Library.

BOWSER, PATRICK P.

1974. *African Slave Trade in Colonial Peru 1524–1650.* Stanford, CA: Stanford University Press.

BROCKINGTON, LOLITA GUTIERREZ

2000. "The African Diaspora in the Eastern Andes: Adaptation, Agency, and Fugitive Action, 1573–1677." *Americas* 57, no. 2:204–224.

BRUNDAGE, BURR CARTWRIGHT

1975. *Two Earths, Two Heavens.* Albuquerque: University of New Mexico Press.

BURGER, RICHARD

1992. *Chavin and the Origins of Andean Civilization.* London: Thames and Hudson.

CASTELLS, MANUEL

1996. *The Rise of the Network Society.* Vol. 1 of *The Information Age: Economy, Society, and Culture.* Malden, MA: Blackwell.

1997. *The Power of Identity.* Vol. 2 of *The Information Age: Economy, Society, and Culture.* Malden, MA: Blackwell.

1998a. *The End of Millennium.* Vol. 3 of *The Information Age: Economy, Society, and Culture.* Malden, MA: Blackwell.

1998b. "Info Tech Project. Information Technology, Globalization, and Social Development." Conference paper prepared for United Nations Research Institute for Social Development (UNRISD) Conference on Information Technologies and Social Development. Geneva, Palais des Nations, June.

2000. "Is the New Economy Socially Sustainable?" Proceedings of the 22nd International Conference on Software Engineering, New York

2001. "Identity and Change in the Network Society." Interview, May 9. Video. In *Conversations with History* video series, organized by Harry Kreisler. Berkeley: University of California, Institute of International Studies. *http://conversations.berkeley.edu/content/manuel-castells.*

CELESTINO, OLINDA

1997. "Transformaciones en los Andes peruanos: Ciclos míticos." (Lima) *Gaceta de Antropología* 13, no. 6.

1998. "Transformaciones en los Andes peruanos: Evangelizaciones." (Lima) *Gaceta de Antropología* 14, no. 5.

CENTRAL INTERREGIONAL DE ARTESANOS DEL PERÚ (CIAP).

N.d. "Procesos de Producción." *http://www.asociacion.ciap.org.*

CIEZA DE LEÓN, PEDRO

1943. *Del señorio de los incas.* Buenos Aires: Editoriales Argentinas. Reprint 1967, Lima: Instituto de Estudios Peruanos. First published 1553.

1945. *La crónica del Perú.* Buenos Aires, Argentina: Espasa Calpe. First published 1553.

COBO, BERNABÉ

1956. *Historia del Nuevo Mundo*, vols. 91–92. Biblioteca de Autores Españoles. Madrid: Ediciones Atlas. First published 1653.

CONKLIN, WILLIAM

2009. "The Iconic Dimension in Tiwanaku Art." In *Tiwanaku*, ed. Margaret Young-Sanchez, 115–132. Denver: Frederick and Jan Mayer Center of Pre-Columbian and Spanish Colonial Art, Denver Museum of Art.

COOK, NOBLE DAVID

1998. *Born to Die: Diseases in the New World Conquest, 1492–1650.* Cambridge, England: Cambridge University Press.

CORNEJO-POLAR, ANTONIO

1998. "Migrant Conditions and Multicultural Intertextuality, the Case of José María Arguedas." In *José María Arguedas, Reconsiderations for Latin American Cultural Studies*, ed. Ciro A. Sandoval and Sandra M. Boschetto Sandoval, 187–199. Monographs in International Studies, Latin America Series, no. 29. Athens: Ohio University Center for International Studies.

CORNEJO-POLAR, A., A. ESCOBAR, M. LEINHART, AND W. ROWE.

1984. *Vigencia y universalidad de José María Arguedas*, Lima: Editorial Horizonte.

COVARRUBIAS, MIGUEL

1954. *The Eagle, the Jaguar, and the Serpent: Indian Art of the Americas.* New York: Alfred A. Knopf.

CUMMINS, TOM

2004. "Silver Threads and Golden Needles: The Inca, the Spanish, and the Sacred World of Humanity." In *The Colonial Andes*, ed. Phipps, Hecht, and Esteras Martín, 2–16.

DAMIÁN, MÁXIMO

N.d. "#7. Danzante. Baile de Tijeras-Pasacalle-Atipananakuy-Wallpa Wajay-Pasta." In *Máximo Damián, El Violin de Ishua.* Audio CD.

DAVIES, LUCY, AND MO FINI

1994. *Arts and Crafts of South America.* San Francisco: Chronicle Books.

DE BERCEO, GONZALO

1965. *Milagros de Nuestra Señora.* Madrid: Editorial Castalia.

DE GANTE, PEDRO

1970. *Catecismo de la doctrina cristiana.* Madrid: Ministerio de Educación y Ciencia, Dirección General de Archivos y Bibliotecas. First published 1565.

DE GRANDIS, RITA

1998. "The Neo-Postcolonial Condition of the Work of Art in Latin America." In *José María Arguedas*, ed. Sandoval and Boschetto Sandoval, 53–69.

DE LAS CASAS, BARTOLOMÉ

1974. *In Defense of the Indians*. DeKalb: Northern Illinois University Press.

DE SOTO, HERNANDO

2001. "The Poor Are the Solution, Not the Problem." Interview. (Acton Institute) *Religion & Liberty* 11, no. 4 (July–August). *http://www.acton.org/pub/religion-liberty/volume-11-number-4/poor-are-solution-not-problem.*

DE SOTO, HERNANDO, WITH E. GHERSI AND M. GHIBELLINI

1987. *El otro sendero*, Lima: Instituto de Libertad y Democracia.

DE VITORIA, FRANCISCO

1960. *Obras*. Madrid: Editorial Católica. First published early 16th century.

DEAN, CAROLYN

1999. *Inka Bodies and the Body of Christ*. Durham, NC: Duke University Press.

DEE, JONATHAN

2003. "The Summer of Screamo." *New York Times Magazine*, July 29, pp. 26–30.

DIAMOND, JARED

1998. *Guns, Germs, and Steel*. New York: W. W. Norton.

DOBYNS, HENRY, AND PAUL L. DOUGHTY

1976. *Peru, a Cultural History*. New York: Oxford University Press.

DOUGHTY, PAUL

1969. "Consideraciones para el desarrollo en los Andes peruanos." In *La comunidad andina*, ed. Jose R. Sabogal Wiesse, 223–255. Ediciones Especiales, no. 51. Mexico City: Instituto Indigenista Interamericano.

DUBOIS, W.E.B.

1994. *The Souls of Black Folk*. New York: Dover. First published 1903 by A. C. McClurg.

EL COMERCIO

2003. "La dispensa de los incas." Poster. May.

ELIADE, MIRCEA

1954. *The Myth of the Eternal Return: Cosmos and History*. New York: Bollington Foundation. First published 1949 in French as *Le Mythe de l'eternel retour: archetypes et repétition*, Paris: Nouvelle revue française (NRF) libraire Gallimard.

EVANÁN POMA, PRIMITIVO, JUAN GUALBERTO QUISPE, AND SALVADOR PALOMINO FLORES

1994. "Construcción de casas y pintura de tablas en la comunidad de Sarhua, Perú. Ponencia" [Wasi Ruwaypi Tabla Apakuykuy]. Paper presented at the Guaman Poma, Nuevas Perspectivas symposium, National Museum of Denmark, Copenhagen, June 29–July 1.

FABIAN, JOHANNES

1983. *Time and Other: How Anthropology Makes Its Object*. New York: Columbia University Press.

FALLER, MARTINA, AND MARIO CUELLAR

2009. "Metáforas del tiempo en quechua." In *Actas del IV Congreso Nacional de Investigaciones Linguistico- Filológicas*. CD ROM. Lima: Universidad Ricardo Palma.

FIGUEROA, LUIS, DIRECTOR

1982. *Yawar fiesta*. Film based on the novel by José María Arguedas.

FLINDELL KLARÉN, PETER

2000. *Peru: Society and Nationhood in the Andes.* New York: Oxford University Press.

FOLK ART AND CRAFTS FOUNDATION

2004. Retablos. *http://www.folkart-crafts.org/chapter_3.htm*, last modified November 2007.

FOUCAULT, MICHEL

1965. *Madness and Civilization.* New York: Vintage Books.

FRANQUEMONT, ED

2004. "Jazz, an Andean Symmetry." In *Embedded Symmetries: Natural and Cultural*, ed. Dorothy K. Washburn, 81–95. Albuquerque: University of New Mexico Press.

FREIRE, PAULO

2001. *Pedogogy of the Oppressed.* New York: Continuum. First published 1970 as *Pedagogia do oprimido*, Rio de Janeiro: Paz e Terra.

FRIEDMAN, JONATHAN

1994. *Cultural Identity and Global Process.* London: Sage.

FUGUET, ALBERTO

2001. "This Revolution Is Being Televised." *New York Times Magazine*, February 25, pp. 35–37.

GARCÍA CANCEL, RICARDO

2000. "Las culturas del barroco." (Madrid) *La Aventura de la Historia* 2, no. 16 (February 16): 52–56.

GARCILASO DE LA VEGA, INCA

1960. *Comentarios reales de los Incas*, vol. 1. Lima: Universidad Mayor Nacional de San Marcos.

GAUR, ALBERTINE

1992. *A History of Writing*, New York: Cross River.

GIBRAN, KHALIL

2007. *The Collected Works.* New York: Alfred A. Knopf.

GIFFORD, DOUGLAS

1986. *Time Metaphors in Aymara and Quechua.* St. Andrews, Scotland: University of St. Andrews.

GIOIA, TED

2006. *Work Songs.* Durham, NC: Duke University Press.

GRABURN, NELSON

1976. *Ethnic and Tourist Arts: Cultural Expressions from the Fourth World.* Berkeley: University of California Press.

1999. "Ethnic and Tourist Arts Revisited." In *Unpacking Culture*, ed. R. B. Phillips and C. B. Steiner. Berkeley: University of California Press.

GROSS, CHARLES G.

1999. "A Hole in the Head." *Neuroscientist* 5, no. 4:263–269. Available at www.princeton.edu/~cggross/neuroscientist_99_hole.pdf.

GUAMÁN POMA DE AYALA, FELIPE JUAN

1988. *Nueva coronica y buen gobierno.* Comments by John V. Murra, Rolena Adorno, and Jorge L. Urioste. Translated from Quechua to Spanish by Jorge L. Urioste. Madrid: Siglo Veintiuno. First published 1603.

HAHNEL, ROBIN

1998. "Capitalist Globalism in Crisis, Part I: Boom and Bust." *New York Times Magazine*, August 18, pp. 2, 4.

HARNER, MICHAEL J.

1968. "The Sound of Rushing Water." In *Natural History* 77 (6): 28–33, 60–61.

1973. Editor, *Hallucinogens and Shamanism*. New York: Oxford University Press.

1982. *The Way of the Shaman*. Toronto: Bantam.

HECKMAN, ANDREA M.

2003. *Woven Stories: Andean Textiles and Rituals*. Albuquerque: University of New Mexico Press.

HENRICI, JANE

2003. "Non-Governmental Organizations and Craft Producers." *Andean Visual Anthropology*, special issue, ed. Mary Strong and Paul Hockings. *Visual Anthropology* 16, no. 2–3 (April–September): 289–313.

HERRING, HUBERT

1968. *A History of Latin America*. New York: Alfred A. Knopf.

HERTZ, ROBERT

1973. "The Pre-Eminence of the Right Hand: A Study in Religious Polarity." In *Right and Left*, ed. Rodney Needham, 3–32. Chicago: University of Chicago Press.

HEYERDAHL, THOR

1950. *Kon Tiki*. Chicago: Rand McNally.

HOOPES, JOHN W.

2009. "From Tiwanaku to Macchu Picchu: Ushnus and the Architecture of Creation." In *Tiwanaku*, ed. Margaret Young-Sanchez, 247–272. Denver: Frederick and Jan Mayer Center of Pre-Columbian and Spanish Colonial Art, Denver Art Museum.

HYDE, PAUL R.

2008. "On Mircea Eliade and the Myth of the Eternal Return." http://www.paul-hyde-author.com/eliade.html.

INSTITUTO DE ESTUDIOS RIOJANOS

2005. "Nájera, legado medieval." *La Rioja: tierra abierta*. Exhibition catalogue.

JACKSON, MARGARET A.

2008. *Moche Art and Visual Culture in Ancient Peru*. Albuquerque: University of New Mexico Press.

JIMÉNEZ BORJA, ARTURO

1941. "Mate peruano." (Lima) *Museo de la Cultura Peruana* 42–43:21–25.

1948. "Mate peruano." (Lima) *Revista del Museo Nacional* 17:34–73.

KARMASON, MARILYN G., WITH JOAN B. STACKE

2002. *Majolica: A Complete History and Illustrated Survey*. New York: Henry N. Abrams.

KATO, TAKAHIRO

2001. "Historia tejida por los sueños: Formación de la imagen del Niño Compadrito." In *Dioses y demonios de Cuzco*, ed. Hiroyasu Tomoeda, Luis Millones, and Takahiro Kato, 99–155. Lima: Fondo Editorial Congreso del Perú.

KEMPER COLUMBUS, CLAUDETTE

1998. "Tricksters in the Fishmeal Factory: Fragmentation in Arguedas' Last Novel." In *José María Arguedas*, ed. Sandoval and Boschetto-Sandoval, 167–185.

KROEBER, ALFRED LOUIS

1930. *Archeological Explorations in Peru*. Part 2, "The Northern Coast." (Field Museum of Natural History, Chicago) *Anthropology Memoirs* 2, no. 2:45–116.

LANNING, EDWARD P.

1967. *Peru before the Incas*. Englewood Cliffs, NJ: Prentice Hall.

LISTER, FLORENCE C.

2003. *Maiolica Olé: Spanish and Mexican Maiolica*. Albuquerque: University of New Mexico Press.

LOPE DE VEGA Y CARPIO, FÉLIX ARTURO

2002. *Fuenteovejuna*. Madrid: Idea Equipo Editorial. First published 1611–1613.

LÓPEZ ALBUJAR, ENRIQUE

1937. *Nuevos cuadernos andinos*. Santiago, Chile: Ediciones Ercilla.

LÓPEZ DE GÓMARA, FRANCISCO

1979. *Historia general de las Indias y vida de Hernán Cortes*. Ayacucho, Peru: Biblioteca Ayachucho. Part 1 of *Historia de las indias y la conquista de México*, first published 1552–1553.

2003. *Historia de la conquista de México*. Mexico City: Oceano de México. Part 2 of *Historia de las indias y la conquista de México*, first published 1552–1553.

LÓPEZ ANTAY, IGNACIO, AND EULALIA LÓPEZ ANTAY

N.d. "Retablos López Antay." Manuscript.

LÓPEZ IBOR, MARTA

1990. *Los judíos en España*. Madrid: Biblioteca Básica, Grupo Anaya.

MACERA, PABLO

1977. *Trabajos de historia*. Vol. 2–3. Lima: Instituto Nacional de Cultura.

MACERA, PABLO, AND ROSAURA ANDÁZABAL

1999. *Flora y fauna de Sarhua. Pintura y palabra: el pintor narrador Carmelón Berrocal Evanán*. Lima: Universidad Nacional Mayor de San Marcos.

MANRIQUE, NELSON

2000. "Racismo en el Perú." Video. In *Tradiciones culturales e identidad en el Perú*, vol. 1. Lima: Congreso de la República.

MARZAL, MANUEL

2000. "Los rostros de Dios en el catolicismo peruano." Video. In *Tradiciones culturales e identidad en el Perú*, vol. 2. Lima: Congreso de la República.

MARTÍNEZ ALESANCO, JESÚS MARÍA

2003. *La danza de los zancos desde 1603–2003 in Anguiano (400 años de documentos)*. Logroño, Spain: Ayuntamiento de Anguiano, Gobierno de La Rioja.

MATTHIESSEN, PETER

1992. *In the Spirit of Crazy Horse*. New York: Penguin Books.

MCDONALD BOYER, RUTH

1976. "Gourd Decoration in Highland Peru." In *Ethnic and Tourist Arts*, ed. N.H.H. Graburn, 183–197. Berkeley: University of California Press.

MELIS, ANTONIO

1998. Foreword to *José María Arguedas*, ed. Sandoval and Boschetto-Sandoval, 37.

MENDIZABAL LOSACK, EMILIO

1964. "La difusión y reinterpretación de las cajas de imaginero ayacuchanas." (Lima) *Folklore Americano*, no. 11–12:116–334.

MENDOZA, ZOILA

2000. *Shaping Society through Dance*. Chicago: University of Chicago Press.

MEYERSON, JULIA

1990. *Tambo*. Austin: University of Texas Press.

MILLONES, LUIS

2000. *Dioses familiares. Festivales populares en el Perú contemporáneo.* Lima: Fondo Editorial del Congreso del Perú.

2003. "Danzantes de Ayacucho." In *Atlas departamental del Perú*, 97–101. Lima: Editoriales Paisa.

MILLONES, LUIS, AND MARY LOUISE PRATT

1990. *El Amor Brujo: Images of Culture and Love in the Andes.* Vol. 10 of Foreign and Comparative Studies. Syracuse, NY: Syracuse University Press.

MITCHELL, WILLIAM P., WITH BARBARA H. JAYE

1996. "Pictographs in the Andes: The Huntington Free Library Quechua Catechism." *Latin American Indian Literatures Journal* 12, no. 1:1–42.

MORALES CHÁVEZ, CECILIA

1981. "Apuntes sobre el mate burilado en Ayacucho." Paper. Dirección Departamental de Industria, Turismo e Integración, Sub-Dirección de Artesania. Ayacucho: Universidad San Cristobal de Huamanga.

MORPHY, HOWARD, EDITOR

1989. *Animals in Art.* London: Unwin Hyman.

MORRIS, CRAIG, AND ADRIANA VON HAGEN

1993. *The Inca Empire and Its Andean Origins.* New York: Abbeville Press, American Museum of Natural History.

MOSELEY, MICHAEL

1992. *The Incas and Their Ancestors.* London: Thames and Hudson.

MURRA, JOHN V.

1972. "El control vertical de un máximo de pisos ecológicos de las sociedades andinas." In *Revista de la Provincia de León de Huanaco*, ed. John V. Murra, 427–476. Huanaco, Peru: Universidad Nacional Hermilio Valdizán.

MUSEO DE ARTE POPULAR DE AYACUCHO

2002. *Mates andinos de ayer y hoy.* Museum catalogue. Ayacucho, Peru.

NATIONAL AUDUBON SOCIETY

1991. *Field Guide to the Night Sky.* New York: Chanticleer.

NEEDHAM, RODNEY, EDITOR

1973. *Right and Left.* Chicago: University of Chicago Press.

NEW YORK ACADEMY OF MEDICINE

1865. Proceedings, December 6. *Bulletin of the New York Academy of Medicine* 2 (1862–1866): 530.

NUÑEZ, R. E., AND EVE SWEETSER

2006. "With the Future behind Them. Convergent Evidence from Aymara Language and Gesture in the Cross Linguistic Comparison of Spatial Construals of Time." *Cognitive Science* 30:1–49.

NÚÑEZ REBAZA, LUCY

1990. *Los dansaq.* Lima: Museo Nacional de la Cultura Peruana.

N.d. "La danza de las tijeras." *Cuadernos de la Música Peruana* 3, no. 5:4–5.

ORTÍZ RESCONIERE, ALEJANDRO

2000. "La persona en los Andes." Video. In *Tradiciones culturales*, vol. 2. Lima: Congreso de la República.

PAREDES CANDIA, ANTONIO

1972. "Cuurmi y Cantu." In *Narraciones hispanoamericanas de tradición oral*, 228–280. Madrid: Instituto Nacional del Libro Español.

PASCUAL, RAFAEL

2003. "Manuel Castells, el cartógrafo de la aldea global, FRC." *Revista de Debat Politic* 1 (October): 85–106.

PERU, CONGRESO DE LA REPÚBLICA

2000. *Tradiciones culturales e identidad en el Perú*. 2 vols. Video.

PHIPPS, ELENA

2004. "Cumbi to Tapestry: Collection, Innovation, and Transformation of Colonial Andean Tapestry Tradition." In *The Colonial Andes*, ed. Phipps, Hecht, and Esteras Martín, 72–100.

PHIPPS, ELENA, JOHANNA HECHT, AND CRISTINA ESTERAS MARTÍN, EDITORS

2004. *The Colonial Andes: Tapestries and Silverwork, 1530–1830*. New York, New Haven: Metropolitan Museum of Art, Yale University Press.

PIERCE, DONNA, AND RONALD OTSUKA

2006. *Asia and Spanish America. The Trans-Pacific Artistic and Cultural Exchange, 1500–1850*. Symposium series, Frederick and Jan Mayer Center of Pre-Columbian and Spanish Colonial Art, Denver Art Museum, 2006. Norman: University of Oklahoma Press.

PRIESNITZ, WENDY

N.d. "Alternative Traders Put People First." *Natural Life Magazine*, no. 37. *http://www.naturallifemagazine.com*.

PUBLIC BROADCASTING SERVICE (PBS), *NOVA*

2010. *Ghosts of Macchu Picchu*. Video. February.

PULGAR VIDAL, JAVIER

1968. *Geografía del Perú*, Lima: Universidad Nacional Mayor de San Marcos.

1987. *Geografía del Perú: las ocho regiones naturales*. Lima: Promoción Editorial Inca.

RAGHAVAN, CHAKRAVARTHI

2000. "Andean Pacts New IDR Regime Shaped in US Interests?" Third World Network (TWN). October 8. *http://www.twnside.org.sg/title/andean.htm*.

REICHE, MARÍA

1993. *Contribuciones a la geometría y astronomía en el antiguo Perú*. Lima: Epigrafe Editores, by María Reiche with Renate Reiche.

ROHR-ROUENDAAL, PETRA

1997. *Where There Is No Artist: Development Drawings and How to Use Them*. London: Intermediate Technology.

ROOSEVELT, ANNA

1999. "The Development of Prehistoric Complex Societies: Amazonia, a Tropical Forest." In *Complex Politics in the Ancient Tropical World*, ed. E. A. Bacus, L. J. Lucero, and J. Allen, 13–24. Arlington, VA: American Anthropological Association.

ROWE, JOHN H.

1943. "Chanapata, la cultura pre-incaica del Cuzco." (Cuzco *Tupac Amaru*, year 11, vol. 2, nos. 2–3 (May): 41–43.

1961. "The Chronology of Inca Wooden Cups." In *Essays in Precolumbian Art and Archeology*, ed. S. Lothrop, 317–341. Cambridge: Harvard University Press.

ROWE, WILLIAM, AND VIVIAN SCHELLING

1993. *Memory and Modernity: Popular Culture in Latin America*. London: Verso.

SABOGAL DIÉGUEZ, JOSÉ

1945. *Mates burilados. Arte vernaculo peruano*. Buenos Aires: Editorial Nova.

1949. *El toro en las artes populares del Perú*. Lima: Ministerio de Educación Pública, Museo de la Cultura Peruana.

SABOGAL WIESSE, JOSÉ R.

1969a, editor. *La comunidad andina*. Ediciones Especiales, no. 51. Mexico City: Instituto Indigenista Interamericano.

1969b. "El subprefacto, los carneros, y Chacón." In *La comunidad andina*, ed. Sabogal Weisse, 167–189.

1979. "Arte vernáculo en Huamanga: testimonio de tres artesanos." Taller de Coyuntura Agraria, no. 16. La Molina, Peru: Universidad Nacional Agraria, Centro de Investigaciones Socio-económicas. First presented February 1978 at Gainesville, FL.

SAID, EDWARD

1979. *Orientalism*, New York: Vintage.

SALOMÓN, F., H. ARAUJO, R. HARRIS, W. D. MIGNOLO, AND G. URTON

2001. "How Andean 'Writing without Words' Works." *Current Anthropology* 42:1–27.

SALOMON, FRANK

2004a. "Andean Opulence: Indigenous Ideas about Wealth in Colonial Peru." In *The Colonial Andes*, ed. Phipps, Hecht, and Esteras Martín, 115–123.

2004b. *The Cord Keepers: Khipus and Cultural Life in a Peruvian Village*. Durham, NC: Duke University Press.

SALOMON, FRANK, AND GEORGE L. URIOSTE, TRANSLATORS

1991. *The Huarochirí Manuscript: Testament of Ancient and Colonial Religion*. Austin: University of Texas Press.

SANDOVAL, CIRO A., AND SANDRA M. BOSCHETTO-SANDOVAL

1998a. "José María Arguedas: El Sexto." In *José María Arguedas*, ed. Sandoval and Boschetto Sandoval, 138–166.

1998b, editors. *José María Arguedas. Reconsiderations for Latin American Cultural Studies*. Monographs in International Studies, Latin American Series, no. 29. Athens: Ohio University Center for International Studies.

SELER, EDWARD

1923. "Viaje arqueológico en Peru y Bolivia." (Lima) *Inca* 1, no. 2 (April–June): 355–374.

SILVERMAN, GAIL P.

1998. *El tejido andino: el libro de sabiduría*. Lima: Fondo de Cultura Económica, Banco Central de la Reserva.

STARN, O., C. DE GREGORI, AND R. KIRK, EDITORS

1995. *The Peru Reader*. Durham, NC: Duke University Press.

STASTNY, FRANCISCO

1981. *Las artes populares del Perú*. Lima: Ediciones Edubanco.

STRONG, MARY

1998. "Big Pictures: Ethnic Identity as a Mutable Concept in New York City Street Murals." Special issue, Mary Strong, guest editor, and Paul Hockings, editor. *Visual Anthropology* 2, no. 1–2: 9–54.

2003a. "Powers Within: Artists and Anthropologists Work Together to Create Andean Mythic Beasts and Elements of Nature in Their Own Image." *Andean Visual Anthropology*, special issue, ed. Mary Strong and Paul Hockings. *Visual Anthropology* 16, no. 2–3 (April–September): 113–158.

2003b. "Public Displays and Double Meanings: 500 Years of Glocal Street Festivals." Poster presentation, AAA meetings.

2009. "Art and Mind: Working on Murals." In *Viewpoints*, ed. Strong and Wilder, 297–327.

STRONG, MARY, AND LAENA WILDER, EDITORS

2009. *Viewpoints: Visual Anthropologists at Work*. Austin: University of Texas Press.

TAMAYO ACOSTA, JUAN JOSÉ

1989. *Para comprender la teología de la liberación*. Estella, Spain: Editorial Verbo Divino.

TAPIA, ANDRÉS T.

2002. "Economist Hernando de Soto Warns Fujimori: Perú's Economy Hinges on Street Entrepreneurs." Pacific News Service, April 18.

TELLO, JULIO CESAR

1933a. "Las ruinas del valle de Nepeña." (Lima) *El Comercio*, October 6, p. 4.

1933b. "Las ruinas del valle de Nepeña II, los testimonios de la más vieja y más adelantada civilización del Peru, recientemente descubierta." (Lima) *El Comercio*, October 9, p. 7.

1933c. "Las ruinas del valle de Nepeña III, de la necesidad de preservar y estudiar los tesoros arqueológicos descubiertos en el valle de Nepeña." (Lima) *El Comercio*, October 14, p. 7.

TOLEDO BRUCKMANN, ERNESTO

2003a. *Retablos en Ayacucho: testimonio de violencia*. Lima: Editorial San Marcos.

2003b. "Taller indígena internacional en Huamanga." *Umalliq*, August 1. Ayacucho, Peru: Prodes.

TOMOEDA, HIROYASU

2001. Estética del ritual andino. In *Dioses y demonios del Cuzco*, ed. Tomoeda, Millones, and Kato, 187–219.

TOMOEDA, HIROYASU, LUIS MILLONES, AND TAKAHIRO KATO

2001. *Dioses y demonios del Cuzco*. Lima: Fondo Editorial del Congreso de Perú.

TRAWICK, PAUL

2001. "The Moral Economy of Water." *American Anthropologist* 103 (2): 361–379.

TRIVELLI, CARLO

2003a. "Desarrollo y afirmación cultural en espacios altoandinos." *Umalliq*. Ayacucho, Peru: Prodes.

2003b. "La historia del toro y del cangrejo." (Lima) *El Comercio*, May 8.

TURNER, VICTOR W.

1969. *The Ritual Process: Structure and Anti Structure*. Louis Henry Morgan Lectures. Chicago: Aldine.

UCKO, P. J.

1989. Foreword to *Animals in Art*, ed. Morphy.

ULFE, MARIA EUGENIA

2005. "Representations of Memory in Peruvian Retablos." Ph.D. dissertation, George Washington University. UMI Microform 3167040, Proquest Information and Learning, Ann Arbor, MI.

UNITED NATIONS DEVELOPMENT PROGRAM (UNDP)

1997. *Human Development Report 1997*, New York: Oxford University Press.

URDANOZ, TEOFILO, ED.

1960. *Obras de Francisco de Vitoria*. Madrid: Biblioteca de Autores Cristianos.

URTON, GARY

1979. *At the Crossroads of the Earth and Sky*. Austin: University of Texas Press.

1981. "Animals and Astronomy in the Quechua Universe." *Proceedings of the American Philosophical Society* 125, no. 2 (April 30): 110–127.

1986. "Calendrical Cycles and Their Projections in Pacariq Tambo, Peru." *Journal of Latin American Lore* 12 (1): 45–64, 281–301.

VALCARCEL, LUIS E.

1967. *Los incas: etnohistoria del Perú antiguo*, Lima: Universidad Nacional Mayor de San Marcos.

VOLINSKY, NAN

2003. "Standing Up: Violin Performance, Technical and Ethnic Resurgence in Saraguaro, Ecuador." *Andean Visual Anthropology*, special issue, ed. Mary Strong and Paul Hockings. *Visual Anthropology* 16, no. 2–3 (April–September): 315–340.

WALLACE, ANTHONY F. C.

1956. "Revitalization Movements." *American Anthropologist* 58 (2): 264–281.

1989. "Plot and the Concept of Culture in Historiography." In *The Relevance of Culture*, ed. F. Morris, 31–39. New York: Bergin and Garven.

WATERMAN, PETER

1999. "The Brave New World of Manuel Castells. What on Earth (or in the Ether) Is Going On?" *Development and Change* 30, no. 2 (April): 357–380.

WHITMAN, WALT

1982. *Complete Poetry and Prose of Walt Whitman*. New York: Library of America.

WILDER, THORNTON

1927. *Bridge of San Luis Rey*. New York: Albert and Charles Boni.

2006. *The Eighth Day*. New York: Harper Perennial Modern Classics.

WILLIAMS, J. DAVID LEWIS

2002a, editor. *Cosmos in Stone*. Lanham, MA: Rowman and Littlefield.

2002b. "Cosmos in Stone: Interpreting Religion and Society through Rock Art." In *Cosmos in Stone*, ed. Williams, 108–110. Lanham, MA: Rowman and Littlefield.

WOLF, ERIC

1959. *Sons of the Shaking Earth*. University of Chicago Press.

YAEGER, JASÓN

2004. "Tiawanaku and the Construction of Inca Imperial Ideology. In *School of American Research Annual Report*," 17. Santa Fe, NM: School of American Research.

YAWAR FIESTA (FILM). SEE FIGUEROA, LUIS.

YOUNG-SANCHEZ, MARGARET, EDITOR

2009. *Tiwanaku*. Denver: Frederick and Jan Mayer Center of Pre-Columbian and Spanish Colonial Art, Denver Art Museum.

ZORN, ELAYNE

1979. "Warping and Weaving on a Four-Stake Ground Loom in the Lake Titicaca Basin Community of Taquile, Peru." In *Looms and Their Products*. Proceedings, Irene Emery Roundtable on Museum Textiles, 1977, ed. Irene Emery and Patricia Fiske, 212–221. Washington, D.C.: Textile Museum.

1987. "Encircling Meaning: Economics and Aesthetics in Taquile, Peru." In *Andean Aesthetics: Textiles of Peru and Bolivia*, compiled by Blenda Femenias, 67–79. Madison: Elvehjem Museum of Art, University of Wisconsin.

ZUIDEMA, R. T.

1964. *The Ceque System of Cusco*, Leiden, Netherlands: E. J. Brill. 1977 1978.

1977–1978. "Shaft Tombs and the Inca Empire." *Journal of the Steward Anthropological Society* 9, nos. 1–2: 13–178.

1981. "Observations of the Solar and Lunar Passages through Zenith and Anti-Zenith at Cuzco." In *Archeoastronomy in the New World*, ed. Ray A. Williamson, 319–342. Los Altos, CA: Ballena.

1983. "Masks in the Incaic Solstice and Equinoctal Rituals." In *The Power of Symbols*, ed. N. R. Crumrine and M. Halpen, 146–153. Vancouver: University of British Columbia Press.

1990. *Inca Civilization in Cuzco*. Austin: University of Texas Press.

2009. "Tiwanaku Iconography and Calendar." In *Tiwanaku*, ed. Margaret Young-Sanchez, 225–247. Denver: Frederick and Jan Mayer Center of Pre-Columbian and Spanish Colonial Art, Denver Art Museum.

Index

Italic page numbers refer to figures.

www.ingramcontent.com/pod-product-compliance
Lightning Source LLC
LaVergne TN
LVHW040825090826
845145LV00001BA/204

* 9 7 8 0 2 9 2 7 5 4 2 5 6 *